Heritage

James Stourton is a senior fellow of the Institute
of Historical Research, University of London.
He is a prize-winning author of several books on
cultural and architectural subjects, including
Great Houses of London. He sat for ten years on
the Heritage Memorial Fund panel, and is
a former chairman of Sotheby's UK.

JAMES STOURTON

Heritage

A HISTORY OF HOW WE CONSERVE OUR PAST

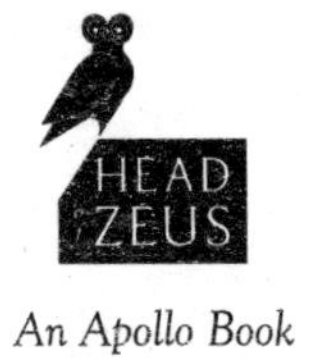

An Apollo Book

First published in the UK in 2022 by Head of Zeus
This paperback edition first published in 2023 by Head of Zeus,
part of Bloomsbury Plc

9 7 5 3 1 2 4 6 8

A catalogue record for this book is available from
the British Library.

p. 68, p. 192, p. 267, p. 369, extracts from works by John Betjeman reproduced by permission
of the John Betjeman Estate; p. 62, extract from *The Waste Land* by T. S. Eliot, reproduced by
permission of Faber and Faber Ltd; p. 219, lines from 'Going, Going', in *High Windows* by
Philip Larkin, reproduced by permission of Faber and Faber Ltd; p. 244, extract from 'Stately
Homes of England', *The Operette* by Noel Coward, © Warner/Chappell Music, reproduced by
permission of Alan Brodie Representation Ltd, www.alanbrodie.com.

Every effort has been made to contact copyright holders for permission to reproduce
material in this book. In the case of any inadvertent oversight, the publishers will include
an appropriate acknowledgement in future editions of this book.

ISBN (PB): 9781838933173
ISBN (E): 9781838933180

Typeset by Divaddict Publishing Solutions Ltd

Printed and bound in Great Britain by
CPI Group (UK) Ltd, Croydon CRO 4YY

Head of Zeus Ltd
5–8 Hardwick Street
London EC1R 4RG
WWW.HEADOFZEUS.COM

To Richard Davenport-Hines

Contents

Preface

History therefore is constituted in large part
by testimonies of loss.[1]

P ETER F RITZSCHE

Heritage is who we are and where we live. It is the place we were born, the street we inhabit, the local park and the places we visit. It is about stretches of countryside, towns and cities, historic churches, treasures in museums, railways and canals – in fact anything from Britain's past deemed worthy of preservation by virtue of its associations, historical value or beauty, the removal or despoliation of which would threaten the quality of our lives and environment. Everybody has their own private and sacred places of heritage: landscapes, music and objects sanctified by memory and association. I am no exception, and it is only fair to the reader to say something of my background, interests and experiences which inform the narrative. As will become apparent, many of the chapters turn out to have more relevance to my own past than I supposed when I began writing.

I was born and brought up in North Yorkshire in a family where heritage appeared against a background of decline. The fortunes of my Roman Catholic forbears had been in decline since the Reformation, although never quite snuffed out. We lived in the shadow of the family Valhalla, a Gothic pile called Allerton Park, which I thought of as Gormenghast until everybody began to refer to it as Hogwarts. It exercised a powerful spell over me as a place of vastness, mystery and secret rooms. The fact that it was a stupendous example of Victorian hubris escaped me then;

the fake was more powerful than the reality, presenting an early lesson that heritage could embody a reinvented identity. Walter Scott has much to answer for.

After my grandfather died in 1965, the house was occupied by priests training for the African missions, and later as a convalescent home, until to everyone's surprise, a romantically minded American bought it in 1983 because it reminded him of Cinderella's castle; Disney had replaced Walter Scott as the cultural driver. Today, renamed Allerton Castle, it is a wedding venue, and noise from the widened A1 motorway screams across the park.

Then there was my mother's family home, Heslington Hall, just outside York, half Elizabethan, half Victorian, barely occupied since the war. My maternal grandfather sold the house and park for a favourable price to one of the heroes of this book, the city councillor and philanthropist J. B. Morrell, as a setting for York University. The Hall took on the role of Senate House, a clear case of social gain trumping heritage loss. The adaptation of both these family houses was a suitable allegory of Britain in a changing world.

As a child my earliest fascination, however, was not yet designated as 'heritage'. It was the rows of steam engines and rolling stock in the railway sidings entering York that first stirred my imagination. Then, at the age of five, I was taken to London, where I made a child-Fauvist drawing of Tower Bridge which my mother turned into a plate – it is the only childhood object that I still possess. As a Roman Catholic, I was sent to be educated at Ampleforth, which had mostly Victorian collegiate architecture but also a distinguished twentieth-century abbey church by Giles Gilbert Scott. This presented a fascinating problem – begun before the war in an updated but nevertheless ornate Gothic Revival style, and then finished after the war in a stripped-down 1950s manner. I would spend the Sunday church services reconstructing the possibilities in my mind.

The school was within the North York Moors National Park, rich in scenery, history and buildings. The jewel was without doubt

Rievaulx Abbey, set in its valley under the terrace and temples of Duncombe Park. 'How England consoles and warms one, in these deep hollows, where the past stands almost stagnant', wrote Virginia Woolf.[2] Nobody described this area better than Herbert Read in his poetic autobiography, *The Contrary Experience*, which first taught me to make the link between landscape, poetry and history. If the North York Moors gave me a life-long love of walking, they also offered architectural discoveries like the ancient crypt of Lastingham, St Mary and magnificent Castle Howard.

At Ampleforth my development was stimulated by the two early giants of heritage, William Morris and John Ruskin. As at most schools, sport was placed on a higher pedestal than art, so I had to become an autodidact. My discovery of Morris changed everything, and I enrolled as the youngest member of the William Morris Society. Under his influence I took up calligraphy and printing, and he led me to John Ruskin and my first encounter with the 1880s conservation movement. I remember the excitement of lugging the two volumes of Collingwood's life of Ruskin back on the bus from a second-hand bookshop in York. Like Ruskin, Morris opened many avenues and introduced me to the idea of building protection, something that seemed oddly irrelevant to the rest of 1960s Britain.

It was watching Kenneth Clark's *Civilisation* that confirmed the direction of my life. My first heritage intervention came in my last year at school, when the *Guardian* published my letter defending the seminal exhibition at the V&A, 'The Destruction of the Country House', against a hostile review – a subject near to my heart, given how close both Allerton and Heslington had come to demolition.

When my parents left Yorkshire, we moved to Angus on the east coast of Scotland, close to the ancient Pictish symbol stones at Aberlemno. The nearest city was Dundee, a powerful spectacle of urban decline in the 1970s, and if I write so much about regeneration in this book it is because of that indelible memory, and my delight in seeing Dundee revive. Dundee was a 'problem' city; Edinburgh, by contrast, was a model of conservation, and the reader will find some of the reasons in this book.

In 1975 I went to read history of art at Cambridge. The faculty was in a ferment of ideas and a powerhouse of the newly invigorated architectural history studies, with lectures by Gavin Stamp, John Harris, Marcus Binney, and from the older generation, John Summerson – all of whom play prominent roles in this book. My tutor, David Watkin, was anti-modernist, determined to prove that Nikolaus Pevsner had got it wrong about *zeitgeist* and architecture, but my university friend, Alan Powers, convinced me that the modern movement should be respected.

From Cambridge I joined Sotheby's paintings department as a cataloguer in 1979. It was an exciting time, when London was the leader of the world art market and Sotheby's evinced a giddy international ambition. The home market, however, was wearily familiar to me – largely the dispersal of country house collections. Two years earlier, the firm had held the Mentmore sale, a triumph for Sotheby's and something of a turning point in the heritage story, as we shall see. But what had become of the disciple of Morris and Ruskin? I kept my hand in, printing books by hot metal in Hackney at weekends, and might have continued. However, at the end of the 1980s my career took me to the continent, where I was predominantly to operate for the next decade and more. If I could no longer print books, I could write them, and the first fruit of my time exploring this new terrain was *Great Smaller Museums of Europe*, a book largely about the transition of art from the private sector to the public and my first real engagement with museums.

In contrast to working in Britain, where I had been mainly dealing with inheritors of 'heritage', on the continent I was talking to new collectors creating their own assemblies, which inspired my second book, *Great Collectors of Our Time: Art Collecting since 1945*. In the new millennium Sotheby's called me back to Britain and it was clear that a very great change had taken place in the home market – it was no longer dominated by old master sales from country houses, but by a new breed of London collector more interested in contemporary art. The creation of Tate Modern, the most important cultural event of my lifetime, perfectly expressed this new direction. I was fascinated by this transition and wrote a book with Charles Sebag-Montefiore, *The British as Art Collectors*, to set the story in context. There was still scope for heritage 'saves' at Sotheby's, and I was proud to have had a hand in the transfer – to an initially very reluctant National Trust – of Sir John Vanbrugh's great house in Northumberland, Seaton Delaval. It was the beginning of their 'we don't accept country houses anymore' phase.

When I was offered the chance to write the official biography of Kenneth Clark (of *Civilisation* fame), I decided to make the career change from poacher to gamekeeper. I left Sotheby's and started to write full time. Clark's God was John Ruskin and this would be a chance for me to reconnect with all my early heroes. Clark took Ruskin's message that beauty, art and access to nature were everybody's birthright into the twentieth century. Through his 1969 television series he did more to open people's eyes than anybody since Ruskin. Significantly, the series heralded the so-called heroic period of conservation in the 1970s. Clark himself became a passionate, if conditional, conservationist. He thought that determining a 'use' for things was more important than merely 'saving' them, and believed that spending money repairing Winchester Cathedral was more valuable than preventing the export of a Titian.

Leaving Sotheby's also allowed me the opportunity to join several heritage committees. I gained hands-on experience of the mechanics of saving heritage on, among others, the Acceptance in Lieu Panel and the National Heritage Memorial Fund.

At times it has seemed as if the end of all heritage endeavour was to transfer objects from the private to the public sphere. It was the post-war Labour chancellor, Stafford Cripps, who saw the limitation of what the state could achieve in this regard. Whereas one half of this book is about the move towards government protection, the other half is about individuals who saved things

– so many of the monuments, landscapes, canals, railways and churches that we are fortunate to enjoy today – because they mattered to them personally.

When the Victorians began to think about conservation, for the term heritage was not yet used in its present meaning, they were referring to cathedrals, castles, villages and certain landscapes. Ruskin and Morris, among others, galvanised the movement, but in the ensuing century and a half we have witnessed, despite their efforts, swathes of despoliation and destruction. This book is an attempt to trace some of these stories and show how the losses became the stimulus to legislative protection. Threat has been the enduring engine of heritage, inspiring outrage and then rescue as each successive generation decides its priorities. Heritage has and always will have a changing pattern around a solid core.

The aims of heritage may be summed up as protection, possession, prevention, promotion and participation. Currently heritage plays many roles: it seeks to preserve landscapes, save works of art, prevent eyesores, campaign against new roads and railways, explain history, sell traditional artefacts, and promote culture of many kinds. In 2012 it was invoked with charm and fantasy at the opening of the Olympic Games to tell us one version of who we are. In the name of heritage, streets are reclaimed from motorists, inner cities regenerated, and wildlife habitats are protected. Today we tie these actions to our quality of life and our attempts to safeguard the planet. As a national movement, heritage is impressive in the numbers it has mustered: hundreds of thousands volunteer for it, millions belong to its organisations, and politicians are careful to pay it lip service.* Heritage is usually seen as one of our great national assets and is one of the main reasons, if not the chief reason, that visitors are drawn to Britain.

Since the 1970s, 'heritage' has encompassed a multiplicity of things, both cultural and commercial, tangible and intangible

---

* Samuel p. 270. According to Heritage Counts 2020 figures, it is estimated that the heritage industry employs 563,000 people directly and indirectly and generates £36.6 billion per annum.

– including oral traditions, food heritage, musical heritage, folk heritage, faith heritage, sporting, and stage art, among others.

Just as each generation has its perception of heritage in a polyvocal and diverse polity, so does every social group. This book, however, is concerned with *tangible* heritage, as preserved in buildings, the countryside, urban areas and works of art, and as placed under protection of the law (or not, as it often turns out) to maintain the quality of our cultural and natural environment.

So, many things, from food heritage to musical memory, the rich plurality of storytelling traditions and much else, lies outside this study, although it is important to recognise that the tangible and intangible are intertwined and cannot be viewed in isolation. This is well demonstrated by the Rhodes Must Fall and Black Lives Matter movements. No heritage subject has been more widely debated. When I began writing this book, although the ideas behind it had long been simmering in the background, the phrase Black Lives Matter had not been coined, and Covid-19 did not exist. Together they have had enormous bearing on the heritage story and will no doubt be seen in future as a turning point, a self-reflective sea-change as profound as the democratisation of heritage in the 1960s and 1970s. If movements like BLM have made us reconsider our history and who writes the narratives, Covid-19 showed us how precious heritage is by temporarily depriving us of access to museums, landscapes and other sites of significance, while also fostering a feeling of gratitude for public parks and local assets.

This book is not a history of heritage (although it is structured as a series of histories). It focuses on the most active periods of conservation, those times when the threats to our heritage were at their greatest – throughout the 1880s, and from the 1960s until the end of the 1980s. The human threats today are more insidious: the current mission creep of developers in the centre of every city, the loss of characterful buildings to new tower blocks, and the failure to protect Conservation Areas. Most grievous of all are the threats to the countryside and greenfield sites. Today it is less about what is being demolished than the pressure to build, alter and push the boundaries, aided and abetted by successive governments seeking to stimulate the economy. Writing this book has proved to me that wherever we are, somebody is probably trying to change the look of where we live. Whether this is good or bad, we must try and ensure that it is compatible with the greatest threat of them all: climate change.

Stour Provost, 2021

Introduction

Heritage is no longer confined to the rich and
powerful: it belongs to everyone.

Dᴀᴠɪᴅ Lᴏᴡᴇɴᴛʜᴀʟ[1]

At 9.02 a.m. on a gloomy October day in 1982, in a specially constructed cradle, the ship's frame of the Mary Rose broke the surface, watched by 10 million home viewers.[*] Heritage had never attracted that kind of audience before. A fifth of the nation held its breath as a corner of the lifting gear collapsed, but the hull was not significantly damaged. The raising of Henry VIII's flagship from the sea floor was the world's most ambitious archaeological project and gripped the public imagination. Almost half the hull proved to be perfectly preserved, a time capsule filled with cannons, longbows, sailors' chests, coins, games, musical instruments, and, most poignantly, the remains of 179 crew entombed in its silt. The discovery of the *Mary Rose* sparked intense public interest in the ordinary sailors – their ethnicities, eating habits, and everyday lives. The story had everything: Henry VIII, a sea battle, a disaster, the opening of a tomb in real time on television, artefacts, and the recreation of the sailors' lives. It cemented the love affair between television and archaeology. And it marked the important moment when the emphasis in heritage shifted from the art treasures of the rich to the artefacts and representation of ordinary lives.

Three years before the raising of the *Mary Rose*, the traditional

---

[*] Sixty million internationally.

heritage lobby had turned its energy to Mentmore Towers in Buckinghamshire. This Rothschild treasure house, up for sale following the death of the Earl of Rosebery, was filled with ornate French furniture, old master paintings and *objets d'art*. There had been concerted efforts to save them for the nation, which would have cost a fraction of the price they later fetched at public auction. But, while the drama of saving Mentmore may have galvanised the denizens of Mayfair, it failed to ignite the necessary government support. Accordingly, its contents were dispersed across the globe and the house was acquired by the Maharishi Foundation to become a centre of transcendental meditation. The failure to save Mentmore contrasted sharply with the popular success of the *Mary Rose*, and though Patrick Wright in *On Living in an Old Country* exaggerated what he called the face-off between 'Brideshead and the Tower Blocks', it clearly reflects the redefinition of a newly democratised heritage. The parameters of heritage were shifting, and so was the machinery that supported it. The battle was lost, but the war had only just begun. The recriminations that erupted over the failure at Mentmore called into question the way in which heritage crises were being handled, and out of the ashes of Mentmore's loss emerged the National Heritage Memorial Fund, which in turn seeded that magic money tree, the National Lottery.

In fact, the Mentmore affair, like so many heritage episodes throughout British history, followed a classic pattern. First there is a gathering threat, then a public protest, triggering interventions. When the protest and interventions fail and the loss is grievous, it stimulates a reaction, most typically a change in the law or the formation of some new heritage body or movement. The chapters of this book explore this pattern and some of the *causes célèbres* that have prompted the resulting protections for works of art, buildings, landscapes, and whole districts of cities – most things, in fact, that make up the nation's tangible heritage.

It will be seen throughout this book that the threats which generated these crises were in turn driven by the great cultural disrupters of their times, beginning with those of the Victorians, who introduced the railway, and expanded industrialisation and urbanisation. The disrupters that followed in the twentieth century include the development of the road network and penetration of car ownership, two world wars, indiscriminate town planning, intensive farming and deindustrialisation. Today we have the new disruptions of our time: climate change, population growth, Covid-19, and the pressure for a new consensus on what heritage is – the demands to look again at imperial history and the impact of race, colour, class and equality on how to present the past. It has been a bumpy ride, for if most conservation victories have been achieved through crisis management, victory has never been a certain or permanent outcome – the wins and losses can be counted in equal measure. It is striking how many of the solutions were the result of private initiative.

If there was one threat that can be said to have sparked the birth of the modern heritage movement, it was Lord Spencer's announcement in 1864 that he intended to enclose Wimbledon Common. This brought England's first environmental campaign group into being: the Commons Preservation Society. In this case, the success of the protesters led to the saving of other commons around London through the Metropolitan Commons Act (1866). Failure was often the spur to action. When Robert Hunter joined forces with Octavia Hill to save John Evelyn's garden at Sayes Court, they did not succeed, but it led to their founding the National Trust. Similarly, the threat of over-restoration at Burford Church and the over-zealous work at Tewkesbury Abbey drove William Morris to form the Society for the Protection of Ancient Buildings (SPAB). It took the sale and export of great paintings such as Titian's *Rape of Europa* to bring the National Arts Collections Fund (NACF) into being. The sight of indiscriminate and unchecked development between the wars inspired Patrick Abercrombie to establish the Council for the Preservation of Rural England (CPRE), and the threat of the destruction of Robert Adam's great Adelphi Terrace was midwife to the Georgian Group.

Throughout history, the machinery of government has

inevitably been less nimble than the footwork of individuals, and it was a tiny number of MPs and peers who attempted to push protective legislation through – again, usually in response to a threat. In order to prevent the Avebury Stones from being swamped by housing, Sir John Lubbock MP had to buy them himself, before lobbying for the passing of the first Ancient Monuments Act. The threat of the wholesale dismantling and exporting of Tattershall Castle led to a tightening of this legislation, as did the shameful despoliation of the area surrounding Hadrian's Wall. Underneath all this we see the power of the concerned and determined individual to make the vital difference: Octavia Hill, William Morris, Robert Hunter, Sir John Lubbock, Lord Curzon, Clough Williams-Ellis, Patrick Abercrombie, Tom Rolt, Dame Jennifer Jenkins, Nan Fairbrother, Marcus Binney and Billa Harrod and many others had a profound effect in changing attitudes and getting things done.

If the heritage movement has a totem it is the Euston Arch, which, though long since dismembered and its blocks used as fill in a flood relief channel, has become more important in death than in life; it is a reminder of what happens when conservationists don't win the argument. Indeed, demolitions such as this were like the early Christian martyrs to the movement, inspiring converts. Another was the 1960s loss of Eldon Square in Newcastle, a sight which so shocked Labour minister Richard Crossman that he was won over on the spot to the cause of conservation. As a result, he commissioned a report on four historic cities, Bath, Chester, Chichester and York, and with his Conservative colleague, Duncan Sandys MP, set up the first Conservation Areas. Similarly, it was the demolition of the former Lloyd's Building that brought the Thirties Society into being, although it was the far more keenly felt loss of the 1920s Firestone Factory shortly afterwards that galvanised Michael Heseltine to accelerate his listing programme and tighten the system. The pattern of this political response to threat and loss was reproduced locally – the neglect and vandalism to lonely St

Peter's Church at Corpusty, for example, was the spark for Billa Harrod to establish the influential Norfolk Churches Trust.

What these crises reveal is the British propensity to be most interested in heritage when it is threatened. In this we are not unique. As the American geographer J. B. Jackson pointed out:

It seems clear that the whole preservation and restoration movement is much more than a means of promoting tourism or sentimentalising over an obscure part of the past – though it is also both those things. We are learning to see it as a new interpretation of history (or recently rediscovered). It sees history not as the continuity but as a dramatic discontinuity, a kind of cosmic drama. First there is that golden age, the time of harmonious beginnings. That ensures a period when the old days are forgotten, and the golden age falls into neglect. Finally comes a time when we re-discover and seek to restore the world around us to something like its former beauty…But there has to be that interval of neglect, there has to be discontinuity; It is religiously and artistically essential […] There has to be (in our new concept of history) an interim of death or rejection before there can be renewal and reform. The old order has to die before there can be a born-again landscape.[2]

This pattern of mutability was established early.

The Victorians

The heritage movement in Britain as we know it began with the Victorians. They had inherited a world without any checks or laws to prevent landscapes, buildings or cities being destroyed, or art treasures being sold abroad.* Whereas in other European

---

* The first time a heritage question was asked in parliament was by John Wilkes in 1777 over the Houghton Hall paintings that were sold to Catherine the Great.

countries the impetus to protect heritage gained more government support, in Britain it was the private sector that was to take the initiative.[3] This first heroic period of conservation was created and led by a small band of activists during the 1880s. To their boldness and vision, we owe such astonishingly successful and enduring bodies as the SPAB, the National Trust, the NACF, the germ of English Heritage, and later the CPRE. This is a story of dogged and sometimes angry groups of Victorian idealists persuading parliament and governments to take responsibility to save historic and beautiful sites and treasures. Alan Powers observes that 'the story of conservation is often told as the parallel progress of voluntary association and legislative and administrative action, combined with media pressure, in a combination that seems to be unique to Britain'.[4] Why does the story take flight during the 1880s?

'England in 1880 was aware of a new apprehension about the future', writes Helen Merrell Lynd. Winston Churchill called it the end of an epoch, the death of the old certainties of the Whigs, a period of turmoil, which 'marks the beginning of a new phase in the recurrent struggle for individual freedom'.[5] The confidence of the Victorians was faltering with foreign competition and a decline in world trade. At home, the growth of cities and urban squalor exposed the limitations of economic liberalism and *laissez-faire*. Few could be immune to the impact of poverty. Social progress came in the form of the Employers' Liability Act (1880), which legislated that prosperity had to be balanced with welfare. In the great cities of the Midlands and the north there was a programme of 'collectivism' that responded to the notion of responsibility for citizens' welfare in the broadest sense. The model was Birmingham, which had extended municipal ownership during the 1880s to parks, gardens, museums, art galleries, libraries, baths, technical schools, concert halls, and, most significantly, housing and hospitals.[6] Not every city was as enlightened as Birmingham, and it would require individuals to take most of the initiatives. Toynbee Hall in London's East End opened in 1884, a powerhouse of ideas and education, founded by Henrietta Barnett and her husband, who would later put her theories into practice at Hampstead Garden Suburb. Environment and welfare became inextricably linked, addressing questions of how we live and the quality of our life. They, like those other Victorians, John Ruskin and William Morris, asked: what are the ingredients of a good life? The answer was access to fresh air, green spaces, sanitation and beauty as a birthright. It was not for nothing that Morris wrote his utopian story *News from Nowhere* in this decade, published in 1890.

The Victorians turned conservation into a movement that attempted to improve people's lives through their environment, and this remains today a priority of the nation's heritage endeavours under the heading of 'well-being'. The three founders of the National Trust were all inspired by the idea that the people should have access to green spaces: Robert Hunter protecting Wimbledon Common, Canon Rawnsley in his attempts to preserve the Lake District, and Octavia Hill opening up green spaces for poor city children. Indeed, among the most successful and lasting philanthropic inheritances from the Victorians are our public parks and gardens. Today there are reckoned to be 27,000 of them in the UK.[7]

Chris Miele has suggested that such protection 'was an act of defiance against capitalism'.[8] Although in central London and most cities capitalism won, in Victorian Edinburgh, Glasgow, Guildford and Norwich we can observe the first stirrings of civic responsibility for the built environment. Moreover, if the Victorians were destructive – especially when they built railway tracks and stations – they were also creating much of the fabric of what today is regarded as quintessential heritage: great public buildings, municipal town halls, museums and libraries, ornate Gothic Revival churches, canals, mills, terraces of housing, and public parks.

It took them time to understand the social impact of their railways, and at first it was the desecration of landscape that caused the most anguish. It is often suggested that the railways cemented the preservationist bodies, as it aroused the energies of the greatest of all Victorian prophets and the father of the heritage movement, John Ruskin. He lashed out in *Modern Painters* with words that still have resonance: 'Wherever I look or travel in England or abroad, I see that men, wherever they can reach, destroy all beauty. They seem to have no other desire or hope but to have large houses and to be able to move fast. Every perfect and lovely spot which they can touch, they defile.'[9] Ruskin believed that art, beauty and morality were indivisible, and that ugliness was wicked. As Clive Aslet put it, 'we have him as much as anyone to thank that, while much has been lost, much also survives'.[10]

Although many Victorian heritage endeavours included a radical tinge, at the other end of the spectrum was the question of portable heritage in the hands of the great aristocratic families. At what level did they feel a sense of public responsibility towards the works of art they owned? They nearly all lent them to the spectacular 1857 Manchester Art Treasures exhibition, and admitted two indefatigable German art historians to inspect their art collections: Gustav Waagen and J. D. Passavant, who documented the privately owned paintings of England at their zenith.* Perhaps their published catalogues encouraged the idea that even Italian and Dutch pictures could become British heritage through long-term possession. Nonetheless, sales of such works to overseas collectors had already begun, and continued relentlessly. The loss of Bellini's *Feast of the Gods*, one of the greatest old master paintings ever to leave Britain, reveals a political calculation at work. The chancellor, Austen Chamberlain, refused to assist owing to a railway strike, and to a perceived notion that the working class was disenfranchised from heritage or opposed to it. This tension between 'elite' heritage

---

* The owners were also happy to collaborate with the Historical Manuscripts Commission set up by Royal Warrant in 1869, formed to document historical papers in private hands. The inspectors, initially seen as snoopers, gained the trust of aristocratic owners because by 1884 they had reported on 424 private muniment rooms in seventeen detailed volumes.

and popular pleasures echoes down to the Heritage Lottery Fund.* The private sector would finally have to step in to save masterpieces, and in 1903 the NACF was formed to do exactly that.

One of the distinctive points of the British experience of heritage has been the degree of collaboration between the public or quasi-public and private sectors. When Sir John Lubbock attempted to pass legislation to list and offer guidance on ancient monuments on their land, many landowners were wary. Indeed, all proposed heritage legislation came up against the impregnable defence of the rights of private property, and landowners were innately suspicious of state intervention. The original Ancient Monuments Act of 1882 was toothless, relying merely on the ability of the first Inspector of Ancient Monuments, Augustus Pitt Rivers, to make landowners want to care for their monuments. When effective laws could not be passed, the only possible way forward was through persuasion and offers of collaboration. Fortunately, the agency responsible, the Office of Works, understood this well. It led the way by striking deals over royal palaces with the monarchy. This partnership model was repeated with the War Office over historic castles, and subsequently with landowners over their ruined abbeys, towers and monuments. In this way, the first national heritage estate was formed, aimed at enabling public access, and eventually leading to the spectacular inventory of properties held by English Heritage today.

In parallel came the growing number of properties held by the National Trust. Sometimes misleadingly described as England's 'noblest nationalisation', the Trust has always maintained

---

* Yeats signalled this question in his poem 'To a Wealthy Man':
And did Guidobaldo, when he made
That grammar school of courtesies
Where wit and beauty learned their trade
Upon Urbino's windy hill,
Had sent no runners to and fro
That he might learn the shepherds' will.

an uneasy equilibrium between its buildings and art and the countryside, and between the socialism inherent in its aims, and the benevolence of the landowners on whom it has relied for properties. However, in its early days it seemed unlikely to turn into anything much more than a small charitable body, and in 1898 it had only made two acquisitions. One of them, Toys Hill in Kent, one of the finest views in southern England, was given by Richardson Evans in memory of Frederick Feeney. That beautiful stretches of land could be made over in memory of the dead was a novel idea, and this would later be taken up after the civilian and military losses of World War II, with the Land Fund founded in 1946. The National Trust's country-house scheme, established in 1937, achieved a beautiful solution to the triangular problem of dealing with crippling death duties, allowing families to stay in their historic homes, and providing public access; in effect it is a form of voluntary nationalisation. Similarly, the national parks, the Acceptance in Lieu scheme for works of art, and the law of treasure trove for metal detectorists, are pragmatic collaborative solutions to heritage problems that benefit both public and private interests. Many of these solutions involving such partnerships developed over a long period.*

Those Blue Remembered Hills...

A striking feature of the interwar years is the ascendancy of countryside preservation over that of towns and cities, described in the chapter 'The Search for Arcadia'. It is during this period that Italy, France and Germany took a different course, making a conscious effort to preserve their historic towns by passing

---

* Other countries have their own solutions: the French have their *Dation* system, like the British AIL scheme, and the Americans give tax concessions for gifts to museums. Both the USA and Italy have National Trust equivalents, but they have not had the success in membership or gifts.

protective measures, but doing less to preserve their countryside. In 1924 France had formed *La Demeure Historique*, a syndicate of the owners of historic buildings (both urban and rural) who successfully lobbied government for grants. Nothing like this would exist in Britain until after World War II.

Andrew Motion observed that 'the English landscape is our great collaborative masterpiece and our greatest gift to the wide world, greater even than Shakespeare'.[11] Observers from Wordsworth and Ruskin to Octavia Hill and Patrick Abercrombie instinctively understood that 'because our greatest achievement is to have made the English landscape, our greatest responsibility is to save it.'[12] The creation of the CPRE in 1926, not to mention the outpouring of books celebrating villages and landscapes, all ensured that this remained the focus of protection; the car represented an even more insidious threat in the twentieth century than the railways had in the century before. The development of the road network and the changes it brought are described in Chapter Two, sometimes through the eye of *Country Life*, a magazine written for town folk to enjoy a (generally) halcyon take on the countryside. Meanwhile London was subjected to virtually unrestricted redevelopment.

Looking at government interventions on behalf of the nation's heritage either side of World War II, there is a distinct sense of Old and New Testament. World War II had by far the greater impact on heritage both in terms of its destruction and, in the aftermath, the institution of a legal and aesthetic framework that would make heritage a national preoccupation. The statism engendered by the war enabled the 1945 Labour government to lay the foundations for nearly all current heritage protection, although this would not become fully effective until the 1980s. In the meantime, Britain was about to experience a destructive force even more powerful than the Blitz: that of post-war reconstruction.

The war caused government, architects and urban planners to consider the question posed by the RIBA in 1943: how much can you say is really worthy of preservation? The answer, it seemed, was only the best individual buildings. A new world was to be built on the ashes of the old, retaining, as one planner put it, 'a few monuments as museum pieces'.* Progress, health and a more sanitary environment were promoted as the antidote to the squalor and congestion of historic cities and buildings of the past. This post-war attitude was exemplified by the architectural historian John Summerson, whose interest lay in buildings that were both attributable to leading architects and influential in terms of driving design. He saw little worth in 'group value', the street or townscape taken as a whole. This approach undervalued, for instance, terraced housing and surroundings which would later become the cornerstones on which Conservation Areas would be designated. Interestingly, the archaeologists were moving in the opposite direction, away from the search for the grand palace or exceptional Roman villa, appreciating instead the group value of a site, such as the remains of ordinary dwellings in early cities at Winchester and York. Correctly, they had anticipated the future in their preoccupation with 'how people lived'.

The zeal of the modern movement to erase the old world and rebuild a new one resulted in a comprehensive plan for the redevelopment of nearly every city in Britain. In the words of Gavin Stamp this was 'a form of terror' which inevitably provoked resistance and discredited its architects.[13] In the meantime, the planners were reconfiguring cities like Plymouth and Newcastle. The chapter on Birmingham is a case history of what happened when planners were given full powers to rebuild a great city with unrestricted access for the car. The perceived need for an inner ring road – a recurrent element in nearly all city planning strategies in the post-war era – had a devastating effect on old cathedral cities such as Worcester and Exeter. By 1969 Kenneth Clark could place planners on his roll call of the enemies of

---

* Herbert Manzoni, the planner who transformed Birmingham. Andrew Saint quotes a civil servant in 1946: 'A very limited category of superlative quality and possibly unique or [...] a selection of representative specimens of their period or type.' Hunter/Saint p. 129.

civilisation.[14] Relentlessly, historic towns and buildings would go on being mutilated until the 1970s. There were grants available to local councils for creating new housing, whereas none existed for preserving and renovating old properties until 1969.

One of the earliest and most effective decriers of this destruction was the angry architectural critic Ian Nairn, who believed that 'the planning offensive was started in a mood of idealism which assumed two things: that rules would be used flexibly and intelligently, and that England was of unlimited size'.[15] In Nairn's view the problems arose when planning 'was tied down step by step with local government [...] this chained it to the very points where democracy is most likely to give the lowest common denominator, not the highest common multiple.'[16]

In post-war Britain, despite the idealism, local councils often turned out to be a destructive force. Birmingham had the attentions of Frank Price and his planner, Herbert Manzoni, for whom the historic fabric of the city was all that stood between them and the New Jerusalem. Most infamous was T. Dan Smith in Newcastle, who combined a passion for planning with corrupt practices. The most tragically destructive council of all was Bath, for whom preservation was an impediment to prosperity. Lord Goodman said of them, 'stupidity is even more difficult to control than evil'.[17] What the so-called Sack of Bath revealed was the ineffectiveness of legislation and consequences of 'masterpiece' thinking. It also exposed the pernicious way in which heritage was cast, particularly by local government and developers, as something frozen, an obstacle to achieving the desired future.* Moreover, heritage was bedevilled at this period by a vague perception that somehow it was a pensioner on the

---

* Alan Bennett amusingly characterised it in 1967: 'How many times in the last 10 years has one seen the same drawing: that spacious sun-baked piazza, the motor-cars tucked vaguely away somewhere, those fine flourishing trees, those outdoor restaurants, the whole thronged with Precinct People, a race of tall, long-headed men. Municipal Masai, who lounge about every architect's drawing in a languor.' Otto Saumarez Smith, p. 57.

state. Yet in complete contrast to the councillors of Bath, we see the benign influence and philanthropic attentions of J. B. Morrell in York, who so vastly benefited the fabric of that city. He and the Civic Trust reinvented its fortunes.

Even among the most fervent apostles of the modern movement, doubt was beginning to creep in. What Peter Smithson described as the 'heroic period of modern architecture' was followed by what Alan Powers dubbed the 'heroic period of conservation'. The planner Colin Buchanan was something of a visionary in his understanding that the increased use of the car was incompatible with environmental standards and quality of life. As early as 1958 he had recognised the 'terrible price' of the new mobility and wrote apocalyptically: 'It is not the traffic movement but civilised town life that is at stake.' His final epiphany would come at the inquiry into the proposed new London airport at the pretty village of Cublington.[18] Each of the main political parties had MPs both hostile and sympathetic to the conservation movement: while the Conservative minister Peter Walker deplored the sentimental public desire to retain all that exists and oppose all that is new, on the Labour benches Anthony Crosland complained that conservationists were 'hostile to growth and indifferent to the needs of ordinary people'.[19]

★ ★ ★

In its search for spiritual values, the idealism of post-war Britain led the Labour chancellor Hugh Dalton to establish the Land Fund in 1946, which he financed supposedly with the sale of surplus army equipment. Here for the first time was a dedicated fund for 'the enrichment of national life', and in the spirit of the property held by the National Trust at Toys Hill, its remit was to acquire, as a memorial to the dead of the two world wars, land and, later, houses. Significantly, it was endowed with its own capital (or so it was believed) and therefore appeared free from the need to petition future chancellors for money at sensitive times such as recessions or emotive strikes. Although the Land Fund saved many important properties, disastrously, it came under

Treasury control – which slowly choked it to death. But its spirit lived on and was later to inspire the Heritage Memorial Fund and the Heritage Lottery Fund, which were set up independent of Treasury control. Heritage in post-war Britain, however, had all the appearance of being very top-down and elitist until, as we shall see, an army of enthusiasts reclaimed the canals and railways.

The post-war era saw a shift in power from landowners to the state with the nationalisation of development rights and the imposition of what historians have called 'the 1947 system'. This was part of a macroeconomic plan which included the protection of habitats and beauty spots, yet at the same time encouraged national self-sufficiency, productivity, and mechanisation – three noble ideas which soon proved to be at odds with one another. Progressives had been speaking since the 1930s of the well-being and spiritual values that accrued to pastoral landscapes, and post-war legislation – above all the National Parks Act – was the fulfilment of this idea. Our own contemporary concept of heritage and well-being is founded on this notion, which stretches back to Octavia Hill. But on the other hand, not only were modern farming methods destroying rural scenery, habitats and hedgerows, but the countryside was under a new pressure from motorways that swept through, with their junctions, feeder roads and giant roundabouts to nearby towns and villages. From the 1970s the battleground became new roads and motorways, notably the M3 at Winchester. The bypass was especially problematic, as it saved towns but spoiled their hinterlands and views. The *conservation versus progress* argument became noisiest at Newbury in 1996, when the A34 bypass united grassroots activists and county ladies in protest.

If the destruction to the countryside was a cumulative process, the effects of the sinking of the oil tanker *Torrey Canyon* in 1967 were both immediate and lasting. This event galvanised the environmental movement into life and gained popular support for it. If most heritage alarms can be counted as local or national issues, the environment was nothing if not global and required, then as now, global solutions. Landscape became moral territory, and this was underlined by the United Nations Conference on the Environment, held in Stockholm in 1972. As Max Nicholson observed, 'the task of Environmental Conservation is peculiar, if not unique. It has to achieve a vast and complex but definable result within a time limit that is relatively brief, although inconveniently longer than is customary for most normal human programmes'.[20] The report on the proposed Cublington airport provides a fascinating example of the limits of growth. Colin Buchanan's conclusion that the social gain was not commensurate to the environmental and heritage loss raises the fascinating problem of measurement. How do you calculate such losses and gains? This is one of the central challenges of heritage today. How much are we prepared to forgo to protect the integrity of our environment?

The 1970s Backlash

If the pre-war conservation movement was largely directed at landscape, it was the post-war attack on our cities that was to concentrate the minds of a younger generation of activists: Ian Nairn, Marcus Binney, Gavin Stamp and Simon Jenkins. They brought a shift of focus in terms of both date and type of building that needed to be protected. Before the end of World War II, few would have attempted to save a Victorian building, but so many of the great conservation battles – St Pancras Station, the Albert Dock in Liverpool and the Euston Arch itself – proved that Victorian architecture was being reappraised. With this came a new interest in the stupendous architecture of the Industrial Revolution: its mills, factories and canals which – from the 1980s onwards, when urban regeneration began – were to become the new focus of heritage in Liverpool, Birmingham and Manchester. The founding of the Victorian Society in 1957 was a major event which – brought together by Anne, Lady Rosse – included many famous names of the older generation of conservation: James Lees-Milne, John Betjeman and Nikolaus Pevsner.

Architects have usually seen amenity societies as a plague on their existence, which in the words of Sir Giles Scott, 'harass the unfortunate artist and hamper the production of the work.'[21] But it was the scale of redevelopment throughout the twentieth century that gave birth to such societies and galvanised them to make the case for preservation. The Georgian Group was formed in the 1930s to challenge the then prevalent view that architecture stopped in 1700; the Thirties Society was founded in 1979 to defend such interwar buildings which stood outside the approved canon of the modern movement -- but it soon expanded its remit and became the Twentieth Century Society. As Gavin Stamp observed: 'to a remarkable extent the history of conservation has been the art of keeping one step ahead of public opinion'.[22]

During the 1970s, 'planning through public protest' acquired a new prevalence and force, proving that well-organised residents could defeat the planners.* Those traditional guardians of heritage who ran the Victorian Society were now joined in alliance by the New Left. Together they proved to be a formidable force. It was, as Simon Thurley described, 'a period when the focus on conservation moved from the State to the individual. The initiative shifted from a small number of specialist campaigning societies – passionate but with limited support – who got governments to change the law through their friends in parliament, to bodies enjoying massive popular support that could not be ignored by politicians.'[23] The campaign to save Covent Garden and its market buildings was a turning point, reversing as it did the top-down methods of post-war planning and becoming the new plan of attack for many future battles. Rod Hackney's neighbourhood challenge in Macclesfield was another case in point, and that story reminds us of the small but highly significant change in the

* There were in fact successful public agitations going back to Richmond Hill at the turn of the twentieth century.

law, the 1969 Housing Act, which passed in the aftermath of the Ronan Point collapse, providing grants for the restoration of properties. This is the period in which the language changes from 'slum clearance', which had held sway since Victorian times, to the 'improvement' of existing buildings and streets.

Government was woken up to the growing interest in area and character. The culmination of this new sensibility was the creation and passing of the Conservation Areas legislation, which required cooperation from both sides of the House of Commons in 1967.* The triple alliance of Richard Crossman on the Labour benches and Duncan Sandys on the Conservative side enabled its passage through the House of Commons, assisted by Wayland Kennet (Labour) in the Lords. This period underlines the importance of both listing and of individual ministerial resolve: Crossman and Sandys were outstanding in this respect. In the chapters on York and Bath we can see the impact of Conservation Area legislation, the difference being that in York the councillors, albeit after initial hostility, strenuously promoted them, while in Bath the councillors were the problem against which the legislation struggled to operate. The Birmingham chapter shows how, sadly, even today the Conservation Areas are being ignored or downgraded.

Britain was not alone in its new-found interest in heritage conservation. The UNESCO World Heritage Convention in 1972 brought together in a single document the concepts of

---

* The French were ahead in Conservation Areas and took the idea a little further. Their seminal example was the Marais district in Paris where they undertook an enhancement plan for 450 acres of the city, including buying up the more important buildings. This was one of forty *Secteurs Sauvegardés* created in France in 1962 through *La loi Malraux*, named after the Minister of Culture.

nature conservation and the preservation of cultural properties.* It defined the kind of natural and cultural sites which could be considered for inscription on the World Heritage List, and set out for each country its duties in not only identifying potential sites but in protecting and preserving them. Britain signed the Convention, and as a result the designation of sites such as Ironbridge Gorge has brought greater public awareness and funding to the local economy. Occasionally UNESCO has threatened to delist urban sites which have become degraded by damaging development. This was the case with the Tower of London and the Palace of Westminster, which avoided delisting in 2009 and 2013 respectively in the wake of intrusive tower block proposals. UNESCO have also cast a wary eye over developments in Bath and Liverpool, but while Bath is concerned not to lose the status, Liverpool was unconcerned to lose it in 2021. The recent mayor of Liverpool, Joe Anderson, blithely used to comment that: 'not one person who comes to visit our city comes to see the UNESCO certificate on my wall.'[24]

The year 1975 is usually seen as the turning of the tide in conservation. Before that date there was always an assumption that a campaign might be lost, but by this date public opinion, the press and politicians had aligned to give their support. It was a euphoric time for conservationists. The year was designated European Architectural Heritage Year and celebrated with commemorative postage stamps, souvenirs and, in Britain at least, 'something of the character of a village fete'.[25] The Civic Trust was appointed to curate a series of events in Britain and the first 'heritage centres' were established in Faversham, York and Chester. Suddenly heritage became highly marketable, and goods from lamps to marmalade were promoted as 'heritage'. As

---

* The idea of combining conservation of cultural sites with those of nature comes from the USA. A White House Conference in Washington, D.C. in 1965 called for a 'World Heritage Trust' that would stimulate international cooperation to protect 'the world's superb natural and scenic areas and historic sites for the present and the future of the entire world citizenry'.

one civil servant rightly observed: 'It was perhaps the beginning of the populist concern for conservation which increasingly supplanted the elitist tradition of conservation in Britain.'[26] 1975 was also the year of Dan Cruickshank and Colin Amery's book *The Rape of Britain*, which revealed the shocking extent of what had been lost in the previous twenty years.

There was one heritage sector that was enjoying something of a revival. Country houses had certainly had a tumultuous post-war history. Forward-thinking owners such as the Duke of Bedford at Woburn pioneered the concept of the family day out, introducing and explaining heritage in a way that was fun for all ages, from safari parks to Rembrandt and retail. During the 1960s the National Trust, still digesting all the great houses it had recently absorbed, held a conservationist point of view but was going through a not-so-quiet revolution on a drive to expand its membership. While it could count only 7,000 members in 1945, rising to 100,000 in 1960, by 1981 it hit the magic number of 1 million, prompting the suddenly ubiquitous car stickers, 'I'm one in a million'. Indeed, it was with the growth of family weekends planned around the car that the National Trust came into its own, which prompted Roy Strong's reflection: 'I concluded the cult of heritage coincided with the decline of the place once occupied by the Church of England in the mental mythology of the middle classes. The worship of God has been replaced by one of heritage.' [27] Heritage sites were now, in the eyes of many, tourist destinations. However, in 1965, in a return to its earlier priorities of landscape and coastline, the National Trust launched 'Enterprise Neptune' to safeguard as much as possible of the rapidly disappearing unspoiled coasts of Britain.

When Mentmore was allowed to be broken up, the National Heritage Memorial Fund was formed out of the resulting crisis, in 1980. What the country received was an independent body dedicated to saving tracts of land, houses, works of art, historic airfields, boats and anything else that might have a memorial value. Nor was this the only organisation to be founded by government with a heritage suffix. It was to be followed by

English Heritage, and later under John Major, the Department of National Heritage, and the National Heritage Lottery Fund. This was the zenith of government's preoccupation with heritage. During the 1980s there was one minister on whose shoulders the mantle of Crossman and Sandys came to rest: Michael Heseltine, a heritage dynamo who was frequently at odds with his prime minister and cabinet colleagues, especially over the fate of Liverpool. His reaction to crises was both immediate and ambitious, and his operations in Liverpool alone earn him a place in the heritage pantheon.*

The Thatcher period was one of intense questioning about the economics of heritage, as with all areas of public life. Until this time all governments had accepted museums and heritage sites as pensioners on the state, but no longer. Why couldn't the success of the National Trust and the private sector be replicated in the public sector? Their answer was to create English Heritage, a glossy rebranding of the Ministry of Public Buildings and Works. In terms of visitor numbers and presentation, it had a long way to catch up with the Trust and the members of the recently formed Historic Houses Association. It learned quickly despite its awkward triple responsibilities as curator of the nation's heritage estate, grant-giver, and lister and enforcer of ancient monuments and historic building protection. There never was a golden age in heritage conservation, but by the end of the 1980s improved legislation, advances in listing, well established Conservation Areas, and experienced heritage bodies were all in place.

However, despite this promising landscape, the fate of English Heritage was not a happy one. Heritage was a lesser priority under New Labour, and the resources of English Heritage were puny beside those of the new behemoth, the Heritage Lottery Fund. It found itself fighting on all three fronts: protecting funding for its curatorial responsibilities,

---

* In the early 1980s, Heseltine introduced a simple but successful heritage test: permission would not normally be given to demolish a listed building unless it had been offered for sale, preferably freehold.

grant-giving to historic properties, and defending its role in the planning system – now seen as 'Orwellian' and a blockage to development. New Labour had little time for what it perceived as heritage nostalgia, and promptly reduced the previous government's heritage enthusiasms in favour of its preferred 'creative industries', the heady and economically successful mix of pop culture, advertising agencies, and Brit Pack artists, all adding up to Cool Britannia. English Heritage was seen by both the Blair and Cameron governments as something to be broken up, dismembered, or sold. Since that time politicians of both main parties have attempted to undermine the planning laws to promote a prosperity agenda through a building boom. As Jocelyn Stevens reflected in his valedictory report as chairman of English Heritage: 'My first realisation [was] that saving the heritage was a continuous battle and that central government was one of the heritage's deadliest enemies.'[28]

The anti-heritage backlash had in fact been simmering for some time. As Patrick Wright noted: 'In Britain as elsewhere, activists, writers, and politicians have long been both claiming and fiercely rejecting the idea of "heritage".'[29] For most intellectuals, the association of the term with a form of jingoistic patriotism and its identity with a triumphalist historical narrative of the Arthur Bryant type was enough to put them off. The plethora of polemical books published during the 1980s, including Wright's *On Living in an Old Country*, David Lowenthal's *The Past is a Foreign Country*, and Robert Hewison's *The Heritage Industry** emerged at a time of

---

* The origin of the term 'heritage industry' is not straightforward: originally appearing as a heading for an article about the Arts Council in New Society in 1981, its first use in any meaningful sense was by Colin Ward in a 1985 review of Patrick Wright's seminal book *On Living in an Old Country*. The term, however, only caught on with Robert Hewison's 1987 book. The nomenclature is discussed in an unpublished article by Hewison 'Afterword/ Afterwards: The Heritage Industry Revisited, 2018' which the author kindly showed me.

intense questioning about the value and meaning of the past, made piquant by Margaret Thatcher's seemingly conflicted attitude, both iconoclastic and sentimental. Intellectuals shared a sense that heritage was perpetuating untruthful history. In Lowenthal's words, 'Heritage is not history: heritage is what people make of their history to make themselves feel good.'[30] The tangled web between the uses of 'identity' heritage and the projection of tangible heritage has never been resolved and the debate has been hugely stimulated by movements like Black Lives Matter. However, the conflating of heritage with community concerns by the Heritage Lottery Fund went some way to paper over the question.

The most politically forthright was Hewison, who wielded the term heritage with scorn. His essential objection was that it was falsely encouraging a repackaged, commodified past that played to a sentimentalised view of a lost golden age, as exemplified, for instance, by Ridley Scott's TV commercial for Hovis. By doing so heritage perpetrated conservative nostalgia for a country in palpable economic decline that was searching for escape. Hewison's book provided a counterblast. While his critics pointed out that he tended to imply that all heritage activities imparted a uniform set of values, usually of nostalgic character, Simon Jenkins in the *Sunday Times* was more pungent, describing the book as 'the wail of post-war socialist dogma gone sour' (Hewison gamely commented: 'sounds pretty accurate').[31] It was a brilliant polemic, but it made no attempt to describe or understand the conservation and curatorial backbone of heritage: the need to preserve towns and cities and the problems of preventing the spoliation of the countryside. His contention that the growth of new museums was symbolic of national decline would be put to the test during the Blair years when, thanks to the Lottery, new museums like Tate Modern became flagship cultural drivers of urban regeneration.

★ ★ ★

The arrival of the National Heritage Lottery Fund changed the game, with its unprecedented transfusion of money into the cultural bloodstream. The watchword of 'additionality' was devised so that grants would be over and above what government would ordinarily fund, *but not in place of it*. However, soon this began to blur. What was evident from the beginning was that, as the funds came directly from the public, there would be a close scrutiny of how the millions were spent, and considerable sensitivity about elite projects. Heritage became connected with social values and community benefit in a way that Octavia Hill would have applauded. The Urban Parks Programme, for instance, became one of its most successful and popular projects. At first the British Lottery remained free of government intervention to a degree that surprised European lottery functionaries; ministers merely provided the policy direction on 'people, activities and access'. Over the years, however, government meddling grew – the grants became more conditional, and bodies such as English Heritage were starved of funds in order that the Lottery should pick up the bills instead. Moreover, government saddled the Lottery with its various millennium projects; it is certain that the Lottery provided the government with an excuse not to fund museum development.

With its recent change of names, the National Lottery Heritage Fund suggests a change of emphasis, less about heritage itself and more about public engagement with heritage. As one recent chairman, Peter Luff, put it to the author: 'For me the heritage is always about people, which means it's not always the finest examples of something that need to be saved, but the ones that have changed – or could change – lives most. Listing or expert approval is not necessarily a measure of heritage worth, but of academic preference. Heritage is not synonymous with excellence.'[32] This would not matter if Historic England (once a part of English Heritage) were properly funded. At present it is far too heavily reliant on the Lottery for its conservation projects, which has a different set of priorities. The loss of funding for Historic England is an urgent problem – it is their job, not that of the NLHF, to keep the fabric of the nation in repair.

Volunteerism

There have been many post-World War II heritage achievements: comprehensive listing of buildings and monuments, the introduction of Conservation Areas, the development of non-elite heritage, urban regeneration, and the accompanying explosion in visitor numbers to heritage sites. Perhaps the most unsung achievement has been the astonishing growth of volunteerism. Octavia Hill used to say that 'gifts of time' were as important as gifts of money, and without the volunteers, the National Trust would not have been able to grow and operate in its present form. Volunteerism vastly expanded post-1945, when heritage bodies came to rely on it at all levels: as the muscle needed to clear and restore canals, and to repair and drive steam trains; for guiding in historic properties, keeping churches open, or the hours (and legal skills) required to rebut a planning application. The importance of civic society volunteers working tirelessly to protect and enhance their locality cannot be overstated. They hold councils and developers to account and where they do not exist – I give some examples in Birmingham – rules are ignored.

In his book *The Sack of Bath*, Adam Fergusson eloquently describes the cost, stress and time spent in the attempt to fight a proposed threat. Simon Jenkins calls volunteers 'culture's fifth column and its golden goose [...] volunteers are the foundation on which most arts organisations depend, though some don't know it'.[33] The National Trust relies on more than 61,000 volunteers who give more than 4.6 million hours of free labour each year; without them the organisation would cease to function.[34] Jenkins points out the disadvantages of volunteers: they're hard to discipline, can be irritating, and contrary to contemporary requirements they tend to be white, middle class and seldom young.* However, the journalist Matthew Parris, writing about his local Derbyshire cultural spots, has described 'the selfless enthusiasts, volunteers, people who look after things, people who want us to see and enjoy the small treasures that they care for [...] a national army of benevolent men and women are neither forgotten nor hidden, but they are modest'.[35]

The dependence on volunteers is also manifestly true of the Church of England. Its churches require around 32,000 churchwardens (giving approximately 1.5 million hours a year) who take on the responsibility on behalf of their Parochial Church Council (PCC). To explore churches this book examines those in Greater Manchester and, as a demographic counterpoint, those in Norfolk. The first thing that strikes the observer is that the temples of the Church of England, in contrast to those of continental Europe, are self-financing and self-governing. The volunteers of the Diocese of Norwich are a shining example of what well-organised and motivated communities can achieve. The Norfolk story underlines the truth, demonstrated by Billa Harrod at Corpusty, that while it takes many people to close a church it needs only one determined person to save it. Succession planning is the problem, and the question is whether the next generation of volunteers will come forward. This is equally true of civic societies. For most areas of heritage, churches, archaeology, and for the National Trust, volunteers form the bedrock of support that keeps them functioning; in some sectors volunteers are the bosses, the workers and everything in between.

The chapter on canals, narrowboats and heritage railways describes the triumph of volunteerism – providing a regular supply of skilled labour all day, every day of the season. When asked how much a volunteer railway paid its engine drivers,

---

* The Art Fund, for one, abolished their regional volunteer network which was out of tune with the direction of the organisation. A Heritage Lottery Fund review in 2017 revealed that volunteer profiles showed they were 98 per cent white British, 44 per cent over sixty, and 69 per cent holding at least one degree.

the answer came: 'minus £50 a trip – and a two-year waiting list'.[36] Volunteer railways are a part of the post-war heritage story which grew from the grassroots up. Teenagers graduated to them from childhood model railways, and no heritage sector has attracted more young people. One of the most inspiring stories in this book is that of the rescue of the Bluebell Railway, which was the achievement of four teenagers. Such restorations attracted volunteers from across the country and tapped into something deeper than community, a sense that anybody could create heritage: 'hands-on heritage' might have been the motto. This was one sector where you could delight in the smiling faces of children enjoying the fruits of your labour.

Beyond the hard work and pleasure, volunteer railways faced the same type of pivotal questions that all heritage organisations must address, whether at Kenilworth Castle or Cawston church: whom are they serving? Enthusiasts, tourists, or locals going about their usual business? How authentic must the experience be? Restored old engines or cheaper new ones? Steam or electric? Railways, like canals, highlight an important heritage distinction between objects and systems. In the preface I referenced Kenneth Clark's support for 'use' over simply 'saving'. Buildings that have a function, like the Whitechapel Bell Foundry, only have meaning if they continue to make bells.* Should the *Cutty Sark* be saved if it cannot sail? There is no definitive answer to this question, but it should always be posed.

Regeneration

Most of the movements that have driven heritage were invented or developed by the Victorians. But the idea of regeneration is very much of our time. It involves the repurposing of former

---

* The Whitechapel Bell Foundry was closed in 2017, the building sold to a developer to be converted to a luxury hotel, and has been the subject of a conservationist battle ever since.

industrial buildings and their wider locale, making old and new architecture work together to create a new sense of place. This has been the most progressive aspect of heritage in recent times, and it dispels the notion that conservation and economic growth are incompatible. It proves that enterprise and free market economics can harness the historic built environment as a locomotive for positive change. 'Cumulatively', writes John Pendlebury, 'this shifted heritage protection from being marginal to being a central element of town planning, something which has continued into this century. It is an inescapable and powerful shaping force in the evolution of our towns and cities.'[37] Once concerned with preserving important monuments, heritage was now seen as the means of regenerating towns and cities as part and parcel of economic and social development. Once an economic passenger, heritage was now pulling the train.

The most ambitious regeneration projects – Battersea Power Station excepted – addressed whole sections of the declining industrial districts of great cities. In the latter half of the twentieth century, 'the city' was pathologised as sick, moribund, and often dangerous. Stanley Kubrick's film *A Clockwork Orange* (1972) well expressed this dystopian view. Dockland areas were particularly affected, and it was at Liverpool – a city with a powerful cultural backstory – that we observe the first stirrings of change, exemplified by the restoration of Albert Dock and establishment of Tate Liverpool. Cultural assets were revaluated, and the success of Liverpool became the forerunner to classic regeneration projects at Gateshead, Manchester, King's Cross and now Dundee.

The change in a district such as Manchester's Ancoats between 2000 and 2020 was astonishing. The idea that anyone other than a football crowd would fly there from Milan for a weekend city break would have been risible until recently. But developers have discovered that 'heritage' gives a competitive advantage, and people now visit for leisure, shopping and culture. When used wisely, the historic built environment is a powerful catalyst and accelerant to the making of magnetic places. Sometimes this requires an outside stimulant, such as the faster railway now serving a revived Margate. In the nineteenth century, culture and heritage followed economic success, but today they are harnessed as the driver of area's regeneration – in Dundee, it is hoped the new V&A will attract a £1 billion investment in the city.

In regeneration, conservation and progress, in the past viewed as difficult bedfellows, found a mutual accommodation, transforming the redundant into the useful, and the dark and dilapidated into pleasing environments for all activities. What are the ingredients of success? A waterline helps certainly, the framework of an old dock or canal basin, a strong group of former industrial buildings, and a balance of new occupants and uses. King's Cross and Birmingham's Brindleyplace bring design, production, living and consumption together. Such places reflect the wider changes in Britain over the last half century, in which architectural, creative and service skills have taken over Britain's industrial base, the country dubbed by Mark Leonard as 'Creative Island [...] blossoming in film, design, architecture, music, computer games and fashion'.

Perhaps the greatest loss is mystery, the very poetry that Larkin found in the blackened warehouses of the backstreet canals. When the self-educated architectural historian John Harris described his childhood forays with Uncle Sid searching for trout streams around post-war Middlesex, it is easy to be moved by the descriptions of dishevelled old parks with beautiful gate piers leading to the ghostly remains of a demolished house, or to one awaiting execution. Today there are few parts of historic Britain that have not been restored and polished. One of the most inspiring recent conservation stories is that of Gwrych Castle in Wales, whose Preservation Trust was established in 1997 by the twelve-year-old Mark Baker when his heart was stirred on his way to school by the sight of the castle's forlorn state.* Perhaps J.

---

* With support from the Heritage Memorial Fund, in 2019 Mark Barker saw off various proposals to develop the grounds and finally the Trust secured a lease to welcome visitors.

B. Jackson was right: 'The old order has to die before there can be a born-again landscape […] the neighbourhood has to be a slum before we can rediscover it and gentrify it.'[38]

Heritage is a process, depending as it does on the ascribing of value to memories and ideas and the things that represent them, against a background of ever-changing menaces and stresses. Today it is climate change that threatens disruption to the landscapes and monuments of the past. But the discussion has moved from the impacts of climate change on heritage (and the need for special exemptions), to the critical role of heritage in a lower-carbon economy. The mantra has become that the greenest building is the one that is already there. Everybody is now a conservationist, and the urge to protect the environment has unprecedented popular approval as well as government agreement. But as is usual with government, it giveth with one hand and taketh away with the other. In the final chapter I outline some of the outstanding threats to our cities and countryside: the devouring demand for housing on greenfield sites, the over-dependence on developers in the planning system, the weakness of local and national government protective bodies, the neglect of Conservation Areas, and the tower block problem. For as David Cannadine reflects, 'the unfinished history of conservation in England has an unnervingly equivocal ending'.[39]

CHAPTER I

The First Threats

It is again no question of expediency or feeling
whether we shall preserve the buildings of past
times or not. We have no right whatsoever to touch them.
They are not ours. They belong partly to those
who built them, and partly to all the generations
of mankind who are to follow us.

JOHN RUSKIN[1]

The heritage movement in Great Britain was born with a radical tinge. It is the progeny of a small group of passionate campaigners who were largely driven by a Christian Socialist impulse. A striking feature of their period, which extended roughly from the 1860s until the death of Queen Victoria in 1901, was the reluctance of parliament to become involved in preservation. Britain was ruled by an oligarchy of landowners – they believed their rights were enshrined in the Magna Carta – who rejected the idea of parliamentary intervention in matters of private property. It took one tenacious MP ten years to get an Act through parliament that recognised even the smallest degree of state responsibility for ancient monuments. In 1944 the *Manchester Guardian* could look back on these early struggles and see them in terms of the ongoing war: 'the fight against the sacrifice of beauty in the nineteenth century was a pretty desperate guerilla warfare. A noble building or a fine landscape threatened by private or public greed had to rely for its defence on groups of sensitive people who had enough public spirit to make an agitation'.[2] Right up until the 1940s, heritage had to rely upon a small enlightened minority to shout, beg, protest and donate. It is largely thanks to their vision and tenacity that the British heritage movement was born.

Their trigger for action was always the threat to a landscape or building that was about to be mutilated or destroyed: the enclosure of a common, the savage over-restoration of a church, the loss of a townscape or a green space, or the desecration of an ancient monument. European governments were ahead in safeguarding their monuments, and across the continent discussions were taking place about the best means of conserving historic buildings – 'between 1870 and 1914 a new, almost obsessive, preoccupation with legislation emerged'.[3] In Prussia protective legislation passed as early as 1815, and was strengthened in 1835. In France, the post of *Inspecteur des Monuments Historiques* was created in 1830 to compile an inventory of all the country's historic buildings. Even the USA began to consider areas of conservation from 1832. As early as 1841 a Select Committee of the House of Commons considered the protection of national monuments, 'which it understood primarily as memorials to illustrious individuals', but nothing came of it then.[4] Britain's first heritage campaigns were not only later, but they were also more about nature than culture, motivated by a desire to save green spaces: these became the first battlegrounds.

Earl Spencer inadvertently fired the opening shot when in 1864 he proposed a bill to enclose Wimbledon Common as a public park, releasing Putney Heath with its ponds for development. At that time, commons were stretches of land over which 'commoners' held ancient rights such as grazing, fishing and the collection of fuel. However, since the sixteenth century, the enclosure of such lands had eroded these rights, and this remained a sensitive matter. Lord Spencer's bill aroused considerable opposition and stirred radicals into action. With the active support of John Stuart Mill and William Morris, England's first environmental campaign group, the Commons Preservation Society (CPS), was formed the following year. Its founder, the Liberal MP George Shaw-Lefevre, identified around seventy commons and greens of various sizes within fifteen miles of London, all of them in jeopardy. He proposed, and was granted, a Select Committee to investigate their preservation. The committee rejected the idea of Lord Spencer's bill and duly recommended an end to enclosures of common space within the suggested radius of central London. It was a crucial victory, and the CPS was to win more in the future, including the protection of Hampstead Heath, Epping Forest and Berkhamsted Common. Berkhamsted was a particularly bruising battle, in which Shaw-Lefevre resorted to bringing in a trainload of navvies to pull down the new fences that had enclosed the common.

David Cannadine notes that it was in fact in the last twenty or so years of Queen Victoria's reign that many national traditions or 'talismans of identity' were invented – Sherlock Holmes, Gilbert and Sullivan, bacon and eggs. They coincide with the appearance of so many private initiatives and voluntary bodies addressing heritage issues, of which the Commons Preservation Society was but one. These bodies speak of the confidence, activism and philanthropy of the Victorian middle classes. Their survival and growth into the following century suggest that they were responding to a deep-seated urge to record and protect both the tangible and intangible qualities of the places around them, threatened by the pace of change in Victorian Britain. They became the foundations of the heritage movement that we recognise today: the Society for the Protection of Ancient Buildings (SPAB); *The Survey of London* and *The Victoria History of the Counties of England*; the National Footpaths Preservation Society; *The Dictionary of National Biography*; the Royal Society for the Protection of Birds (RSPB); *Country Life* magazine; and above all the National Trust, which was to become the most successful voluntary heritage organisation in the world.

Octavia and Miranda Hill

The several roots of the National Trust run deep: one of them was the Kyrle Society, founded in 1875 by Miranda Hill. With philanthropic Christian Socialist values, it sought to beautify overcrowded working-class districts of the big cities under the banner 'Bring Beauty Home to the Poor'. Between 1800 and 1900 the population of England and Wales increased threefold, and the proportion living in cities also more than trebled, putting them under the immense pressures of overcrowding and loss of greenery.[*] The society was to provide art, books, music and above all access to green spaces.[†] Miranda's sister, Octavia Hill, moved by the degradation and misery she saw in London's East End, became its treasurer. This turned into a mission – 'how can the poor live?' Octavia asked herself. In the belief that people's behaviour was profoundly influenced by their environment, she determined to provide them with more wholesome lives through better housing and the enjoyment of nature. A social visionary, her priorities were clean housing, dignity, employment and access to green spaces. Octavia was a gentle, clever woman, whose tactful manner belied her great energy and determination, and whose charm persuaded people to do whatever she wanted. She worked with volunteers, endlessly fundraising and lobbying to launch her schemes for housing the poor with proper sanitation. By 1874 she had over 3,000 tenancies in fifteen separate areas of London, gave

[*] Between 1800 and 1900 the population of England and Wales tripled from under 9 to over 30 million people. At the beginning of the century 25 per cent lived in the cities and by the end of it 80 per cent. The railway had 6,000 miles of track in 1852, which trebled by 1912.
[†] Since 1847, when Joseph Paxton designed the world's first publicly funded civic park in Birkenhead, Victorian social reformers had made parks in slum areas, and placed access to fresh air and the provision of green spaces for the poor very high on their agenda.

employment to women rent-collectors, and returned a healthy 5 per cent a year for her investors, among them John Ruskin.

Octavia Hill's schemes were much dependent on what she called open air sitting rooms, and it was in order to save London's disappearing green spaces that she became involved in the preservation movement. She started with the fields around Swiss Cottage, which she persuaded the owner to sell to her if she could raise the money; she did, whereupon he reneged on the deal. It was around this time that a fateful encounter took place: she met and became friendly with the CPS's remarkable lawyer, Robert Hunter. Under five feet tall, he was a diminutive dynamo with a lively conscience and an outstanding intellect that drew him to social causes. Together they forged a powerful partnership. Swiss Cottage had been lost, but they succeeded in preserving the more important Parliament Hill Fields on Hampstead Heath. Hunter was involved in saving Epping Forest, an ancient hunting ground, from enclosure. It was taken into public care by Act of Parliament in 1878. When, four years later, Queen Victoria visited it, she stood in Chingford and declared, 'It gives me the greatest satisfaction to dedicate this beautiful forest to the use and enjoyment of my people for all time', after which it became known as 'The People's Forest'.

The National Trust

The catalyst for the formation of the National Trust was John Evelyn's garden at Sayes Court in Deptford. The diarist's descendants offered the remains of the estate to Octavia Hill in 1884 to safeguard its future, but there was no legal apparatus to hold the property. The CPS could not help, as it had no corporate status, and therefore was unable to purchase or hold any land it wanted to protect. Hill and Hunter realised that there needed to be a recognised independent body that could hold property in perpetuity. What would they call it? Octavia Hill proposed: 'Commons and Gardens Trust?' Hunter simply pencilled on her letter: '? National Trust. R. H.' It was a brilliant coinage. Writing of Sayes Court in his National Trust history, Merlin Waterson observed: 'It would be hard to conceive of a property which encompassed so many of the future purposes of the National Trust. The garden was of exceptional importance, the historical associations fascinating, and it was a valuable open space in the heart of London Docks.'[5] The Trust never did receive Sayes Court, but a part of the estate nevertheless became a municipal park.

It took another ten years for the National Trust to come into being, and a third powerful character to give it impetus. It was Ruskin who introduced Canon Hardwicke Rawnsley to Octavia Hill, describing her as 'the best lady abbess you can find for London work'.[6] Rawnsley shared her passion for helping impoverished children. When he became vicar of St Margaret's, Wray, beside Lake Windermere, he joined the protest against what Wordsworth called the 'rash assault' of tourism and day-trippers. However, the flashpoint for Rawnsley was neither tourism nor mining,[*] but the proposal in 1877 to construct a reservoir at Thirlmere to supply water to Manchester via an aqueduct; the lake would have to be dammed and the valley flooded. Even though the objectors of the Thirlmere Defence Association included heavyweights such as Thomas Carlyle, Matthew Arnold and William Morris, it failed. It had, however, succeeded in establishing a momentum. For Rawnsley, like Hill and Hunter, had become convinced that the only secure means of protecting land for public enjoyment was not by lobbying or legislation, but through ownership.

The Lake District had been hallowed by Wordsworth, whose poetic genius found inspiration there, and this makes him the patron saint of the National Trust. In 1810 he had published a bestseller *Guide Through the District of the Lakes*, which showed people where to go and how to find the right viewpoint, but by 1844 he was campaigning against a proposed railway line between

---

* The Lake District was exploited not just for tourism but also by commerce: slate quarrying and mining for copper.

Kendal and Windermere, which would spoil a wilderness he described as 'rich with liberty'. He made the striking observation that the Lake District was 'a sort of national property in which every man has a right and interest who has an eye to perceive and a heart to enjoy'.[7] It was not until the National Parks Act in 1949 that this sentiment would be fully realised.

Ruskin took up the cry, memorably launching one of his famous diatribes when in 1863 the railway was built through Monsal Dale in the Peak District:

There was a rocky valley between Buxton and Bakewell [...] you might have seen the Gods there, morning and evening – Apollo and all the sweet Muses…..You cared neither for gods nor grass, but for cash (which you did not know the way to get); you thought you could get it by what *The Times* calls 'Railroad Enterprise'. You enterprised a railroad through the valley, you blasted its rocks away, heaped thousands of tons of shale into its lovely stream. The valley is gone, and the Gods with it; and now, every fool in Buxton can be in Bakewell in half an hour, and every fool in Bakewell at Buxton; which you think a lucrative process of exchange – you Fools everywhere![8]

It was the Lake District that caused Ruskin the most anxiety. He remarked that, 'the stupid herds of modern tourists let themselves be emptied, like coals from a sack, at Windermere and Keswick'.[9] Preserving the Lake District would be a great concern and, notwithstanding Ruskin (with whom paradox is never far away), access would be the one of the first great motivating forces of the nascent heritage lobby, one that retains its force today.

Meanwhile in parliament, James Bryce presented his Access to Mountains Bill eight times in the House of Commons between 1884 and 1905, always without success. William Morris was certain where the problem lay: 'my firm opinion is that we shall be quite helpless against the landowners as long as there is any private ownership of land'.[10] One MP, Henry Labouchère, stood up in parliament to defend them: 'I protest against these attacks on property. Is my Hon. Friend prepared to pay for the national playground he is going to establish for the benefit of sentimentalists, poets and aesthetes?'[11]

David Cannadine has described the National Trust as the pursuit of politics by other means. It is in this context that its foundation in 1895 should be set and understood. The pervasive influence of Ruskin and Morris had established the idea that the preservation of nature, the transmission of ancient handcrafts, the elimination of ugliness, and orderly, benign social progress were all interlinked. In July 1895, the National Trust was ratified at a meeting at Grosvenor House. The three founders were fortunate to have the Liberal politician, the Duke of Westminster, as their first chairman, which made the embryonic organisation acceptable to the landowners who in future would need to become their collaborators. The duke showed prescience at the meeting when he said: 'Mark my words, Miss Hill, this is going to be a very big thing.' Although the Trust and its Robert-Hunter propagators were then seen as radical, they knew how to activate friends in high places, and Octavia Hill persuaded Princess Louise, Queen Victoria's feminist fourth daughter, a supporter of the arts and education, to attend the ceremony marking the acquisition of the Trust's first property in the Lake District, Brandelhow, in 1902.*

The earliest gift to the Trust was in Wales, four and a half acres of grazing land overlooking Cardigan Bay presented by a local lady and friend of Ruskin, Mrs Fanny Talbot. They bought their first building soon after, the thatched medieval Clergy House at Alfriston, Sussex, which cost £10. Questions were raised, then as now, about the expense of maintenance. This came into

* There had been a wobble four years earlier when Canon Rawnsley was offered the Anglican bishopric in the French colony of Madagascar; 'we want you at home,' cried Westminster and Rawnsley refused the offer. He was to be honorary secretary until his death, overseeing the acquisition of large areas of countryside, especially in his beloved Lake District.

particular focus in 1907 when the Trust acquired its first country house, Barrington Court in Somerset, which was paid for with a legacy. The restoration costs went far beyond anything envisaged, and this, for a while, made the Trust nervous of country houses. By 1907 the Trust owned 2,000 acres and twelve buildings, and in the same year it was recognised by an Act of Parliament, which enabled it to preserve 'lands and tenements of beauty or historic interest' on property that was to be 'inalienable', on behalf of the people of England. *The Times* hoped these extraordinary new powers would 'furnish a great inducement to donors who, for the first time, would be able to feel quite certain of the permanent possession by the public of everything worth preserving that the Trust is able to secure'. [12] It would take another fourteen years before Scotland had a similar organisation.

William Morris and the SPAB

In 1881 William Morris gave an address entitled 'Art and the Beauty of the Earth' in which he stated, 'we must turn this land from the grimy back-yard of a workshop into a garden [...] time was when it was beautiful from end to end, and now you have to pick your way carefully to avoid coming across blotches of hideous-ness'. [13] He deplored the dehumanising aspects of the industrial age and looked back to the world of medieval artisans, advocating a return to traditional methods and materials in craft and building, while always drawing on a strong sense of locality. The Arts and Crafts movement directed architects towards improving society (without a religious element), and finding the solution to that ever-present question of low-cost housing. Morris was as concerned about preserving the past as directing the present. This would lead him, after a visit to Burford Church in 1876, to establish the Society for the Preservation of Ancient Buildings (SPAB). He had been shocked by the way in which his former master, the architect George Street, was restoring the Norman and fifteenth-century church. Ever since the Canterbury

Cathedral fire in 1174, builders and planners have faced the question of what to preserve or replace.* In their enthusiasm for restoration, eminent architects like Street believed that it was a fine way to train young architects. In *The Seven Lamps of Architecture* Ruskin had warned, 'do not let us talk of restoration. The thing is a lie from beginning to end'. And nor was Street the only problem. The following year Morris wrote a letter to *The Athenaeum* magazine:

> my eye just now caught the word 'restoration' in the morning paper, and, looking closer I saw that this time it is nothing less than the Minster of Tewkesbury that is to be destroyed by Sir Gilbert Scott. Is it altogether too late to do something to save it and whatever else of beautiful or historical is still left us on the sites of the ancient buildings were once so famous for? [...] What I wish for, therefore, is that an association should be set on foot to keep a watch on old monuments, to protect against all 'restoration' that means more than keeping out wind and weather, and by all means, literary and other, to awaken a feeling that our ancient buildings are not mere ecclesiastical toys, but secret monuments of the nation's growth and hope.[14]

The SPAB was formed to combat the zeal, piety and wealth of the Victorian patrons who wished to restore Britain's medieval churches. The society put the case for conservation as opposed to such modernisation. For Morris this meant a minimalist approach to do no more than was strictly necessary to keep a building wind and weather tight. He was never again to accept a commission on behalf of Morris & Company to place new stained glass in old churches. Particularly shocking was the work at St Albans Cathedral by Lord Grimthorpe, an amateur who paid £100,000 to restore it to his own designs, a clumsy

---

* The instruction given to the restorers was to preserve as much as possible of the original fabric. It has been suggested that this was the result of conservatism rather than conservationism.

and inappropriate intervention. *The Builder* magazine called it 'railway station Gothic' and correctly called him 'an architectural pretender who can pay for the privilege of abusing [...] the building which is the property of the nation.'[15] The SPAB tried to legally challenge the restoration and they also fought a battle with the Dean and Chapter of Exeter Cathedral, who appeared to believe that the more money expended, the greater virtue there was in the work.[16]

The SPAB created a benchmark in conservation – then as now their most dreaded phrase remains 'restored to its former glory'. Their approach to conservation focuses on maintaining the fabric of the building rather than restoring to the original design. Their philosophy respects the different layers of style and history and may be summed up by the sentiment 'leave it alone'. They acquired the nickname 'anti-scrape', and indeed they mourned a lost patina. In 1877 the SPAB produced their manifesto: 'prop a perilous wall or mend a leaky roof by such means as are obviously meant for support or covering'. The foundation of the SPAB was followed in France by something similar, *Société des Amis des Monuments Parisiens*, referred to at the time as a 'French SPAB' although they did not see it like that. It was more concerned about the complete loss of buildings like the Tuileries.

One of the most interesting aspects of the foundation of the SPAB was the precedent of voluntary action it established. Its members debated the merits of a system of state control, such as existed in France, but never reached much of a conclusion – Morris sat in the middle because he doubted the value of state intervention. For at least one historian, William Morris and the SPAB 'are the nearest things we in the [conservation] movement have to a foundation myth. They function as twin totems, furnishing an otherwise diverse coalition with a common ancestry and sense of shared purpose'.[17] Certainly Morris's letter to *The Athenaeum* forms part of the incunabula of British conservation. The formation of SPAB marks a milestone in the idea of a commonly held national architectural heritage and the elucidation of the responsibilities ownership of historic buildings brings. Today, while deploring the insensitive restoration of hundreds of mediaeval churches, we nevertheless can often appreciate the insertion of a lady chapel by J. L. Pearson or the appearance of Morris stained glass in a medieval church.

Sir John Lubbock

John Lubbock (1834–1913), later 1st Baron Avebury, was a Liberal MP who can claim the honour of persuading a reluctant parliament into passing legislation which has become the fount of all modern heritage protection law. As he explained, 'we cannot put Stonehenge or the Wansdyke into a museum – all the more reason why we should watch over them where they are'.[18] Lubbock was a Victorian activist, ubiquitous on committees, with a reforming zeal that covered a vast range of activities. It is said that thirty bills passed through parliament thanks to his energies.* When he became interested in archaeology and was informed that the Danes had finer methods, he learned Danish and went to Denmark to study them. Then in 1871 the Rector of Avebury wrote to him because the monuments in his parish had been acquired by a building society which was selling plots for the construction of housing. Lubbock once again proved that only private enterprise had the willingness and speed to act; he purchased a large part of the stone circle complex at Avebury himself to prevent any further building.

Private and individual action sowed the seeds of heritage, but it could do nothing about ancient monuments on other people's land. Only government intervention would have any effect, and this was late in coming and initially toothless. In 1873 Lubbock proposed a private member's bill for an Ancient Monuments Act, which failed to pass. Lubbocks' bill was given a hard time; archaeologists and antiquaries were not regarded with favour by landowners, but viewed as predatory trespassers. Sir Charles

---

* Including the Wild Birds Protection Act of 1880.

Legard called the proposed bill 'legalising burglary by daylight [...] invading the right of private property'.[19] Lubbock was not deterred, introducing the bill on no less than eight occasions between 1873–1880 without success. *The Times* sardonically noted that the bill would be 'as roughly treated as the monuments that it seeks to preserve'.[20] It became laughingly known as 'the monumentally ancient act'.

The Act finally received royal assent in August 1882 under Gladstone. It enabled the state to purchase historic sites, or take them into guardianship, and made damage punishable by a fine. But as Simon Thurley has pointed out, 'Stonehenge could have been demolished for as little as five pounds under the Act'.[21] The 1882 Act attached a list of sixty-eight ancient monuments that the Office of Works – the government department traditionally responsible for Crown property – might take into its care by ownership. It was, however, merely permissive, and had no teeth. As Thurley wrote, 'thus the mountain of ten years of debate produced the molehill of an act'.[22] But at least the government now had skin in the game, although compared to France or Germany, compulsion in Britain remained low.[23]

General Augustus Pitt Rivers

It was generally agreed that the effectiveness of the Act would much depend on the quality of the person appointed to oversee the guardianship. Gladstone appointed General Pitt Rivers as the first Inspector of Ancient Monuments in 1883, and it was an inspired choice. As one of the fathers of modern archaeology, Pitt Rivers brought military organisation as well as a scientific mind to the subject and pioneered the documentation of the physical context of finds. He was a polymath with a startling range of interests, and a major collector of ethnography, as his museum in Oxford attests. Bertrand Russell noted that 'he spent every penny he could spare on excavating antiquities, much to the annoyance of his large family'.[24] His long-suffering wife once organised a luncheon party only to find that her husband, not wishing to be disturbed, had closed the park gates. Pitt Rivers was an indefatigable classifier and lister who believed that creating a national record of prehistoric remains was one of the most useful tasks he could undertake.

It was hoped that the position of Pitt Rivers as a great Dorset landowner – he owned 27,000 acres – might give him weight and authority with his fellow landowners, particularly as he could only achieve results through persuasion and voluntary cooperation. During his first year thirteen scheduled (listed) sites were taken to guardianship. The first monument to be acquired was the megalith Kit's Coty House, in Kent. It was being defaced by visitors and Pitt Rivers ordered a strong iron fence to be placed around it, which annoyed the Treasury, who had been assured that protecting monuments would not involve any expense. They reluctantly coughed up the £100 for spiked railings, whose installation had the unexpected consequence of impaling a Cambridge undergraduate – he had scaled them to pose for a photograph atop the monument, and then fallen.

Pitt Rivers did not look back on his time as inspector in a positive light. In 1891 he told Lubbock: 'I feel that my time has been a good deal wasted.' He believed that 'neither Govt. nor parliament care a button for ancient monuments, but the majority of owners take an interest in their own monuments as family possessions'.[25] He thought that everything should be done to encourage owners to do the work themselves, with local archaeological bodies keeping an eye on their condition, since 'no inspector of ancient monuments can stand sentry over all the monuments in Great Britain'.[26] Fairly typical was the response when the commissioners suggested to the owner of the ruins of Glastonbury Abbey that his property needed repair. His answer was 'well, they are ruins now, and if they fall they will be ruined still, won't they? What more do you want?'[27] The Liberal politician, Lord Crewe, believed that ancient monuments were more neglected in England than Italy for the simple reason that

England had no tourists and was not therefore dependent on them for revenue. However, by 1900, forty-three scheduled sites had been taken into state guardianship and these formed the basis of the National Heritage Collection.

Henry Cockburn and Patrick Geddes

Towns and cities were also beginning to consider their heritage in the light of rapid redevelopment. Two remarkable campaigners put Edinburgh at the forefront: the eminent judge Henry Cockburn, and the biologist and polymath Patrick Geddes. Cockburn worked to protect the beauty of the city, notably resisting construction of new buildings on the southerly side of Princes Street thereby preserving its open character – a monument of romantic town planning. The Cockburn Association (which later became Edinburgh's Civic Trust) was founded in 1875 to continue the legacy of his work and is one of the first architectural conservation and planning monitoring organisations. If much of Cockburn's work was to protect the New Town, it would fall to Geddes to revive the neglected Old Town. He founded the Environment Society in 1884 to save and regenerate parts of Edinburgh's Old Town (an area in steep decline since the creation of the New Town) by cultivating waste ground using volunteer labour. One crucial point that Geddes realised – like the pioneers of community architecture in the 1970s – that for success it was essential to involve the local community. Geddes was at one with Ruskin, Morris and Octavia Hill in believing that behaviour was influenced by environment. To that end, he bought and restored slum tenements before leasing them as halls of residence to students.

If we are looking today for a historical figure bestriding the different interest groups, operating locally at the micro scale while thinking globally, nobody fits the role better than Patrick Geddes, whose disciples continue to regret that his diversity makes him difficult to explain briefly. Yet in terms of the expanded field of nature conservation and built heritage considered here, his urban interventions for slum dwellers in Edinburgh Old Town, his vision for recreation linked to education in Pittencrieff Park, Dunfermline, and his 'conservative surgery' in the overcrowded cities of India begin to show his belief, in Colin Ward's words, 'that the only really useful planning was ordinary, practical, day-to-day activity, rather than campaigns to persuade governments to do things'.[28]

In the wake of Cockburn and Geddes, several civic groups and preservation trusts were formed around the country: Glasgow (1896), Guildford (1896), and Liverpool (1909), but London had to wait until 1912. Building protection came piecemeal to the capital; during the 1880s, a letter to the SPAB complained that the London authorities 'care nothing, the property owners less, save to make big shops, with plate glass fronts, build them as cheaply as possible and make money'.[29] This is not entirely fair, as Andrew Saint has pointed out; much of the development in the capital between 1870 and 1914 was very good.[30] The London authorities, however, did take action at the appearance of a fourteen-storey building in Queen Anne's Gate which prompted complaints from Queen Victoria, whose view of the Palace of Westminster from Buckingham Palace was obstructed. This precipitated the 1894 Act which imposed a height limit of 80 feet to the cornice or parapet of London buildings. The other notable piece of London legislation was the protection of one of its most hallowed views.

The Lass of Richmond Hill

Richmond Hill was the first view to be protected by an Act of Parliament in 1902. It is a view in one direction of the winding River Thames – which reminded some of the Tiber – and in another the dome of St Paul's was visible. The view had been painted by Richard Wilson and by Turner, and since 1816 a steamboat service had taken visitors to Richmond for pleasure.

It was the prospect of development that made the Richmond Corporation anxious to protect its precious view. *Punch* magazine depicted the 'Lass of Richmond Hill' being saved from the 'Jerry-Builder Dragon'.[31] The sale of the little river island of Petersham Ait brought matters to a head when the owner threatened to sell to an advertising company. The *Daily Mail* thundered that 'the view from Richmond Hill is the world's view, not Richmond's only'. Moreover, Marble Hill House was threatened to become the centre of a housing estate and the builders began to lay out the sewers and roads. All these developments were thwarted by local opposition campaigns, and in 1902 an Act of Parliament was passed protecting the view from Richmond Hill. Marble Hill was opened as a public park the following year.

Central London was under even greater pressure than the picturesque suburbs: engineering works, embankments, new thoroughfares, and railways were chipping away at its fabric. Concerns were raised in parliament over the loss of Northumberland House and the removal of Temple Bar. The demolition of the former in 1874 to create a route from Trafalgar Square to the Thames passed with surprisingly little objection. Northumberland House was a venerable Jacobean palace belonging to the Percy family, who in the eighteenth century had commissioned a grand suite of rooms by Robert Adam. The London building specifically acquired for preservation was York House Watergate, erected in 1626 by Nicholas Stone to designs by Balthazar Gerbier as the river entrance to York House. The house had been demolished back in the 1670s and when the Embankment was created in 1886 the question arose as to who owned the gate. The Metropolitan Board of Works thought it should be repositioned to embellish the new Embankment wall, where it would only be seen from the water. This gave way to the view that it should be re-erected to serve as a gateway to the gardens created over the reclaimed foreshore. Morris, as secretary of the SPAB, wrote to express his disagreement at this 'unnecessary, mischievous and damaging proposal'. His solution was to leave the gate exactly where it had always stood, and it happily remains there to this day, marking the original width of the river.*

The achievements of a handful of individuals in the second half of Queen Victoria's reign were extraordinary. That Britain was behind other countries in building protection was made forcibly clear by Gerard Baldwin Brown's book, *The Care of Ancient Monuments* (1905), in which the author pointed to effective legislation in Denmark (nearly a hundred years old) and in various German states as well as Sweden, Portugal, France and Greece. Conservation in Britain would need all the support it could get as the new century dawned, and it would broaden its base beyond the radical campaigners of the 1860s and 1870s to involve Conservative imperialists such as Lord Curzon and Lord Milner and Liberal grandees such as Lord Dufferin and Lord Rosebery. As late as 1912, during a debate in the House of Lords, Lord Curzon could lament that there was nothing 'under our existing law' to prevent the owner of Stonehenge from selling it tomorrow 'to an American syndicate to be erected in Central Park in New York'.[32] He would in large part provide the solution to the problem.

* The London County Council (LCC) was formed in 1889. One of its early decisions was to identify the need for an inventory of historic buildings, and the first of the series of parish volumes of the *Survey of London* was published in 1900 and was to constitute a record at a level of detail and scholarship unmatched by any city.

CHAPTER 2

The Search for Arcadia

O England country of my heart's desire,
Land of the hedgerow and the village spire.

E. V. LUCAS

In 1934 J. B. Priestley described what he called the three Englands:

There was first, Old England, the country of the cathedrals and minsters and manor houses and inns, of parson and Squire; guide-book and quaint highways and byways England…Then, I decided, there is the 19th century England, the industrial England of coal, iron, steel, cotton, wool, railway [...] The third England, I concluded, was the new post-war [World War I] England, belonging far more to the age itself than to this particular island. America, I supposed, was its real birthplace. This is the England of arterial and by-pass roads, of filling stations and factories that look like exhibition buildings, of giant cinemas and dance-halls and cafes, bungalows with tiny garages, cocktail bars, Woolworths, motor-coaches, wireless, hiking, factory girls looking like actresses, greyhound racing and dirt tracks, swimming pools, and everything given away for cigarette coupons.[1]

It was an acute sense of the loss of Priestley's Old England that sanctified the countryside between the wars but left the cities to the mercy of commerce. This loss, which was magnified as the effects of the arterial and bypass roads became evident, drove the various groups who lobbied government for the preservation of the countryside. The rural scene had long been the subject of a sentimental cult since the Romantic movement, and this was reinforced during World War I, evinced by its war poetry. Recruitment posters had shown rolling hills and hamlets, as if it were the English countryside rather than Flanders that the men were called to protect. When the poet Edward Thomas enlisted in 1915 and was asked what he was fighting for, he picked up a handful of English soil and replied, 'for this'. While other countries, particularly France and Italy, would make a concerted effort to preserve their great cities, in England it was to be the countryside that was saved. The cities, especially London, would be redeveloped without much attempt at control until the mid-1930s. As Thomas Hardy so eloquently expressed it: 'God was palpably present in the country and the devil had gone with the world to the town.'[2]

By the time World War I was over, the fighting had dissolved four empires and precipitated the Russian Revolution. Britons were demobilised into a world that had greatly changed, and the two decades that followed were periods of intense social and economic upheaval in which both rural and urban landscapes were transformed. It is here that we meet the third England to which Priestley referred, with its arterial and bypass roads, its filling stations and factories, motor-coaches and bungalows with garages. For in large part, it was the new reach of the motorcar that brought about these transformations. Whereas the countryside had previously belonged to country folk, now it was within reach of everybody who could afford a car or a bus fare.

These developments added to the groundswell of ruralism; for some, like R. H. Mottram, it was simple: 'We wanted 1914 back.'[3] However, ruralism could be seen at many levels, from the success of the wistful Batsford 'Heritage' books, which reimagined a vision of old-time village England, to the all-important founding of the Council for the Preservation of Rural England. This is mainly a story of the south, as nobody then worried much about the fabric of Priestley's second England, the industrial north and

Midlands. Perhaps because he was a boy from the suburbs himself, Priestley did not register the new rural revivalism implicit in the development of the garden suburb and garden city, a *via media* between town and country, and it was here that Octavia Hill's followers addressed their attentions in the hope of creating ideal conditions for living.[*]

Country Life Magazine

One of the best barometers of what was happening in the countryside was in the weekly magazine *Country Life*. Founded in 1897, it was aimed from the outset at city-dwellers who hankered for the country, playing to the idea of 'ours being an island race whereof even the town dweller is a countryman at heart'.[4] The magazine's appeal was visual and most people, then as now, flicked through its alluring pictures. Technical advances in cameras and photography as well as half-tone block printing had made such a publication possible. From the outset it had a strong architectural component, so that in 1913 Lord Runciman could describe it as 'the architectural conscience of the nation'. No magazine better expressed the search for Arcadia which is such a feature of the period, and offered the fantasy if not the means of becoming a part of it through its appealing weekly house advertisements.

Country Life promulgated the view shared by so many writers, John Ruskin among them, that life in the country was better. Public schoolboys nurtured on Horace and Virgil believed that

---

[*] To Alan Powers it was the 'application of creative and liberal social thinking to the design of buildings and cities which was arguably Britain's most distinctive contribution to the modern movement worldwide'. The influence of the garden suburb permeated the planning philosophy throughout the UK of low-density, low-rise housing and irregular streets, with open spaces and owner-occupied. Garden suburbs began with great promise but as Powers observed 'had gone terribly wrong by the 1930s'. See Powers, p. 63.

contentment lay in the rural idyll, and this had been reinforced by the eighteenth-century parkland Arcadias abutting estate villages and acres of fine plantations. These values were shared across the political divide, but with a slightly different emphasis. Stanley Baldwin famously claimed that 'to me England is the country and the country is England' (although, as Neville Chamberlain pointed out, for all his much-vaunted passion for the countryside, Baldwin could not recognise anything more than the most obvious birds or flowers).[5] At the other end of the spectrum, William Morris and his followers envisaged villages of honest craftsmen practising their skills. *Country Life* embraced both views, even if it was more attuned to the world of the manor house.

Epitomising the fashionable reversal against Victorian taste, *Country Life* set out a vision of English heritage as Tudor and Georgian. It put old country houses at the core of its mission, and celebrated Baddesley, Knole, and Little Morton Hall as emblems of nationhood; during the 1920s, Henry Avray Tipping's scholarly articles helped to make such houses central to the story of British architectural history.* But it was not all rosy; as early as 1910, the magazine had been recording and mourning the break-up of great estates. After 1917, as sales multiplied, it observed, 'The countryside is changing from month to month. Estates are in the process of disruption.'[6] The death of heirs at the front had taken the stuffing out of many families, who gave up the effort to maintain their estates. Post-war it is surprising to find many famous houses available to let: Levens Hall, Ragley Hall, Leeds Castle, Corsham Court, Knole and Blickling. Even the richest landowners were affected: Lord Spencer closed Althorp and the Duke of Northumberland temporarily left Alnwick, saying in 1922, 'I am, like so many other people, obliged to take measures of retrenchment owing to the excessively heavy burden of taxation.'[7]

---

* Anybody who collects old books on country houses will be aware of Avray Tipping, whose intelligence and strong personality persuaded many owners of country houses to feature in the magazine.

Between 1919 and 1930 death duties rose to 40 per cent and then 50 per cent. An often quoted statistic is that between 1918 and 1922 a quarter of England's land area came to market. By the 1930s the country house market was saturated, and the houses were more likely to find institutional uses, many becoming schools or hotels. Moreover, beyond the pages of *Country Life*, sympathy for landowners was waning.

The spirit of William Morris and Canon Rawnsley was still alive, in a rising demand for a 'right to roam'. Not only was this now growing steadily, but so was a new resentment at the way people were still excluded by landowners in favour of grouse shooting. It was noted that in 1930 half of the population of England lived within fifty miles of the Derbyshire Peak District, but only 1 per cent of its open moorland was legally open to all. To the swelling ranks of campaigners for access, it was landowners, lauded as they might be by *Country Life*, who were the great obstacle. Indeed, landowners play an ambiguous role in the heritage story: on the one hand they saved great swathes of landscape from speculative builders and development, but on the other they tended to fight any attempts to permit access across their land by ramblers. With escalating frustration, especially among industrial workers in Manchester, a mass trespass was organised in 1932 on the Duke of Devonshire's moor at Kinder Scout in the Peak District, which led to a confrontation with his gamekeepers, followed by various arrests. All this was grist to the publicity mill, and decades later Roy Hattersley would call it 'the most successful direct action in British history'.[8] It was a milestone on the way to state recognition that access to the wilder parts of the UK needed to be opened up, and ultimately it pointed to the formation of Britain's national parks. Between the wars, landscape became the most politicised aspect of conservation.

Roads

The 'third England' that Priestley identified was in large part the consequence of the car. The great disrupter of the age, the car represented the biggest threat – and opportunity – for the countryside. Through the development of the road network, it was the decisive factor in turning the countryside into a national playground. From 78,000 cars in 1918, the numbers swelled to 1 million by 1930, and this doubled again within three years, all contributing to what T. S. Eliot called 'the sound of horns and motors'. The Ministry of Transport (established in 1919) began to classify roads, and ten years later instituted the Trunk Roads programme to provide arterial roads and bypasses. There was even an organisation founded in 1928, the Roads Beautifying Association, in the hope of creating well-designed and attractive routes around London and making petrol stations attractive – a challenge, given their need to stand out enough to give the approaching driver adequate warning.* Styles varied between Art Deco and faux Arts and Crafts. One of them became famous, the Ace of Spades Garage and Road House, which came with its own polo ground and riding school and which stood on the Kingston Bypass, Britain's first dual carriageway. It caught the eye of Noel Coward, who wrote a song: 'Give me the Kingston Bypass on a Saturday Afternoon'. The car, however, had many critics, such as Professor Joad of *The Brains Trust*, who opined of roadside advertising, 'this riot of blatant reckless hustling is alien to the historic English temperament'.[9]

An unexpected consequence of the car, and to a lesser extent the railway, was the astonishing rash of hoardings that appeared all over the country, especially in the towns. Small tobacco shops could sport as many as twenty garish metal advertisements and railway stations were especially vulnerable. One unsung hero who worked tirelessly to improve the quality of the rural and urban environment was the businessman Harry Peach. Inspired

* The first one opened at Aldermaston in 1920, operated by the AA.

by William Lethaby and the nineteenth-century heritage radicals, it was said of Peach that 'more than any other person he made the preservation of Rural England a popular issue in the late 1920s'.10 He went to war against advertising in Leicester, staging a number of small skirmishes of town tidying until the London Midland railway wanted to sell advertising space on the bridge opposite the London Road station. Peach lost this battle, but it was the catalyst for the formation of the Leicester Society in 1929. The year before, Peach had walked into the Covent Garden offices of the publisher Noel Carrington with a plan to start a campaign to prevent billboards and improve design. They teamed up with one of the most extraordinary figures of the time, the architect Clough Williams-Ellis, to produce a series of pamphlets. *A Cautionary Guide to St Albans* was followed by a similar one on Oxford. These showed photographs of the good and the bad and offered a corrective to the rash of heritage books of the period extolling the beauties of England. One of their most successful pamphlets was *The Village Pump,* about garages, which caught the attention of Shell. Peach was a founder member of the Design and Industries Association (DIA), an outgrowth of the Arts and Crafts movement but accepting of machines. His aim to foster good design in ordinary things echoed Morris, reminding the DIA to concentrate 'on the humble as well as the great' and remain focused on what he called the pots and pans – he designed urban litterbins and gave particular attention to lettering.

But the urban environment that Peach fought so hard to improve was spilling out into the countryside. There was a new and fast-expanding battleground which Priestley identified:

first we construct a specially broad and straight road [...] as soon as the road is finished...firms of builders buy the land on each side of the road, and begin hastily throwing up hundreds of bungalows and the like...so that very soon the road that was made to escape the town has become a sort of town itself. This is called Ribbon Development and it is going on all over England.11

The difference, Priestley thought, between the nineteenth and the twentieth centuries was that whereas the former concentrated on what he called 'the nasty attack on a few districts, it [the twentieth century] has set to work to ruin the look of the whole island'.[12]

The battle to preserve a rural heritage was being lost in the suburbs and on the coast, where development was unchecked. Who was standing up for the countryside? The National Trust had no wish to become a militant protest movement, so initially it was left to *Country Life*, which took up the role in a limited way. As early as July 1925, its pages drew attention to the thousands of bungalows and cheap houses that were springing up 'badly built, badly designed, devastating the landscape [...] The result is a menace to the countryside'.[13] The magazine supported zoning, which would allocate land for building or preservation. The following year it entered the battle for the South Downs: 'the debauch of cheap and vulgar exploitation of all the most magnificent stretch of Downs between Brighton and Newhaven [...] the motor bicycle and the small motorcar have made possible the variegated paper bungalow in places 50 miles from town. Indeed, no corner of England is really safe'.[14] A shanty town emerged on the cliffs east of Brighton which was known as Peacehaven and at first had no roads, power or sanitation. Most of the huts were self-built, dominated by caravans and wooden shanties. Over 3,000 people created dwellings there, out of anything from army huts to railway carriages.

St George to the Rescue of Rural England

These 'Wild West' developments shocked the man who would become Britain's planner-in-chief, Patrick Abercrombie. He was alarmed by the growing tendency for speculators to acquire and divide pieces of land in attractive rural locations, and then sell them as 'plot lands' to individuals who wanted a bungalow in the countryside. He lamented that 'soon this green and pleasant land will only be glimpsed through an almost continuous hedge of bungalows and houses'.[15] In reaction he founded, with the architect Guy Dauber, the Council for the Preservation of Rural England (CPRE) in 1926. They portrayed themselves on a 1928 postcard as St George, patron saint of England, rescuing the countryside.

Abercrombie became 'by a long way the most influential of the environmental campaigners'.[16] The son of a Manchester stockbroker, he apprenticed to architects in Manchester and Liverpool before becoming professor of civic design at the University of Liverpool in 1915. His first success came a year later when he won a competition to redesign Dublin, and later he created similar plans for Plymouth, Hull, Sheffield, Bath, Edinburgh and Bournemouth. He is a contradictory figure who wrote polemical pamphlets against ribbon development, but at the same time his sweeping plans for reinventing cities show that his priorities lay in the preservation of rural scenery, not with historic town centres. This is part of the reason why today we can still marvel at the preservation of our countryside, but sigh at what has been lost in our great cities; for, along with most of his fellow countrymen, he accorded landscape a higher value than historic townscape.*

Nonetheless, the avowed object of the CPRE was to educate people to protect both town and country. It aimed 'to preserve beauty and see that what is added to the face of the land is not unbeautiful' and believed that the big landowners were the best stewards to protect the countryside. As a senior government minister Neville Chamberlain gave it powerful support, and soon county branches were set up in nearly every district of England and run by volunteers. It campaigned for national principles with local application to prevent ribbon development, badly sited

---

* There were some interwar attempts at preserving townscape, notably at Elm Hill in Norwich.

advertising hoardings and electric pylons, and urban sprawl.[*] It produced a series of practical design guides, showing what good and bad building looked like and encouraging vernacular traditions, along with the use of local stone. Part of its success was the combining of a romantic appreciation of natural and architectural heritage with the modernist zeal for advancement.[17] It was against this background that Clough Williams-Ellis wrote his polemic *England and the Octopus* in 1928, in which he exposed the poor quality of most housing developments, in particular what he called the 'blasphemous bungalows'.

The 'octopus' in question was London, whose tentacles stretched out endlessly in all directions. The author created his own 'Devil's Dictionary' against advertising hoardings, broadcasting masts, golf courses and petrol pumps. *England and the Octopus* ran through several editions and was described by the author as 'an angry book, written by an angry young man'.[†] James Lees-Milne later described Clough as 'a man of fantasy, with long whiskers [...] He is cranky, hearty, arty and disarming.'[18] What makes Williams-Ellis especially interesting is that he created his own Arcadia in 1925 on the Welsh coast at Portmeirion, 'first conceived as a serious demonstration about placing buildings in landscape'.[19] He designed and constructed the village, incorporating salvaged stone from abandoned buildings.

In 1927 Christopher Hussey, one of the *Country Life* writers, published *The Picturesque*, an influential book that explained how from the eighteenth century writers, poets, painters and patrons

---

* It was aided in this endeavour by SCAPA, the Society for Checking the Abuses of Public Advertising, formed in 1893 to protest against the proliferation of advertising hoardings. It had some success in getting two acts on the statute book to take action against this blight. Its early members included William Morris, Rudyard Kipling, William Holman Hunt, Arthur Quiller-Couch and John Everett Millais. Morris's last public speech before his death, in 1896, was at a meeting of the society.

† *England and the Octopus* inspired a group of young women to form an action group, Ferguson's Gang. Taking up Williams-Ellis's call for action, they saved several rural properties from demolition – see Chapter Three.

came to see landscape through new eyes, a uniquely English contribution to European aesthetics. Hussey defined picturesque architecture as not so much a style, but a method of using and combining styles. This is exactly what Clough Williams-Ellis was doing in creating his vision of a Mediterranean fishing port on the North Wales coast.

How did Whitehall respond to all this campaigning? Firstly, with the ineffective 1932 Planning Act, which gave power to restrict rural as well as urban development. However, it was not until the Ribbon Development Act of 1935 that effective legislation was passed that prevented the building of houses less than 200 feet from a main road. But it would take another war before the government would properly grasp the nettle of town and country planning.

Arcadia Described

The car was wreaking havoc on the countryside, but was also making its most remote points accessible. As the economic importance of the rural world diminished, so its cultural importance increased. There arose an ardent and at times sentimental yearning to describe the vanishing old England of villages and wayside inns, comparable to the pre-war *Heimat* movement in Germany.[20] Laurie Lee captured the after-effects of World War I: the change to village life, the disappearing horses and wagons, the thinning communities and loss of craftsmen. With them went the dynamic spirit of the village as a self-contained organism – a world which, usually set around a manor house, had been circumscribed by the limitations of the horse, a world of smithies, stables and farriers. Not all villages were now hermetic, self-sufficient units of history, and increasingly they were populated by retirees and commuters. The village was becoming a new kind of suburb.

The Arts and Crafts movement had attempted to keep the idyll alive after the arrival of train travel. C. R. Ashbee and

Ernest Gimson set up workshops in the Cotswolds to practise traditional crafts and building. The celebrated historian G. M. Trevelyan propagated this view of a vanished idyll ruined by the Industrial Revolution. Businessmen, commercialisation and industry were set in counterpoint to the timeless spiritual values and changing seasons of the rural scene, with the honest yeoman praised as the model Everyman. This wistful mood was exploited by a publishing boom when Longmans announced its volumes on 'English Heritage' and Batsford followed with its better-known series, the 'English Life' and 'British Heritage' books. They purveyed the roses at the cottage door version of heritage, which could be visited by car, describing the church and the manor house. As early as 1904, Rudyard Kipling had expressed the view that 'the chief end of my car, so far as I'm concerned, is the discovery of England'.[21] The publishing wave of guides would make this a reality for the post-World War I middle class. Perhaps the most famous of all these explorations was H. V. Morton's *In Search of England* of 1927, which ran through sixteen editions. Morton was inspired to write it while he was delirious in a hospital in Palestine, dreaming of woodsmoke and elms, and the jingle of a team slowly coming home from the fields. Thanks to the car, he believed that more people than in any previous generation are seeing the real country for the first time.

The first 'heritage' advertising came from the oil giant, Shell, whose 'Lorry Bills' employed a galaxy of artistic talent to persuade people to visit historic sites and beauty spots – by car, of course. Their press advertisements were famous for their captions such as 'Stonehenge Wilts but Shell goes on forever' or this by John Betjeman, 'Fishguard Wales but Shell's run by experts'. Under the editorship of Betjeman, the company launched their own Shell Guides in 1933. He described the England of those days as rich in 'undisturbed villages, where streets wandered out into commons and woodlands [...] away from the railway line there was a country silence so deep that it went back to Chaucer'.[22] The guides placed both new and old photographs alongside well-written, opinionated descriptions. The authors were generally poets and writers – and the artist John Piper was one of them. They relished 'decrepit glory', pleasing decay and a sense of patina. Ian Hislop later called Shell Guides 'a storehouse of national identity', albeit to a minority.

London and the Bulldozer

And all that day in murky London Wall
The thought of Ruislip kept him warm inside

Betjeman imagined City workers finding comfort in their new suburban villas; Arcadia might extend to certain suburbs, but not to the city itself. For the capital, dulled by a sense of mutability and the inevitability of change, was under attack from developers and had few defenders until the mid-1930s brought the formation of the Georgian Group. By then the swansong of the great aristocratic London houses was well under way. Typical was Devonshire House on Piccadilly facing Green Park, which served as the headquarters of the Red Cross during World War I, never to be reopened, and demolished in 1925 to be replaced by a block of luxury flats, a hotel and showroom.[23] This was followed by the loss of Dorchester House, Grosvenor House, Lansdowne House, Norfolk House and Chesterfield House. With them went their furnishings and art collections. Panelled rooms were usually salvaged and often shipped to America; the Norfolk House Music Room went to the V&A. The remains of the art collection were usually dispatched to the country houses to which their owners had now retreated.

There were other grievous losses in London. Foremost among them was Soane's masterpiece, the Bank of England, rebuilt during the 1920s by Herbert Baker. The greatest tragedy of the townscape was the gradual replacement of Nash's majestically sweeping Regent Street; this was the work of the Crown Commissioners, who proved to be the most destructive landlords in the capital. In 1933 they announced a plan to rebuild Nash's Carlton House

Terrace on The Mall to designs by Sir Reginald Blomfield. The novelist George Moore wrote of the commissioners that year: 'the moment they see a fine building they form a plot to pull it down. Yesterday it was Park Lane, today it is Carlton House Terrace, and tomorrow it will be the churches in the Strand. All will be destroyed and nothing of beauty will be left in London to indicate that a once-civilised people who did not make a God of football and motorcars lived in it'.[24] A campaign to save Carlton House Terrace followed, and it may have been the intervention of Queen Mary that saved this most serene of terraces.* What became clear from these developments was that the Society for the Protection of Ancient Buildings was indifferent to buildings after 1714, and a new more aggressive body was required to champion the capital.

It was the destruction of Robert Adam's Adelphi Terrace in 1936 that ignited the anger of Douglas Goldring, a novelist and journalist, who had waged a campaign against its destruction in the pages of the *New Statesman*. He had already noted how supine the SPAB had been in defending the little shops on Bishopsgate 'on the grounds that they had been rebuilt not much more than a century ago and were therefore not "old"'.[25] As it happened, Lord Derwent was proposing a motion in the House of Lords that the Royal Commission on Historical Monuments should extend its work beyond the 1714 cut-off date to cover buildings up to 1830. Derwent and Goldring joined forces to form a provisional wing of the SPAB in 1937. They called it the Georgian Group. Its driving force and publicist-in-chief, however, was Robert Byron, whose outraged intelligence made him a precursor to Ian Nairn and Gavin Stamp.

Robert Byron made a great impression on his contemporaries, who agreed that he looked like Queen Victoria. He wrote a lauded polemic, *How we Celebrate the Coronation* (1937), which

---

* It was not a complete victory, since the Crown Commissioners did succeed in replacing 4 Carlton Gardens at the Trafalgar Square end of Carlton House Terrace.

spoke of 'the ruin of London, for our humiliation before visitors'. He went on to state that 'the value of architecture in England according to official and ecclesiastical standards, varies in proportion to its antiquity, its quaintness, and its holiness. By these standards, a bit of the old Roman wall is of more importance than Nash's Regent Street, and one ruined pointed arch than all Wren's churches put together.'[26] James Lees-Milne observed that Byron would 'resort to any and every weapon, mockery, vituperation, scurrility, pillorying if needs be prime ministers and archbishops, with gloves off'.[27] One of his guerrilla tactics was to list the telephone numbers of those whom he perceived as the villains: the Ecclesiastical Commissioners, the Archbishop of Canterbury, the Bishop of London and the trustees of the British Museum. The relationship with the SPAB was baleful from beginning – the young Turks of the Georgian Group were impatient with the SPAB, who were accustomed to a softly-softly approach. If the SPAB was middle class and arty crafty, the Georgian Group was urbane and smart. Its early members included the more artistic grandees: the Sitwell brothers, Edward Sackville-West, Bryan Guinness and Kenneth Clark. The Georgians were quarrelsome, metropolitan, and positively enjoyed controversy. With their flair for publicity and a shrewd use of the press, they created the template for heritage pressure groups from the 1960s onwards, including Save Britain's Heritage (SAVE).

The organisation turned out to be more than just an action group and would play a significant role in establishing the listed buildings system after the war. One of its early failures was James Wyatt's domed and colonnaded Pantheon in Oxford Street, which was replaced by a new Marks & Spencer store. Despite having virtually no protective legislation to help, the Georgian Group did have some notable successes: they played a pivotal role in saving a pair of Palladian houses in Old Palace Yard, one of the most historic sites in the capital, sandwiched between the Abbey and the Palace of Westminster. Perhaps its greatest triumph was preventing the demolition of the east side of Bedford Square to allow for the expansion of the British Museum. The square happily remains the best preserved Georgian square in the capital.

The Georgian Group was not the only champion of London operating between the wars. In 1921 *The Times* proposed 'a committee of taste composed of sculptors, painters and architects to choose sites for statues and a standing committee of designers to oversee street decorations for occasions of national importance'.[28] It was rather small beer. The French had their Ministry of Fine Arts, which did not offer a comparable precedent to the British, but the American prototype set up in 1910 to monitor development in Washington was admired. The Royal Fine Art Commission (RFAC) was convened in 1924, with a group of aesthetically minded grandees: Sir Lionel Earle from the Ministry of Works, the Earl of Crawford (the go-to peer on aesthetic matters) and two architects, Sir Reginald Blomfield and Sir Aston Webb. The final member was that busybody, Lord Lee of Fareham, who is best remembered for giving Chequers to the nation. Lord Curzon, the most artistic member of the cabinet, was too busy to be directly involved, and indeed wondered whether a commission was really needed. Lord Crawford persuaded him on the ingenious grounds that had such a body previously existed, he would not have to gaze at Sigismund Goetze's shockingly bad paintings, which he passed every day on the stairs at the Foreign Office.

In the early years nobody really understood what the RFAC did. There was much discussion on whether their role was about intervention or assistance, and they decided it was the latter. It commented on matters such as design of firemen's helmets and the sighting of statues. The latter could be surprisingly controversial, particularly Charles Jagger's Royal Artillery memorial at Hyde Park Corner, which was considered alarming in its mixing of stone and bronze. Worse was the controversy over the siting of the equestrian statue of Earl Haig in the middle of Whitehall, staring at the cenotaph. The RFAC gradually extended its range and claimed a hand in the victory at Carlton House Terrace. Before effective planning controls and the listing system became workable, it was virtually the only court of appeal to prevent developments. Its most lasting achievement in the early years was its role in the choice of Sir Giles Gilbert Scott to design Britain's red telephone kiosks. The body, whose attentions were overwhelmingly focused on London, tried to strike a balance between conservation and development. When the issue of Scotland was raised, Crawford drily commented, 'I do not think that Scotland would accept decisions from so predominantly southern a personnel.'[29]

Thanks to the war and its aftermath, the destruction of the fabric of London would be replicated in cities across Britain: the momentum of rebuilding, development and modernisation was too great to be arrested. London was never to be like Paris or Rome, a city preserved at all costs. The British reserved such sentiments for their rural beauty spots. The historian G. M. Trevelyan made the argument for the landscape in his 1938 booklet, *The Case for National Parks in Great Britain*: 'it is not a question of physical exercise only, it is also a question of spiritual exercise and enjoyment. It is a question of spiritual values'.[30] In the same year, Trevelyan told a CPRE meeting that while other nations were defining themselves through political ideology, racial supremacy or military might, the landscape was central to Britain's national identity: 'natural beauty is the highest common denominator in the spiritual life of today'.[31] After the next world war, a Labour government would enshrine this belief in their national parks law.

CHAPTER 3

Assembling a National Collection

We regard the national monuments to which this bill
refers as part of the heritage and history of the nation.
They are part of the heritage of the nation, because
every citizen feels an interest in them.

LORD CURZON, 1912

On 21 September 1915, as World War I had just entered its second year, a Wiltshire landowner, Cecil Chubb, was sent by his wife to buy some chairs at an auction held by Knight, Frank & Rutley in the New Theatre at Salisbury. He did not buy any chairs, but he did buy – apparently on impulse – lot 15, which was Stonehenge, for £6,600. As Chubb later remarked: 'while I was in the room, I thought a Salisbury man ought to buy it and that is how it was done'. The cause of the sale was the death of the long-time owner, Sir Edmund Antrobus, whose heir had been killed in action in the first month of the war. The notion that Britain's most illustrious ancient monument might be sold at auction and then dismantled and shipped to America had haunted the Tory grandee Lord Curzon, who had warned the House of Lords of such a possibility only three years earlier. Fortunately, even if the war had not made shipping overseas less likely, Chubb had no such designs and made the decision in 1918 to present Stonehenge to the nation, for which he received a baronetcy. He became known locally as 'Viscount Stonehenge'.

Stonehenge could serve as an index of historic attitudes to heritage and conservation. Each century has interpreted Stonehenge according to its own values and interests; Geoffrey of Monmouth in the eleventh century saw it as an act of wizardry, and Inigo Jones in the seventeenth century as the product of the Roman occupation. Nearly every antiquarian historian of note had explored the problem of its interpretation. The evolution and creation of Stonehenge is too complex to admit just one explanation, and 'the oldest stone on the site is unlikely to have meant the same to the people who saw it erected as it did to those who later placed the most recent'.[1] By the seventeenth century the stone circle had become a considerable visitor attraction. Pepys left an account of his visit and the by then already well-developed tourist industry at the site. During the eighteenth century Stonehenge was owned by the Dukes of Queensbury who sold it to the Antrobus family in 1825. With the appointment of the great pioneering archaeologist, Augustus Pitt Rivers, as the first Inspector of Ancient Monuments in 1882, it was inevitable that he would turn his attention to it. He produced a report full of sensible suggestions, predicting that 'sooner or later, more probably sooner than later, most of the stones will fall through natural causes'.[2] Sir Edmund Antrobus, a former colonel in the Grenadier Guards, however, resenting what he saw as government interference, did nothing to shore up the stones and refused all requests for excavation, making it clear that he considered that Stonehenge was safer in private hands. He relented enough to offer the site to the nation in 1898 along with 1,300 acres of land for an exorbitant £125,000, several times the Ancient Monuments department's annual budget. Baulking at the price, the government understandably declined it.

On the last day of the nineteenth century (31 December 1899) two of the stones in the outer circle collapsed, just as Pitt Rivers had predicted. Antrobus sought advice from the Society for the Protection of Ancient Buildings (SPAB) and the Wiltshire Archaeological Society. The result was that the stones were fenced off for the first time and a ticketing system was introduced the following May, at a considerable rate of one shilling per entry. This went against the principles of the Commons, Open Spaces and Footpaths Preservation Society, which argued for freedom of access. Robert Hunter, one of the three founders of the National Trust, was among the protestors: 'To the minds of most persons there is something absurd in the idea that a national possession like Stonehenge should be at the mercy of a private person!'[3]

When the Antrobus family finally relinquished control through the Salisbury sale, the oddest part of the story is not that the most celebrated ancient monument in Europe was placed in a local auction sale (and advertised with a thumbnail picture in *Country Life*), but that the Office of Works, the guardian of monuments on behalf of the state, did not exercise its newly acquired pre-emptive right to purchase an ancient monument when offered for sale. It was no doubt the demands of war that prevented them from acting.* The cumbersomely titled Ancient Monuments Consolidation and Amendment Act of 1913 had provided the power to place monuments under state protection and even ownership.† In addition, the Act expanded the range of existing legislation to 'any monument or part remains of a monument, the preservation of which is a matter of public interest'.[4] As a result, the date 1913 is usually given as the foundation of the National Heritage Collection, the great outdoor museum of the nation, with almost 900 properties today held by English Heritage, Cadw in Wales, and Historic Scotland.

The Office of Works was a truly ancient department that had been established in 1378 to maintain royal residences. By the nineteenth century it had also become responsible for the government's civil properties. Sometimes described as the smallest department in Whitehall, it was organised under a political head, known as the First Commissioner, working with

---

* The budget of the Office of Works was consumed by the war effort, constructing munitions factories and housing for their workers.
† The commissioners could place a preservation order on a monument for eighteen months, but in order to protect it permanently, the preservation order had to be confirmed through an Act of Parliament, at which point compensation equivalent to the market value of the site would be payable.

a senior civil servant, the Secretary.[*] With the passing of the Ancient Monuments Act in 1882, it found itself the guardian of a growing collection of monuments, initially to protect them, but increasingly to provide public access. Over the next thirty years there was a gradual transfer into its care of some of the country's most famous castles and abbeys, not under any programme of acquisition but rather in pragmatic acceptance as historic sites became available. Overseas, France had established the *Commission des Monuments Historiques* as early as 1837, which provided the framework for a comprehensive set of objectives (with an emphasis on Gothic). In Britain ancient monuments were saved (and laws passed) as and when the situation arose. It turned out to be a successful system, largely thanks to a handful of outstanding public servants and the persuasive powers of their political masters. Indeed, the first decades of the twentieth century turned out to be golden years of acquisition.[†]

The Office of Works and its successor, the Ministry of Works, would hold sway over the largest collection of heritage sites, with by far the largest visitor footfall until overtaken by the National Trust during the 1970s. While there would always be rivalry and overlap between the two bodies, they retained a distinct character, the former mainly holding ancient castles, ruined abbeys and archaeological sites, while the National Trust was for the most part concerned about beauty spots, coastline and, increasingly, country houses. The growth of the Trust, which was relatively slow at first, presaged the expansion of the voluntary and philanthropic aspects of heritage that were to be so successful in the UK. It also offered an alternative to those who were less enthused about donating to a government department. The enlargement of the National Trust would depend almost entirely

---

[*] It was reconstituted as a government department in 1851 under that name until 1940, when it became the Ministry of Public Buildings and Works, later incorporated into the Department for the Environment.

[†] In 1913 there were forty-four monuments in the department's care which rose to 273 by 1933, of which 147 were in England.

on the generosity of donors and activists,* yet the collection of sites held by the Office of Works was, to a surprising extent, the result of gifts from landowners like Cecil Chubb – tight budgets offered little alternative.

The growth of the National Heritage Collection was an evolutionary transition whereby former royal residences, military barracks, abandoned castles, archaeological sites and ruined abbeys mutated into public heritage assets whose purpose was increasingly to welcome visitors. The greatest boost to this process (and to visitor numbers) was the result of the pioneering partnerships forged by the Office of Works with the monarch, and various government departments. The range of properties which came into guardianship as a result of these were vastly to add to the possibilities of the department's role.

The first public buildings, except cathedrals, commonly considered as visitor attractions were royal palaces, which had always offered a degree of public access. The Tower of London, long one of the capital's premier attractions, had since Tudor times welcomed visitors to inspect the Royal Menagerie, the Armouries, and after 1669 to enjoy the display of the Crown Jewels. This access impressed foreigners: in 1786 Sophie von La Roche noted 'this seems to me the most outstanding difference between London and Paris; the foreigner is shown the Tower, while he dare not even look at the Bastille'.[5] As the Tower was both a royal palace and a fortress, by the early nineteenth century the increasingly paramount needs of the visitors were causing considerable frustration to the Duke of Wellington, who viewed the Tower as a military establishment. This pressure increased in 1825 with the opening of a new exhibition hall to display the armour, followed by the new Jewel House in 1841. And then, no doubt aware of the huge visitor success of the Tower, Queen Victoria allowed Hampton Court Palace – long

---

* After World War II some major properties, particularly country houses, came to the National Trust via the government's Land Fund and later the Heritage Memorial Fund.

deserted as a royal residence and by now a medley of grace and favour apartments – to be opened without charge to the public in 1837.* Although the ownership of the palace remained with the Crown, the Office of Works was given the responsibility for the opening arrangements. Between Hampton Court and the Tower, the department could now add running tourist attractions to its responsibilities.

The position of royal palaces in the modern era has always been delicately poised between royal prerogative over their use and the willingness of the state to pay for their maintenance. It was that enigmatic éminence grise, Reginald Brett (Lord Esher from 1898), when he was Secretary of the Office of Works, who persuaded Queen Victoria to also transfer the management of Kensington Palace to the Office of Works.† A very modern style of partnership deal was struck whereby the palace would be shared: residential rights were to be reserved for members of the royal family and their households, while the state apartments would be opened to the public by the department. Given the difficulty of getting funds out of the Treasury, it was considered a great coup that £20,000 was offered for the restoration of the palace. This raised the interesting question of just how it should be renovated. Esher took personal control and decided that the rooms in which Queen Victoria had been brought up would be left, and not returned to their eighteenth-century appearance. As for the state rooms, Esher restored them as a furnished palace of the Georgian era, to escape the rather sterile 'picture gallery' effect at Hampton Court. The opening of the palace in 1899 was a success, with almost 350,000 visitors in the first year. Having

---

* In order to make Hampton Court more approaching the prevailing romantic notions of a Tudor palace, the architect, John Lessels, was brought in to make the Tudor parts look more Tudor by removing all the Georgian sash windows from this section of the palace.
† Esher also persuaded her to open the ranger's house at Blackheath and Kew Palace to the public. Since he had worked at the War Office he was useful in that relationship as well.

won the trust of Queen Victoria, Esher succeeded to an even greater extent with her successor, Edward VII, who agreed after the queen's death to transfer the state rooms at Osborne House on the Isle of Wight. Under the new king, Esher would be responsible for turning British royal pageantry, which had previously been rather approximate, into the immaculate performance it remains to this day.

Not all collaborations went as smoothly as at Kensington Palace. The largest single owner of secular historic buildings remained the War Office, with its vast estate of castles, barracks, and coastal fortifications – and its tense relationship with the Office of Works over the Tower of London and Edinburgh Castle. Typical was the row that erupted over the rebuilding of the latter's Portcullis Gate during the 1880s, when the Office of Works had recently been given a limited responsibility for the castle, but the War Office retained control over the greater part of the building. This led to some decisions which illustrate the kind of situation that provoked William Morris to set up the SPAB: the Edinburgh publisher, William Nelson, paid for the restoration of the Great Hall and, most controversially, the Portcullis Gate, under War Office jurisdiction. Despite protests, Nelson used his own architect, the Scot of French parentage, Hippolyte Jean Blanc, whose interpretations were romantic. He created the vista that visitors still enter through, controversial for obliterating medieval work, but accepted by most as original.

Notwithstanding such disputes, in 1898 the Treasury agreed that the responsibility for the maintenance and appearance of several more of the War Office's most hallowed buildings should be passed to the Office of Works, but this did not happen until the reorganisation following the failures of the Boer War. Lord Esher was able to ease the matter through the War Office, where he had previously worked. Thus between 1900–10 several important buildings came under the notional, but rarely complete, control of the Office of Works: an extended remit at the Tower and Edinburgh Castle, and responsibility for the castles of Dover,

Walmer and Deal.* The War Office maintained operational control over most of these facilities for military purposes: Dover Castle remained a fundamental part of national defence as late as World War II, and even today Edinburgh Castle maintains a garrison.† Stirling Castle was taken into state care in 1906 after King Edward VII expressed his concern over the 'irrevocable damage' being done by the soldiers stationed there. It was not until the Argyll and Sutherland Highlanders finally marched out in 1964 that work could begin in earnest to recover the cultural significance of Scotland's finest Renaissance royal apartments.

Despite managing the public parts of these palaces and castles, the Office of Works would always be associated with ancient monuments, ruins and archaeological sites. There was one spectacular series of castles in the British Isles not in the hands of the War Office, but under inattentive municipal care; those great abstract masterpieces of construction built by Edward I to subdue the Welsh: Caernarfon, Conwy and Harlech. They fell to the Office of Works during the early decades of the twentieth century and have ever since presented Welsh nationalists with an image problem as 'those magnificent badges of our subjection'.‡ The only one that was still privately owned was Beaumaris, which had been associated with the Bulkeley family since the sixteenth century. They had incorporated it into their park as an oversize folly and allowed it to fall into a state of

---

* The first visitor attraction that the Office of Works in a sense created was Walmer Castle, bringing in furniture and other objects to foster tourist interest. An entrance fee was charged to keep out 'the worst of the undesirables' and to bring in a modest income.

† Some readers will recall the romantically imagined interiors of the castle barracks featuring in the film *Tunes of Glory,* set during the late 1940s – the reality was much more squalid.

‡ Caernarfon Castle came through an unusual route, as certain responsibilities such as management and care were transferred to the Office of Works by a written agreement with the Constable of the Castle on 1 December 1906. The town walls are a mix of freehold ownership and guardianship arrangements.

neglect until in 1925 Richard Williams-Bulkeley ceded the castle to the Office of Works.

One source of important properties came through a sister department, the Commissioners of Woods. They cared for Crown lands and held many monuments and abbeys, including such historic buildings as Eltham Palace Old Hall, which it duly transferred to the Office of Works. Most great abbeys, however, remained in the hands of private landowners at the beginning of the twentieth century. Interest in ecclesiastical ruins, those 'bare ruined choirs' resulting from the dissolution of the monasteries, had been fuelled by the romantic watercolours of Girtin and Turner as well as a pioneering book of photographs, *Ruined Abbeys and Castles of Great Britain* by William and Mary Howitt (1862). William Gilpin had already declared in 1786 that 'a ruin is a sacred thing'. The landowners had been mixed in their appreciation – some, like William Aislabie, the owner of Fountains Abbey, had incorporated such remains into their landscape parks. However, by the end of the nineteenth century, with the increase of railway tourism, many landowners regarded ancient monuments as problems, attracting both snooping visitors as well as state interference.

Perhaps the most eulogised of all the abbeys was Tintern in South Wales, a revered pilgrimage destination for picturesque tourism, hallowed by Wordsworth and Turner alike. Tintern was in the ownership of the Dukes of Beaufort until 1901 when the abbey was, rather surprisingly, purchased by the Crown for £15,000, which transferred it to the Office of Works in 1914. Another of the most spectacular acquisitions came as a result of World War I: the great Cistercian foundation, Rievaulx Abbey in Yorkshire, dating mostly from the thirteenth century. Its owner, Lord Feversham, had died leading the battalion he raised from his Helmsley estate into the Battle of Flers-Courcelette (1916). This brought what Charles Peers, Inspector of Ancient Monuments, described as 'perhaps the most beautiful of all our ruined abbeys'.[6] Three years later, the Duke of Buccleuch handed over Melrose Abbey to the guardianship of the Office of Works so that now

England, Scotland and Wales each had an outstanding abbey in public ownership.

Tintern Abbey was the first major repair job undertaken by the Office of Works and caused some heart-searching about methods of preservation and presentation. The ivy-clad park ruin romanticism of the Victorian era would no longer suffice – such monuments now required a clarity of presentation that would make them easier to explain and to preserve. It was agreed that 'the loss to the imagination would be more than repaid by the gain to the intellect'.[7] Tintern established a pattern: cleansing the site of later accretions and buildings (which might today be judged of value), editing the landscape by cutting down trees, and, in this particular case, reinforcing the structure with a braced steel frame. This attracted SPAB criticism: 'the building is no longer alive [...] everything is now fixed, solid and secure, a mediaeval ruin frozen, as if by cold storage in perpetuity'.[8] For them the repairs had gone too far. One criticism that has never entirely gone away is a belief that the Office of Works and its successors tend to manicure the sites, especially with their fondness for smooth lawns. Such care has removed some of the picturesque romance of the site and gave the department a reputation for antiseptic presentation.

Tattershall Castle

The expansion of the Office of Works had exposed the limitations of the existing protective legislation. However, it would take a crisis to ensure the passage through parliament of the important amendment of 1913. This was the sale and mutilation of 'the finest piece of mediaeval brickwork in England', Tattershall Castle in Lincolnshire. The drama must be understood in the context of the increasing exodus of panelled rooms to America. From the 1890s, when Americans started to buy and ship historic fixtures as well as great paintings from British aristocratic collections, an anxiety arose that collectors might also wish to acquire old houses to dismantle and export to the United States. This fear appeared to come true when Tattershall Castle was put up for sale in 1910. A syndicate had already removed important fireplaces and was expected to dismantle the building and find a buyer in America. It took the intervention of Lord Curzon to prevent this happening. Informed that there was only twenty-four hours to save Tattershall, he rushed to Lincolnshire and made a private offer, which was accepted. He then set about tracking down the missing fireplaces, which he managed to return to their rooms. This was one of the first occasions when there was a serious attempt to retain a work of art in this country.

Lord Curzon is easier to respect than love, but it must be acknowledged that he was a prince of heritage conservation. His interest had been awakened in India. Pandit Nehru once remarked that after all the other viceroys had been forgotten, Curzon would be remembered for restoring all that was beautiful in his country. Curzon sat on a great many arts-related committees and showed an energetic interest in conservation.[*] Having acquired Tattershall, he brought in the SPAB to restore the castle and left it to the National Trust on his death in 1925. He realised, like Lord Avebury before him, that the only way to achieve his goals was 'to cut the Gordian knot by buying it myself'. His intervention was timely, as parliament was about to debate the deficiencies of the Ancient Monuments Act, and the Tattershall Castle affair underlined the need for wider protective legislation.[†]

---

[*] Apart from Tattershall, Lord Curzon also restored Government House in Calcutta, Walmer Castle, Hackwood Park, Montacute, Bodiam Castle and Kedleston Hall. There is a story that Lord Curzon invited his prospective second wife to the country, blindfolded her and took her through some trees to surprise her with Bodiam Castle, and then invited her to marry him.

[†] It should be noted that the 1900 Ancient Monuments Act had been a step in the right direction, giving the Office of Works the ability to charge an entrance fee to inspect ancient monuments. The Act also brought medieval buildings into the picture.

In the debate Curzon spoke the words found at the head of this chapter, adding that such monuments: 'are part of the history of the nation because they are documents just as valuable in reading the records of the past as is any manuscript'.[9] He urged that the new Act should encompass inhabited buildings, such as manor houses, 'and then, descending the scale, the smaller buildings, whether they be bridges, market crosses, cottages or even barns, which carry on their face the precious story of the past'.[10] Curzon was successful, and the Act extended the range of state guardianship to include medieval structures and any monument that was worthy of preservation by reason of historic, architectural, artistic or archaeological interest.[*] The Duke of Rutland spoke for many landowners when he complained about the meddling, spying and loss of liberty. However, the Act brought together representatives from the learned societies to advise on the use of the new preservation orders that might have applied to Stonehenge two years later. Notwithstanding the failure to act at Stonehenge, the passing of this bill in 1913 is regarded as a key event in the development of the nation's collection of monuments. Henceforth there would be a clear division in the responsibilities of the Office of Works: protecting and listing monuments on the one hand, and opening and explaining them for visitors on the other.

Hadrian's Wall

After Stonehenge, Hadrian's Wall was the ancient monument that excited the greatest national curiosity. It had been repeatedly robbed since the Middle Ages, with sections used

---

* Kirby Muxloe Castle in Leicestershire, really a fortified house, was the first privately owned castle to be taken into the care of the Office of Works. The 1913 Act established a separate advisory body for Scotland, with James Richardson as its secretary. The most curious aspect of the 1913 Act is that ecclesiastical buildings in use were excluded, unlike on the continent.

as a quarry and plundered for building materials. The greatest vandal was General Wade when he constructed one of his military roads in 1746. It was a local landowner, John Clayton, who made the first serious attempt to preserve the wall. He had inherited one of the wall's seventeen larger forts and acquired further sections to safeguard it, so that by the time he died in 1890 his heirs came into possession of the forts of Chesters, Carrawburgh Housesteads, Vindolanda and Carvoran, as well as much of the wall in between. The Clayton family cared for this estate until 1929, when it was split up. Public-spirited landowners saved whatever they could; one of them, Eric Birley, acquired the then virtually unknown Vindolanda Fort, later to become celebrated for the discovery of the tablets – an intimate and moving glimpse into the everyday lives of the men and women from all around the Roman Empire who once formed its garrison.

When Charles Peers, a heroic figures in the history of the Office of Works, was appointed Inspector of Ancient Monuments, the first thing he did was to spend two days inspecting Hadrian's Wall.* He was dismayed to find that local industries were still plundering it. Twenty years later, in 1930, he returned with his minister, George Lansbury.† On this occasion, Peers was more shocked about the degraded state of the area around the wall. Lansbury consulted the prime minister, and this was the catalyst for a new parliamentary bill the following year, sometimes referred to as the Hadrian's Wall Act, that

* Charles Peers (1868–1952) was the son of a clergyman who studied in Germany, travelled widely, and trained as an architect. Preferring the study of old buildings, he became the architectural editor of the scholarly Victoria County History volumes, until in 1901 he took up the position of Inspector of Works.

† Lansbury, a deeply committed Labour politician, as First Commissioner of Works, broke the mould of aristocratic charmers at the Office of Works – George V considered him a dangerous Bolshevik. He was an effective First Commissioner who joined his passion for providing employment with the reconditioning of monuments such as Helmsley Castle.

provided the power to preserve the vicinity of any monument from unsightly development.* The problem at Hadrian's Wall, however, could not be immediately solved since many of the quarries had the legal right to remove stone until their leases ended. Most of Hadrian's Wall remains in private hands to this day, although the best-known sections are owned by English Heritage and the National Trust.

Between the wars, the Office of Works continued adding to its inventory of monuments at the rate of at least five a year. Perhaps the most impressive addition during this period was Kenilworth Castle – not only a great fortress but the site of a fantastic lost garden created to greet Queen Elizabeth I. The Earl of Clarendon sold the castle to the aircraft manufacturer, Sir John Siddeley, who acquired it with a view to public benefaction. He first considered the claims of the National Trust but was uncertain whether they had the means to maintain it properly, and so presented it to the Office of Works instead, for which he was rewarded with a peerage, becoming Baron Kenilworth.

Many of the department's most exciting acquisitions were archaeological sites. None was more intriguing than Skara Brae in the Orkney Isles, the best preserved prehistoric village in northern Europe. It was a storm of exceptional severity in 1850 that exposed these ancient dwellings with all their built-in stone furnishings and domestic items. After an initial excavation and the clearing of a large haul of objects, the site was left undisturbed until 1925, by which time it was in the guardianship of the Office of Works. The archaeologist put in charge of the excavation was a legendary figure, Professor Gordon Childe, a Marxist who was pleased to reveal at Skara Brae a pastoralist, communistic society of 'ordinary people' with no obvious hierarchy.

* The 1931 Ancient Monuments Act.

The National Trust

For the first half of the twentieth century, the National Trust stood somewhat in counterpoise to the Office of Works; it had a different emphasis and was completely dependent upon private benefaction and volunteer activity. The priorities of the Trust as it moved into the new century are recognisable today: open spaces, nature conservancy, and increasingly, the fate of historic buildings. It was a milestone in the heritage movement that a charitable body should be so powerfully protected. The National Trust Act (1907) gave it the provision to hold property inalienably, which could only be disposed of by act of parliament. The problem of disposal was to prove to be of greater relevance in the future than at the time.* Buildings did not form a part of the original vision of Octavia Hill and Robert Hunter. Those buildings that the Trust did acquire were medieval and, excepting Barrington Court, usually modest: the clergy house at Alfriston, the old post office at Tintagel and the Chantry Chapel at Buckingham.

Several buildings of this type came to the Trust from a dashing source, a volunteer group known as 'Ferguson's Gang'. Formed in 1927 under the inspiration of Clough Williams-Ellis's book, *England and the Octopus*, their motto was that 'England is Stonehenge, and not Whitehall'. They were a colourful body of activists, mostly women, who branded themselves as a Robin Hood organisation, anonymously acquiring small historic properties and then handing them over to the National Trust. They adopted whimsical names and once dropped off a card at the Trust's offices which ran: 'we ain't so many – we ain't so few/all of us had this end in view/National Trust – to work for you'. They preferred model everyday buildings such as the eighteenth-century watermill at Shalford in Surrey. They raided Mayfair parties at the invitation of the hostess and behaved like

* It became very relevant during the 1970s when sections of the parks at both Saltram and Petworth were under threat from compulsory purchase for ring roads.

highwaymen, wearing masks and demanding pieces of jewellery. The money was then delivered in characteristic style: on one occasion a masked lady arrived at the National Trust headquarters in London announcing herself as 'Red Biddy', deposited a hundred pounds in silver and left by taxi. They saved many rural properties from demolition and presented the Trust with tracts of coastline, including Frenchman's Creek on Helford River.[*]

Country Houses

The National Trust was beginning to broaden its range of properties, and even ventured into archaeology, the traditional area of the Office of Works.[†] The most unexpected change of direction, however, was the organisation's gradual acceptance of its role as the repository of last resort for country houses. Between the wars, there were already several visitable country houses in public ownership, usually situated in or near towns, which had been taken over to become local museums or show houses. These included Towneley Hall in Burnley and Heaton Hall on the edge of Manchester, both acquired by their civic authorities in 1902, Temple Newsam by Leeds Corporation in 1922, and Wollaton Hall, acquired by Nottingham Council in 1925.[‡] The motivation in the latter two cases was to save the parks as a public amenity,

---

[*] Frenchman's Creek was not until 1946.

[†] Among notable early sites acquired by the National Trust were the stone circles known as the 'Druids' Circle' at Saddleback near Keswick, and the Roman villa at Chedworth, near Cirencester, with its spectacular mosaic pavements.

[‡] The first country house 'save' was the Jacobean Aston Hall and its park on the outskirts of Birmingham, acquired by the city in 1864. It never really knew what to do with the house, which served as a museum and a municipal library and was threatened with demolition in the 1920s. It was saved thanks to a popular campaign with a committee of working men offering many small donations.

but this resulted in buildings also being retained, by no means a given at the time.

The National Trust's first venture with country houses had been a near disaster: the purchase in 1907 of Barrington Court, Somerset, entailed repairs which had almost bankrupted it. The Trust was in no hurry to repeat the experience. Their association with large country houses really began when Ernest Cook, heir to the Thomas Cook travel fortune, bequeathed the unfurnished but irresistible Montacute House in 1931. This new course by the Trust was given impetus by one of the most important speeches in the history of heritage. It was at the Trust's AGM in 1934 that Lord Lothian, a Liberal peer who had once been secretary to Lloyd George, expressed his anxiety about the future of country houses. Lothian urged the Trust to find the means by which it could accept houses while leaving the family in residence. It was a visionary idea that perhaps, on the surface, went against the Trust's egalitarian ideals and predominantly landscape-oriented priorities – but were not country houses also beautiful and historic?

Perhaps surprisingly, the Trust took Lothian's bait and established their country house scheme. However, the organisation recognised the grave threat to their existence, encouraged by *Country Life* writer Christopher Hussey. If such an arrangement were to work, a method would have to be invented to calculate the size of the endowment required from owners that would allow the Trust to support the property – much later this became known as the Chorley formula.* Legislation was passed in 1937 and 1939 to allow owners to transfer their properties to the National Trust free of capital taxes in return for public access (and a considerable part of their fortune for the endowment). This form of voluntary nationalisation was an inspired piece of pragmatism, with outcomes that no other nation has ever been able to reproduce so successfully. In his speech, Lord Lothian

---

* In 1968, when the size of endowment required was increased.

said: 'most of these houses are under sentence of death, and the axe which is destroying them is taxation – especially death duties'.

The speech had an immediate effect, with Sir Charles Trevelyan offering Wallington in Northumberland with 13,000 acres, although it would take some time to reel in that fish. One of the reasons for the success of the scheme was the appointment of a National Trust Secretary, James Lees-Milne, in 1936, who would be the persuader, nanny and guide to the nervous owners of the houses offered. He wrote: 'the lengths to which I have gone, the depths to which I have plumbed, the concessions which I have (once most reluctantly) granted to acquire properties for the National Trust, will not all be known by that august and ungrateful body. It might be shocked by the extreme zeal of its servant, if it did'.[11] Lord Lothian himself gave his own poetically beautiful Jacobean house in Norfolk, Blickling Hall, an example followed by Hatchlands in Surrey, and Stourhead in Wiltshire. One of the most spectacular transfers was that Tudor masterpiece in Kent, Knole, more like a grand Oxford college than a home, which with its astonishing furnishings was the archetype of the 'olden times' mansion. The inspiration for Virginia Woolf's novel, *Orlando*, Knole has always had a special place in the country house pantheon. All these houses had their own peculiar complexities: unbreakable entails, heirs who had to be bought off, multiple ownerships, lack of money for an endowment. The difficulties were labyrinthine, as there was rarely such a thing as an unentailed house.

The inventory of important monuments and houses saved for public benefit was, like so much else – one thinks of the British Museum, and the nation's collection of overseas embassies – seemingly created in an absence of mind. As Michael Heseltine was later to admit: 'there was no deliberate government policy to create a nationally owned heritage'.[12] But the legislative structures established to receive and protect it were of the highest quality, and this no doubt encouraged the benefactions which, by European standards, were extraordinary. By the outbreak of World War II, the Office of Works alone held well over 300 sites, only about half of which were in England. The vast majority of pre-war visitors to these attractions were British and this would not alter until the 1970s, when the international heritage industry took off. By this time, thanks to the assiduity and achievements of the Office of Works and the National Trust, Britain could already offer visitors one of the richest collections of heritage sites in Europe.

CHAPTER 4

The Exodus of Paintings

And all this brought together yesterday,
will be dispersed tomorrow.

THÉOPHILE THORÉ ON THE
ART TREASURES EXHIBITION, 1857

In 1857, on what is now the cricket field of Old Trafford, was held 'the mother of all blockbusters', the Art Treasures of Great Britain exhibition in Manchester, the high water mark of British art collecting.* It revealed the astonishing riches amassed by British collectors over the previous 250 years. Queen Victoria and Prince Albert headed the list of lenders which constituted a veritable *Who's Who* of British collecting. A special railway line and station were constructed to transport the 1.5 million visitors to the doors of the exhibition, which was underwritten by the Bank of England. The catalogue listed 1,079 old master paintings (including twenty-eight supposed Rembrandts), some modern paintings and a vast array of the decorative arts. The impact was international. The French critic Théophile Thoré thought that the exhibition was the equal of the Louvre.[1] Engels even wrote to Karl Marx recommending he bring his wife to see it. Never again was such an immense display of privately owned works of art from private collections to occur, and within a few decades the tide of art would start to retreat from Britain.

The exhibition was made possible by the industry of two

---

* A civic gesture to match London's Great Exhibition of 1851. It was Prince Albert who suggested an exhibition of art rather than industry for Manchester. See Haskell 2000 pp. 82–9 for a succinct account of the exhibition.

German scholars of British private collections, Dr Gustav Waagen and J. D. Passavant; their pioneering efforts made the public aware of the extraordinary riches of British collections.[*] Almost everyone invited to lend agreed to do so as it was widely felt that ownership of great art brought obligations, and indeed the *Manchester Guardian* pointed the finger at the owners of three great treasure houses, Cassiobury, Hatfield and Petworth, who had contributed nothing. This was considered a dereliction of duty which Giles Waterfield recognised as 'a further stage in the concept of private collections becoming part of a national heritage'.[2] Ideas of what formed an international conception of national patrimony had emerged from the Napoleonic Wars with the restitution of goods from Italy. The notion that the aggregate sum of British art collections formed a kind of national heritage crystalised at Manchester, but it would take a very long time and two world wars before measures were taken to safeguard it. What emerged was a crisis-driven system by which politicians and the Treasury gauged the necessity to intervene by the clamour in the press. It suited well the universal propensity to pay most attention to heritage when it is threatened.

There were important sales, exhibitions and even heritage crises long before the Manchester exhibition. The sale of the superb paintings collection from Houghton Hall to Catherine the Great in 1779 prompted John Wilkes to lobby parliament to buy it for the nation as an annex of the British Museum.[3] The dispersal of Charles I's collection during the Commonwealth – the greatest single loss of paintings in British history – meant that unlike most European countries, any future national gallery could not be based on a princely collection like the Louvre or the Uffizi, but would have to be built out of sales and donations from

---

[*] The exhibition was based on the recently published three volumes, *Treasures of Art in Great Britain* by Dr Gustav Waagen, director of the Berlin Gallery, and the old master paintings were selected with German erudition and discrimination by George Scharf who had an English mother and was brought up in London.

private collections. It is worth noting that from the sixteenth century onwards oil paintings gradually supplanted tapestries and illuminated manuscripts as the most valuable portable treasures of European culture, a status they have retained ever since. Robert Benson, of whom we will hear more, would call them the 'big game' of art collecting.

The National Gallery in London was not founded until 1824. It was the unexpected repayment of an Austrian war loan that made possible the purchase for £57,000 of the banker John Julius Angerstein's thirty-eight paintings by Raphael, Titian, Rembrandt and other masters. Having bankrolled the foundation of a collection, parliament was only prepared to offer an annual grant of a mere £2,000 a year for acquisitions.* The grant was raised to £10,000 by the time Sir Charles Eastlake was made director (1855–65), when the gallery entered a golden period of acquisitions, especially of then still affordable early Italian paintings, often spotted by his travelling agent, Otto Mündler. The problems arose at home. When the former prime minister Sir Robert Peel's collection of seventy-seven Dutch paintings was offered for sale in 1871 at £75,000, the gallery could only appeal to the Treasury. This purchase set off a recurrent theme of this chapter, the continuous need to request special grants from a reluctant Treasury.† This unsatisfactory system of saving paintings would remain the norm until the appearance of the Heritage Memorial Fund in 1980 and the National Lottery in 1994.

British art collectors did not have serious competition on the home front until the 1880s, when Wilhelm von Bode attained pre-eminence in the Berlin museums. He found it easier to acquire great Italian pictures on the London market than in

---

* The annual grant might be compared to the £10,000 a year for printed books secured by Anthony Panizzi at the British Museum Library.
† The system in fact began earlier with the grants to the British Museum, starting with the foundation Sloane collection and, most famously, later the Elgin Marbles.

Italy. The British aristocracy was feeling the effects of a severe agricultural depression brought on by cheap grain imports from America. The consequent loss of farming income led to a collapse in land prices while art was rising steeply in value. From now on National Gallery directors would have their hands full trying to prevent paintings from being sold abroad. With no laws to control exports the gallery had to depend on the intelligence network of its trustees to hear when paintings came up for sale, and the patriotism of owners to offer it first refusal. Henceforth the acquisitional focus of British public collections – with a few exceptions – would be trying to save works from British private collections.[*]

Two spectacular sales brought home the weakness of the British position. The first was the Hamilton Palace sale of 1882, the result of the death of the heavily indebted art collector, the Duke of Hamilton, which saw Botticelli's drawings for Dante lost to Berlin amid widespread dismay.[†] In the same year the Settled Land Act was passed which unlocked heirlooms from entailed estates, allowing family trustees to raise money from them. This led to a flood of sales and none so important as the sale of old master paintings from Blenheim Palace in 1885. The Duke of Marlborough offered the National Gallery the pick of his collection for a stratospheric £400,000. The heritage crisis that followed set the template for similar crises in the future: deputations to the chancellor, extensive press coverage, questions in parliament, and reminders of the loss of Charles I's collection. At this time of high unemployment, political concerns were

---

[*] Nicholas Penny points out the most remarkable exception was the purchase for 'the future National Gallery' in 1811 by the British Institution of Benjamin West's huge *Christ Healing the Sick* to save it from export to America, for which it had been originally commissioned.

[†] This was despite a special exchequer grant of £15,000 which saved thirteen paintings, of which the most important was Velazquez's *Philip IV*.

focused on the plight of the working classes.* All of which resulted in only £87,500 being made available to save Raphael's *Ansidei Madonna* and van Dyck's *Charles I on Horseback* while the Treasury reduced the National Gallery purchase grant to £5,000. So, when in 1890 Holbein's *Ambassadors* was offered from Lord Radnor's collection, the gallery did not have sufficient funds. Lord Rothschild, Sir Edward Guinness and Charles Cotes stepped in and offered half the amount, thus setting the precedent for another now familiar process, that of private donors coming to the rescue to fund national acquisitions. Happily, the other half was supplied by the Treasury.

Landowners were incensed when in 1894 the Liberal chancellor, Sir William Harcourt, introduced death duties at what seemed at the time an exorbitant top rate of 8 per cent for estates valued at over £1 million. His political opponent, the former prime minister Lord Salisbury, threatened to send his own works of art to America and Russia. By this time, major paintings were already starting to trickle out of the country. That year Mrs Gardner of Boston bought Lord Ashburnham's Botticelli *The Story of Lucretia*, an outrider of the many Italian Renaissance paintings that would cross the Atlantic, a love affair kindled by the authority of the American *wunderkind* Bernard Berenson.

That same year negotiations began for the most painful loss of them all. Titian's *The Rape of Europa* had come to England in 1793 as part of the Orleans Collection, the greatest group of paintings brought into the country since Charles I purchased the Gonzaga Collection. The Orleans paintings were bounty of the French Revolution. The *Rape* was now at Cobham Hall, owned by the 6th Lord Darnley, whose uncle, the eminent art historian Lionel Cust, wrote to a trustee of the National Gallery in 1894 indicating that Darnley would accept £15,000 for the painting. This was rejected, probably on grounds of price, and also may have been a matter of preference, as the gallery had a

---

* The arguments against the purchase are strangely familiar: unemployment, the need to raise the defence budget, and a war on terror in Afghanistan.

good collection of Titian's earlier work, which was then more fashionable. In the opinion of a recent director, Nicholas Penny: 'It is the one painting above all that the National Gallery in London regrets losing.'[4]

After this rejection by the National Gallery, the dealer Colnaghi opened negotiations with Berenson to sell *The Rape of Europa* to Mrs Gardner. Lord Darnley affected nonchalance, announcing that his painting was not for sale, but did nothing to forestall an offer being made, doubtless hoping for more. Such exploratory offers fast became the norm in the flirtatious relationship between the art trade – acting on behalf of American buyers – and the British nobility. While usually rejected, these were welcomed by their recipients, mindful of future needs. Robert Witt, a founder of the National Art Collections Fund, attributed the relentless drain of art to the combination of taxation and *temptation*.[5]

In 1896 Lord Darnley finally accepted £14,000 from Colnaghi, who in collusion with Berenson sold it on to Mrs Gardner for £20,000.* Although the sale was widely regretted in England, Berenson was cock-a-hoop writing to Mrs Gardner: 'the Titian Europa is the finest Italian picture ever again to be sold'.[6] The loss of the painting, felt more keenly afterwards, represented something of a retrospective turning point. Titian was the artist most admired by the Whitehall circle of Charles I, and among the cream of the Orleans paintings were the Titians that were acquired by the Duke of Bridgewater. As we shall see, these last Titians have remained high on the wish list of the National Gallery ever since.† *The Rape* was probably the most important painting to leave Britain since the time of Charles I, and as Penny remarked, its loss 'exposed the hopeless situation at the National

---

* Berenson dishonestly told Colnaghi that it was sold for £18,000 and thus took a double commission.
† The author was informed that such is the importance of the former Bridgewater, now Sutherland Collection, and the heritage implications if there were to be a sale, that the potential threat used to form part of an incoming prime minister's briefing.

Gallery and the extreme difficulty for them even had the trustees shown more spirit'.[7]

The same year as the Titian sale the government acknowledged the drain of 'objects of historic interest' through death duties by deferring payment of this tax on certain works of national or historic importance until they were actually sold.[*] Thus began the long evolution of the tax system known as 'conditional exemption' which still operates today, and which was eventually to become, *mutatis mutandis*, an effective means of retaining works of art in their historic settings. Lady Sackville, who was to inherit part of the Wallace Collection, claimed the credit for persuading the chancellor to approve this measure, which as she proudly observed 'will save Knole'. The system, since amended and improved many times, effectively semi-nationalised important works of art, since the state now owned the proportion of them equivalent to the deferred tax. The reciprocal provision for this tax deferral of providing public access to the work in question was only introduced in the 1970s by appointment and not made an absolute requirement until 1998.

One of the most pervasive tastes to cross the Atlantic had been pioneered by the Rothschilds – grand full-length British portraits often paired with historic French furniture. One of the earliest such portraits to leave England for America was van Dyck's *Portrait of James Stuart, Duke of Richmond and Lennox*, bought in 1889 by Henry Marquand who wrote to the seller, Lord Methuen, that it would help educate a new country. The main 'educator' would in fact turn out to be the dealer Joseph, later Lord Duveen, who by 1910 or so acquired a dominating position in the international art market to a degree difficult to imagine today. Lord Duveen made a brilliantly successful career playing the *grand seigneur* in America and the buffoon in England – it was hard to resist his ebullient personality. Kenneth Clark observed 'it has been well

---

* The Finance Act (1896), but it was not until the Finance Act of 1910 that these advantages were extended to objects of artistic interest, whether settled or not, and to all forms of duty.

said of the late Lord Duveen that he had got the better of every art dealer in the world except that great syndicate of art dealers, the House of Lords'.[8]

Duveen promoted the taste for British eighteenth-century portraits and gave them a cachet never achieved since. It was believed that Pierpont Morgan's purchase in around 1900 of Reynolds's majestic *Portrait of Lady Elizabeth Delmé and Her Children* started the craze in America. They were bought in quantity by both Henry Clay Frick and Andrew Mellon and few great American museums are without a fine group of them. It was not just Americans who bought them. Lady Dorothy Nevill remarked that the new-money British collectors of the time also surrounded themselves with 'the beautiful eighteenth-century portraits of the class they have conquered'.[9]

During the first decade of the twentieth century the trickle of art to America turned into a flood and the National Gallery found itself powerless to act. It was particularly galling that even their trustees were selling abroad. Lord Lansdowne, chairman of the trustees, did offer the gallery first refusal for Rembrandt's *Mill* at £100,000 but it had only £2,300 in its coffers at the time. His fellow trustee, the Earl of Carlisle, led a deputation to the prime minister without avail. The *Mill* started the valedictory tradition of exhibiting pictures at the gallery prior to export; 50,000 visitors came to bid farewell. Lord Carlisle, one of the best trustees that the gallery has ever had, did not even inform its director when he sold his Velazquez of *Baltasar Carlos With a Dwarf* to a dealer in 1900 before going to the Boston Museum of Fine Arts a year later.

What had happened to the owners' sense of responsibility that had been so evident during the 1857 Manchester exhibition? The imposition of capital taxation meant that many owners felt relieved of any obligations to the nation.* The first loyalty

---

* Collectors like Lord Fitzwilliam who had given their collections to the nation in the past usually did so because they had no children.

of most aristocrats was to their family and castle.* However, a younger generation was beginning to see things differently. Henry James in his 1911 novel *The Outcry* insinuates the question of responsibility in the guardianship of great art treasures. The grandee in the story, Lord Theign, does not see that he has to answer to anybody for what he does with his treasures, but he is quietly reprimanded by his daughter who says 'we look at the thing in a much larger way…It's of our treasure itself we talk, and what can be *done* in such cases […] What we've set our hearts on is working for England'. To landowners, deeply suspicious of the state's encroachment, the rights of private property had been ingrained since Magna Carta.

It was against the background of the ever-growing economic power wielded by American collectors that the National Art Collections Fund (NACF) was founded in 1903. Broadly based on *Les Amis du Louvre*, it was an attempt to save works of art – mostly paintings – for the nation. Their first test came early: Velazquez's *Rokeby Venus* was offered through Agnew's for £45,000 in 1906. The Fund opened an appeal with a letter to *The Times* which lambasted the 'apathy of our National Gallery authorities' and admiringly referenced the Berlin museums. The Fund raised £15,000, followed by a single donation of £10,000, but still the Treasury would not assist. It was the last-minute intervention of Edward VII who anonymously pledged £8,000 that saved the painting. According to Kenneth Clark the NACF was effectively the saviour of the National Gallery until World War II and beyond. It was established to buy what was perceived as national heritage as well as modern works from abroad, but the former was a higher priority.[10] Lloyd George's so-called People's Budget of 1909 raised income tax for the rich, and death duties to 15 per cent. He attempted to sweeten the pill the following year by offering

---

* This was echoed as recently as 2003 when the Duke of Northumberland, criticised for selling Raphael's *Madonna of the Pinks* to the Getty, exclaimed: 'I have my own National Gallery to support.' Philanthropy and art flourished in countries like America where dynastic obligations count for less.

tax deferral concessions in favour of items that were of *artistic* as well as historic importance, but this did nothing to assuage the anger of owners. The Duke of Norfolk cited the budget as his reason for selling Holbein's *Portrait of Christina of Denmark*. The National Gallery was given one month to raise £72,000 before the painting would be sold to Frick. There was a press furore, shocked that the duke could behave so unpatriotically. An appeal launched by the NACF raised £32,000 and the prime minister pledged £10,000, but the asking price could not be reached. On the eve of the deadline an English lady on holiday in a German spa – who had read about it in the newspapers – offered the shortfall of £40,000. Her identity is held secret to this day.

The same year the Holbein was saved, *The Times* ran an article about the drain of works of art from country houses.[*] Sir Robert Witt estimated that in 1909–10 art to the value of £1.2 million left Britain.[11] He observed that the annual grant to the National Gallery was £5,000 while the British Museum had an annual grant of £22,000 and the Victoria and Albert Museum about £12,000. He wondered – perhaps with the Oscar Wilde scandal still in mind – whether there was a sense in Britain that 'art softens, that our national grit will be enfeebled by increased devotion to aesthetic pleasures, though mistaken, is too prevalent to be ignored'.[12]

Alarmed by the flood of masterpieces going to America, in 1913 the former Viceroy of India, Lord Curzon, chaired a committee to examine the retention of works of art. It tackled three questions: Which were the paintings and where were they? On what principles should the gaps in the National Gallery be filled? How to identify future old masters? The committee had no doubt about the causes of the problem: the 1872 Settled Land Act, and death duties. The most startling part of the report was

---

[*] 'The Drain of Works of Art from Great Britain', part 1, *The Times* 21 May 1909. This matter had an added urgency because the same year the United States lifted the tariff on the import of works of art which precipitated Morgan to move his collection from London to New York.

the list drawn up by Sir Claude Phillips (Appendix V) of about 500 paintings exported between 1880 and 1914 of which 90 per cent had been shipped to America and the rest to Germany. The greatest loss of works by one artist was sixty-two (mostly genuine) Rembrandts. The greatest loss in terms of the proportion of a single oeuvre was that of Vermeer, with six lost to the USA and one to Germany.

The Curzon Committee considered many solutions: a Paramount List, a duty on works of art sales or exports, raising the National Gallery's grant from £5,000 to £25,000, and the earmarking of the sums raised through death duties on works of art for future gallery purchases. They predictably vetoed anything that interfered with rights of property or the free market. They recognised the implausibility of claiming a work of art brought into the country a hundred years earlier had since become 'so English that the law can be legitimately invoked to prevent it from ever going abroad again'.[13] The results were disappointing, as one historian acknowledged: 'All in all, the Curzon Report did little other than provide extensive evidence of how serious the problem of art exports had become.'[14]

For international art dealers, World War I was a time for rich pickings as young heirs fell at the front. 'In troubled waters', the great dealer William Buchanan had said during the Napoleonic Wars, 'we catch the most fish.' It also turned out to be a case of the finest fish, as the Duke of Northumberland parted with Bellini's *Feast of the Gods* from Alnwick Castle in 1916. Berenson heartlessly exclaimed 'bless the war' and told Mrs Gardner, 'I am sure that [the painting] is greater than any that has yet gone over to America. I won't say that it is the greatest picture in the world, but I will say that the world has no greater.'[15] The chancellor, Austen Chamberlain, went to examine it, but with a railway strike in progress he told the National Gallery director Charles Holmes that he did not feel justified in advancing the amount.[16] It later became an ornament of the new National Gallery in Washington, where Andrew Mellon's collection demonstrated how extensive had been the transfer of paintings across the Atlantic.

It was not until 1922 under the directorship of Charles Holmes that the National Gallery drew up its first 'paramount list', which comprised only seven paintings, including three of the former Bridgewater (now Duke of Sutherland) Titians, Holbein's *Henry VIII,* owned by Lord Spencer, and the *Wilton Diptych*. These were paintings that, in theory, the Treasury would save at all costs if an export crisis arose. The Paramount List would be revised and expanded every few years, but it carried no legal force and some still got away. The trustees, who should have known better, continued to sell their own paintings abroad, as we shall see, without reference to the gallery they were meant to represent.

Holmes thought that the main problem was the time it took to sell a picture to the gallery: 'the dealers generally were shy of exposing their treasures to the long-drawn discussions, the rumours, the semi-publicity and the almost inevitable refusal [...] "No one ever thinks of offering pictures to you" one prominent dealer told me'.[17] It was not all bad news, however. In 1929 two works on the Paramount List were saved: Titian's *Vendramin Family,* bought from the Duke of Northumberland, and the *Wilton Diptych,* bought from Lord Pembroke (numbers three and four on the list). Winston Churchill as chancellor agreed to pay for half of both paintings, but it was the following Labour government that would have to honour his promise.[18] One picture that ought to have been on the list was Turner's *The Burning of the Houses of Parliament,* which had gone to the Philadelphia Museum of Art the year before.* Kenneth Clark thought it was one of the very few paintings that should have been forcibly retained in the country.

The transatlantic taste for English portraits reached its apogee with the dramatic export of Gainsborough's *The Blue Boy* in 1921, the result of an opportunistic swoop by Duveen on the Duke of

---

* A remarkable exception to the transfer of paintings to America or the National Gallery was Titian's *Death of Actaeon* for which Lord Lascelles paid £60,000 in 1923, an unprecedented sum for an Englishman.

Westminster when almost incredibly he needed money. Duveen sold it for \$620,000, or £148,000, to Henry Huntington, who formed a superb group of portraits at his museum in California. Duveen exhibited *The Blue Boy* at the National Gallery before it left England, when Holmes scribbled 'Au Revoir' on the back. Cole Porter wrote a comic elegy, 'The Blue Boy Blues':

> For I'm the Blue Boy, the beautiful Blue Boy
> And I am forced to admit, I'm feeling a bit depressed
> A silver dollar took me and my collar
> To show the slow cowboys just how boys
> In England used to be dressed…

Duveen also managed to winkle a group of five paintings out of Lord Spencer's home, Althorp, in 1925, including two by Reynolds, a Gainsborough, van Dyck's *Daedalus and Icarus* and a Frans Hals, all for export. But the dealer's greatest coup during this era was his purchase for \$3 million in a 1927 sale of the exceptionally fine collection of 114 Italian old masters owned by the banker and National Gallery trustee Robert Benson. This included Giorgione's *Holy Family* and Bellini's *St Jerome Reading* (NG Washington), but none were initially offered to the gallery.[*] Today Benson's pictures are dispersed across many leading museums in North America.[†]

One painting on every Paramount List since 1927 was van Eyck's *Three Marys at the Sepulchre* in Sir Herbert Cook's collection housed at Doughty House on Richmond Hill. Assembled in the late nineteenth century, this included Renaissance masterpieces and Rembrandt's beguiling *Portrait of 'Titus'*. The family had close links with the gallery and various promises were believed

---

[*] In 1927 Duveen offered Holmes a choice of three paintings from the Benson collection for the Gallery. He chose Correggio's early *Christ Taking Leave of His Mother*, which Duveen may have found harder to sell in the USA.

[†] Duveen is probably the only dealer in modern times to handle two Raphaels, from the collection of Earl Cowper at Panshanger.

to have been made by Sir Herbert, so when he died in 1939 it was shocked to discover that his executors put family obligations first. 'They are Shits', wrote the chairman of its trustees, Lord Crawford, in a rare outburst.[19] The van Eyck was sold to a Dutch collector and is now in the Museum Boijmans Van Beuningen in Rotterdam. The *'Titus'* remained in the collection until 1965, when its sale at Christie's to the Los Angeles collector Norton Simon resulted in a bizarre fiasco.*

When Kenneth Clark was director of the gallery (1934–45) he bemoaned the uselessness of the Paramount List. On Treasury instructions, it was kept confidential, which Clark thought was a mistake: 'we were strictly enjoined not to tell the owners. As a result, at least three of the pictures were sold secretly overseas'.[20] The most grievous loss was Lord Spencer's Holbein of *Henry VIII*, the only surviving autograph painting by the artist of the monarch, sold to Baron Thyssen without reference to the gallery. Clark was generally fortunate that owners such as the Duke of Buccleuch (Rubens' *Watering Place*) and Lord Radnor (Poussin's *The Adoration of the Golden Calf*) did give the gallery first refusal, and with the help of the NACF Clark could act swiftly. He acknowledged his reliance on the NACF, which always came to his rescue. Later in life he thought it ridiculous that large sums were always available to save a Titian, which in his view belonged to the world, rather than to restore a cathedral, of greater national importance.[21]

World War II provided an unexpected benefit for the retention of works of art: the Trading with the Enemy Act 1939 was the most significant piece of legislation to preserve works of art in Britain. It was not designed as a heritage measure, but the law proved so effective that it was still in place when Rab Butler, the then chancellor, asked a committee chaired by Lord Waverley to re-examine it. They performed their task well. The result

---

* Simon gave absurdly complicated bidding instructions to Christie's that predictably went wrong, and the process had to be repeated. It gained huge publicity, which may have been Simon's motivation all along.

was the formation in 1952 of the Export Reviewing Committee operating under what became known as the Waverley criteria, which assessed whether an item proposed for export was either:

1. Closely associated with our history and national life?
2. Of outstanding aesthetic importance or art historical interest?
3. Of outstanding significance to the study of some branch of learning or history?

These criteria have stood the test of time. The system allowed museums the breathing space to raise money, the problem identified by Charles Holmes in the 1920s. Today the committee still has the power to stop exports for six months (extendable if an effort to raise funds is underway). The nation is then obliged to match the export price.

The other great improvement to the heritage system for works of art was the improvement to the Acceptance in Lieu system, the means of preserving works of art in their historic setting. Set up as early as 1910, it had proved unworkable owing to the Inland Revenue's insistence on being paid back for the loss of hard currency. It was not until in 1946 that a solution was found, when the Labour chancellor, Hugh Dalton, established the Land Fund to be used for the enrichment of national life. Here for the first time was the money not only to compensate the Treasury for the loss of tax, but also to extend the system by acquiring works of art for the state with a special deal or *douceur*. This came in by degrees. Dalton originally had tracts of beautiful scenery and coastline in mind, but he extended the fund's remit to save two country houses for the National Trust, which he strongly supported. Works of art were an afterthought when the contents of Petworth, a house and park already owned by the Trust, were threatened with dispersal, and so the system was extended to allow them to remain in their historic setting.

The death of the 10th Duke of Devonshire in 1950 precipitated the greatest potential heritage crisis since Hamilton Palace and the Blenheim pictures in the 1880s. With death duties payable at 80 per cent on large estates the inevitable sales led to a further development in cultural tax law. The government initially proposed that Chatsworth should be nationalised and made the responsibility of the V&A. The idea was not pursued, but a series of great works of art were accepted in lieu of tax for allocation to national collections.* These included Holbein's full-length cartoon for *Henry VIII* and a picture on every Paramount List, Memling's *Donne Triptych*. The importance of the Acceptance in Lieu (AIL) system in the mutually beneficial transfer of works of art from the private to the public sector can hardly be overstated. Its principal beneficiaries were the public museums and galleries whose collections were enhanced at no cost to themselves.

How successful were these new initiatives at preventing the exodus of art? The answer is fairly successful when the impetus was there to save items, but such victories came after hard-fought and noisy battles. A glance at a list of the twenty-nine outstanding works of art sold between 1945 and 1974, in the Cornforth Report (for the Historic Houses Association), shows that seventeen, just over half, were retained by museums in Britain.[22] One of the noisiest cases was Goya's *Portrait of the Duke of Wellington*, sold by the Duke of Leeds at Sotheby's in 1961 to the New York collectors Charles and Jayne Wrightsman for £140,000. Controversy raged as to whether the painting should be saved for the nation, and indeed whether or not it was a good likeness of the duke, or even a good Goya. The director of the National Gallery at the time was unenthusiastic and dismissed it as a matter for the Portrait Gallery (whose purchase grant was only £4,000 a year). Finally, after a long press campaign, the gallery was shamed into

---

* The first work of art accepted in lieu was in 1957, van der Weyden's *Pietà* from the Earl of Powis's collection for the National Gallery. The scheme tiptoed towards its present design when in the 1960s allocations were extended to regional museums.

reluctantly buying it with the aid of a special Treasury grant of £40,000.[*]

The following year another crisis loomed that stimulated the first truly grassroots fundraising campaign for a work of art in Britain. Unusually, this was not from a private collection but the Royal Academy, which decided to sell its Leonardo cartoon of the *Virgin and Child with St Anne and St John the Baptist* to the National Gallery for £800,000. The Treasury refused to help, so soon after the Goya fiasco, and there followed a popular campaign including 'over a thousand schools holding sales – mostly baking cakes – to raise money'.[23] Instead of the usual big donors, the Leonardo was saved by the accumulation of small sums – the largest being a mere £1,000. The Treasury finally caught the mood and agreed to match the public's generosity. The greatest failure of the period was the export to the Metropolitan Museum in New York of Lord Radnor's Velazquez *Portrait of Juan de Pareja* after its sale in 1970 at Christie's for the enormous sum of £2,310,000, the first time any work of art had made over £1 million at auction. The failure to retain the Velazquez was followed in 1972 by the successful export stop on behalf of the National Gallery of Titian's *Death of Actaeon* after its sale to the J. Paul Getty Museum in California.[24]

The Treasury special grant system was becoming politically more difficult. Five had been given between 1954 and 1961 and when in 1961 a special grant was provided for a pair of decorative late Renoir paintings of *Dancing Girls*, acquired from a French collection, there was a furore. The prime minister, Harold Macmillan, asked that in future such grants should only be used 'to keep what is in England' and this was the last occasion when the Treasury funded a foreign purchase.[25] This policy of 'British first' was implicit in the Acceptance in Lieu system, and later became a stated principle of the National Heritage Memorial

---

[*] Famously, the controversy did not end there, as the painting was stolen by an amateur thief, Kempton Bunton, from the National Gallery nineteen days after its arrival.

Fund.* The formation of the latter in 1980 in the aftermath of the loss of the Rothschild treasures at Mentmore went some way to providing the means of saving important paintings without recourse to the Treasury, as was intended. The arrival of the Lottery completed this process of removing buying art from the political process, although it has not been without its own internal politics.

Today fewer important paintings or works of art are lost through export than at any previous time (although this is less true below the top tier). Of course, it will be correctly argued that most of the greatest works of art have already been exported or entered national collections. The store of great works of art in private collections is much reduced. The system that slowly developed for saving works of art was a pragmatic solution and, like so many government heritage interventions, it worked more successfully after 1945 in a new era that was resigned to accepting the stronger state control. From this period came the magnificent transfers to the National Trust, the rekindling of the AIL system with its redistribution of art to national and regional museums, and the ability of the Export Reviewing Committee to pause the process and give time for fundraising. What no system could do was compensate for the economic problems that the country seemed continuously to face after 1918, or the apathy of almost all politicians to the national patrimony.

The Italians imposed their own export restrictions in 1909 (much earlier in the Papal State) but it was argued by those opposed to such laws in Britain that the Italians had actually created the art which was leaving their country, which was seldom the case at home. Parliament, particularly the House of Lords, was filled with landowners who fiercely resisted the state's

* It is worth noting that despite the 'British first' policy, Paul Mellon was able to assemble an outstanding collection of British paintings including such extraordinary works as Turner's *The Dort Packet Boat Becalmed,* bought directly from the Fawkes family of Farnley Hall, where it had hung since it was painted. It left Britain in 1966 without much effort being made to save it.

encroachment on the rights of private property, whether art or land, just as they had resisted all the early heritage acts to protect monuments on private land. The protection of private property and the free market were Holy Writ, and this underpinned cultural law, or the lack of it, until 1939. The most striking and perhaps melancholy fact was revealed by the Curzon Report that during the thirty-four years between 1880 and 1914, when Britain was still wealthy, more important paintings left the country than in the 106-year period since.

Brave New World

*All over the country the grime, muddle and decay
of our Victorian heritage is being replaced and the
quality of urban life uplifted.*

HAROLD WILSON

Between 1940 and the mid-1960s the look of Britain changed forever. The Blitz almost destroyed cities like Coventry and Plymouth while others, like London, were left scarred and damaged. But what really transformed the country was the scale and manner of the rebuilding: vast high-rise housing estates on the edge of cities, office tower blocks and shopping precincts within. The confidence and speed with which this extraordinary growth was achieved swept aside or punctured much of the built heritage. The past was thought to be an impediment to the desired future. It was soon apparent, however, that a great deal of the new architecture was neither as permanent nor as pleasing as what it had replaced. 'Brave New Worlds', as Gavin Stamp observed, 'have a way of looking rather shabby and sad before too long.'[1] It would lead to a profound backlash (see Chapter Seven) and a desire to bring more of the public voice, and a greater respect for the past, into the planning system.

The hopes and ideals of a new post-war healthy Britain were embedded in an exhibition that opened in January 1943 at the National Gallery in London, organised by the RIBA: 'The Rebuilding of Britain'. *Country Life* called it the visual equivalent of *The Beveridge Report* (1942). Both assumed a colossal change would take place in the appearance and running of the country.

It was estimated that between 4 and 5 million new homes would be needed. The RIBA booklet accompanying the exhibition is the prospectus for a new world, with a gospel of rebuilding and modern architecture. It opened with a critique on the past, houses 'built without regard to the welfare of their occupants or their neighbours', describing them as 'monotonous and lifeless'. The RIBA estimated that one in five buildings in Britain had been damaged during the war and offered the challenge: 'Are we going to make this rebuilding an opportunity for real re-planning or are we going to patch up our ruins higgledy-piggledy with some architectural finery here and there, and say that is the best we can do?'[2] They posed the question: 'How much can you say is really worthy of preservation?'[3]

The question was apt, because when cities are left in ruins somebody must decide which buildings are worth salvaging and rebuilding. James Lees-Milne described the war damage in London when he visited the SPAB office in Great Ormond Street: 'all around, where whole squares and streets of houses existed a short time ago, are now empty blankets of snow'.[4] The City of London churches (mostly by Wren) were a special problem of their own.[5] All forty-eight of them within the Square Mile were to some extent damaged: some, like St Mildred, Bread Street, had been completely destroyed; others like, Christ Church, Newgate Street were left as shells but with their towers still standing; but most, like St Bride's, Fleet Street, needed rebuilding or restoring.

During the Blitz there arose an initiative to record historic buildings prior to their damage, both to assess their importance and as an aid for repair. The National Buildings Record was established by Walter Godfrey and John Summerson in early 1941 to document historic buildings under threat from aerial bombardment. It encompassed good buildings up to 1850, but only exceptional ones thereafter. This activity was expanded through the 1944 Town and Country Planning Act, which gave local and central government the power to list historic buildings – but without any powers of enforcement. Despite this, the 1944

Act was the most important piece of heritage legislation since Lubbock's Bill of 1882 and is the foundation of our current system of statutory control. Its central feature is the List of Buildings of Special Architectural or Historic Interest and from that day on, owners would have to seek permission before making alterations to individually listed buildings, though there was nothing yet about area protection.[*]

But Britain in 1945 was a country looking forward, desirous to create a healthier, more sanitary world. The nation saw cities full of soot-blackened, bomb-damaged housing that needed replacing. This was an old attitude going back to 1900 given new urgency: 'For it was held that town planning in the twentieth century was essentially an enlightened restoration to order out of chaos, and to quality out of squalor [...] as a corrective against errant, nineteenth-century philistinism.'[6] The state would be the main driver in this process, and it would take one more important parliamentary bill to gain control of development. There was a widely held belief, in Colin Buchanan's words, that:

> market forces in land, left to their own devices, fail utterly to produce a humane environment. The Town and Country Planning Act of 1947 marked the turning point. It rejected the market approach. It removed once and for all an owner's right to do what he liked with his land, and put in its place the concept of the community managing and regulating the national estate for its own convenience and delight.[7]

* An amendment proposed by Lord Salisbury in 1947 made listing a statutory duty of government. Initially buildings would fall into three grades, which would later be amended to two grades with the lesser occasionally being starred. In the course of the debate Lord Salisbury referred to 'the national heritage', probably the first use of this term in parliament – see Delafons, p. 60. Lord Curzon as early as 1912 had referred to national monuments as part of the heritage and history of the nation. See Hansard House of Lords, 30 April 1912.

These two parliamentary bills (1944 and 1947) constitute a major step forward in the government taking control of the built landscape and the countryside. It was, as one civil servant observed, 'a faltering start and it took another twenty years to complete the structure'.[8]

What is most striking about the period is the cleavage between the utopian public housing schemes and the red in tooth and claw developer-led London office boom, which immediately followed the abolition of building licensing (and the end of rationing materials) in 1954. The key people were now on the one side the city architects and planners, and on the other developers. The new consensus, as Lionel Esher put it, 'embraced not only the architects but also the planning committees and the commercial organizations on which they depended for policy decisions'.[9] By the 1960s the image of the city was vertical, multi-layered and designed to provide car access. A language emerged of distributor roads, spaghetti junctions, multi-level, tower-and-podium, streets in the air, and pedestrian-decked traffic architecture. A grid of expressways would crisscross the city for access, and all this would create the framework to enable high-density living. There were those, like Patrick Abercrombie, who tried to find a *via media*, as Esher put it, 'to accommodate the two extremes – English Garden City sentimentality and German *Zeilenbau*', the rows of housing slabs favoured by Walter Gropius.[10] The two obsessions of planners were what to do about traffic and how to deal with population densities. Traffic would be the province of Colin Buchanan, and population that of Patrick Abercrombie.

Sir Patrick Abercrombie

Sir Patrick Abercrombie and Sir Colin Buchanan were Britain's most prestigious planners and their influence ran everywhere. They are awkward figures to assess because nearly all their most ambitious plans were watered down, and their positions were sometimes self-contradictory. Barbara Castle bluntly told Buchanan – and the same was even more true of Abercrombie – that the government would never be able to find the money for his schemes. They belonged to different generations: Abercrombie (1879–1957) was a Lancashire boy, brought up on the Arts and Crafts movement, who wore a monocle, enjoyed good claret, and founded the CPRE in 1926. Clough Williams-Ellis called him a genial wizard. He is essentially a pre-war figure who kept alive the radial planning, adherence to inner and outer rings, and the garden city area designations of Ebenezer Howard to arrange the parts of the city so that in his own words 'they form one satisfactory mechanism, each part performing its function in the best way'.[11]

Abercrombie's early career was in Chester, a town whose complex web of streets he claimed had a great influence on his thinking, and we can see something of this organic development in his smaller pre-war town projects. In his larger post-war schemes, such as Plymouth, we see the other side of his planning – his admiration for the simplicity of Georgian squares which he wanted to translate into Alker Tripp's precincts and grids.[*] Abercrombie's creation of Armada Way, Plymouth, imposes a formal rather Beaux Arts sterility and nobody has found the result very inspiring.

Plymouth had presented Abercrombie and the architects with a *tabula rasa* on which to plan, but this was not the case in London. His most celebrated scheme, the County of London Plan (1943), was conceived at the request of the Minister of Town and Country Planning who, like many others, saw the Blitz as an opportunity to tidy up London. Several architectural plans had been put forward during the war: at one extreme was the MARS Group plan in which the City was recast in a grid, contrasting with the Royal Academy planning committee's Beaux Arts proposals, dominated by grand avenues and *rond-points*. With much talk

* Alker Tripp (1883–1954), artist and member of the civil staff of Scotland Yard, Assistant Commissioner of Police 1932–47.

of boldness, the Ministry of Town and Country Planning made a 'safe' choice in appointing Abercrombie, who was to restrict himself to the ground plan rather than the architecture. His scheme was a call for order, to remove 'untidy sprawl' and create open green spaces and sanitary housing in neighbourhood units, with commerce and industry, leisure, shopping and civic activities all neatly separated.

But in the end London rebuilt itself in the way it always has – piecemeal – and strategic planning in central London was limited to trying to resolve specific problems such as Piccadilly Circus. Abercrombie is sometimes described as the second man who was not allowed to re-plan London, but here and there sections or hangovers of his plans can be found: Churchill Gardens in Pimlico and the Lansbury Estate in Poplar, and perhaps there is even an echo of his plans in the creation of the Westway (which so brutally punched through North Kensington), and the M25. One part was realised: the decentralisation of 1 million people to eight entirely new towns in an outer country ring, including two unheard of locations – Stevenage and Harlow – which offer the purest and most successful manifestations of Abercrombie's post-war vision.

Sir Colin Buchanan

Charismatic, sometimes aloof, Colin Buchanan (1907–2001) was the child of empire, born in Simla of a long line of Scots civil engineers. In 1946 he joined the newly formed Ministry of Town and Country Planning where he was soon promoted to the planning inspectorate. Among others, he handled the inquiry on the redevelopment of Piccadilly Circus. Buchanan's big break came in 1961 when the ambitious Minister of Transport, Ernest Marples, appointed him advisor on traffic and planning. Two years later Buchanan produced his celebrated *Traffic in Towns* report – which became a surprise bestseller when republished as a Penguin Special.* The most famous illustration showed a scheme skirting Georgian Fitzroy Square in Bloomsbury with a classic vertical segregation of cars and pedestrians allowing, it was hoped, for 'convenient shopping'. This 'deck' system was much favoured as part of what Buchanan called 'traffic architecture', but such schemes generally remained on the drawing board. The Brunswick Centre in Bloomsbury and similar schemes in Birmingham, Coventry and Newcastle came closest to realisation.

Traffic in Towns stated that there were 6.6 million cars in Britain (excluding buses and lorries) and 'it does not need any gift of prophecy to foresee that the governments of the future will be increasingly preoccupied with the wishes of the car-owners'.[12] However, Buchanan recognised that at the present rate of growth it would be necessary to demolish half the physical fabric of the inner city to cope with the car. His report can be, and indeed was, read in different ways. Perhaps because it was written for Marples there is an upbeat optimism in many of its statements, notably the belief that technology and increasing resources from growing prosperity would produce solutions, but a careful reading suggests a more nuanced message.†

Buchanan recognised that there were difficult choices to be made, and success depended on what kind of place people wanted to live in. He proposed setting absolute environmental standards which would limit the amount of traffic that could be accommodated. The priority was less how to keep the traffic moving than the quality of the urban environment and thus the quality of life. Buchanan realised this was a stark choice: reduce car use and enhance the quality of life by improving public transport

---

* There was a precedent: a wartime publication, Thomas Sharp's 1940 Pelican paperback *Town Planning*, which sold a quarter of a million copies.
† Marples wrote, 'the old Roman concept of a road, a pavement and a building – the way we have been building for over 1,000 years – is now outdated'. Quoted *Times Literary Supplement* 25 October 2019, p. 33.

and pedestrianising city centres, or simply allow cars to dominate by building tunnels and motorways right through the heart of historic cities. The latter is what happened at Birmingham. In its environmental concerns Buchanan's report was greatly ahead of its time.

While Buchanan examined various regional towns and cities, including Leeds and Newbury, he recognised that 'the study of Norwich indicates the kind of approach which we think must be adopted in the case of areas of historic or architectural interest. It is based on frank acceptance of the fact that, if major physical changes are out of the question, then there must be a reduction of accessibility, with the possibility of considerably more circuitous journeys for drivers.'[13] Buchanan liked to use the analogy of hospital circulation with its constituent parts, some of which would be restricted access and others would be free to all. His recommendations lay somewhere between the two extreme positions of demolition (required for new traffic schemes) and restriction.* Buchanan was increasingly ambivalent about some of the schemes that he was asked to advise on, notably over the Cublington London airport proposal.

New Housing

The Attlee government took office in 1945 in an atmosphere of hope and optimism despite a grey present. They were, as Hugh Dalton put it, 'walking with destiny'. The housing minister Lewis Silkin advised 'plan boldly'. After World War I only 10 per cent of the population had been in council housing, but by 1971 almost 30 per cent rented from local housing authorities, and between 1955 and 1975, 1.3 million people were rehoused from slum dwellings into new estates.[14] Post-war public housing has acquired a bad name – much of it justified. It is considered a

---

* Among the outcomes of his Report were the appearance of yellow lines and parking meters in London, as well as the Hyde Park underpass.

social and architectural failure. On the other hand, there were some successful estates, such as the above-mentioned Churchill Gardens in Pimlico and Lansbury Estate in Poplar,* both built on vast bomb-damaged sites, which hold their own with the best of the past. Today the former is listed Grade II and the latter a Conservation Area. The most depressing spectacle in retrospect is the wanton destruction of old, mostly Victorian, housing stock that disappeared under a planner's pencil in cities like Birmingham, Glasgow and Liverpool. These terraces and tenements had often been overdue for maintenance and modernisation before the war. Six years after, they were rat-infested, rotting and insanitary. There was much talk of eliminating dirt and decay.†

Perhaps the most poignant case is Glasgow, where the Gorbals had the reputation of being the most infamous slum in Britain. Following the Bruce Report (1945), its stone-built tenements were earmarked for demolition. They were sound (and often fine) buildings that desperately needed modernising – but this was never considered as an option. A new city was planned on the periphery with over a hundred high-rise blocks, several by distinguished architects, including Robert Matthew and Basil Spence. Most notorious were the monumental dystopian blocks of the Red Road estate by Sam Bunton which were opened in 1966. All have been demolished since.

* The Lansbury Estate was a part of the 'Live Architecture' exhibition at the Festival of Britain, illustrating British housing and town planning. It is sometimes said to come closest to New Town principles with the involvement of both Frederick Gibberd and Geoffrey Jellicoe.
† See Chapter Sixteen for an account of the destruction of the fine nineteenth-century artisan housing by the Liverpool architect Richard Owens, and its replacement with the mediocre towers once known as 'the Piggeries' by the city architect, Ronald Bradbury.

The London Developer Boom

While the East End of London was being rebuilt with new housing, the West End and the City were given a facelift thanks to the astonishing office and hotel expansion that followed the Conservative election victory in 1951 (heralding thirteen unbroken years of Conservative administration). To ignite the economy, the housing minister, Harold Macmillan, embarked on a bonfire of controls to encourage rebuilding. He abolished the 100 per cent development charge and opened the gates to the property boom that followed in London. Bombing in the capital had destroyed 9.5 million square feet, about a tenth of the whole. The hunger for new office space could hardly be satisfied. Government, desperately short of offices, had been initially the main customer, paying fixed rates of six shillings and six pence a square foot. In this climate of shortage and need with requirements for speed and low cost, the quality was generally poor – the new buildings were designed, unlike their North American counterparts, to last only twenty years.[*]

What followed, so eloquently described in Oliver Marriott's book, *The Property Boom*, was one of those short bursts of activity which has occasionally overtaken London and transformed the look of the city. Two things made this boom so pervasive: the scale of the operation and the sophistication of the credit system within a favourable economic climate. Vast wealth was channelled into the hands of a few individuals. Simon Jenkins believes that the developer was accorded 'a mystical value out of all proportion to the expertise and effort involved in his activities'.[15] Pension funds and insurance companies, always on the lookout for somewhere to invest money, were impressed by the quick returns. Labour savant Anthony Crosland complained in 1962 that 'greedy men abetted by a complacent Government are prowling over Britain

---

[*] An exception is the first post-war City building of any distinction, Sir Albert Richardson's Bracken House for the *Financial Times* in Cannon Street (1955–9).

and devastating it [...] Excited by speculative gain the property developers furiously rebuilt the urban centres with unplanned and aesthetically tawdry office blocks.'[16]

In 1968, the town planner Thomas Sharp wrote: 'the other enemy that threatens [...] is the new fashion for high buildings'.[17] Tall buildings, then as now, were one of the most vexing heritage conundrums facing every city and London in particular. There has never been a coherent policy on how and where they should be sited. New York with its grid plan was well able to create intelligible relationships between skyscrapers, whereas the London version had to fit in wherever it could.* The first structure that smashed through the planning height restrictions was Howard Robertson's monolithic Shell Building, opened in 1962, modelled on the idea of the Rockefeller Center in New York. Until that date, London buildings had been restricted to a height of 84 feet to the cornice (or 100 feet to roofline, allowing two floors of dormers, which may account for the popularity of *Le style Rothschild*), the reach of a fireman's ladder, as imposed by the London Building Act of 1894.† The tall buildings that followed were a very mixed bag; sometimes, like the Vickers (now Millbank) Tower, these are elegant and well placed, while others, like the American-designed Hilton Hotel, were more controversially sited. For centuries nothing spoiled the treeline of Hyde Park, until in the 1960s two buildings, the Hilton and Basil Spence's Knightsbridge Barracks, broke it. The former received planning permission owing to the shortage of modern luxury hotels in London and at that time it was believed that these were essential to attract American businessmen. Only a hotel could have got permission on that site, overlooking Buckingham Palace.

* The first true skyscraper had to wait until Seifert's NatWest Tower (opened 1981) on Broad Street which acted as a nucleus around which twenty years later a cluster would form as part of City of London policy.
† Following the construction of the fourteen-storey Queen Anne's Mansions in Westminster which so upset Queen Victoria.

Many oddly sited tower blocks were the result of the partnership model as suggested in ministry circulars, whereby a local council would achieve many of its desired planning goals by working with developers, in return for the granting of otherwise inadmissible planning agreements. A typical case was Joe Levy, who held properties on the Euston Road. In exchange for giving the front of his site to Camden Council to enable the creation of the Euston Road underpass, Levy was given permission to build the strangely isolated Euston Tower. This was the beginning of a system that is still with us, of 'community benefit'. In the hands of a clever developer this could have both good and bad consequences.

Plot ratio was the all-important formula for the developer – the relationship between the area of the site and the gross floor area of the building.[*] The architect was judged on his ability to achieve the maximum. This required an understanding of national local planning regulations, with all their loopholes – and an ability to negotiate. The most notorious players in this game were the buccaneering developer Harry Hyams and his architect, Richard Seifert, a former pupil of Albert Richardson. 'The trouble with Seifert', as one commentator observed, 'was that he knew some of the regulations far better than the London County Council (LCC) itself. Every now and then we had to bring in clauses to stop up the loopholes exposed by Seifert, we called them "Seifert clauses."'[18] The special skill of Hyams and Seifert was to understand what the LCC needed, and then acquire sites at nodal points which they would offer back to the council in return for being allowed to create buildings of greater height and density than the controls normally allowed. Planning permission was, it turned out, negotiable if you provided the answer to a planner's need. The chance to build Centre Point arose because of the LCC's desire to rearrange the land at the

---

* This measure was introduced with the support of architects and planners to allow more flexibility in design, better daylighting, and, they hoped, a more interesting and attractive streetscape.

junction of Oxford Street and Tottenham Court Road – and they sought a private partnership to pay for it. Hyams offered a neat solution: buying out the other interested parties. The LCC could have its roundabout and Hyams got his planning permission, with almost twice the normal plot ratio in return.[19] Centre Point (1963–7) was the building that gave developers a bad name.* Today it is listed Grade II, admired as a piece of 1960s speculative building.

Tall buildings were an obsession of the Royal Fine Art Commission (RFAC), the body that was meant to keep an eye on aesthetics, but which had only an advisory rather than a statutory role. However, 'that pallid but prestigious body', with its architectural knights and peers, turned out to be a bit of a mouse – often spoiling good designs with its interventions, such as reducing New Zealand House in the Haymarket, and thereby destroying its proportions. It was described as 'an apathetic guardian of architectural standards'.[20] Betjeman, who sat on the committee, generally found it frustrating, exclaiming: 'I wish we gave as much time to the subject of old buildings to tinkering with the designs of new and often uninteresting blocks of offices and flats.'[21] Kenneth Clark ruefully commented that all they did was to tell architects to remove ornament, because after 'the debauches of the nineteenth century our architects have such indigestion that they are condemned to a diet of Ryvita and Vichy water'.[22]

* Hyams famously would keep buildings empty, because in a market where the rents were rising, it helped his tax position with no rates payable on 'empties'. He would wait for the market to catch up with his expectations. There was no Capital Gains Tax at the time, so the economic model was designed to credit income in the form of capital gains.

Newcastle

One city that wanted to be a showcase of city planning and modernity was Newcastle. This was a flawed concept from the start, because the city was not a *tabula rasa*. Like Bath and Edinburgh, it contained a historic centre, the result of superb town planning in the past, the nineteenth-century collaboration between the developer Richard Grainger and his architect, John Dobson. The planning bug was to rear its head again in post-war Newcastle, but with mixed results. The city's 1963 development plan – a classic of its time, with the creation of pedestrian footways separate from vehicle freeways and the channelling of through-traffic in centralised motorways. It was the inspiration of T. Dan Smith (1915–93), who became leader of the council and chairman of the planning committee in 1958. He was a charismatic, quick-witted politician, round-faced, twinkly-eyed and always ready with an earthy quip from his famously runaway mouth.[23] The son of a miner and a conscientious objector in the war, Smith set up as a house painter. Known for cutting corners, he was branded 'one-coat Smith', but despite that he was soon running seven companies. He joined the Newcastle Labour Party, rising swiftly to the top, and his strong character and intimidating physical presence did not brook much opposition.

Smith's zeal for planning fed his ambition to create the 'Brasilia of the north'. It was on a visit to Coventry that Smith was impressed by a young planner, Wilfred Burns, whom he persuaded to come to Newcastle to establish a new city planning department in 1960. Burns believed in big solutions; great swathes of the city would have to go. All would be redeemed by the modern futuristic city that would rise out of the ruins. As John Pendlebury wrote, 'in no city was there more evangelical zeal for the benefits of town planning'.[24] Smith believed that planning was more than pulling down houses, but was, as he put it, 'a dialogue on the enrichment of life',[25] and was even named Planner of the Year by *The Architectural Review* in 1962.

The 1963 Development Plan well expressed the romanticism

of the time about roads. There were to be raised roads above the motorway, notably Percy Street, and elevated walkways. With the opening of the new and unloved Eldon Square Shopping Centre, the 1963 plan was modified. A central feature was to promote Newcastle as the regional shopping capital and provide not only glitzy new shopping precincts but adequate parking. The plan made the hollow claim that the impact of the new shopping centre would be 'equally as great as that which the schemes of Dobson and Grainger had in the past'.[26] The greatest casualty was the partial demolition of the Regency housing terraces of Eldon Square. None of the local amenity societies raised a finger until, on a visit to Newcastle, the Minister of Housing Richard Crossman was appalled by the impending loss, making him an instant convert to the cause of conservation (see Chapter Seven).

Only a part of the 1963 plan was completed. This was largely owing to delays in implementation – some of the proposals which would have had the biggest impact on Newcastle were never realised, and those that did go ahead were modified.[27] Dobson's Royal Arcade was another casualty to one of the surviving elements of the plan. Swan House (1961), now renamed 55 Degrees North – an office block wonderfully redolent of the period – was built at the centre of a roundabout, a section of Burns's part-realised north–south motorway route to bring traffic from the Tyne Bridge, skirting the centre. In theory the new routes were to provide a frame around the city centre, which even Smith recognised had a special character and needed to be preserved.*

There were Newcastle successes: the most striking post-war building is the Civic Centre, opened in 1967 by the city architects G. W. Kenyon, whose clean lines look strongly to Scandinavian models, a confident marker for the future. This building set the model for the provision of artworks and public buildings in the city. Smith explained that he gave the artist Victor Pasmore a

---

* As early as 1962 there was 'A Plan for the Preservation of Buildings of Architectural or Historic Interest'.

free hand in the Rates Hall because 'I wanted people to go there, albeit reluctantly, to pay their rates, and to come face to face with Pasmore's abstract art.'[28] In other rooms are tapestries by John Piper and murals by Elizabeth Wise. It was certainly a pioneering approach, with so many contemporary artists commissioned. One of the attractive features of Smith was his Ruskinian belief in the arts as a way of improving people's lives.

Alas, T. Dan Smith's name became synonymous with local council malfeasance owing to his corrupt relationship with the amoral architect John Poulson. With a large practice based in Pontefract, Poulson believed that all planning was a matter of price; everybody was corruptible. His practice paid Smith's public relations companies £156,000 in fees over a decade to ensure that the contracts fell into the right hands. It was Poulson's bankruptcy hearings that brought Smith down, revealing the extent of their corruption on deals outside Newcastle, and landing him in prison.

But if Newcastle suffered a bad case of the planners it also provided a solution. The antidote to the housing problems in Glasgow and Liverpool and the effects of islands of buildings in a sea of open space was a return to medium and low-rise schemes. The best-known and admired example is Newcastle's elegant Byker housing estate (1969–81) – the poster boy of post-war housing – encompassing 200 acres with a population today of 9,500.* The architect, Ralph Erskine, was a humanist who lived much of his life in Sweden, where he had been impressed by the successful marriage of architecture and social policy. He declared that 'housing is a small "a" architecture. It should be friendly, intimate and have little there to make it monumental'.[29] Erskine insisted that from the beginning the local community was involved in the planning, and as such Byker is hailed as a milestone in the development of community architecture. His main challenge was an adjacent proposed dual carriageway.

---

* This was not one of T. Dan Smith's estates but commissioned during the brief Conservative administration of the city.

To deal with this, Erskine designed the famous Byker Wall, a dramatic polychromatic affair – like a Spanish medieval city wall – turning its back on the road. There are many surprises about visiting Byker: the scale of the estate, the variety of flats and houses, the colour, the sense of fun and the interesting use of materials. It is today listed Grade II*.

1963 is usually seen as the high point of the Brave New World, in the trajectory of an ambitious set of ideas.[30] It was the year of Buchanan's report *Traffic in Towns*, the year of Larkin's poem 'Annus Mirabilis' and the year when Ian Nairn optimistically saw the Liverpool re-planning as 'drawing its vitality from some common resurgence' with the Mersey Sound and the emergence of the Beatles. But the story was soon to turn sour. When Kenneth Clark, in his landmark 1969 series *Civilisation*, listed 'all those forces which impair our humanity' alongside lies, tanks, tear gas, he added *planners*.[31] This was indeed a fall from grace. When the RIBA invited George Tremlett, chairman of the Greater London Council housing committee, to give the keynote address at its conference in 1978, he did not pull his punches:

> the fact that I have made no secret these past twelve years of my disrespect for the architectural profession's work in inner London makes me a surprising guest [...] Yours was the hand that signed the paper that felled a city. Above all we will not lend our name to any architectural project which is not sympathetic to the environment. We will not build high-rise blocks. We will not build high-density developments. We will not demolish whole communities.[32]

In fact he was closing the stable door long after the horse had bolted. The era of tower block public housing was over, and the era of the vanilla Lego estate was beginning. Market forces were back in charge.

CHAPTER 6

Birmingham and Anti-Heritage

You've got very badly to want to get rid of the old,
before anything new will appear.

D. H. LAWRENCE, *WOMEN IN LOVE*

Birmingham, 'the second city', has received more respect than affection. One of Jane Austen's more disagreeable characters in *Emma* exclaims: 'They came from Birmingham, which is not a place to promise much [...] one has not great hopes from Birmingham.' It is not an historic cathedral city, but rather a city of scientific discovery, canals and workshops. Memories of Matthew Boulton and the Lunar Society are held sacred. Economic progress developed with metalworking, manufacturing, and the network of waterways. It was never a metropolis of great factories like the Yorkshire mill towns but rather a city of small workshops reflecting the 'city of a thousand trades' moniker. Birmingham was ascendant in the late nineteenth century, when it was judged to be 'the best-governed city in the world'. Architecturally, the city centre is surprisingly small – the suburbs spread much further and it is an exceptionally low-density city. Birmingham has always assimilated newcomers firstly from the countryside, Wales and Ireland, and more recently from the West Indies, India and Pakistan. Birmingham is an interesting case of a city that went out of its way to de-heritage itself in the 1960s.

The first thing that strikes all visitors is that Birmingham is a city with a love-hate relationship with the car. Dual carriageways pierce the heart of the city, dissect neighbourhoods and – until recently – throttled the city centre with a concrete collar. But for all that, the traffic does not flow smoothly, and no city is more frustrating to access by car. Neighbouring buildings are cut off from one another and heritage assets are isolated on thunderous urban clearways. Many good buildings are set in a degraded context – none more than Pugin's St Chad's Roman Catholic cathedral. Isolation is the word that keeps coming to mind in the city when examining its buildings. Even the instantly recognisable Bull Ring Rotunda by James Roberts, once the symbol of the new modern aspiring city, is now a stranded curiosity. The problem in Birmingham today is context.

Architecturally, Birmingham could never compete with Liverpool or Manchester, but it has much to admire. There are still pockets of the old eighteenth-century town, notably St Philip's, now the cathedral, an outstanding baroque design by Thomas Archer with its spectacular Burne-Jones windows. The city centre was comprehensively rebuilt by the Victorians in a mixture of Italianate, Flemish Gothic and French Renaissance style. Typical are the law courts faced in terracotta, a popular material because it could easily be cleaned. By far the grandest building is the town hall, a Roman temple of startling purity (Hansom & Welch 1832–4) that lands like a giant spaceship in Victoria Square. The suburbs have one jewel of international importance, the Arts and Crafts model village of Bournville, developed by George Cadbury from 1894, the best working-class suburb in England. Mercifully, the planners left this gem alone while they performed on the city centre the most dramatic intervention imposed on any great city in the post-war period.

'Birmingham is almost a new city', wrote Ian Nairn in 1967.[1] He thought no other town except Croydon had changed its looks so radically. The city enthusiastically embraced the spirit of the time. Birmingham was to be the city of the future, like Newcastle – the British answer to Brasilia – and nowhere was this better expressed than in a short film, *Telly Savalas Looks at*

Birmingham (which can still be enjoyed on the internet). His optimism was sadly misplaced. Birmingham was the classic case of a city seeking to renew itself through redevelopment. It began with the assumption that there was little worth preserving. It is sometimes pointed out that the city's strategy was an engineer's strategy – primarily functional, without taking into account either aesthetic or social considerations. The aim was to benefit the transit and accommodation of the motor car, on which Birmingham believed its prosperity hinged.

The post-war story of the city is dominated by two larger than life characters whose confident vision of the future drove the changes: Herbert Manzoni, the city engineer and surveyor (1935–63), and the pugnacious Labour councillor and sometime Lord Mayor, Frank Price. The Duke of Edinburgh, seeing Price advancing towards him one day, exclaimed, 'here comes trouble!' Price had grown up in a Birmingham back-to-back and he wanted to rid the city of such slums (which would be valued today) and turn it into the most modern city in the country. He described in his memoirs 'the mammoth task of clearing away 1000s of occupied slum properties […] it was to be the biggest comprehensive redevelopment program ever staged in Great Britain.'[2] Manzoni felt no sentiment for the historic fabric of the city: 'I have never been very certain as to the value of tangible links with the past', he said in 1957, adding, 'As to Birmingham's buildings, there is little of real worth in our architecture. Its replacement should be an improvement, providing we keep a few monuments as museum pieces to past ages.'[3]

After the housing shortage it was to the roads that they next turned their attention. This went to the heart of the city's self-image. Birmingham manufactured cars and had a large vehicle assembly industry, so that Frank Price could maintain that 'we were Britain's car city'. For him 'catering for the car and improving the standards of our public transport was a priority'.[4] In 1955, when Birmingham was about to embark on the major road improvements, the city sent a delegation to America to see how things were done in Chicago, Pittsburgh, Philadelphia and New York. How fatally attractive must have been the flowing freeways and flyovers in these wealthy high-rise cities.

The Birmingham inner ring road, with its combination of underpasses and flyovers, was approved a year later with a 75 per cent grant from central government. The first section was opened in March 1960 by the ubiquitous Tory minister Ernest Marples, the complete circuit opened by the Queen in 1971. Large areas of the inner city had been destroyed, but just as damaging was the dissection of neighbourhoods and the psychological effect on the city. As Nairn pointed out apropos Birmingham, 'ring roads are powerful instruments for good or ill, and what they can do in architectural and social terms is, I am quite sure, unappreciated by those who draw them so blithely on a map, purely as a means for relieving traffic congestion'.[5]

At the heart of the city's brave new world was the rebuilt Bull Ring partially completed in 1963, an ambitious development of offices and shops to be a public/private enterprise with car park, bus station, and market stalls etc.[*] It was billed to be 'Europe's most advanced shopping centre', entirely covered over, a pioneer perhaps, but one that had not been properly tested. As one critic put it: 'the Bull Ring gives the impression that a highly sophisticated designer with a Meccano set, tied down to a restrictive brief, was the originator of the structure [...] the Bull Ring's complexity gave the developers a severe headache'.[6] The problem with the Bull Ring was that it was too large, badly designed and awkward to access. The shops were poorly chosen and the ambience had little shopping appeal. It ran into immediate commercial trouble. One councilor described it as 'the biggest white elephant in the history of Birmingham'.

Birmingham did not have a great architectural school to fall

---

[*] The Bull Ring Centre, built 1961–7, was designed by Sydney Greenwood and T. J. Hirst.

back on, but the property boom threw up two good architects, John Madin and Graham Winteringham. Madin's central library was, according to Andy Foster, 'the first library in Western Europe to be designed as a complete cultural centre including exhibition areas, lecture hall, children's and music departments under one roof'.[7] Perhaps the most successful and lasting intervention of modern architecture was over at Birmingham University, which employed several distinguished architects, notably Casson, Conder and Partners, Chamberlin, Powell and Bon, and Arup Associates. But by the end of the decade the boom was over and the economy stalled. Birmingham entered the 1970s with the reputation of a 'difficult' city. To counteract this the National Exhibition Centre, a successful out-of-town solution, was opened by the Queen in 1976 and has been expanding ever since.

Conservation came to Birmingham with the founding of the West Midlands Group of the Victorian Society in 1967. Many fine buildings had already gone, notably the city's two Victorian railway stations. The turning point came with the saving of the post office, listed in 1972. The following year a proposal was put forward to replace it with a tower by Seifert & Partners, which was granted permission. The Victorian Society went into battle and the seven-year campaign which followed, in which they put forward an alternative scheme, was successful. It is now a standard procedure to provide an alternative scheme, but in those days it was still a novelty.

Other turning points were the Prince of Wales's 1984 'carbuncle' speech attacking modern architecture which, according to Foster, had great influence in the city. Four years after the speech came the Highbury Initiative, a meeting of international savants gathered to discuss improvements to Birmingham city centre and attract investment. Such gatherings, full of good intentions, usually leave little trace but this was different – it had an effect far beyond anybody's hopes. The immediate result was a scheme to open up the 'concrete collar' of the inner ring road and pedestrianise much of the city centre. The removal of the eastern half of the ring road changed the psyche of the city centre, no longer hemmed in by a concrete moat. The man largely responsible for the Highbury Initiative and reshaping the city during the 1980s and 1990s was a Labour leader of the council: Dick (Sir Richard) Knowles, leader from 1984 to 1993. A plumber by trade, Knowles enjoyed Victorian architecture and kept a shelf of Pevsners in his study. He oversaw the destruction of much of Price and Manzoni's Birmingham.

There have been many conservation success stories during the intervening years: the heart of the city offers the much-improved space around Archer's cathedral with Colmore Row providing a fine parade of Victorian buildings on one side.* In 1987 the 1960s Bull Ring Centre was cited for redevelopment. The new proposals brought forth the body known as 'Birmingham for People', which tried to move the city away from the 'big is beautiful' ideology which had been so much a part of Birmingham thinking since the war. The council always had a predilection for ambitious, eye-catching projects of varying quality, such as the International Convention Centre, Birmingham's Symphony Hall, and the Brindleyplace redevelopment.

The city was once again on the front foot, but as so often in the past the results were mixed. Alas, the council's recent attempt at civic grandeur, the rearrangement of Centenary Square, was an expensive near miss. At its heart is the new library with the Symphony Hall to one side and the Birmingham Museum and Art Gallery on the other. We should applaud any city which builds a new library, but this came at a high cost and the motivation may not have been entirely cultural. The city announced their intention to demolish their best post-war twentieth-century building, John Madin's brutalist library, to

---

* Colmore Row was secured with the saving of the Grand Hotel, listed in 2004.

update it for the digital age.* But they also wanted to develop the site. English Heritage twice attempted to list the building (critics said it sat on an awkward site) but were prevented by council lobbying. No councillor was prepared to defend Madin's building. Finally, the secretary of state, Margaret Hodge, turned down listing application against the advice of both the Twentieth Century Society and English Heritage. To celebrate its short life a wake was held by its admirers in Chamberlain Square starting at 11 a.m. on Saturday 31 January 2015. Warm clothes, a candle, food and drink were recommended.

Birmingham in 2021

Like many cities, Birmingham has had to sell off prime sites to fill the hole in funding – as one might expect. However, if ever there was a trophy creation it is Centenary Square and the new library. The library is wrapped in mechanical symbols that over-make the point. As Rowan Moore observed: 'there is a way of building now that is all about packages and wrapping, which, though it sounds nice – sort of Christmassy – does not always result in the most beautiful gifts to the fabric of British cities.'[8] The square is an unappealing space (but rescuable one day when the tram station is finished) with forty-three meaningless, very tall lighting columns that distract and take up space where trees and benches might humanise it.

Birmingham's Victorian buildings in the city centre are in a generally fine state of preservation, but there is a pressure to redevelop. There is a slow insidious erosion of character in all too many Birmingham Conservation Areas. In Digbeth and Deritend Conservation Area a huge planning permission has been granted for the demolition of more than half the buildings in the area.

---

* The Madin library itself replaced a Victorian building by Martin & Chamberlain and the present building incorporates the Jacobethan Shakespeare Memorial Room.

Typical is the thirty-five-storey tower being built on the Colmore Row site of John Madin's NatWest Tower. Will it be better? Hard to say at this stage (2019), but it certainly uses more space and opens the way to other developments. It is a continuous battle between the developers and the conservationists which the former is winning – pushing for more height, sometimes decades of revisions to the application, a relentless drip drip to wear down opposition. Most developers today realise that they must talk the language of conservation while at the same time they push the boundaries. Even the indignities inflicted on St Chad's are not over – a high-rise twenty-one-storey Shadwell Tower is planned to overshadow Pugin's cathedral, set on the Birmingham and Fazeley Canal, wildly out of scale with the rest of the Gun Quarter.

Birmingham has one great triumph of conservation: the Jewellery Quarter. This old artisan district represents the way the city sees itself and its history: a light industrial area where everyone would come to buy jewellery and metalware. The quarter has at its heart the only Georgian square left in the city.[*] The regeneration was encouraged and given recognition when English Heritage published a report in 2000. The area still has many workshops (some survival, a few revival) but conversion to residential is slowly taking over. It is a fragile balance and the residential gentrification will be increasingly at odds with the old industries. If the twenty-acre Northwood Street housing scheme, in train since 2002, goes ahead it will decisively impact the flavour of the area. The greatest risk to the district is land value and HS2.[†] If the Jewellery Quarter is a triumph of conservation and regeneration, Brindleyplace, with a masterplan originally by Terry Farrell and modified by John Chatwin, is the city's most ambitious new development. It is the old canal district using the

---

[*] The only other Georgian square – Old Square – was demolished in the 1920s and 1960s.

[†] If anyone doubts the pressure of development on the area they should peruse the section of the *Hockley Flyer* website – 'the Voice of the Jewellery Quarter' – on planning applications.

old warehouses converted to bars and restaurants and new offices in a neo-classical vein with touches of Venice and Schinkel. This successful regeneration project is a child of its time and much enjoyed by the locals.

What of the far-flung suburbs? The best suburban delight, Bournville, is unscathed and full of sweetness and light, but even that has a main road running through its heart. The capacious suburbs of the city offer other delights, such as Newman's Birmingham Oratory: rich and Italianate, for a prelate who was an architectural classicist. For Goths there is Pearson's St Alban's – surprisingly only Grade II* for an obviously Grade I church – an Anglo-Catholic oasis surrounded by twentieth-century banality in what is now a largely Muslim neighbourhood. St Augustine's, by the impressive nineteenth-century local architect J. A. Chatwin, is one of the few that sits in an entirely sympathetic setting. One particularly successful adaptation is the Green Lane library and swimming baths, a fine Victorian building in the local redbrick and terracotta Gothic-Jacobean style (1893–1902), into a mosque – the Green Lane Masjid, which won the Victorian Society's 2017 Conservation Award.

But all is not well in the suburbs. There are thirty Conservation Areas in Birmingham of which only eleven are subject to an Article 4 direction which give extra protection to sensitive architectural detail. Without this protection residents are unlikely to get permission to demolish but can do practically anything else. There is a slow insidious erosion of character in all too many Birmingham Conservation Areas. In what might have been the Grosvenor Estate of Birmingham, Calthorpe Estates, commercial development has been allowed to spoil the character of the city's best middle-class suburb.

The desire to strip out, modernise, alter the fenestration, use inappropriate rendering, put up prominent satellite dishes and build porches are typical changes which on an individual basis make little impact, but in the aggregate amount to a district where it is no longer worth enforcing the rules, leading to an 'if they can do it why can't I?' mentality. An official attitude of 'we cannot cope' and 'we are where we are' has overtaken the situation and the belief that they are too degraded and no longer viable as Conservation Areas.[*]

Birmingham Council's 'Planning and Regeneration Department' has been reducing the city's Conservation Areas. Ideal Village, an Edwardian area – with lots of UPVC and house improvement but not always to the tune of Historic England's guidelines, has been removed. Austin Village, a unique area of World War I prefab wooden houses shipped from the Aladdin Company in Michigan, replete with US wild-west style open balconies, for the war workers brought in to make munitions, hangs by a thread. Planning officers have been given the power to get rid of it without consulting councillors. Finally, Barnsley Road in Edgbaston, with houses of around 1900 by the Arts and Crafts architect J. L. Ball, has been cut down in area, after the planners allowed big demolitions, including an Arts and Crafts house by Ball's relative, Ernest Barnsley. New Conservation Areas have been blocked. One in Acocks Green has been refused, even though former planning officers encouraged it, and it has much local support.

Local conservationists look with admiration at how neighbouring Dudley has tackled similar problems with a detailed survey and a marked respect for the built heritage. It requires political will, an adequate supply of building officers and good local resident associations who are prepared to support

---

* I was informed of one case, 22 Ladywood Road, Four Oaks, by W. H. Bidlake, 1900, a magnificent Arts and Crafts house by Bidlake at the top of his form. Described and illustrated at length in Muthesius's *Das Englische Haus* of 1904, so of European importance, the house was altered, degraded and the subject of a blizzard of planning applications, the building stripped out, followed by a fire. The fire service investigated the blaze but did not find enough evidence to prosecute anyone for arson. The city never took strong action against the owner and now the building is a shell and allowed to rot.

conservation disciplines.* The city appears to go one step forward and then two steps backwards. Birmingham for most of the last seventy years has been in thrall to a prosperity agenda that has trumped conservation. Does Birmingham really appreciate its heritage assets? Yes, until a developer looms into view. Today the story is one of mission creep both in the city centre and the suburbs – different in intention and scale, but does the city have the will to hold the line with either? One architectural historian, Tim Bridges, suggested to the author that the Birmingham mentality is shaped by craft: build, use and replace.

* This is the case at Greenfield Road, Harborne, a mixture of working-class terraces and grander houses including some by good architects such as J. H. Chamberlain and George Ingall.

CHAPTER 7

The Backlash: The Heroic Period of Conservation

*The conservation of the urban environment is one of the
very few fields of public policy in Britain since the war where
public opinion has risen in revolt and demanded,
on specific occasions over and over again, the authorities
mend their ways and produce something better.*[1]

SIMON JENKINS

Just before 6 o'clock in the morning of 16 May 1968, Ivy
Hodge, a fifty-six-year-old cake decorator, went to the kitchen
of her flat on the 18th floor of Ronan Point in Newham, East
London, to make a cup of tea. Leaning over her cooker, she lit a
match. An explosion ripped through the kitchen, blowing apart
the concrete panels that formed its outer walls and causing the
entire corner of the twenty-two-storey building to collapse like a
house of cards.[2]

Thankfully Ivy survived, but it was to prove to be a shattering
blow for system-build tower block housing, and the turning
point from subsidising high-rise new builds to providing grants
to upgrade existing housing. The event was the catalyst to passing
the 1969 Housing Act – improvement replaced development as
the focus of planning attention. The public had woken up to
the social and aesthetic consequences of the new landscape being
developed around them.

The period from 1960 to 1975 has been called the 'Heroic
Period of Conservation' and it sprang from disillusionment on
several fronts: the social and planning failure of the poorer-quality

utopian housing schemes, the insensitive redevelopment of historic towns and cities, suffocating ring roads, and the loss of familiar landmarks. For the first time it was felt that what was being destroyed would be replaced by something worse. By the time Colin Amery and Dan Cruickshank produced their paperback bible of doom, *The Rape of Britain*, in 1975, the full horror of the damage inflicted on thirty cities and towns in Britain since 1945 was evident. The authors' main proposition was that more damage was done to these towns by planners and local councils than by Nazi bombers. They had no doubt that the car was the villain, but that was only half the story. From 1954 onwards there were individuals and a few government ministers who had begun to see what was happening and blow the whistle.*

The great conservation battles would be fought on many fronts, notably in Bath and London, where concerted opposition prevented development schemes for Piccadilly Circus, Covent Garden and later Spitalfields. But there were casualties such as Eldon Square in Newcastle. Individual monuments were also lost, such as Euston Arch (in 1961) and the Firestone Factory (in 1980), but every loss was so much martyr's blood, allowing conservationists to hone the tactics required to fight the next battle. It was a period that saw important initiatives from Civic Trusts and Conservation Areas, the vast extension of the listing of historic buildings that for the first time offered real protection to the built environment.

Although many of the battles would be spearheaded by the amenity societies, populated for the most part by an older generation of conservationists, there was a generational change. The counterculture that opposed the Vietnam War, supported

---

* The 1962 annual report by that equivocal body, the Royal Fine Art Commission, stated: 'It is not, we believe, at present realised what shocking schemes are afoot for mutilating some of the most beautiful historic towns – notably Bath, Salisbury and Cirencester – owing very largely to traffic flow over all other factors.'

CND and the earth activists created a climate of revolt against and a questioning of prevailing orthodoxies. Young architectural historians and critics brought energy and urgency to the cause, as became particularly evident in the battles fought by the nascent Victorian and Thirties societies. If pre-war conservationists had concentrated on saving Georgian architecture, the destruction of terraces in Newcastle, Liverpool and Bath showed that even this battle was far from won, but the most striking element of the 1960s was the shift of focus towards Victorian architecture. The great conservation battles of the era, the Euston Arch and St Pancras Station, and the growing appreciation of cities like Manchester and Liverpool are powerful demonstrations of this tidal change. Protection of interwar and post-war architecture would take a little longer.

The first grenades of the counterattack were thrown by a hard-drinking, angry journalist, born in Bedford, who romantically claimed to come from Newcastle. In 1954, after national service in the RAF flying jet fighters called Meteors, Ian Nairn joined *The Architectural Review*. The following year he produced a special issue of the magazine entitled *Outrage*, one of the earliest and most powerful polemical attacks on the sad state of the landscape. There had been nothing like it: a car journey from Carlisle to Southampton cataloguing the architectural and landscape horrors he found, and photographing them all to create an album of visual misery. Nairn railed against the minutiae of the scene: poor lamp standards, dumping grounds, wire fences, advertising hoardings, pylons and inappropriate municipal flower beds. Even one of the great views of England, Oxford from Boars Hill, was spoiled: 'a magnificent skyline framed between concrete lamp standards and with a foreground of pylons, railways and allotments'.[3]

Nairn described *Outrage* as 'a prophecy of doom – the doom of an England reduced to universal Subtopia, a mean and middle state, neither town nor country, an even spread of abandoned aerodromes and fake rusticity, wire fences, traffic roundabouts, gratuitous notice-boards, car parks and things in fields.'[4] Above all it was the sameness of the new landscape: 'the defence of individuality of places is the defence of the individuality of ourselves'. Nairn was not initially anti-modernist: he liked the old and new acting to the advantage of both. 'Modern architecture', Nairn liked to say, 'has its own set of broken election promises.' Bankrupt post-war Britain was not prepared to spend money on architecture: 'The outstanding and appalling fact about modern architecture is that it is just not good enough, it is not standing up to use or climate, either in the single buildings or the whole environment.'[5]

From 1964 Nairn delighted readers of the *Observer* with his architectural column, but he reached his largest audience through television. He was not a natural performer, being rather awkward, but was authentic, passionate, and often angry – he exploded with rage on camera when he saw the state of St Saviour's Church, Astley Bridge in Bolton. Nairn was the most influential architectural critic of his generation. He had none of the whimsy or humour of John Betjeman but a raw humanity that made him love pubs and drink too much – he died of cirrhosis of the liver. Gavin Stamp was to keep alive Nairn's angry journalism through his 'Piloti' column in *Private Eye*. When Nairn was invited to join the newly formed Civic Trust, he refused as he did not want to be contaminated.

The Civic Trust was the brainchild of Duncan Sandys MP, Churchill's son-in-law. Sandys was an efficient political operator who had steered the Clean Air Act through parliament. His tastes were Georgian: he was to be appalled by the destruction in Bath. His interest in conservation was very much against the tide of his own party, who were swept along by Harold Macmillan's drive to modernise Britain and reach housing targets whatever the compromise of quality. Sandys perceived that there needed to be a body separate from government which could bring together all the various local civic societies and speak on their behalf, a sister organisation to the CPRE that would deal with urban as opposed to rural England. The Civic Trust was inaugurated at Lambeth Palace in July 1957 at a reception for 300 people.

The developing listing system emphasised individual buildings of merit, taking little account of their historic surroundings.* But where did this leave a familiar urban landscape without particularly important buildings like Piccadilly Circus? Typically, the Civic Trust piloted schemes such as Magdalen Street in Norwich where a run of historic buildings was considered in unison.† It offered both a facelift and a design guide, backed up with grants. The accent was on civic pride and offering practical models for new uses. Later generations have often criticised the detail, but the important point is that the Civic Trust encouraged the idea that modern architecture and conservation were not in opposition to one another but could be used imaginatively together. By the mid-1960s the Trust had some 700 affiliated societies and developers were forced to pay attention (to understand how effective and influential a local civic society could be, see Chapter Eight on York). There is no doubt that the Trust focused on the easy and picturesque towns and did not attempt much in the great industrial cities of the north. Perhaps its greatest achievement was its central role in the formation of the 1967 Civic Amenities Act, which gave us Conservation Areas. This required cooperation from both sides of the House of Commons.

When Harold Wilson won the election in 1964, he appointed Richard Crossman as his Minister of Housing and Local Government. Fiercely independent, intellectual and often brusque, Crossman was not the man to accept prevailing orthodoxies. His diaries, an important document of the times, describe his growing awareness that something was radically wrong with the 'demolish and develop' attitude to historic towns.

* From the formation of the National Buildings Record established in 1941 to document historic buildings under threat from aerial bombardment, through the Historic Buildings Council (1947), the emphasis of conservation was on the important individual building, a policy endorsed by one of the leading architectural historians of the day, John Summerson.

† The Norwich Society had pioneered this approach at Elm Hill from 1927.

Responsibility for listing historic buildings came under his remit, but listing had fallen into abeyance when the pro-development stance of the previous Conservative government had seen the number of officers reduced from twenty-four to nine nationally. Even where listing had been completed, it was not always effective, as there were on average over 500 notices to demolish every year. Moreover, preservation orders were rarely enforced because local governments were worried about the compensation clauses for which they might become liable. Overall there is no doubt that historic buildings were regarded as a nuisance – the prevailing attitude saw preservation as uneconomic and even an impediment to prosperity.

The year after the election, Crossman visited Newcastle. He was proudly told about the impending partial demolition of Regency Eldon Square being carried out in his name. He was appalled, and it was here that he had a conservation epiphany. He reflected on how much was slipping between the cracks because of the division of responsibility between his own ministry and the Ministry of Works; the law was inadequate and not functioning properly. Crossman received little support from his senior civil servants. He observed that the permanent secretary, Dame Evelyn Sharp, 'counted herself a modern iconoclast' and was in no doubt whose side she was on in the 'clear-cut conflict between "modern" planning and "reactionary" preservation'.[6] However, Crossman noted in his diary that a 'Townscape Group' were 'working on a new policy document' which suggested that 'preservation of ancient buildings should be concerned not merely with individual listing buildings but also with groups or streets or small areas of town.'[7]

The year after his fateful visit to Newcastle, Crossman called a conference on historic buildings at Churchill College, Cambridge (an edifice he described as having been 'designed at great expense by architects who hated college life or else knew nothing about it').[8] Five towns were selected for pilot studies: Bath, Chester, Chichester, King's Lynn and York. The aim was to demonstrate how town centre redevelopment was compatible with the preservation of ancient buildings. They would focus on areas rather than individual buildings, and would be positive in strategies for action, rather than negative prevention. The ministry and the local council were to share the costs of the report equally; King's Lynn dropped out because their local authority refused to pay its share. York wavered for the same reason – the city council viewed the project as an implied criticism. Fortunately, York's powerful Civic Trust was in favour and found backing from the city's chocolate manufacturers, Terry's, who agreed to meet half of the city council's costs. Crossman ended up with an agreement to make four studies: York – which would be the first to report in 1968 – followed by Chichester, Bath and Chester.

It was fortunate that such a senior and forceful minister as Crossman began to take an interest at this critical moment, and that his interest was mirrored on the Conservative benches by Duncan Sandys. In an unexpected stroke of luck, Sandys drew first place in a ballot for the right to introduce a members' bill in the House of Commons. After some hesitation he decided to sponsor the broadly named Civic Amenities Act (1967), and the result was the introduction of Conservation Areas.[*] It was not easy getting the legislation through, and Sandys was forced to compromise on one small but important point. The minister proposed that development within a Conservation Area should only be allowed to 'conserve and enhance', but he was forced to settle for 'or enhance', which caused many headaches in future by developers claiming enhancement without conservation.[†]

Nevertheless, the Act was the first to recognise the importance of harmony in a district which might not have outstanding

---

[*] Conservation Area legislation came with the Civic Amenities Act 1967 but even then it was still possible to demolish unlisted buildings in a Conservation Area without permission until the Town and Country Planning Act 1972, which was further strengthened by the Town and Country Amenities Act 1974.

[†] This was the reasoning behind the application to demolish No 1 Poultry in London.

buildings, and in which the whole was greater than the parts. Four Conservation Areas were initially designated, the first being Stamford, followed by parts of Plymouth and Exeter. This rose rapidly to 138 the following year, with fifty-two in London alone.[*] Crossman and Sandys, ably assisted by Labour's Wayland Young, Lord Kennet in the House of Lords, effected a revolution which proves – if it was not obvious already – that conservation flourishes when it has strong all-party support from national government as well as local government.[†] Those two years after the Cambridge conference have been described as the most important post-war years for the conservationists, with a stream of important legislation that still operates today.

Campaigns were of particular significance. Between 1958 and 1968 there were six full-scale plans for revamping Piccadilly Circus put forward by developers, notably Jack Cotton. Pevsner called it 'the ill-shaped rock on which the hopes of many twentieth-century improvers foundered'.[9] Colin Buchanan presided over a public inquiry which rejected one plan: 'Piccadilly Circus attracts people from the ends of the earth as it is, and if comprehensive redevelopment is to take place, then it should be to a standard that really justifies a journey from the ends of the earth.'[10] For the first time the Civic Trust, the press and public opinion were all marshalled to prevent the scheme. From now on it would be 'planning through public protest'. Piccadilly Circus attracted much public interest, a much-loved assembly point for visitors,

[*] Alongside this initiative the 1968 Town and Country Planning Act strengthened the cause and made it harder to undermine listing. Lord Kennet had observed that officials often instinctively took the side of property owners, but the Act acknowledged 'group value' as a justification for listing and it included fixtures in the listed protection. Equally important for the future was a clause in the Act that the amenity societies – such as the Georgian Group – became statutory consultees so that local authorities were obliged to advertise listed building applications.

[†] Kennet was impressed by the French system of *zone protégée* set up by André Malraux in 1962 that protected a one-kilometre diameter circle around every monument and *site classé*.

but what about those great Victorian buildings variously referred to as elephants and wedding cakes? They found their champion in the Victorian Society.

The Victorian Society

Few amenity societies were more effective or would fight harder battles than the Victorian Society, which held its first meeting in 1957. Conservation was still in the hands of a small number of concerned activists and the overlap with the Georgian Group is striking: John Betjeman, James Lees-Milne, Christopher Hussey, Ralph Dutton and Lord Esher (the first chairman). The scholars were Mark Girouard and Nikolaus Pevsner, who were to do so much through their publications to change the appreciation of this period. One of the earliest writers on Victorian architecture, Kenneth Clark, warned them, 'your list will have to be severely critical, otherwise you will find yourself called in to try to save two-thirds of the town halls in the Midlands, practically all the Insurance Offices in the country and many other buildings'.[11] Today they would all be regarded as worthy of preservation.

The Victorian Society lost many of its early campaigns, fighting not just developers but ingrained artistic prejudice. The gradual revival of Victorian art and architecture took many forms: the writings and cartoons of Osbert Lancaster, exhibitions of Victorian painters, promotion by the colour sections of the Sunday magazines, Sotheby's opened a saleroom dedicated to Victoriana in Belgravia, and films like the 1968 musical *Oliver!* found a new glamour in the period. One name more than any other, however, is attached to this story: John Betjeman. He was an early appreciator, certainly, but not the first: that was H. S. Goodhart-Rendel, whom Kenneth Clark described as 'the father of us all'. To Betjeman, Goodhart-Rendel's slim masterpiece *English Architecture Since the Regency* was 'like St Paul's Epistles: you can find more and more in it every time you turn back to it.'[12]

Anyone who studies Betjeman's writings and television output will be struck by how catholic his range of interests was. The poet had a sensitive appreciation of his surroundings, which being largely Victorian he gave the same affectionate scrutiny as other periods. More importantly, at a time when people were discovering the continent of Europe, Betjeman made them look at their own country anew. He rarely wrote about the great heritage set pieces but spoke in favour of the merits of out-of-the-way churches, the Isle of Man, Belfast City Hall, and Swindon. His television programmes of the 1960s convey his love of the unfashionable, and how he brought humour to conservation by ridiculing developers by parodying their patter. The most notable example was his 1965 BBC television play *Pity About the Abbey*, lampooning a proposal to demolish Westminster Abbey to make way for a new government Treasury building, a part of a new 'Westminster Roundabout'. *

Betjeman became the go-to celebrity for all conservation battles and he invariably did what he was asked to do, especially for young people. The impact of his interventions can rarely be ascertained but they greatly lifted the morale of the campaigners. His intercession was certainly critical at Holy Trinity, Sloane Street, helping to save J. D. Sedding's great 'cathedral of the Arts and Crafts'. The most painful loss to him was 'the removal [in 1956] of the Imperial Institute and the splendid range of South Kensington buildings by the most eminent architects of mid and later Victorian times by London University'.[13] The other great loss that ignited one of the first great campaigns of the Victorian Society was the glorious Coal Exchange in Lower Thames Street

---

* This was not far-fetched since in 1963 the Conservative Minister of Public Buildings and Works, Geoffrey Rippon, announced that Sir George Gilbert Scott's Foreign Office building would be demolished. Sir Leslie Martin, a leading modernist architect, created a plan that encompassed the whole area between St James's Park and the river, a grid of ziggurats and towers linked by high-level glazed gallerias. It was only Britain's declining economic position that ditched the scheme, which had all-party support.

by J. B. Bunning. This was the victim of the desire to widen the east–west artery of the City. The choice was either to demolish the Coal Exchange or remove a section from the back of the rather dull Regency Custom House, which had a higher listing. As Betjeman pointed out, if the Coal Exchange had been by Wren or Chambers it would be saved, but being Victorian nobody cared.

Betjeman is invariably coupled with Nikolaus Pevsner, the stringent German professor versus the English literary aesthete. That characterisation is far too glib since their interests and causes were remarkably similar but had a different emphasis. When Pevsner launched his Buildings of England series in 1951, it stood in counterpoint to Betjeman's Shell Guides. If Pevsner's inventory of national buildings is, necessarily, drily architectural, Betjeman enjoyed literary and historical associations, as well as local legends. Betjeman was not a little silly about 'the Herr Doktor Professor' but they joined forces when it mattered, such as for the Euston Arch campaign.

Their *cause célèbre* was the demolition in 1962 of this master-piece by Philip Hardwick.* There had been plans since the 1930s to rebuild Euston Station and relocate its most spectacular feature, the 70-foot entrance 'arch' erected in 1837, supported by four fluted Doric columns, which surprisingly stood at the side of the station where the cars entered. *The Times* broke the story that the London County Council would not object to the removal of the arch for the electrification of the London–Manchester line. British Rail was trying to promote an image of modernity and desired that stations capture the excitement of airports, so they had little time for symbols of the age of steam. At Euston they wanted to build a new station with longer platforms.

The Victorian Society accepted that the arch could not be saved in its present position and petitioned for it to be re-erected on the Euston Road where it could be admired by all. Ernest

---

* In 1958 the Victorian Society asked British Rail if it could hold its AGM in the boardroom of Euston Station – a request that was refused.

Marples, the progressive transport minister, told the House of Commons that this would cost £190,000 compared with £12,000 to demolish it. Nobody was prepared to foot the bill. The sum involved was, as the Victorian Society later noted, 'rather less than the Treasury paid out about the same time for the purchase of two indifferent Renoirs, which no one was threatening to destroy'.[14] John Betjeman ruefully noted that railway enthusiasts were more interested in engines than buildings.

When Betjeman was asked why it mattered, he simply replied, 'It was the first bit of railway architecture in the world of any size [...] and if it were moved forward in front of the new Euston station it would be the most magnificent public monument in London.'[15] *The Times* published an editorial headed 'Not Worth Saving' which contradicted their architectural correspondent J. M. Richards. It was thought that this article was the decisive influence on the prime minister, Harold Macmillan's, refusal. The officers of the Victorian Society even went to see him, sitting alongside Marples. The Victorians were rebuffed by the prime minister who cited the cause of progress. Much was learned from this failure, however: they had left everything too late, had not raised sufficient funds and needed to be better prepared and more aggressive. The Victorians believed that 'even our lost battles are not altogether fruitless, for on each occasion, successful or not, we recruit more and more disciples to the cause.'[16] The Euston Arch has been more important in death than in life, becoming the Alamo of the conservation movement.

The Victorian Society was better prepared when, in 1966, British Railways announced plans to integrate the lines running into St Pancras and King's Cross, demolishing in the process George Gilbert Scott's fairytale hotel building at St Pancras, long converted to dismal offices. What it planned to do with Barlow's spectacular train shed was not clear. The Victorian Society's argument against demolition was that St Pancras should be preserved as an epitome of 'the greatest period of British history', when the country was at the zenith of influence and power.[17] There were conservationists like John Summerson who found Scott's design both nauseating and unworthy of special protection, but public opinion was against them.[18] The following year, St Pancras was listed Grade I and the building was saved from demolition. It was fortunate that none of the plans made in the wake of that decision came to fruition and the building slumbered through the next three decades to find a triumphant return to its original purpose serving as a hotel for the Eurostar service. St Pancras had demonstrated the power of listing and the increasing importance of public opinion. Both would be decisive in the next campaign, one of far greater complexity and with wider ramifications.

Covent Garden

The battleground now moved to Covent Garden. The Greater London Council (GLC) formed a consortium in 1965 with Westminster and Camden councils to redevelop the area around the market with mega-structures, enormous roads and walkways. Their report published three years later dutifully listed all the local tradesmen: violin makers, the booksellers, stamp dealers, the publishers, the printers, the theatres and of course the Opera House, although none of them had been consulted. Tradesmen and residents rallied around the energetic vicar of St Martin-in-the-Fields church, the Revd Austen Williams, and they formed the Covent Garden Community Association. The story became the seminal example of a neighbourhood against the planners. Owing to its high-profile national appeal (the film *My Fair Lady*, set in the market, had been released the previous year), Covent Garden attracted enormous publicity and the battle is sometimes seen as a turning point in the shift of conservation from professionals to the local community and an attempt to reverse the top-down methods of post-war planning.[19] The grandee guardians of heritage were joined by the New Left in alliance.

The Covent Garden plan was subverted by the same government minister, Geoffrey Rippon, who had wanted to demolish the Foreign Office. He asked his officials to list several strategically placed buildings across the area, and Covent Garden was made a Conservation Area under the new Civic Amenities Act. The neighbourhood was fortunate in having determined and articulate residents who did not care that there was no greenery, the Holy Grail of all planners. They asked that their *quartier* should 'provide living, shopping and leisure facilities for the people who work in the entertainments industry, rather than tourist attractions [...] Covent Garden is not part of the West End'.[20] The residential population was retained but the tourists poured in as well. The defeat of planning at Covent Garden was seen as a political victory as well as a conservationist one. As Lionel Esher observed, what emerged was an attitude rather than a plan. That attitude was to be much in evidence during the battle to save Spitalfields in the late 1970s.[*]

Edinburgh

North of the border, a crisis point was being reached in Edinburgh's once visionary Enlightenment quarter, the New Town, which held some 11,500 properties, mostly residential, covering 318 hectares. The conservation effort came not a minute too soon. There had been several alarm calls during the 1950s and 1960s: firstly the university had demolished part of the noble George Square (prompting the creation of the Scottish Georgian

---

[*] Poverty and the benign neglect that so often goes with it had preserved Spitalfields until the 1960s, when owing to the encroaching City of London, it began to attract developers. Conservationists squatted in the houses while the demolition men were outside. The Spitalfields Trust was formed in 1977 by Mark Girouard, among others, to buy properties with a revolving fund, apply first aid, and resell to enthusiasts; to whom the ownership of a Georgian house became a hobby, a way of life and an obsession. The Bengali community and Brick Lane Market were the neighbours and provided colourful shops and restaurants.

Society). There followed the brutal insertion of a graceless shopping centre, and finally the two finest buildings on Princes Street were demolished, William Burn's New Club and David Rhind's Italianate Scottish Life Association Building. After 1970 the city's protection came to rest in the excellent hands of the Edinburgh New Town Conservation Committee, formed in the wake of the Civic Amenities Act three years earlier.[21] It started with the simple belief that Edinburgh provided one of the three best townscapes in Europe, the others being Venice and Leningrad. The physical proximity of Edinburgh's various conservation bodies greatly helped, and the Civic Trust set about recruiting a team of over 120 architects, surveyors and engineers, galvanising them to examine the fabric of every property, particularly the leaning chimney stacks, the flaking stone on the facades, the sorry state of carved and cast balconies, balustrades and cornices, and the degraded rooflines and fenestration. All this work was undertaken on the simple principle of cost sharing between the Edinburgh Corporation, the government and the owners of the properties themselves. Grants were offered in inverse proportion to rateable value, so that the poorest should receive most help.

SAVE Britain's Heritage (SAVE)

1975, European Architectural Heritage Year, was something of a turning point. Apart from international recognition of the problem, that year saw the previously mentioned publication of Colin Amery and Dan Cruickshank, *The Rape of Britain*. But in the long run the most important development that year was the foundation of SAVE, following the V&A's 'Destruction of the Country House' exhibition the year before. It was the brainchild of Marcus Binney, one of the show's organisers, an architectural historian and former editor of *Country Life*. Binney is a professional activist with considerable PR and theatrical skills, a genial figure who combines diffidence with courage and a will of iron. He has demonstrated great determination in being prepared to sustain fights through the courts for a decade or more to prevent demolitions at The Grange (when he legally challenged the secretary of state) and No 1 Poultry. SAVE was founded on a wing and a prayer and has always existed on donations. We will meet SAVE in several chapters of this book and it plays a significant role in the heritage story after 1975.

Binney was joined by the architectural historian John Harris (who had helped to curate 'The Destruction of the Country House' exhibition), and the journalist and future editor of *The Times* Simon Jenkins, who has shown consistent interest in building losses and planning blights. Jenkins described SAVE as the shock troops of the heritage world, and it is easy to see why. They went to war against anyone who proposed to knock down a listed building and frequently against those who should be upholding the law: ministers and local councils. Their weapon was press releases, often with arresting Victorian billboard typography – they lived on the gunpowder of publicity. Jenkins described the constituent parts as: 'good punchy copy, statistics and a juicy quote'. SAVE was effectively a press office, issuing photographs and bulletins which the newspapers were only too pleased to report. It was staffed with well-informed and dedicated young people who learned how to gain media attention. From the very beginning SAVE was concerned with all kinds of architecture. Its most impressive achievements would lie in saving northern mills and other industrial buildings, but their first report focused on Victorian artisan terraced houses.

SAVE had a simple philosophy: whatever the building type, every structure can be adapted, reused or regenerated given a good architect and a willingness to try. The message was always *preservation pays*. In Binney's words, no good building, however large, should have to be a pensioner of the state. They mounted pioneering travelling exhibitions starting with 'Off the Rails' (1977) to draw attention to the destruction of railway buildings, followed by 'Satanic Mills' (1979) and one on pubs, 'Time, Gentleman, Please!' Exhibitions were supplemented by reports with catchy titles like *What! Conservation in Gateshead* or *Leeds,*

Must Old Mean Bad? and *Bright Future: The Re-use of Industrial Buildings.* Early victories included saving George Gilbert Scott's All Souls at Haley Hill, Bolton, and Manningham Mills, Bradford.* The successful battle honours of SAVE are too long to enumerate but seared by one epic campaign that lasted for a decade.

Mansion House Square

One of the longest and most keenly fought battles by SAVE was in the heart of the City of London over a proposal unveiled in 1968 to demolish a group of characterful Victorian mercantile buildings next to the Mansion House on Poultry and Victoria Streets, and replace them with a Mies van der Rohe glass tower, similar to his celebrated Seagram Building in New York. This was a trophy scheme by an important modern architect who died aged eighty-four the following year.† As one civil servant put it, the matter 'began as a planning issue concerned with (aesthetic) design control and ended as one concerned with conservation'.[22] The developer, the well-connected Peter Palumbo, no doubt believed that such a gleaming design would overcome any planning objections for the destruction of, among others, eight Grade II listed buildings within the Bank Conservation Area. He was still assembling the site. The plan was widely supported, especially in the architectural profession, but others were sceptical. The matter was examined by the Royal Fine Art Commission (RFAC), the nation's committee of taste, who were divided. John Summerson thought that the tower would bring drama into the City, but opponents thought it was on the wrong site and pointed to the proximity of St Paul's, always the lodestar of City

* St Francis Xavier in Liverpool even dedicated a stained glass window to SAVE.

† Gavin Stamp described it as an 'essentially old fashioned design – conceived in the 1960s but representing the 1940s'. *The Spectator,* 4 May 1985, p. 18.

height restrictions. As so often, the RFAC tried to have it both ways, approving the design but suggesting a height reduction which would have destroyed its proportions – a measure of its confusion. The City of London, as planning authority, refused planning permission. The case went to the secretary of state, the application dragged on and attitudes changed in the interval.

Two public inquiries were held – at the first in 1984 the secretary of state, Patrick Jenkin, rejected the Mies tower proposal but with the curious rider that he did not 'rule out development of this site if there were acceptable proposals for replacing the existing buildings'.[23] This opened the way for Palumbo to present James Stirling's postmodern design. The second inquiry (1988) focused 'on whether the listed buildings were of such importance as to outweigh the case for redevelopment, and whether the proposed new building [by Stirling] was of sufficient quality to override the case for conservation'.[24] The secretary of state ruled in favour of the Stirling scheme and the demolition of the best of the Victorian buildings. SAVE alongside other amenity bodies and English Heritage fought the proposal. From the very beginning they had offered an alternative scheme by Terry Farrell that well demonstrated the new urbanism by following the grain of the city and was particularly mindful of pedestrian space. SAVE took legal action, losing in the High Court, winning in the Court of Appeal, but finally losing in the House of Lords with costs against them of £90,000.* The Stirling building, completed in 1997, does neither the architect nor the site justice, but is now itself listed and a showy part of the City landscape. The saga is an example of baleful political interference with planning rules. It would foreshadow many more campaigns down to our own time where developers used big names to push through their schemes for good or ill.

---

* Binney 2005 p. 222. This was the most dangerous moment in SAVE's history and disaster was only averted by frantic fundraising.

The Thirties Society and the Twentieth Century Society

Marcus Binney became a founding father of the Thirties Society in 1979, which filled an important gap in conservation. The catalyst had been an unsuccessful attempt to save Sir Edwin Cooper's classical Lloyd's of London building from demolition in favour of the Richard Rogers high-tech design. In the end Cooper's portico was saved and Binney supported the Rogers scheme. The listing of twentieth-century buildings was in its infancy, and only a few pre-1939 buildings had been listed under the advice of Nikolaus Pevsner in 1970. His personal preference was for the pioneers of the modern movement, and he had ignored many interesting buildings including one that galvanised the newly formed society with far more emotional resonance than the Lloyd's building.

One style popular with the public was Art Deco, an excellent example of which was the Firestone Factory on the Great West Road with its Egyptian temple design. Bevis Hillier, the Thirties Society's first chairman, takes up the story: 'When Firestone decided to cease [tyre] production in Brentford, they sold the land for development. A call from the Department for the Environment to the developers [Trafalgar House PLC] alerted them that the minister, Michael Heseltine, was going to list the building on the Tuesday following the August Monday Bank Holiday; on Sunday bulldozers were sent in to demolish the façade. It was a calculated act of philistinism.'[25] Simon Jenkins wrote in the first *Thirties Society Journal*: 'I can recall few buildings of the last decade whose destruction has produced more spontaneous outrage from laymen'.[26] This gave helpful publicity to the nascent society. Michael Heseltine, enraged by the Firestone demolition, brought forward the massively enhanced listing programme.

One of the merits of the Thirties Society from its inception was its pluralism; it showed interest in the full range of styles, from classical and neo-Tudor to Art Deco and modernism. As the scope of the society's work widened it was decided to rename it the Twentieth Century Society, and as such it went on to create a sympathetic climate of opinion for post-war buildings.[*] The society was successful in campaigning, SAVE-style, to prevent the wholesale destruction of Giles Gilbert Scott's famous red telephone kiosks, later raising the alarm about the loss of outdoor swimming pools with the report *Farewell My Lido* in 1991.

If the interwar buildings now felt more secure there remained the problem of extending listing to post-war. The 1939 cut-off for listed buildings was becoming a problem, and the society pressed for action. The matter was brought into focus during the 1980s when three important mid-century buildings were threatened with demolition or alteration: Giles Gilbert Scott's Bankside Power Station (now Tate Modern), the National Union of Mineworkers building on Euston Road and Albert Richardson's 1958 masterpiece, Bracken House, on Cannon Street. (Scotland had a more flexible thirty-year moving dateline which offered a useful precedent.) Bracken House became the first test case and was duly listed in 1988, triggering the change to the system. But as Elain Harwood noted: 'after the positive outcome for Bracken House, the next stage of post-war listing […] came as a set-back. After soliciting suggestions from amenity societies and readers of the *Sunday Times*, English Heritage proposed 70 buildings from the early 1950s. The government had – and still has – the final say on listing, and it accepted only 18 of these recommendations.'[†] The press often chose to pillory post-war listing, but English Heritage took care to manage the presentation of each new tranche of listing proposals, and the process coincided with a generational change during the 1990s towards admiration of recently despised modern buildings of the 1950s and 1960s.[‡]

---

[*] The name change was in 1992. The strapline was always 'to protect buildings after 1914'.

[†] Ministers still frequently refuse recommendations on the basis of their own inexpert personal judgement. Harwood 2015, p. 11.

[‡] The Twentieth Century Society had a conspicuous success when the spectacular, threatened, but still fully functioning 1969 Preston bus station was listed and saved.

One recommendation that was especially controversial was the listing of the monumental Park Hill Flats in Sheffield of 1957–61 (whose subsequent complex restoration project became the subject of a television programme made with the support of English Heritage).* This need for protection was in the context of the demolition taking place all over Britain of shoddy post-war housing – the final backlash. The largest demolitions were the Le Corbusian Hulme Crescents in Manchester, and towers of Red Road in Glasgow, where the problem of non-functioning lifts, vandalism, and cracks had multiplied. As one architect commented: 'what we did not realise when we were building things of this nature is that they involved very high maintenance costs. And that cost was impossible for the local authority to deal with'.[27]

The tide of conservation was already turning by the 1980s. According to one historic buildings inspector, Derek Sherborn, comprehensive listing and ministerial resolve was at the heart of the change. He recalled the worst days of the 1970s when, according to him, at one point there were only four people listing the whole of England and Wales.[28] In Sherborn's opinion, 'of the political parties, far more Labour ministers actively supported preservation, but of all the ministers one really great contribution came from Michael Heseltine. Duncan Sandys was useful because he invented the idea of the Conservation Areas in the act of 1967 and found the Civic Trust. But the Conservation Area concept had to be given legislative teeth'. An important stepping stone was the formation of the Department for the Environment in 1970, a ministry that had the power and money to act with the right minister at the helm. In Sherborn's view, 'It was Michael Heseltine who ordered that means be found to produce a comprehensive list of buildings of special interest, and he pioneered the foundation of English Heritage

---

* As Andrew Saint put it: 'What is to be done with this powerful, problematic yet memorable and by no means unloved housing estate, lowering from his hilltop over Sheffield?'

as an organisation of experts standing outside the normal civil service.'[29] The heroic period of conservation was over, the systems and organisations were in place by the 1980s and from now on it would be a case of holding the line against governments of both stripes who viewed listing as an obstacle to the planning system, and therefore economic prosperity.

CHAPTER 8

Rescuing a City: York

*It is fair to say that conservation took root in York
just in time to preserve the essential qualities of
the ancient city – and that it arrived in most other
English cities just too late.*

PETER ADDYMAN[1]

In the mid-1960s the architectural pundit Ian Nairn made a TV programme about York. He described it as a dying city in which the car had taken over. The presenter looked down from the heights of Clifford's Tower and was appalled – everywhere he saw parked cars. He called the city 'a dismal failure' and recent developments 'dreadful' and 'unforgiveable'. York was indeed depopulating within its mediaeval city walls. Nairn wondered whether the new university could possibly make any difference. And yet within a few years the city was to become the poster boy for the conservation movement, and Pevsner was able to write: 'York provides England's prime example of the economic benefits of preserving the historic fabric and the aesthetic benefits of positive conservation.'[2] What happened?

Nairn was right. York had recently been cursed with poor-quality building developments, and traffic was paralysing the city centre. Moreover, a destructive inner ring road was planned.* But if Nairn had spent longer in the city, he would

---

* York had been here before. Between 1825 and 1835 there was a move to demolish the city walls and bars (gates) and in an early example of popular preservation, the residents prevented their destruction. The York Footpath Association was founded in 1827 and acted as a catalyst for the restoration of the walls.

have become aware of its most priceless intangible asset – the Civic Trust, the volunteer body which more than any other was to steer York through the pressures of the post-war era, utterly determined to protect and develop the city in a sensitive manner. Indeed, York was to lead the way by its exemplary civic engagement and by embracing the most significant legislation to protect towns and cities: the designation of Conservation Areas. Across the land, Civic Trusts would turn out to be the local volunteer body that would ensure Conservation Areas would be respected, and would save what was left of Britain's best urban landscapes. Dovetailing into these advances in historic building protection, York became the subject of a far-reaching report by Lord Esher, a key document that tells us much about changing attitudes.

Nowhere can the powerful effect of this new interest in the townscape be seen to better advantage than York. No ancient cathedral city has a richer history, with so many layers: Roman, Viking, Norman, Medieval, Georgian and Industrial. The city was transformed in 1839 by the opening of its first railway line and by the end of the century effectively became a railway town, with 6,000 employees. The other transformative industry, confectionery, was the result of the Quaker presence, with the establishment of the Terry and Rowntree factories in the mid-century, which became the main employer in the city. The Rowntree family exercised an especially benign influence, promoting social justice and good housing for their workforce. Philanthropy was to run through the family and its firm, and many of the key figures in the influential York Civic Trust were senior employees.[*]

York was bombed in World War II, with 9,500 houses damaged. It was the target for a series of Baedeker raids that also affected Bath, Norwich and Canterbury. Post-war it still had the

---

[*] Joseph's son, Seebohm Rowntree, published his seminal *Poverty: A Study of Town Life* (1901). With a small group of volunteers he had spent a decade studying 11,560 families.

ambience of a county town with a farmers' market for which 6,000 sheep and cattle were herded into the centre every week. By the early 1960s the city was visibly declining: the traffic made it awkward as an agricultural market, and its railway engineering works were becoming redundant. Much hope was placed on the new university opened on its fringes in 1963. But as one sceptical resident told an academic: 'You should know, as you start this institution, that York has seen off the Romans, the Anglo-Saxons, the Vikings, the Normans and the Roundheads, and if you think your university will make the slightest difference to the place, forget it now!'[3] It was only the support of the Civic Trust and its chairman, J. B. Morrell (who presented the site), that made it happen. Their report quoted a remark made about Dijon (with which York was later twinned): 'mainly because it has a university, Dijon is a young and gay town; and yet kept the atmosphere of mediaeval times.'[4]

York was among the first cities* in Britain to establish a Civic Trust, as early as 1946. The idea was so effective that it was taken up by Duncan Sandys who in 1957 created a national Civic Trust, a federation of local societies dedicated to the protection of historic buildings and their settings. Within three years 300 such societies had been registered, a number which doubled by 1967. York offered an excellent model. As Alan Powers has written: 'the Civic Trust encouraged the idea that modern architecture and conservation were not in opposition to one another and helped to foster a new strain of sensitive modern practice.'[5] From the time of their inception Civic Trusts were to become the vital counterpart of the Conservation Area. They still hold local government to account today, with a

* Birmingham had a civic society as early as 1918 but its aims were more about community progress than conservation. The Bath Preservation Trust was founded in 1934. Three years later the Bath Corporation Act initiated the creation of a list of protected buildings to be drawn up in conjunction with the BPT, making it effectively the first of the Civic Trusts.

membership that act as the eyes and ears of what is happening on the ground.

Of all Civic Trusts, York's has exercised the most beneficial influence, describing its purpose as 'everything which might profit the history, beauty, reputation and the happiness of York'.* Its achievements have thus gone far beyond protecting the built environment, even to acquiring works for the York Art Gallery. The Trust would accept temporary ownership of buildings at risk until a better use was available and would encourage good design and craftsmanship in new buildings. In this it was only partially successful, since very little of quality was built outside the university, one exception being the foyer of the Theatre Royal by Patrick Gwynne.

The founding members of the York Civic Trust had a Victorian sense of obligation towards their city, underpinned by philanthropy and social purpose. The leading figure in the story is J. B. Morrell, perhaps the outstanding regional civic figure in post-war Britain. He came under the benevolent influence of Joseph Rowntree while working at the factory and maintained a fierce belief in the enrichment of the lives of citizens through art and heritage. During the war Morrell had written his own utopian blueprint for York's future, *City of our Dreams* (1940, expanded 1955). Besides serving as the first chairman of York Civic Trust, he was forty years a city councillor and twice Liberal Lord Mayor of York. Morrell established the Castle Museum, in a beautiful building by John Carr of York (a former women's prison), and he made an outstanding contribution to the development of the City Art Gallery. He and his brother Cuthbert established their own trust to save many local historic buildings from demolition, eventually becoming the York Conservation Trust (which today

---

* Pevsner believed that the Civic Trust 'cannot be underestimated with regard to its work for the conservation of York's historic buildings and townscape'. Pevsner and Neave, p. 123.

owns over 100 mainly listed buildings). He declined the offers of a seat in parliament and of a knighthood.*

The first task of the York Civic Trust was to restore the city's famous medieval street, the Shambles, one of the earliest local authority-led urban conservation schemes in the country. This was followed by the restoration of the medieval walls and the four 'bars' (city gates). One of the Trust's most lasting legacies was the purchase and restoration of Fairfax House which, with its superb interiors by John Carr, has a fair claim to be the finest provincial eighteenth-century town house in England. The building was in a forlorn state, having served as a cinema and a dance hall. The Trust brought in a local architect, Francis Johnson, to restore the fabric and filled the rooms with treasures (including the Terry Collection of eighteenth-century furniture), turning it into one of the most rewarding sights in the city.

With such a well-established, active and forward-looking Civic Trust, it seemed natural that York would be offered the chance to be one of the first to adopt Conservation Areas, but the city council were against it. These independent Yorkshiremen did not want to be told what to do by an outsider. Besides, many of the ideas embedded in the concept of Conservation Areas had in fact already been anticipated in a local 1964 report by a remarkable York planning officer, June Hargreaves (and were later adopted within the Civic Amenities Act). As a result, York Council had set up its own town scheme to preserve the ancient walled city, so it did not welcome the idea of a Conservation Area and its attendant costs. Once again it was the support of the Civic Trust that swung the argument. In parallel with this overdue legislation came the Crossman Churchill College Report. Although not directly connected, the two initiatives informed each other and should be read as part of the new climate of conservation. Lord

* He was notably assisted by the scholarly Dean of York, Eric Milner White, who came from King's College, Cambridge, in 1941. Few individuals were to have such benign effect on their adopted city and his studio ceramic collection remains a highlight of the art gallery.

Esher, a grandee who happened to be a modernist architect, was appointed to write the York report.

Lionel Esher is better remembered today for his writings than his architecture. He authored one of the earliest dirges about the state of the countryside, *Landscape in Distress* (1965), while his book *A Broken Wave: the Rebuilding of England 1940–1980* is a classic work on post-war architecture and reveals his ambivalence about his own profession. He wrote his York report anticipating the arrival of Conservation Areas.

Esher described how he came to accept the project:

> two years earlier, impressed by the public outcry at the damage done to the heart of Worcester redevelopment, (Richard) Crossman decided to commission some studies of major historic city centres as exemplars of how such places might survive the stresses of the twentieth century. After some argument with local authorities, not all of which wished to be guinea pigs, I was offered the choice of Chester, Bath or York. York, I was told, would be the most worthwhile but difficult, as the City Council was hostile. So I chose it, on the understanding that this would not be just another exercise on paper, but a live demonstration with government money (£2 million were spoken of) of conservation and renewal in action.[6]

On arrival in York Esher was greeted in a blunt fashion by Bill Burke, the Labour leader of the council: 'we don't like consultants here'.

The Conservative leader, who doubled as the city engineer and planning officer, was no better. He felt the appointment was a criticism of his department and therefore maintained a polite obstructiveness. Apart from anything else York had a more urgent problem to deal with; the Minster's foundations were sinking with the very real possibility of collapse. Esher, however, gained support where it mattered and, as John Shannon, chairman of the Civic Trust, who came to his rescue, later reflected, 'not only was the report to become a blueprint for the development of the city in future years, but there is little doubt that it was the main factor in attracting government grants amounting to many millions of pounds over the years'.[7] The council came to heel. Esher estimated the net cost for all his recommendations would be £2.1 million, with an expectation of a 50 per cent government grant.

Esher was careful to salute the excellent work already done in York with the refurbishment of the Assembly Rooms and the reconstruction of the Shambles. He extolled the importance of the learned and voluntary societies: the Yorkshire Philosophical Society, the Yorkshire Architectural and York Archaeological Society, the York Georgian Society and, 'widely recognised as the outstanding body of its kind in the country', York's Civic Trust. Notwithstanding the Minster, Esher recognised that 'the visual wealth of York is in the secular city, one of the richest and most complex townscapes in the world. It is the most mediaeval in feeling of all English cities, city of streets rather than spaces, and its streets are narrow'.[8] The architect in Esher was keen to make clear that 'a city is not a work of art' and did not want it to be a stage set. He wanted the commercial heart to remain alive, to eliminate decay, congestion and noise, while retaining the best buildings to be economically self-conserving. The buzzword was 'liveability'.

Esher realised that by far the greatest obstacle to rehabilitation of the historic core of York was its traffic. He was an early advocate of exclusion zones and the development of attractive public transport. He rejected the plan for a four-lane carriageway beside the city walls and believed that 'an inner ring road is unsuitable for *through* traffic', advocating a loop on the city circumference which is what eventually was built.

Esher was keen to stress that 'conservation is and always has been a part of planning'.[9] He divided the walled city into eight sectors, each considered with its own separate identity. Keen not to compromise York's success as a shopping town, Esher advocated four multi-storey car parks within less than five minutes walking time from the centre. The Conservation

Area was expected to cover more than half the area of the walled city, with a requirement for funding to protect all buildings that contributed to the townscape value. He recognised that small shops and boutiques serve as some of the most effective guardians of character, while big stores and offices can be agents of destruction. Esher recommended an 'inner enclave' should be restricted to pedestrians and paved, closed to vehicles between 10 a.m. to 5 p.m. and this was adopted in 1971. He also advocated the introduction of a residents' parking permit scheme.

Another of Esher's recommendations was to secure the skyline, so that buildings should be erected with a roofline slightly lower than that of the Minster.[10] In this he was at one with Bill Burke, who had already declared: 'over my dead body will we have bloody tower blocks in York.'[11] Anybody who has ever approached the city from the north will remember the prospect from Brandsby of the Vale of York laid out like a Dutch landscape painting. From that distance only the Minster tower pierced the horizon. That remains almost true today, although the sightlines remain under constant threat. One modern hotel on the south side of the Ouse has been permitted to break the skyline – when, as with the Hilton in London, this was felt necessary for investment.[12]

One of the main objectives of the Esher report was to address the depopulation of the city centre within the walls, which had fallen as low as 3,498 by 1961. The plan was to raise this figure to 6,000 by regenerating derelict buildings and empty sites. And fortunately, the university needed central housing. It was pointed out that it cost £1,440 to house a student in a new building but only £460 in a converted building in Micklegate. As an architect Esher wanted to see more new development in the centre, but not all his recommendations were accepted; the city only went halfway with him on the destruction of Aldwark, described as a 'derelict hinterland [...] in need of comprehensive development'. One very successful housing development that Esher did initiate was within the walls in Bedern, formerly an area of poor workshops and lean-tos, around the magnificent fourteenth-century Bedern Hall which is still the heart of the community.

When the time came for the launch of his report, Esher travelled up to York by train with his assistant Harry Teggin. Esher mentioned to Teggin that he was not going to plug the document, which he felt should speak for itself. Teggin stepped off the train at Grantham, refusing to go any further until Esher promised to put his weight behind the report. It was only as the guard's whistle blew that Esher agreed, and Teggin resumed his seat. Unveiling the report had in fact stirred so much interest in York that the *Northern Echo* broke the press embargo to be the first with the story. The meeting was a triumphant success and Esher received a standing ovation.

The outcome of *York: A Study in Conservation* (1968) was that the city had changed its destiny. It passed from an identity associated with manufacturing, administration and agriculture to one more devoted to tourism. This had not been Esher's central intention, which was 'to improve the living conditions and reanimate the city through the exclusion of unnecessary traffic'. In today's terms the report has some shortcomings: it does not set the city in either a national or international context and it offers no understanding of the city's importance as an archaeological site (which would turn out to be transformative). Esher recommended the establishment of a local Conservation Section – whose first task would be to define the boundaries of the Conservation Areas – to maintain the level of preservation.[*] Esher's report remains a hugely significant document of the time and of all the Crossman Reports, it is the one most frequently referenced. It certainly prevented the worst excesses of heritage destruction, particularly the inner ring road. With its belief that economic value could be derived from conservation, the report has served the city well. Peter Addyman was correct in saying: 'It is fair to say that conservation took root in York just in time to

---

[*] The Esher Report has been criticised for being too sanguine in believing that conservation, once established, would look after itself. He did, however, warn readers of the ongoing costs – see Chapters Nine and Ten.

preserve the essential qualities of the ancient city – and that it arrived in most other English cities just too late.'[13]

When Ian Nairn issued his jeremiad against York in the mid-1960s, he looked down from Clifford's Tower and despaired. While almost everything in the city has improved in the intervening years, the huge open-air car park that drew Nairn's spleen is still there and remains the subject of debate. The old castle – it was only named Clifford's Tower later – rises at one end of a stately composition of buildings by the great eighteenth-century architect John Carr of York, and it includes his former women's prison, which now serves as the Castle Museum, while his noble assize building is happily still serving its original purpose. This is the grandest piece of eighteenth-century planning in York. Since the time of the Esher Report there have been plans to replace the car park, of which the least costly option has been to build a commercial shopping development. The Civic Trust opposed this solution, which was refused planning permission by the secretary of state in 2003. A more sensitive plan to extend the museum envisages the area as a powerful public space, somewhat in the manner of Somerset House. All that is needed is £30 million.

Like everywhere else in Britain, York needs more housing, but it has the additional problem of low-lying estates built on the floodplain of the Ouse and the Foss; climate change is wreaking havoc with York's housing. Most of the new homes built in York have been of poor quality – with one notable exception. The Joseph Rowntree Housing Trust, which inherited responsibility for the ideal village of New Earswick, decided to develop what they describe as a twenty-first-century version. The result is Derwenthorpe, a new village two miles east of York. It spreads 540 well-designed homes over a 22-hectare site, a mixed and environmentally sustainable community with the social housing 'pepper-potted' around the estate. Despite virtuous intentions and excellent design, twelve years of objections and protests had to be faced down before the Rowntree Trust could start building. Derwenthorpe has been a success and its residents love it.

What is the Civic Trust concerned about today? With a city centre so small and full of pedestrians, outdoor seating and café culture has become a problem for mobility and traffic congestion continues to blight the centre. To that extent, the city is a victim of its own success, attracting 7 million visitors a year (although only 2 million of these ever spend time in a museum).

The ratio of office to residential conversions is a problem, and the city needs more economic drivers. The largest development on the horizon is the York Central Scheme, forty-five hectares of brown field land on former railway sidings. The development is planned to include 2,500 homes and a major expansion of the National Railway Museum. However, the quality of the design is not inspiring and there is a problem of access to the rest of the city.

York does not attract expensive developments. The Civic Trust commented that the National Planning Policy Framework (NPPF) means council planners are limited in their ability to insist on anything more than a 'just about acceptable' standard of architectural design. Worse is the ability of developers to change their design: new development continually strives to be higher and with greater massing than that of York's historic streetscape and Conservation Areas.

Their 2018–19 report states that 'long and earnest debate about appropriate heights and the impact on views will amount to nothing when the developer knows that an argument about changed economic circumstances will allow a restriction to be (literally) lifted.'[14] The report is particularly critical of the Hungate development, in which the developers have returned to the city's planners seeking greater height and density than was approved. As the report ruefully concludes, 'for those with sufficient chutzpah, such compliance is optional'.[15]

In 2016 Ron Cooke, a former vice-chancellor of York University and professor of geography,* published a report for the Civic Trust on the state of York's built environment. Cooke

* And former chair of York Civic Trust.

examined several streets in detail, their vistas, street furniture, and the quality of conservation. He compared the city favourably against Chester but set it unfavourably against that show-city Bruges: 'the key contrast with York is that in Bruges appearance seems to be a *higher priority* and, above all it has been *continuously sustained* by investment in both personnel and infrastructure'. He commented that the Department for Conservation and Heritage in Bruges has twenty staff but York cannot make any such claims.* Despite this, compared to most English cities, the historic centre of York is in good condition, with many streets such as Walmgate and Fossgate much improved since Pevsner first described them in the 1960s. The Minster still dominates the city from most vantage points.† Today York has a collection of over 1,500 listed buildings, thirty-five Conservation Areas, and retains its medieval ground plan. With a such powerful and vocal Civic Trust, the Conservation Areas are well protected.

* While perhaps not of a similar level as Bruges, the University of York Department of Archaeology has come on in leaps and bounds on this front, with numerous MA programmes for historic building conservation and cultural heritage management in particular.
† Sometimes views are lost – the Fishergate Travelodge inexcusably blocks the view of the Minster from the southern approaches.

CHAPTER 9

The Sack of Bath

If there are such things as national treasures, Bath
is one of them [...] At the present rate every month is vital,
and in eighteen months it may be too late.[1]

KENNETH CLARK WRITING IN 1972

It is an astonishing fact that the Georgian terraces of Bath were still being demolished as recently as the 1970s. The city offers the starkest example of conservationists going to war against the local council, planners and architects, whose declared intention was to keep historic Bath 'a living city'. The intemperate disagreements spilled into the national press, and only with the publication of that powerful polemic, Adam Fergusson's *The Sack of Bath* (1973), was the destruction finally halted. This is the most striking story of a conservation backlash in a historic city since World War II.

Until the 1950s the world held few more perfectly preserved eighteenth-century cities than Bath. Built with a harmony of style and grace, it was the product of great architects working on a scenic landscape. And all on top of a Roman city that had grown around a temple and bathing complex, where the Roman Great Bath and sacred spring are still standing. As the architect Peter Smithson put it, 'Bath is Rome in England: on Seven Hills, founded by the Romans, and re-founded in conscious imitation of Roman civic virtues in the eighteenth century.'[2] Bath's peculiar social organisation as a seasonal spa city meant that it had an unusually large number of gentlemen's houses. But Bath was about more than grand houses, it also had superb early nineteenth-century artisan housing, and it was these streets that were to be the battleground where the developers did their worst. The city's Grade III buildings[*] and the many hundreds more that were unlisted received no mercy from Bath City Council, and several Grade II buildings went at the same time.

Bath was always the spa city *par excellence* of Britain. The fashionable season that burgeoned in the early eighteenth century encouraged the beautification of Bath, but there were geographical and geological factors as well. The city lies in a loop of the River Avon where enclosing hills both restrict its development and provide the picturesque setting for its escalating crescents and terraces. They also served as the quarry for some of the most beautiful building stone in England, a pale cream oolitic limestone which weathers to a beautiful honey colour, lending an astonishing homogeneity to the city and reinforcing the consistency of the Georgian architectural vision.

John Wood the Elder (1704–54), the architect responsible for so much of the city's distinction, settled in Bath in 1727, the same year that his son, who would carry on his work, was born. They were both architects of powerful originality. Wood senior had a vision of a great Roman town, but one that paid homage to a mythical local Druidic antiquity. The city fathers were initially sceptical about his plans and pronounced them 'chimerical' until they could see a source of profit in them.[†] Wood began building speculative terraces in 1740 with Queen Square but it was not for another fourteen years that he undertook his greatest achievement, the Circus, where he took inspiration from the Roman colosseum and Druid stone circles. The Assembly Rooms, where society came together for public dances, were built 1769–71. Many architects were to contribute to the beauty and development of the city, and although the style of buildings developed from Wood's authoritative

* A now defunct grade.
† The River Avon was made navigable to Bath during the period, and as the century wore on journey times from London dramatically decreased, from thirty-six hours in the mid-century to ten hours by 1790. Forsyth, p. 31.

Palladian manner into something lighter, they all worked within a Georgian aesthetic, subordinating individual expression to the unity of the whole. As James Lees-Milne pointed out, 'the extraordinary thing about Bath is its being a city of one period. Bath took shape literally within 100 years notwithstanding its extremely long history'.[3] Wood's son built the city's greatest astonishment in 1767–74, the Royal Crescent – like the Circus, the first of its kind.

Bath owes much of its character and growth to the assiduity of property developers, and yet it is one of the most coherent and beautifully planned cities in Europe. The land on the other side of the river was owned by the Pulteney family, and its development was assured once they obtained permission to build a bridge to a design by Robert Adam, completed in 1774. Much of artisan Bath was built across the river in the early nineteenth century. It is often pointed out that in Bath, the grand was not permitted to dominate the humble.

The collapse of the Bath Bank in 1793 was the first real check in the city's expansion and several builders went bankrupt. This and the French wars caused building activity to cease. During the nineteenth century the city lost much of its fashionable allure to Cheltenham and Malvern, which scooped the spa traffic. This protected Bath from ambitious Victorian rebuilding. There was an attempt to revive the spa, and the Empire Hotel stands as a memorial to this period. Although the city became a genteel retirement spot, it also had a modest commercial and industrial expansion, to which the surviving artisan terraces still bear witness; Milk Street and Corn Street, however, were demolished.

The Early Twentieth Century

Robert Atkinson was commissioned by Bath Corporation in 1915 to draw up an improvement scheme, an abortive attempt to revive visitor numbers. The aim was to compete with continental spas, providing facilities that would encourage visitors to stay for three weeks at a time. Atkinson was an eclectic architect best known today for his Art Deco cinemas, but for Bath he adopted a Roman Imperial style. Atkinson's centrepiece was a Forum for public outdoor performances, surrounded by civic palaces standing at the end of a broad boulevard that connected with a triumphal arch, leading to a new railway station that would bring tourists into the city centre. The monumental size of the buildings would have been completely out of scale with eighteenth-century Bath. Moreover, the plan had a classical symmetry unsympathetic to the elliptical contours of the Georgian city.

Of great significance, the Bath Preservation Trust (BPT) was founded in 1934, and it would be the main champion of Georgian Bath in its post-war battles with the local government. Three years later – the same year that the Georgian Group was formed – the Bath Corporation Act provided for a list of 1,251 protected buildings to be drawn up in conjunction with the BPT, usually hailed as the first introduction of a systematic conservation in Britain. This was an important milestone in the protection of the nation's historic urban fabric.

However, Bath suffered the attentions of the Luftwaffe in one of the Baedeker raids in April 1942.[*] There was bomb damage mainly in the south of the city: 329 buildings were destroyed and a further 732 demolished. The city engineer estimated that over 19,000 buildings had some degree of damage. The main loss was the Assembly Rooms, which had just been restored. The manner of the rebuilding would be argued over for twelve years – an early indication of the differences to come.

* The so-called Baedeker raids were revenge for the British bombing of Lübeck.

Post-1945

To advise on the reconstruction of the city, Sir Patrick Abercrombie, Britain's planner-in-chief, was brought in by the corporation.[*] His *A Plan for Bath* faced the same problem that every planner has to come to terms with in Bath, that of its enclosed topography. With his passion for zoning, Abercrombie proposed dividing the city into ten precincts according to their function, with connecting ring roads that would have caused the demolition of what he referred to as 'poor housing' and 'disposable Georgian utility buildings'. He was actually impressed by the quality of such buildings, which he thought should be preserved 'unless [they] must give way to essential major planning improvements'.[4] At the time there was a general belief that the days of large houses, like those in the Royal Crescent, were numbered. One of Abercrombie's boldest suggestions was therefore to repurpose the middle of the Royal Crescent as the centre of civic administration, attaching a vast building to the rear as a new council chamber. Very little of Abercrombie's plan was carried out, and it would be left to Sir Colin Buchanan to take up the challenge a decade later.

Despite Abercrombie's indication that such buildings should be preserved, it was the intention of the Bath Corporation in 1960 to sweep away within a decade over 2,000 Georgian houses, mostly from the early nineteenth century. Five hundred had already been demolished since 1951.[5] If the corporation had little respect for the architecture beyond the tourist centre, they did initiate the Bath Terraces Scheme in 1955 to restore the more weathered fronts, beginning with the Circus. Much of the carving was replaced and the original glazing bars reinstated – an interesting decision, and surely the right one. One of its most commendable later initiatives was the recarving of street names by Peter McLennan in the eighteenth-century manner. The

---

[*] Abercrombie had been involved with planning in Bath since 1930 and was consulted in 1935 over what became the 1937 Bath Corporation Act. His plan was published in 1945.

National Trust acquired land around the city to preserve woods and pastures on its edge.

More than anything else what the Bath story revealed was the inadequacy of government legislation in the face of a determined and philistine local council. This was despite a raft of new conservation law, starting with the Civic Amenities Act (1967), by which a townscape could receive for the first time certain protections by being designated a Conservation Area.[*] The following year six Conservation Areas were created in Bath.[†] Regardless of this, hundreds of buildings continued to be demolished every year.[‡] Richard Crossman, the Labour minister, came to Bath in May 1966 to make a speech in which he identified 'a Cold War' in cities like Bath between developers and preservationists. It was in Bath that he announced the selection of five cities where pilot studies would examine the best implementation of conservation policies: Bath, Chester, Chichester, King's Lynn (which soon dropped out) and York. Crossman, and his initiative, were to be pivotal in the conservation story – and in the preservation of these cities.

The continuous destruction of Bath terraces and housing became known as the Sack of Bath. It was not, as the name suggests, a sudden event, rather the cumulative effect of two decades of chipping away at the fabric of Bath, moving into the centre with new shopping precincts, and the proposals of the Buchanan Report. By the early 1960s the amenity societies and preservation groups were falling out with Bath Corporation.

---

[*] The Town and Country Planning Act (1968) overcame the difficulty of councils reluctant to enforce compulsory purchase orders by using building preservation notices. Demolitions were still lawful if the buildings were dangerous – they could be removed in the interest of health and safety, a loophole Bath City Council availed themselves of.

[†] Conservation Areas were variously extended since then and today cover 60 per cent of the city area.

[‡] About 1,000 Georgian buildings – including 350 that were listed – were demolished between 1950 and 1973. See Forsyth, p. 47.

At the time it seemed to the corporation that tourism would not be enough to sustain the local economy, and they wanted to promote economic growth. The battle was fought street by street and the results were often unsatisfactory to both sides – the preservationists won the battle for Beaufort Square, for example, but failed to preserve its entrance.

Bath Corporation were guilty of deliberately leaving properties empty so they would deteriorate to the point where they were unarguably disposable. Morford Street was a particularly sad case: first the glass was smashed, and eventually the roofs and ceilings fell in. Most of the street was replaced by modern housing, with the odd old building with a Venetian window here and there to remind us of its former elegance. Money of course was at the root of the problem. The corporation never had enough money to put its listed buildings into proper order and the tempting grants for new buildings were a much more attractive option. The city architect commented: 'if you want to keep Georgian artisans' houses, then you will have to find Georgian artisans to live in them'.[6] 'Must not preserve for preservation's sake' became the mantra. Some streets, such as sections of Bathwick Hill, had Georgian on one side and modern housing on the other. The problem was exacerbated by the poor quality of the new housing.

Another difficulty was finding an architectural style appropriate to the setting – something that still bedevils Bath. Some new terraces were well-intentioned and of architectural merit, such as Calton Gardens, but turned out to be unhappy in their situation. The same can be said of the Snow Hill housing estate built in 1954–61, its intrusive green copper roofs visible across the city (replacing eighteenth-century streets and buildings) being described as a Scandinavian interpretation of Bath's classicism.[7] There were even some modest tower blocks, typified by Berkeley House (1955–7), compared by Adam Fergusson to a pop group in the middle of a symphony orchestra – although the estate was and remains popular with its residents.

There were several fine modern architects who worked in Bath during the period – notably Peter and Alison Smithson, whose innovative work at the university does not offend the old city. But other architects who should have known better created new developments that were badly sited or unsympathetic to their neighbours. Frederick Gibberd's Bath Technical College (1956–65) is a good building in an unsuitable position. Hugh Casson, architect, friend of the royal family, and the darling of the Establishment, was brought in by Bath City Council to reassure conservationists as a 'safe' modern architect. His interventions, however, were not admired, and as a man used to praise, he became very tetchy over criticism of his well-paid consultancy.* He trumpeted the 'develop or decline' municipal catchphrase. Indeed, Casson was the consultant on one of the most inappropriate buildings of all, the intrusive sport centre (1972), designed by the city architect's department in concrete and reconstituted stone.

Perhaps the gravest modern accretion was the development of the Beaufort (Hilton) Hotel, which still dominates the skyline above Pulteney Bridge. Part of the problem is that Bath stone, so suited to the classical style, is less suitable for contemporary buildings, where 'it serves principally to emphasise their functional nature and causes them to stand out aggressively from their surroundings.'[8] The development that more than any other turned the people of Bath against modern architecture was the SouthGate shopping centre by the Owen Luder partnership (1969–72). The construction of this concrete precinct was preceded by the demolition of no less than ten acres of Georgian and Victorian Bath.† It was so unsatisfactory that it was itself demolished in 2007 to make way for the present neo-Georgian

---

* Both Casson and Gibberd were members of the Royal Fine Art
Commission, designed to protect places like Bath.

† Not all developers were bent on destruction. Older residents fondly
remember Charlie Ware, who evinced a passion for restoring Georgian
houses between parties that lasted several days and earned him the soubriquet
'Champagne Charlie'. There was other good news – in 1967 No. 1 Royal
Crescent was presented to the Bath Preservation Trust. It was to become a
popular tourist attraction, filled with Georgian furniture and works of art.

set of buildings, which raise all kinds of questions about an appropriate style for a modern shopping centre in Bath.* The most admired 1960s intervention is the beautiful Pulteney weir, a successful flood prevention scheme.

But by the late 1960s the Bath Preservation Trust was losing patience with the council, which was effectively ignoring them. The priority was to halt the demolition of all periods of architecture and to prevent the further spread of the brutalist style that the city's planners were perpetrating. The underlying message of the BPT was the insistence that it was not significantly more expensive to adapt and restore than to demolish and start again. Preservation was half the battle; the other half was to ensure that infilling, replacement and surroundings were sympathetic. Adam Fergusson, who alerted the public to what was happening in Bath, ruefully observed that:

The destroyers work from nine to five every day sitting in comfortable offices, figures and plans and projects at their finger-tips or simply in their minds, and they get paid for what they do. The preservers have to make their own time, usually in the evenings or at weekends, when they would prefer to be with their families, acquiring what facts and figures and plans they can get hold of [...] and they have to raise the money for it themselves, organize petitions, and pay for the legal and architectural expenses out of their own pockets.[9]

This is as true today as it was then.

* Designed by Chapman Taylor, the new shopping centre opened in 2009 and won a Georgian Group award. The view in Bath is that it is better than the buildings that preceded it, but is it good enough? The materials are an uneasy combination of real stone with reconstituted stone, and the fenestration is wrong. The street furniture is not of a high enough quality and the lighting, while attempting to be 'Bath', is also wrong. Access to the railway station is not architecturally acknowledged – altogether, the shopping centre is troubling.

The Buchanan Report

Around the same time that the city council was appointing Hugh Casson as a consultant, they had received a report from Abercrombie's successor as Britain's planner-in-chief, Colin Buchanan: *Bath – A Planning and Transport Study* (1965).[*] As the name suggests, this was primarily concerned with traffic circulation, which always going to be problematic given the tension between vehicular flow and heritage impact. But Buchanan was evidently provided with a misleading brief, with maps that did not include all the Grade II and none of the Grade III buildings and left out a part of the Conservation Area.

The Buchanan Report initially had a favourable reaction but opposition gradually mounted, particularly to his opinion that the lesser Georgian buildings were unimportant. Certain parts of the Buchanan plan were achieved, as the obtrusive Beaufort (Hilton) Hotel witnesses. But by far the most contentious recommendation, and the one for which the report is best remembered, was his proposed tunnel to solve the east–west traffic problem through the city. Buchanan's tunnel was to start on Walcot Street, and burrow under the Paragon and Gay Street just below the Circus to emerge on the Bristol Road. Demolitions at the Walcot Road entrance began in 1970. By September James Lees-Milne, a leading member of the BPT, who worked from the library of William Beckford's old house in Lansdown Crescent, was able to write a letter of seething sarcasm to *The Times*:

> your readers may be interested to learn that we are getting on quite nicely with the demolition of the centre of Bath. This year alone we have swept away several acres between Lansdown Road

* This report was followed and extended for a wider audience as one of Richard Crossman's four city conservation studies, *Bath: A Study in Conservation* in 1968. The report stated that Bath contained 1786 Grade I and II buildings and 1,032 Grade III buildings – compared with Edinburgh, 2,998 and 473 respectively, and Oxford, 660 and 310.

and the Circus. The whole southern end of Walcot Street [...] has already gone. We are just beginning on Northgate Street, and it only knocked down two or three houses in Broad Street this month. But [Bath's] New Bond Street's turn is imminent. All the houses are (or were) Georgian, every one.[10]

The following year Lees-Milne, in a calmer frame of mind, wrote in his diary:

I spent this afternoon with members of the Bath Preservation Trust being shown on the spot exactly where the proposed tunnel will go and which buildings will have to be sacrificed. It is extremely difficult to make up one's mind whether all this tremendous work will be worth the effort and damage. Because where old buildings will be spared their proximity to the new through-road will render them uninhabitable. Thus, the terraces on London Road will have a road on both sides of them instead of one side as at present. I was horrified by the poor condition of the houses at the back from where one can see the roofs all tumbling in.[11]

Buchanan's proposal was described as 'a spear thrust in the city's side'. It was not so much the tunnel that was the problem as the system of approach roads and roundabouts, with their effect on the civic environment.[12] Surprisingly, Bath Civic Trust approved the tunnel scheme, making a bizarre reference to 'Victorian twilight areas'. Bath Corporation was split along party lines: the Labour minority opposed the scheme on social and financial grounds and called for a ring road instead. It eventually overturned the scheme, stating that it had not appreciated the extent of the demolition, nor the collateral damage at the tunnel terminals.

After the problem of traffic, Buchanan was most concerned with finding new uses for historic buildings: 'There is insufficient demand for accommodation (especially on the upper floors) to encourage conversion and rehabilitation. Developers therefore have not been encouraged to do such work. This general unsuitability for present day use and the lack of a profit motive to encourage developers or others to adapt premises for suitable uses, leads to property lying vacant and then to physical decay.'[13] Here the university was seen to offer a partial solution with the need for student lodgings.

Bath in Extremis 1972/3

Matters came to a head in 1972. Adam Fergusson wrote a passionate article in *The Times* Saturday Review in April quoting the city clerk who had asked whether Bath was 'a city for living in or a Georgian mausoleum?'[14] While commending Bath's beauty, Fergusson also took a well-aimed swipe at Hugh Casson, who defended himself in *The Times* a few days later: 'No one expects a lover to be fair', he said, mistaking the lover in question for James Lees-Milne. Casson continued: 'But when all is said (so much) and done (so little) we returned to the fact that the problems of Bath are not so much architectural as economic, social, moral and political.'[15] Lees-Milne decided to enter the fray with a letter of his own, picking up on many of the points Casson had made: 'the historic centres of Rome and Paris have not yet been wrecked. Believe me the inhabitants have the equivalent of their supermarkets, but the contrivers of these places are obliged by law to adapt and subordinate them to the ancient palaces and monuments'.[16] On the subject of car parks, Lees-Milne commented: 'If architects today are incapable of designing decent-looking ones why not put them underground?'[17]

No one was more alarmed by this hardening of views than Colin Buchanan, who wrote to *The Times* in June 1972: 'Have attitudes to comprehensive development changed? If so with what justification and with what results? [...] No one questioned those areas at the time. But now there seems to be a hullabaloo if so much as a single house is threatened. What has happened?'[18] The answer was simple – the outside world and the architectural profession were becoming involved. Among others, Kenneth Clark, the recent presenter of *Civilisation* and perhaps the biggest gun of all, waded into the debate.* He told Eric James, the vice-chancellor of York University: 'Conservationists have cried "wolf" so often that one tends to think they are exaggerating, but in this case they are understating, because all the depredations [in 1972] have been done since I was there last year, and heaven knows what will have happened by next year'.[19] Clark was especially dismayed that the destruction of the streets in the name of 'welfare' was actually in the financial interests of developers. In May 1973 *The Architectural Review* ran an article, 'Bath in Extremis', which stated that 'every attack on a minor Georgian building is an attack on the architectural unity of Bath'.[20]

Kenneth Clark was happy to use his position in the House of Lords to raise the matter. He pointed a finger at Hugh Casson, for combining the role of paid consultant to Bath Corporation with membership of the Royal Fine Art Commission, which Clark saw as a clear conflict. Inevitably this brought an angry reaction from Casson and a sharp exchange of letters followed.[21] Clark thought the real villain, however, was Bath City Council, with its practice of allowing vacant houses to deteriorate in order to justify pulling them down. He wanted the problem to be taken out of their hands: 'Bath belongs to us all [...] it is a national possession if anything is, and I personally much resent spending huge sums of money on Italian pictures which we do not require and which, if we did not buy them, would not be destroyed but made accessible in some other gallery, when our own great buildings are being pulled down.'[22]

Rescue was on the way, and it came in several forms – first legislative. The 1972 Town and Country Planning Act (Amendment) gave some control over the demolition of unlisted

---

* Kenneth Clark became a vice-chairman of Bath Preservation Trust in 1970.

buildings in Conservation Areas* and provided restoration funds for 'outstanding' Conservation Areas such as those in Bath. The most powerful weapon, however, was the 1973 publication of Adam Fergusson's bombshell, *The Sack of Bath*, which broadcast nationally what was happening in the city. It is a slim book with a poem by John Betjeman:

> Goodbye to old Bath. We who loved you are sorry
> They've carted you off by developers' lorry.

But it was the before and after photographs that were to make the point most eloquently. The author bleakly stated that 'today artisan Bath is largely rubble' and the photographs showed what had replaced it. Fergusson later wrote of his book: '*The Sack of Bath* was the product of the collective cultural blindness of those who ran the city and of the simmering, bursting indignation of those who cared about it.'[23] Their anger was duly directed at the local authority and its advisors. The book's publication halted the redevelopment of the old city. Timothy Mowl believed that 'no single literary defense of an architectural heritage has ever been so immediately effective. At a stroke Bath became aware of the whole of its Georgian stock and of the need to guard the lesser excellences as jealously as the grand set pieces of crescents and terraces [...] Demolition of old buildings came to a virtual full stop'.[24] At the same time the government stepped in and offered money for the conservation of Bath on condition that all demolition should cease, pending an investigation by a number of groups, including the Department for the Environment, Bath Preservation Trust and the Georgian Group. The pendulum had decisively swung in favour of conservation. UNESCO added Bath as a cultural site to its World Heritage list in 1987 citing

---

* This would be extended with the Town and Country Amenities Act 1974, which gave demolition control to all unlisted buildings in Conservation Areas whereas previously it was applied selectively.

the Roman remains, eighteenth-century architecture and town planning, social setting, hot springs and the landscape setting.

Bath Today

The tragedy is that the twentieth century never managed to produce architecture worthy of Bath. For sure there was some fine work done in both Georgian style (the 1921 post office in New Bond Street) and in modernist style (Alison and Peter Smithson's university work) but in general the architecture was either an unimpressive watered-down modernism or bloodless neo-Georgian. The slightly kitsch Podium building (currently Waitrose) attempted a cheerful postmodernism, but this was designed without verve or originality. One of the problems for Bath today is the 'contemporary vernacular' so beloved by the recent city council; another is the use of reconstituted stone, which has no place in a city the quality of Bath. The twentieth century may not have been kind to Bath, but at the turn of the twenty-first century it received a superb piece of contemporary architecture, the New Royal Bath by Nicholas Grimshaw and Partners, working with the conservation architects Donald Insall Associates. The materials, colour, shape and height all blend beautifully on this most sensitive site.

The Stadium

There are currently many proposals for new architectural developments in Bath, the most debated being for a replacement rugby stadium on the riverbank, next to Robert Adam's Pulteney Bridge. In order to provide a subterranean parking concourse and flood-space, the ground itself will need to be raised and the stadium with it, compromising the picturesque views across the river to a residential quarter, which spreads upwards in a *rus in urbe* manner. The idea for the redevelopment of the rugby ground has been germinating for a decade and will no doubt attract UNESCO attention. If the people of Bath have a sporting passion it is for rugby, so the scheme is popular. The BPT's very measured response has been to focus concern over heritage impacts because of the height of the stands, and the associated visual impacts on key views out, over and across the World Heritage Site. They have emphasised that the upper levels must not be allowed to dominate the design, and should allow for some visual transparency of the stadium onto the hills beyond and the creation of sightlines and eye-catcher 'gaps' in the structure. The fear is that a monolithic structure would upset the pattern of the city.

The development pressure on a beautiful city like Bath is always intense. There are several schemes, often meritorious in themselves, which can lead to overdevelopment with buildings sitting high and tight on their sites such as Chivers House, with nine- and seven-storey student accommodation blocks near the Windsor Bridge. Another large housing development, the Western Riverside by Crest Nicholson, of rather dull housing blocks attempting to ape the terrace manner, caused a UNESCO delegation to descend anxiously on Bath. However, it is not all bad news on the river – there is also a proposal to turn a riverside car park into a public amenity and a green space.

Today the Bath Preservation Trust continues its excellent work and acts as a watchdog on all new developments. They are a volunteer organisation who own the Georgian house museum at No. 1 Royal Crescent, Beckford's Lansdown Tower, while their main office in Lady Huntingdon's Chapel also serves as the Museum of Bath Architecture. The Bath Heritage Watchdog is the other main heritage body in the city who also do good work. Through traffic is still the greatest problem – what is to be done? It may never be possible to eliminate it entirely with a bypass, but a congestion charge for non-residents (or everybody?) would go some way to lower traffic levels.

The underlying problem in Bath is the high value of land, which makes every plot a potential goldmine for redevelopment.

A previous Conservative council sold much land, and thereby lost control of it. Typically, developers make harmless-looking proposals, purchase land, then change their proposals with very frequent redrafting and they vary their plans, almost inevitably offering less public housing. The difference today is that while during the Sack of Bath matters were black and white – when a Georgian building was being torn down, it was obvious for all to see and to understand what was happening – today's situations are much more diffuse and the threats often to views and vistas, or to overall contexts. Moreover, few people can follow the complicated planning strategies, the mission creep effected by repeated variations to planning applications, or the context of unitary plans and government housing targets under which all these new developments must be carried out.

CHAPTER 10

The Archaeologists

When their world ended our story began.

MARY ROSE MUSEUM

In many respects the archaeologists were heritage pioneers in the post-war landscape with their demotic concern with public engagement and the embrace of 'ordinary people' history. They absorbed the lessons of anthropology and were pioneers in facing the conundrums posed by the ethics of heritage. They had much to contend with. The post-war expansion of Britain was especially damaging to fragile archaeological sites, now uniquely vulnerable to the potent threats of the time: new towns and housing estates, urban renewal, farming mechanisation and deep ploughing, new motorways and ring roads, gravel extraction and mining for minerals. On the other hand, the war had thrown up never-to-be-repeated opportunities and it was out of bombsites and rebuilding that some of the most rewarding excavations resulted. As early as 1943 the Institute of Archaeology hosted a London conference which set the agenda for the post-war era, and inspired by this renewed sense of mission, the Council for British Archaeology was founded the following year.

Before the war, the public had mostly understood archaeology to be concerned with grand buildings and spectacular objects: Roman towns, villas and mosaics, Anglo-Saxon cemeteries and their treasures. These artefacts were the backbone of museum collections up and down the country. Indeed one of the most inspirational finds in British archaeology had just been unearthed only a few weeks before the outbreak of World War II – the Sutton Hoo burial ship, with its haunting treasures.* There had long been flamboyant archaeologists like Mortimer Wheeler who relished publicity but many, concerned about security, preferred to cloak their activities in discretion to protect sites. Therefore, until the war archaeologists were cautious about publicity and public engagement. But in the post-war era this was to change as the new scale, complexity and pace of excavations called for widespread public support. We can observe this through a series of excavations which were to ignite the public imagination, and make archaeology not only popular as a visitor attraction but also a surprise success on television.

Neither the popularity of archaeology as a subject of television programmes nor as a hobby for people intent on unearthing caches of treasure was predicted. But first archaeologists needed to win enthusiastic support from communities, local and national government and to attract the all-important volunteers on whom the excavations depended. They therefore embarked on a charm offensive. As one of the main players in the story, Martin Biddle, wrote: 'when the public pays the cost of archaeology, whether as taxpayers or ratepayers, public relations are a duty. Public relations are also vital to an activity like archaeology which is in competition with many other perhaps conflicting interests. Good public relations bring ample rewards – in cash, in assistance of every kind, and not least in the status of archaeological activities in the public realm of local and national government.'[1] Public interest fed into the creation of new university departments of archaeology, in which the teaching led to a much greater emphasis on archaeological theorising, both about purpose and function.

In the post-war story two pioneering branches of the subject became ascendant, 'rescue archaeology', important in a fast-developing world, and its first cousin, 'urban archaeology'. The

---

* The Sutton Hoo burial ship and treasure were uncovered in 1939 but did not really have full impact until exhibited at the British Museum in 1947.

accelerating pace of development during the 1960s made it obvious that archaeologists of either branch could only investigate a tiny proportion of potential sites. Aware that it is easier to gain attention and funds when a crisis is declared, a pressure group was formed in 1971 by RESCUE – The British Archaeological Trust, to campaign for government support to permit the excavation of archaeological sites in advance of development. One of their best-known causes has been opposing the planned A303 tunnel near the World Heritage Site of Stonehenge. In urban archaeology, the purviews of the subject were extended from the individual building to the wider settlement and later historical periods were included in studies. Notwithstanding important prehistoric excavations such as that at Star Carr, the scene moves seamlessly from a largely Roman outlook to encompass the Anglo-Saxons, Vikings and medieval Britain.

On the face of it, the subject was well embedded into the fabric of public life: there were archaeologists working for the state at the Ministry of Public Buildings and Works, the universities, the museums and local authorities; and towering over all of them was the British Museum, with its great collections and promotion of the subject. But this force would prove to be pitifully inadequate given the escalation of activity. The solution came from a small number of active professional archaeologists working especially through RESCUE to make that case heard at senior civil service levels. A part of the solution lay in recruiting a force of trained volunteers, to the extent that even today archaeology is substantially reliant on their recruitment.

Meanwhile, highly significant advances in science introduced new methods of analysis and interpretation: radiocarbon dating offered a new reliability, advances in dendrochronology and thermoluminescence were equally important, while the increasing use of photography, particularly aerial, offered new perspectives, and underwater equipment enabled the *Mary Rose* story to be told. New techniques such as DNA analysis (which identified the remains of Richard III) and stable isotope analysis have radically expanded our understanding of the nature and movement of human populations.* This chapter examines a series of excavations which were profoundly significant in the ways in which archaeology was undertaken, perceived and projected as conserving the nation's heritage.

The Temple of Mithras

Bombsites on the City of London presented a special problem: the urgent need to restore economic activity quickly had to be balanced against the paramount importance of such sites to archaeologists. Mortimer Wheeler, the doyen of the profession, wrote: 'with hindsight it is easy to see how inadequately planned the whole situation not unnaturally was at this time. The national consciousness had not yet been sufficiently attuned to historical and archaeological thinking'.[2] It was the construction of Bucklersbury House in the shadow of St Paul's in 1954, a fourteen-storey headquarters for Legal & General, that yielded the first archaeological sensation. Here W. F. (Peter) Grimes uncovered the remains of what the nation came to know as the Temple of Mithras (or Mithraeum), which he identified by its characteristic layout and by finds of items associated with the Mithraic religion, including a large sculpted head of the god Mithras himself. Grimes considered that in its latter days the temple might have been converted for Christian worship, which would account for the burial of an extraordinary collection of high-quality sculptures of Roman deities around the site. These sculptures, the finest Roman sculptures found in Britain, attracted vast media interest and were immediately whisked off to the Museum of London (then housed at Lancaster House). The discovery of the marbles changed everything for a previously almost unknown excavation. Over 30,000 visitors came to see

* Also important is the development of photogrammetry, and the non-invasive survey methods Lidar and Ground Penetrating Radar (GPR), in revealing and interpreting standing and below-ground structures.

the Mithras temple site during one week in September 1954; they were invited to contribute but gave less than 1p per head. Archaeologists still had much to learn about how to harness public interest.

In order not to hold up the building development, the remains of the temple were relocated to a nearby site and, to Grimes's dismay, rationalised and even supplemented with new stone. It was said to have been the prime minister, Winston Churchill, who intervened to save the remains. Bucklersbury House was eventually demolished in 2010, and the temple ruins returned to their former home. The new owners, Bloomberg, commissioned a fresh excavation and a splendid museum devoted to the Mithraeum, focusing now on the lives of ordinary citizens.

The discovery of the Temple of Mithras in the 1950s was the find of the decade, important in all kinds of ways, but it represented a pre-war tradition. Although there were important Roman digs after Mithras, notably Sheppard Frere's work at Verulamium, the two examples we will examine to demonstrate the rewards of urban archaeology focus on later periods. It was, as Wheeler put it, in 'cities such as Winchester, Oxford, York, and half a dozen others [that the new generation of archaeologists] can claim to have demonstrated how the thing should be done'.[3]

Winchester

It was the proposal to build the Wessex Hotel on an important site adjacent to Winchester Cathedral that set off one of the most innovative excavations of the post-war period. No city was to receive such close archaeological scrutiny over the next decade as Winchester, and the results were revelatory. Town excavations had taken place before, for instance in the nearby Roman town of Silchester in the late nineteenth century, but the stimulus was provided by post-war rebuilding. As the leader of the Winchester dig Martin Biddle explained: 'the remains of periods later than Roman were very much in evidence and simply could not be ignored, and this led to the current concept of urban archaeology. This sees the town itself, the urban phenomenon, as the centre of interest, rather than any one period of the town's history or any single aspect of its activity'.[4] In 1965, the Council for British Archaeology introduced the concept of historic urban areas, highlighting group value as opposed to individual buildings or sites, an approach that mirrored the development of Conservation Areas in the built landscape. It is at Winchester that we can observe a prime example of urban archaeology in action.

The leading spirit, Martin Biddle, had been responsible for the excavations at Cheam in 1959 of Nonsuch, the most intriguing of Henry VIII's lost palaces. Here Biddle devised a new approach to dealing with the public. It was an excavation in the middle of a public park, to which Biddle attracted 75,000 curious visitors by arranging tours, lectures and timed visits. Biddle had gained his first experience as a schoolboy working under Mortimer Wheeler at St Albans and later with Kathleen Kenyon at Jericho, the quintessential administrative and spiritual capital. One of the big questions at Winchester was how to define a regional capital, whether Winchester had really been one, and if so, when? On arrival in the city, Biddle was offered the support of six council workers. Fortunately, he persuaded some Cambridge friends and colleagues to join him. During their long first summer of excavation in 1961 the wealth of the city's hidden archaeology became evident, and the extent to which it was threatened. During the 1960s, the Winchester excavations were the most extensive archaeological excavations ever undertaken of any British town.

Indeed, the excavation of 1961 became so productive that it was decided to create the Winchester Excavations Committee; an early public meeting attracted an audience of 700. Several critical decisions were soon reached, namely that the city digs would not be subject to any one age, period or layer, would encompass the whole city, and would use written evidence as an adjunct to all its investigations. Biddle has always taken as his motto 'time and chance', asserting that without these, little can be achieved. He was given both at Winchester and was able to excavate on one site for up to ten summer seasons. When his team of volunteers rose to 200 at any one time, they had to be accommodated in an old army camp. It was such scope and continuity that enabled Biddle to come up with results beyond the superficial. He stresses that it is the support of local authorities that is essential for professional archaeologists to achieve research objectives beyond mere rescue requirements.[*]

One purpose of urban archaeology that Biddle likes to endorse is establishing and explaining the normal. A great deal of archaeology and indeed public interest is focused on the exceptional, the unique and the splendid, but town archaeology is as much about understanding the typical evolution of streets to reveal the points of comparison and patterns of habitation and use. Biddle was granted a further ten seasons of digging, and carefully documented the finds in the ten meticulous volumes of Winchester Studies.

The city sits at the head of Southampton Water, the greatest natural harbour in England. For the last 1,600 years it has been dominated by the cathedral. Winchester, sited at the narrowest point of the Itchen Valley settlement, controlled the east–west route in circa 100 BC. It became a fort soon after the Roman invasion and we begin to see the appearance of a north–south route towards the sea. Around AD 70 came a major development – a rampart and ditch enclosing fifty acres with five or possibly six gates. Winchester was to soon grow into the fifth-largest town of Roman Britain, *Venta Belgarum*, and this remains the basis of the modern city. Early finds revealed the Roman forum lying partly below the great Anglo-Saxon churches of the Old and New Minsters, but work was complicated by a high water table

---

[*]   The Winchester excavations by Martin Biddle were financed by the Department for the Environment, and local government, with the remainder from grants and other sources.

running through this – a potential danger to the site. Little is known of the other Roman public buildings and no baths have yet been discovered.

At the end of Roman times, the town dwindled to a husk, with evidence of various settlements from the fifth to seventh centuries scattered along the River Itchen down to the Solent. Winchester became the focus of this wider settlement until in the seventh century a major church was built by the King of Wessex – but why? The locations of both of Winchester's so-called Old and New Minsters had long been lost, and their rediscovery by Biddle and his team, 'so close that a man could scarcely walk between them', was one of the dig's most important achievements. The size of the Old Minster, housing the shrine of St Swithun, was a stupendous revelation. Begun circa AD 650, and expanded and rebuilt over the next 400 years, it had grown into one of the largest churches in Christendom, greater in extent than Charlemagne's great cathedral at Aachen. And then the New Minster, the royal burial church of Alfred and his family begun in 901, proved also to have been on the scale of Cluny or Speyer, or as Eric Fernie described it, 'a church of imperial dimensions'.

Archaeologists like to point out such excavations are often the only source of information we have about the early history of towns, since before the thirteenth century, written records are limited. Dr Johnson offered a challenge to archaeologists when he opined that 'all that is really known of the ancient state of Britain is contained in a few pages'. Biddle's work has proved to the public that the history of a town lies as much below its pavements as in its archives and records.

The Jorvik Settlement

There was one archaeological project in the 1970s that was to capture the national imagination: the discovery and interpretation of the properties found flanking the Viking-age street below Coppergate in York. The excavation of Jorvik, as the

Viking town had been named, transformed the way archaeology was explained from site reports and visits, into an evidence-based reconstruction which in turn became a major tourist attraction.

As a response to the potential disruption to sites from building works in the city, the York Archaeological Trust had been set up in 1972 as the brainchild of Peter Addyman. The imminent redevelopment of Coppergate into a shopping centre lent urgency to the task. Addyman had to persuade city councillors to allow him to undertake early site clearance and excavation – without really knowing what his team would find. He argued that their excavations would increase the local collections, and would supply educational and tourist benefits, as well as provide better understanding of the city's history. This turned out to be a wild understatement.

When Addyman began digging, York's idea of its own early history was centred around its Roman past, when it had been the city of Eboracum. Everybody remembered that Constantine the Great was proclaimed emperor here, and Ebor remained a popular prefix for many local businesses. Few members of the public knew that the subsequent Anglo-Saxon city of Eoforwic had been captured by the Vikings in 867, changed its name to Jorvik, and remained such for half a century; but this was the archaeological phase that Addyman wanted to investigate. Not only was his work to reshape the identity of York, but in the process it would rehabilitate the Vikings, who had an image problem stretching back to their depredations described in the *Anglo-Saxon Chronicle*. Luckily York's water-retaining clay substrate had created anaerobic conditions perfect for the preservation of organic material, and the Coppergate excavation yielded up an entire neighbourhood of the Viking town. The reconstruction of Jorvik as a peaceful settlement of Viking traders, leather workers and craftsmen arrived as a revelation.

The council was initially sceptical of Addyman's plans, but he had excellent communication skills and persuasive charm. He realised that the key was to give the public as much access as possible, even while work was in progress.[5] The site was opened as 'the Viking Dig', and visitors were even given the chance to purchase some of the material found, particularly oyster shells at 20 pence each – selling 20,000 of these considerably helped costs. The emphasis was on the kind of education that made archaeology exciting. Schools were encouraged to send classes, and volunteer guides explained the story with audio-visual aids. Above all the press were mustered, and the BBC's *Blue Peter* made several visits – one with a memorable crawl through a Roman sewer. Councillors approvingly noted the amount of national press coverage Addyman's digs were receiving.

Addyman had a flair for nobbling the right people and fundraising: he recruited Magnus Magnusson and the Prince of Wales, who promised to give them three events in three years. Funds came in from all over the world, which enabled the excavation to continue for five years; half a million people came to peep into the vast pit. Eventually, however, the site had to be handed over to the developer. This might have been the end of the story, but Addyman, greatly encouraged by his American wife, Shelley, countered with an imaginative new scheme. His proposal was to create, below the new Coppergate shopping centre, an underground museum. This would be an evidence-based reconstruction to demonstrate what Viking-age Coppergate might have looked like, and to show the people who would have worked there. The final touch was to turn the experience into a ride, to carry visitors through the reconstruction in time-cars which would ensure both safety and efficient passage. For this Addyman took inspiration from Williamsburg, which offered 'a way of telling a very complicated story well'.[6] He also visited Disney to see how they handled crowd management. Thus in April 1984 the Jorvik Viking Centre opened, and in its first year attracted almost a million visitors.

The time-car brings its rider through a reconstruction of the old multicultural Viking trading centre and the people who inhabited it, who are seen making and selling their crafts, and living among their families. At the end of this ride into the past, the centre displays the actual archaeological finds which have been contextualised in the recreated village. Of this radical new approach, the academic world was supportive; however, the president of the Museums Association condemned Jorvik for generating 'modern mythologies, deodorised and sanitised'.[7] Even the Yorkshire Museum were a little envious, until they were given the most spectacular find: the Anglo-Saxon York Helmet, discovered at Coppergate in 1982.

With the rehabilitation of the Vikings in full swing, an annual Viking festival was established, taking place every February with lectures and re-enactments of Viking ceremonies on the banks of the river. Today Jorvik has welcomed nearly 20 million visitors, and Peter Addyman is justified in his description of York as 'quite simply Britain's largest, deepest, most important and best-preserved urban archaeological site'.[8] Despite the major archaeological discoveries in York, only 2–3 per cent of the city has been excavated, so there remains vastly more to be discovered.

This desire to reconstruct the past encouraged another development: experimental archaeology. It was a gravel extraction pit destined to become a rubbish tip at West Stow in Suffolk that revealed a former Saxon settlement brilliantly excavated over many years by the eminent local archaeologist Stanley West, many of whose observations underpinned the work of the recreators of the village. In 1974 the Anglo-Saxon village was resurrected in a pioneering case of experimental archaeology under the supervision of John Coles, largely relying on his Cambridge students in attempting to understand the 'how' of ancient life. The experiment continues today both as a tourist attraction run by English Heritage and a laboratory of Saxon practical skills overseen by an advisory committee who decide on the projects. These involve crafts such as thatching, pottery and smithing. At West Stow the aim is to educate visitors about Anglo-Saxon life and history with evidence-based reconstruction of their lives.

Television Archaeology and the *Mary Rose*

As early as 1946 archaeology had started appearing on television screens, when Glyn Daniel described various discoveries. The first series devoted to the subject was *Animal, Vegetable, Mineral?* from 1952 to 1959, in which Daniel was joined by the venerable and imposing, moustache-twirling figure of Mortimer Wheeler, elucidating 'mystery' artefacts in a museum. They were gifted performers – Daniel was twice given the accolade of Television Personality of the Year. Wheeler was famous for his refrain, 'Ah, I know this chap. I was there when it was dug up.' This series was followed by *Chronicle* and later by *Time Team,* which educated the public in the methodology and technical parameters of archaeology. *Time Team* in particular was a hugely popular TV series from 1994 until 2014 in which Tony Robinson played Everyman investigating 'ordinary' places such as village greens and back gardens. This was indeed the people's archaeology. These programmes were important in gaining public support so that archaeologists could continue their work.

The most compelling television archaeology story came with the raising of the *Mary Rose* from the waters of the Solent in October 1982. This was accorded sixteen hours of broadcasting over three days, attracting an international audience for the raising of the hull of up to 60 million. The world held its breath as the timbers broke the surface, for there was a fair chance that the remaining frame might shatter, or as one wit put it: 'a slight hiccup on the atypical journey from grave to cradle'.[9] It was the most ambitious marine archaeological project ever undertaken.

The *Mary Rose* had many points of interest. It had been the flagship of King Henry VIII, but it was also a story of everyday sailors. The ship had been loaded in 1545 for the Battle of the Solent with heavy cannons and 2,000 cannonballs. To render the ship stable, guns were positioned low, with their ports only six feet above the waterline. A gust of wind and the failure to close these ports probably let the water in and caused the sinking.

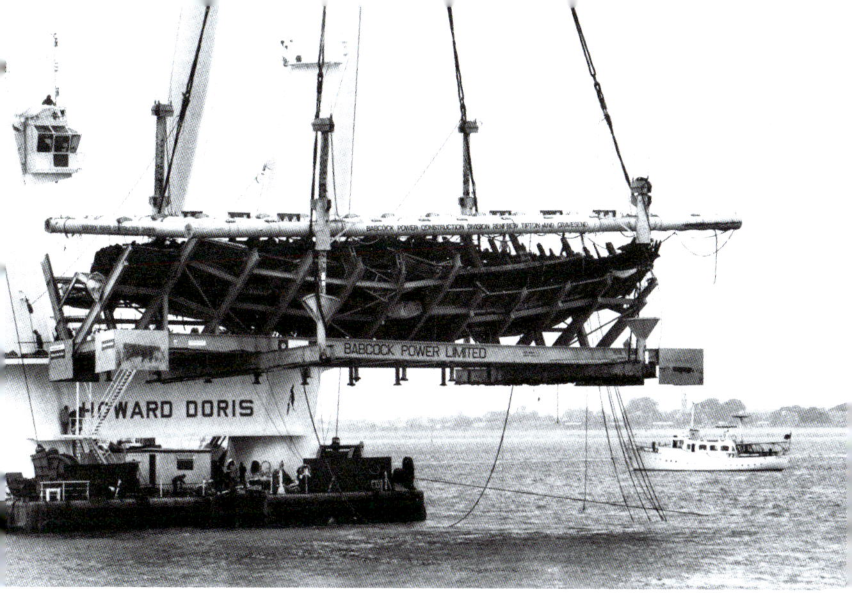

1. In 1982, the *Mary Rose* rose from the deep after 437 years.

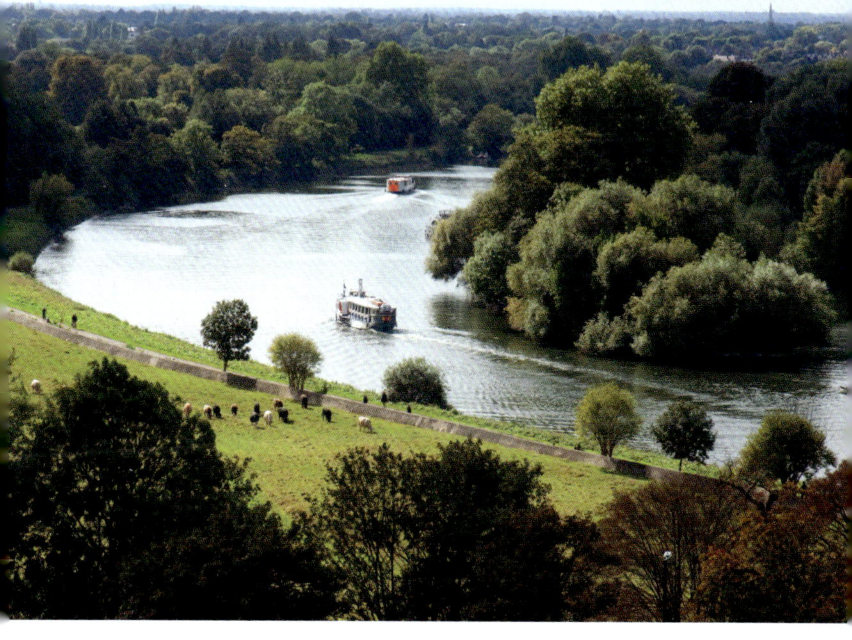

2. The Lass of Richmond Hill.

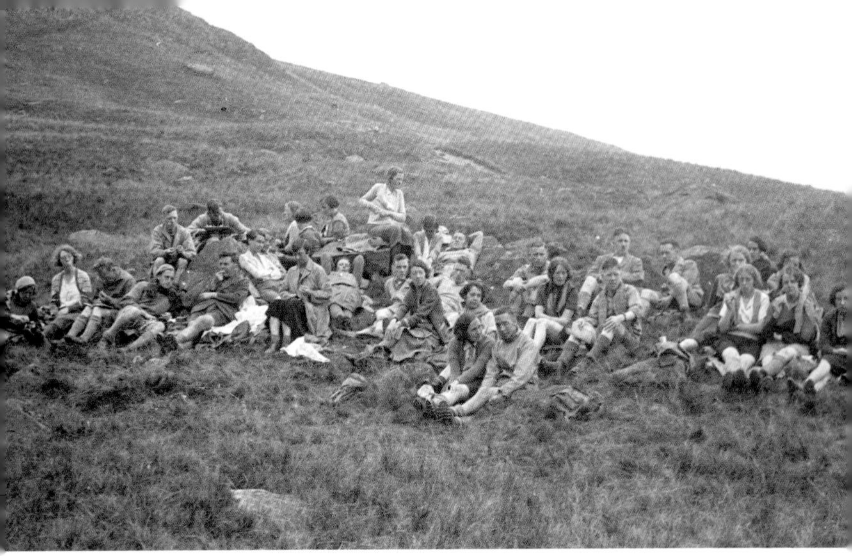

3. The Kinder Scout mass trespass, 1932.

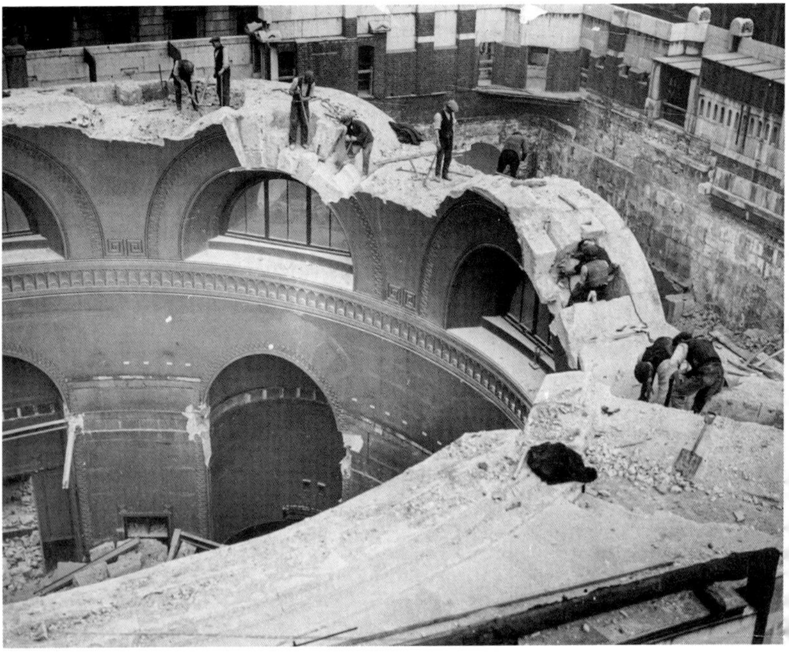

4. Destroying Soane's Bank of England, circa 1926.

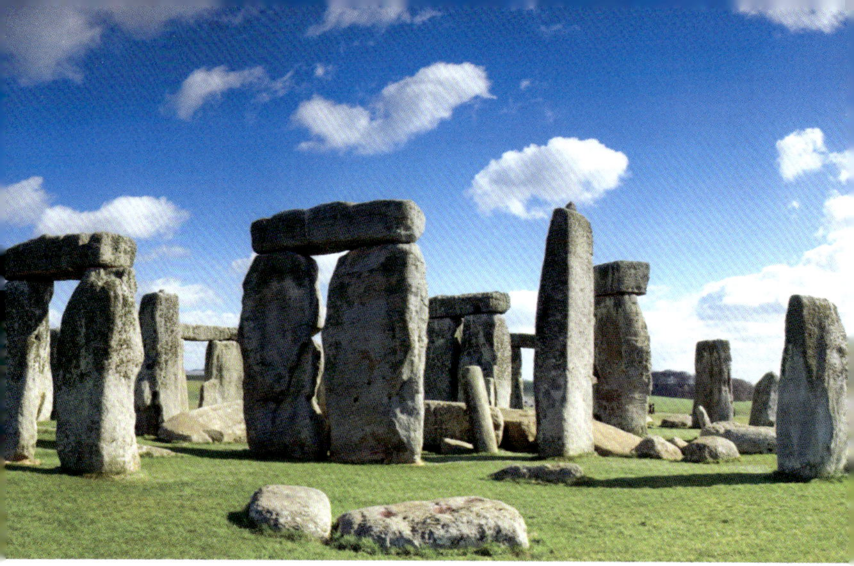

5. Stonehenge joined the national collection in 1918.

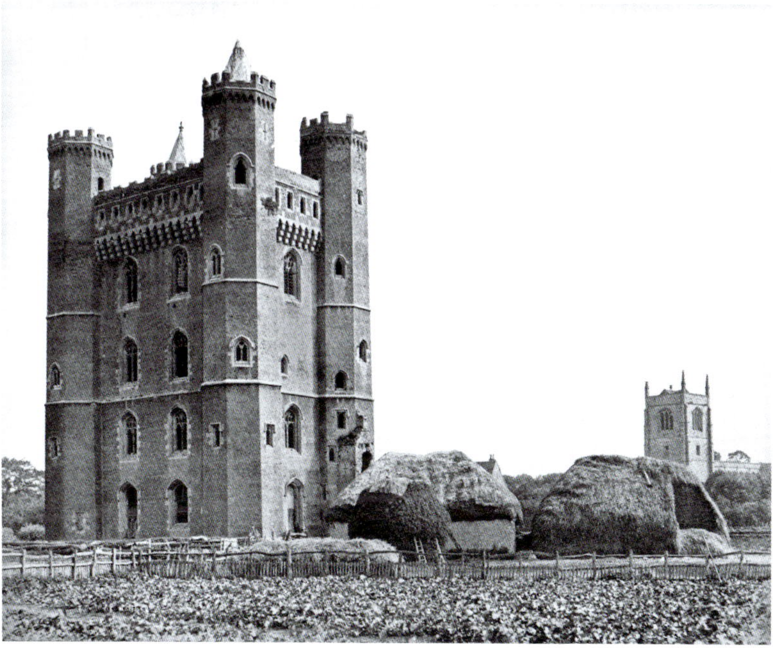

6. Tattershall, saved by Lord Curzon in 1910.

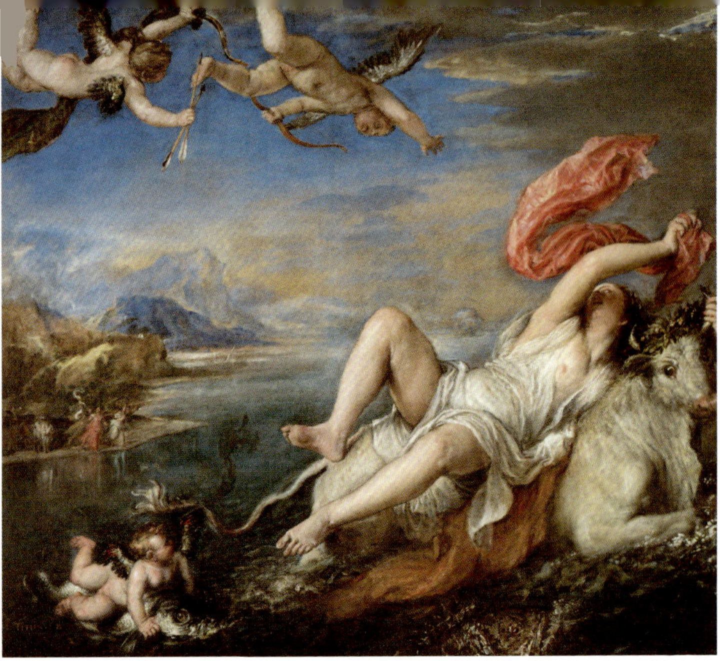

7. The most grievous loss: Titian's *The Rape of Europa*.

8. Buchanan's 'Deck' system separating cars and pedestrians.

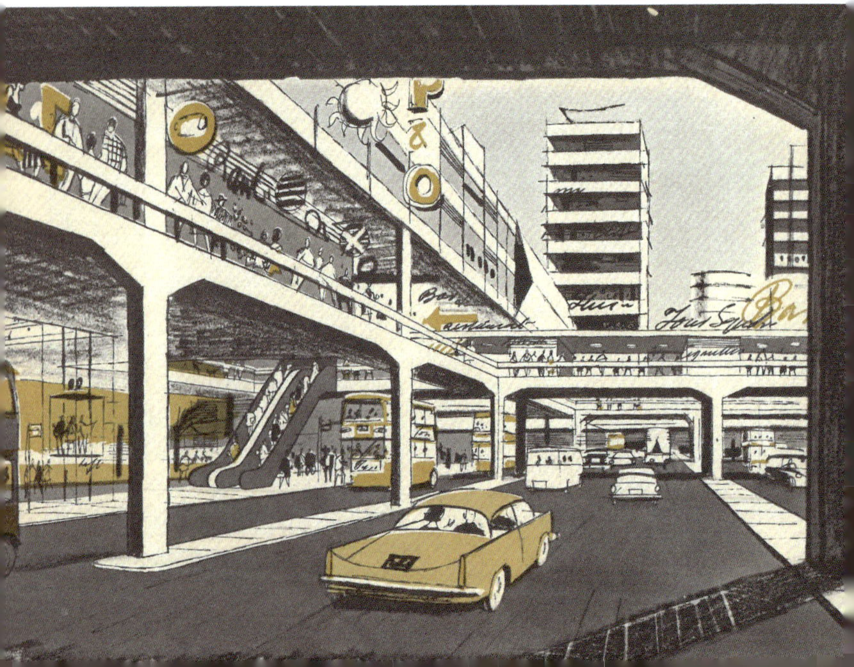

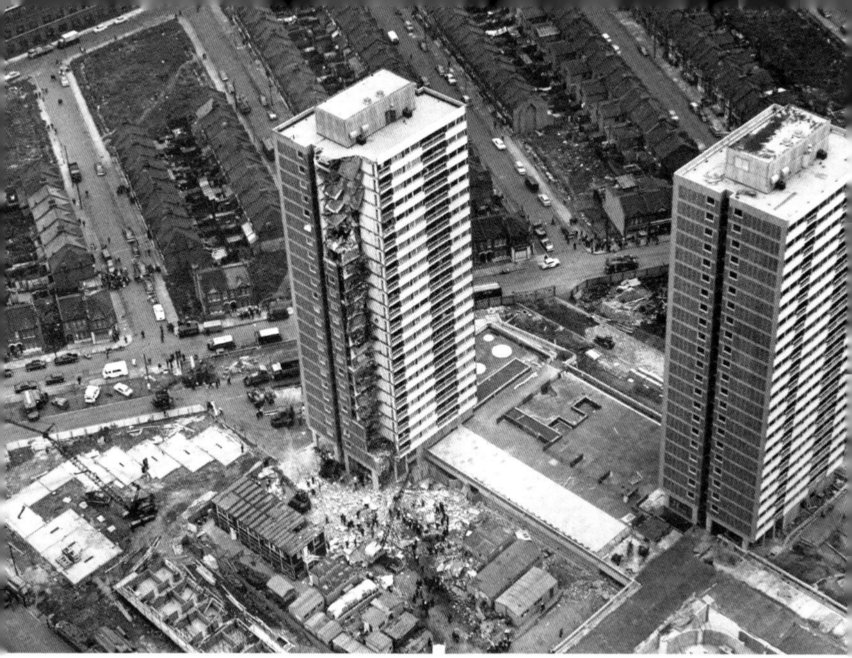

9. Ronan Point: the turning point.

10. Birmingham's Bull Ring Centre, circa 1965.

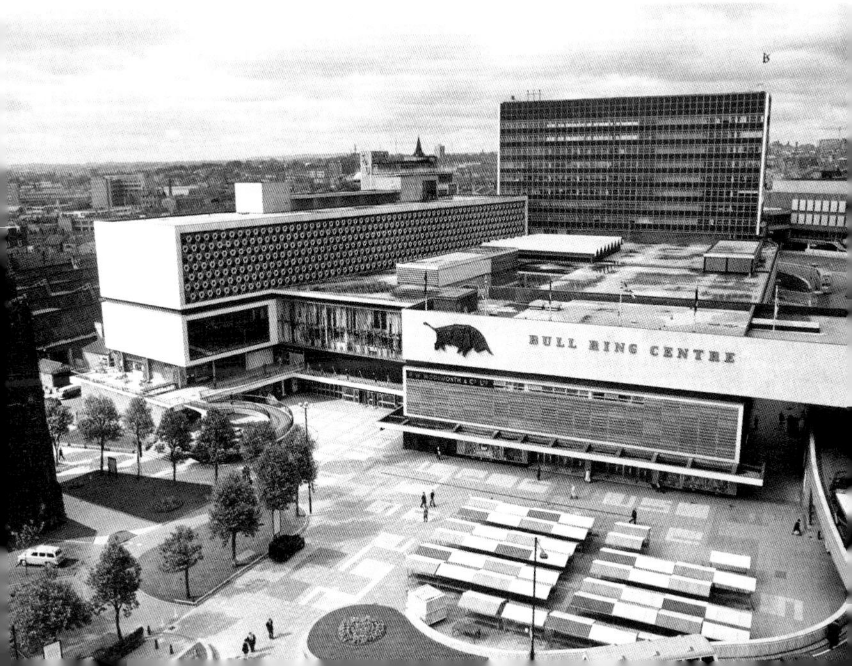

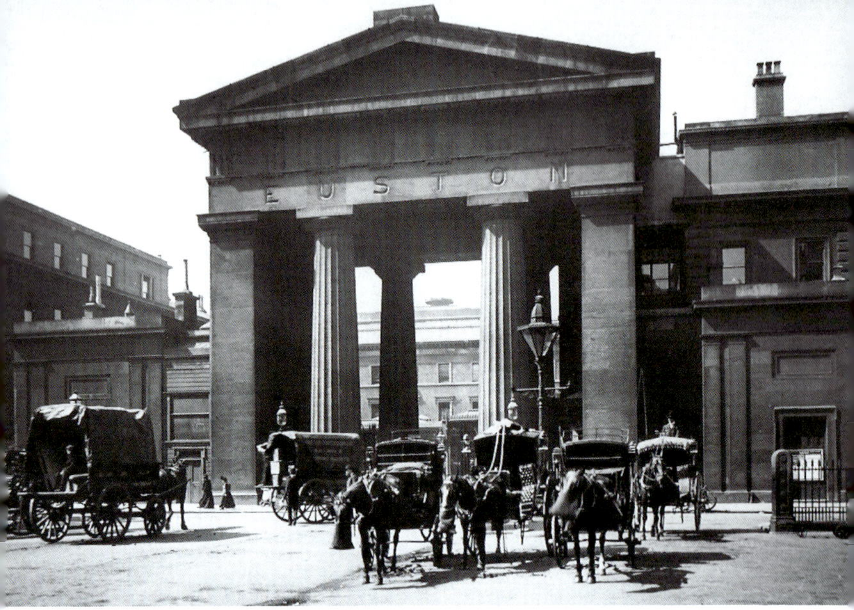

11. The Alamo of the conservation movement: the Euston Arch.

12. Saved: St Pancras.

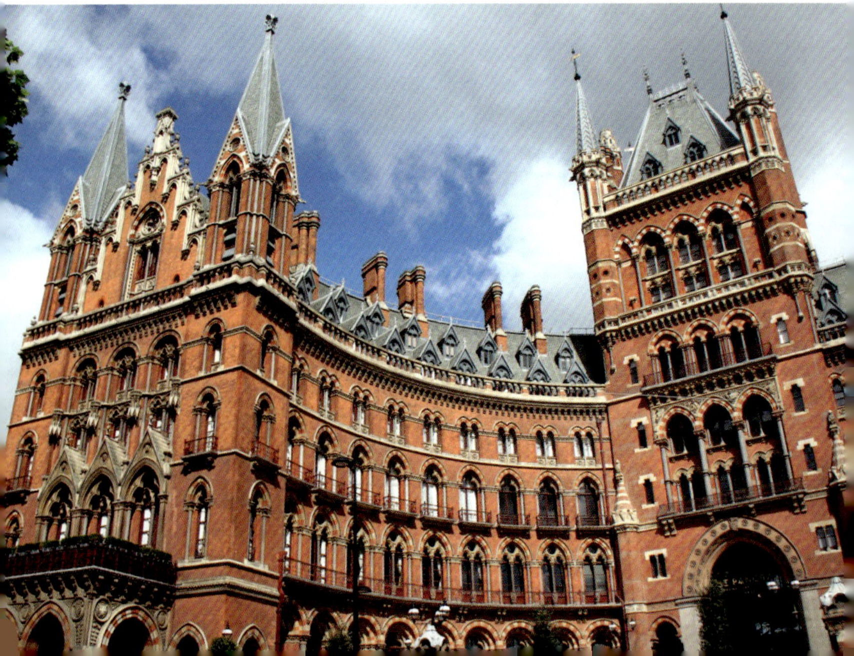

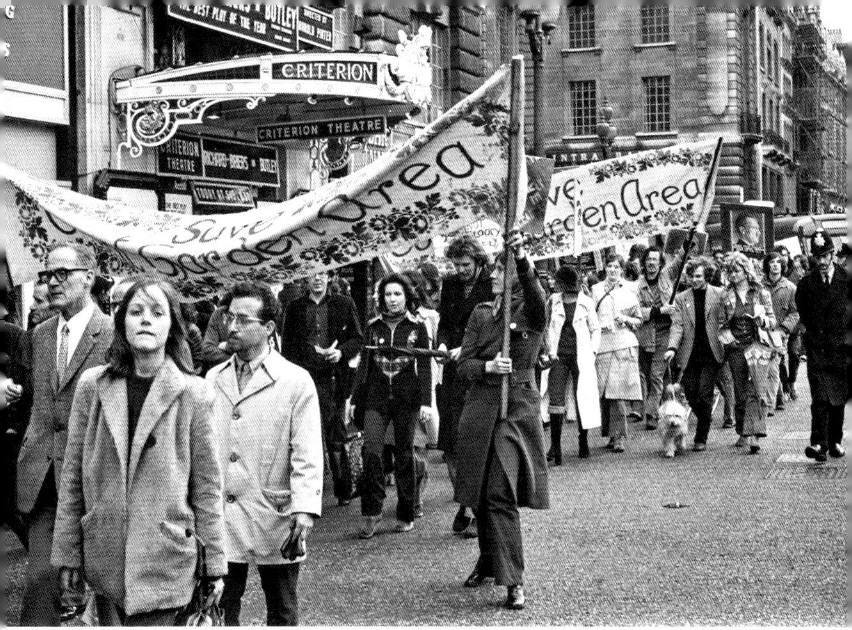

13. Covent Garden residents march against the planners, 1972.

14. Demolished over a bank holiday in 1980: Firestone Factory.

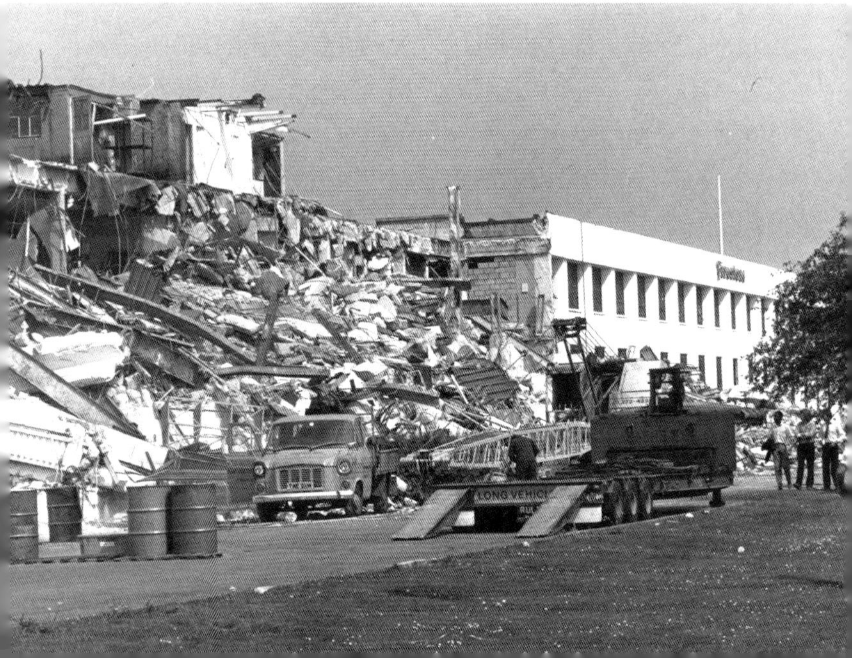

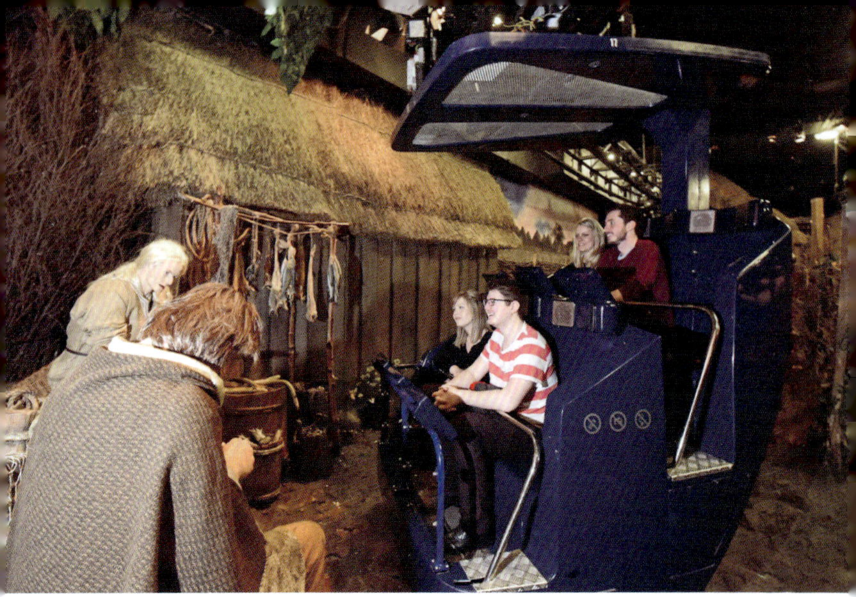

15. Visiting the Vikings in time-cars.

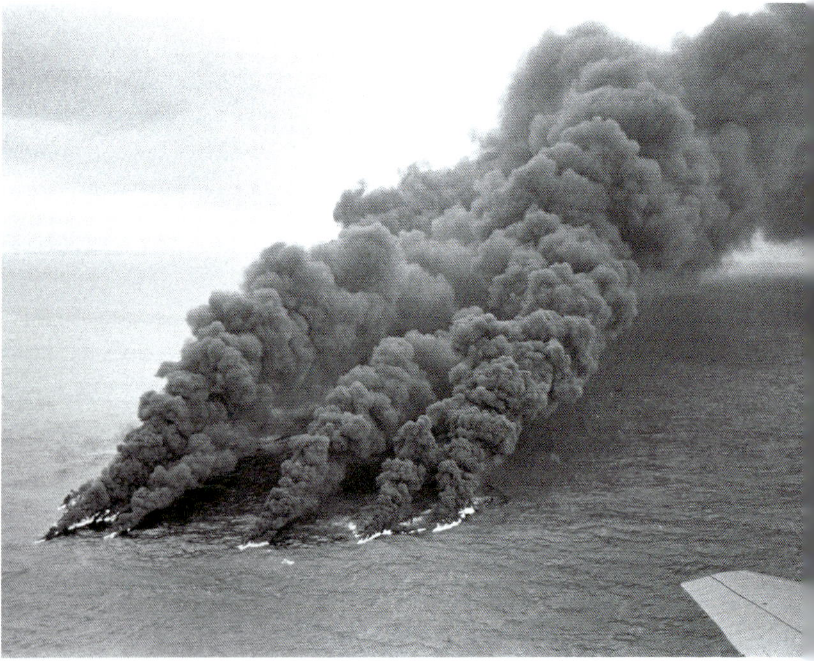

16. The Torrey Canyon hit the headlines in 1967.

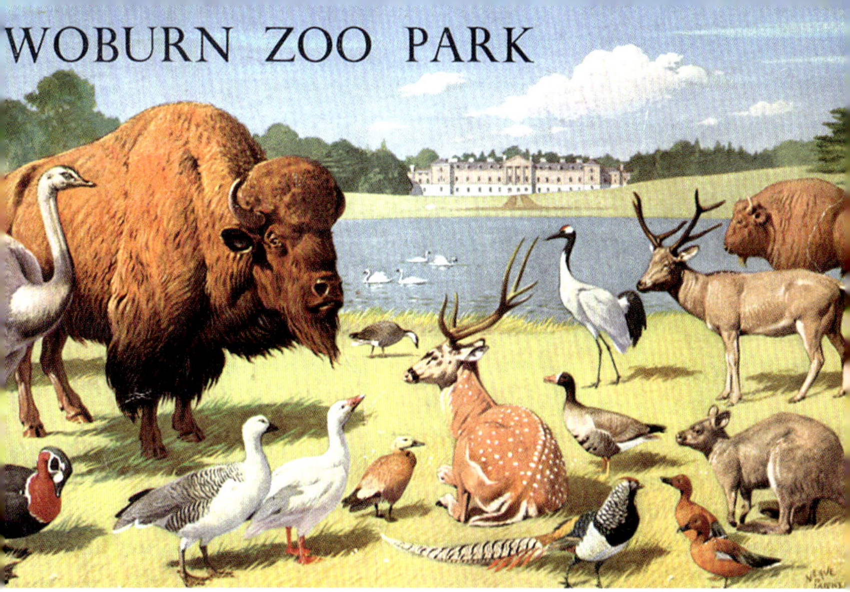

17. A family day out at Woburn.

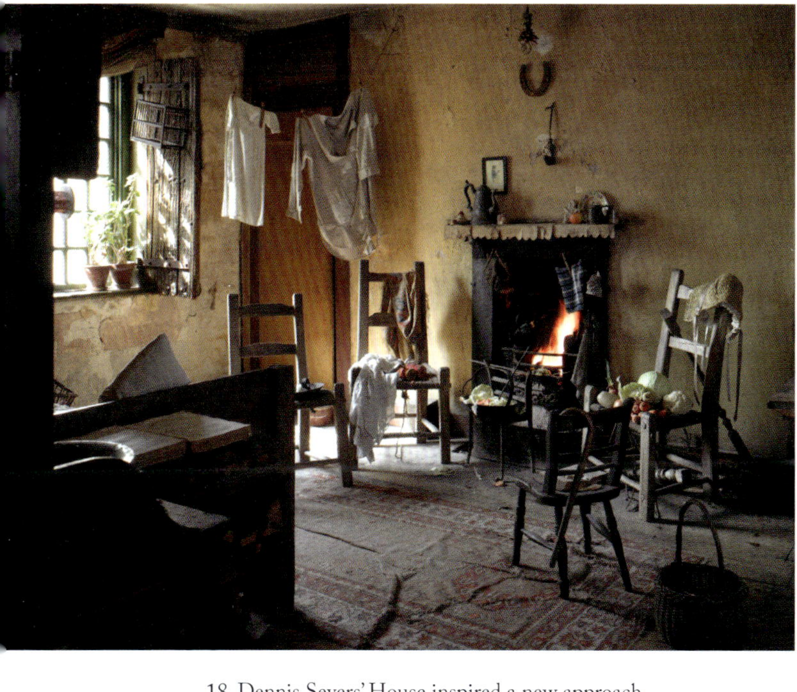

18. Dennis Severs' House inspired a new approach.

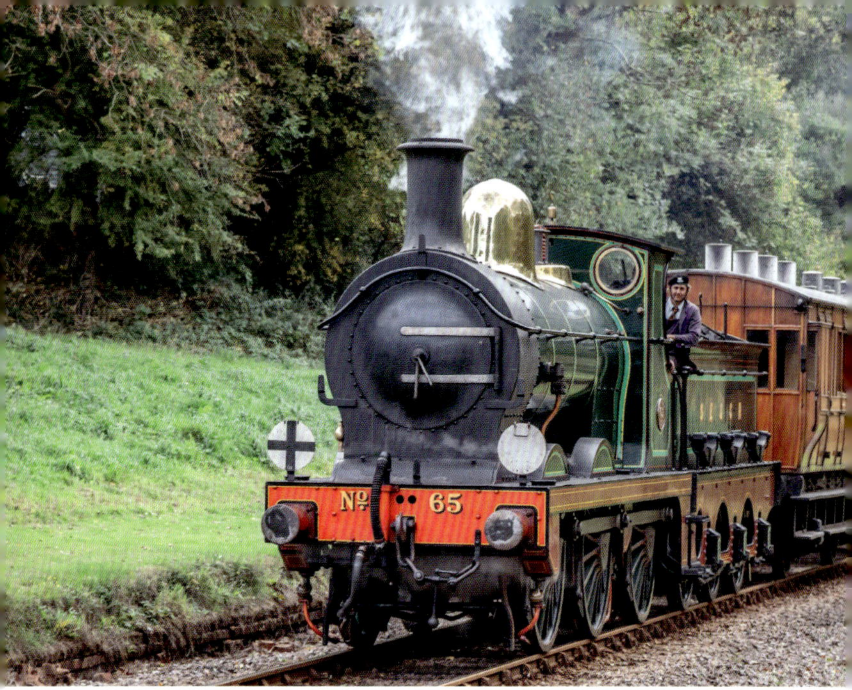

20. One of the wonders of the north: The Piece Hall, Halifax.

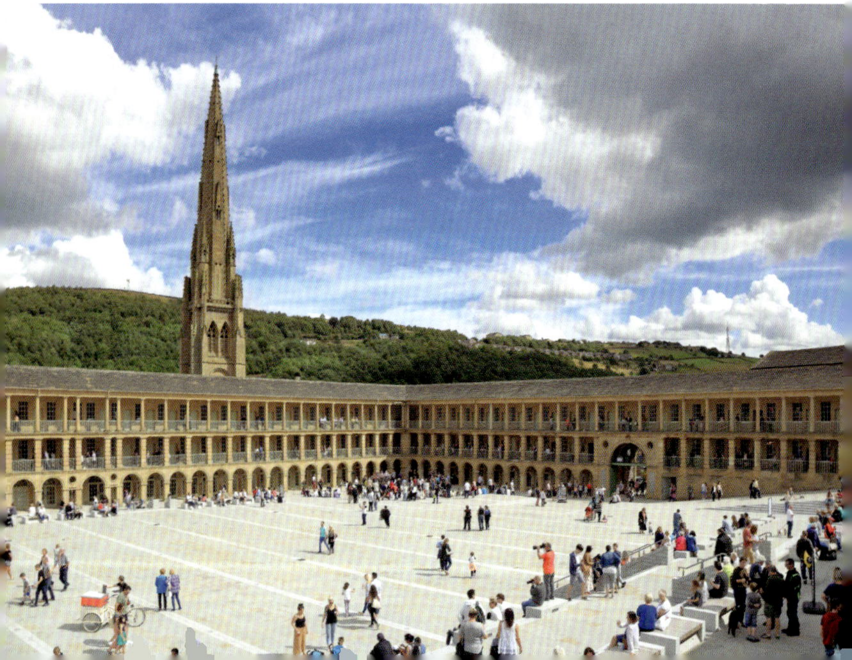

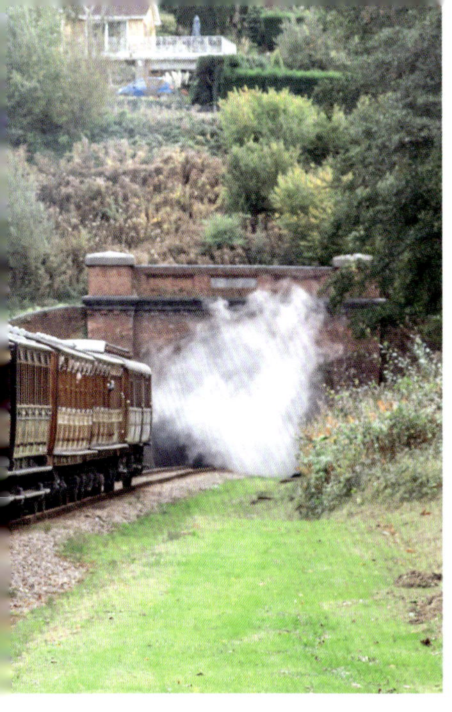

19. The Bluebell Line restored.

21. V&A Dundee with the Discovery.

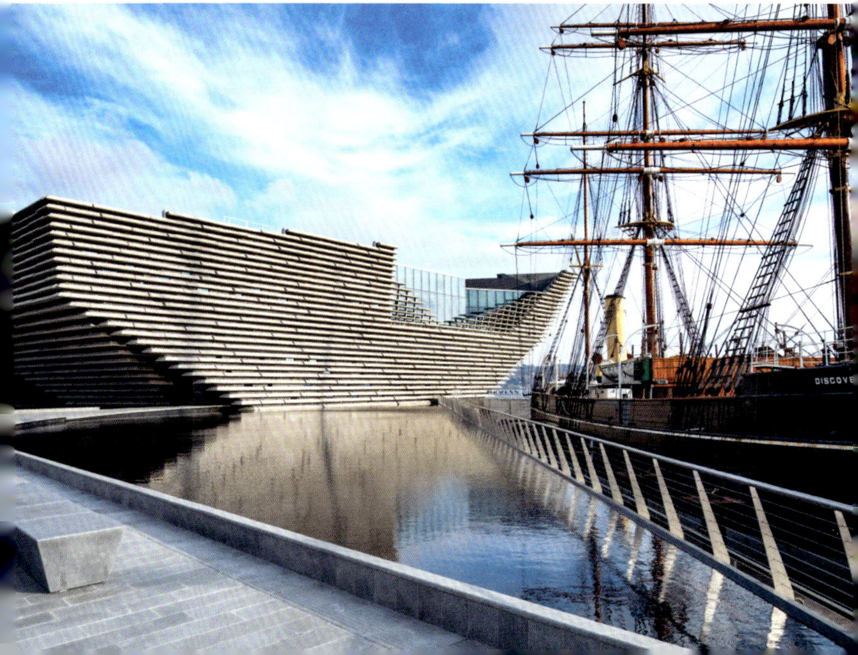

22. The Three Graces.

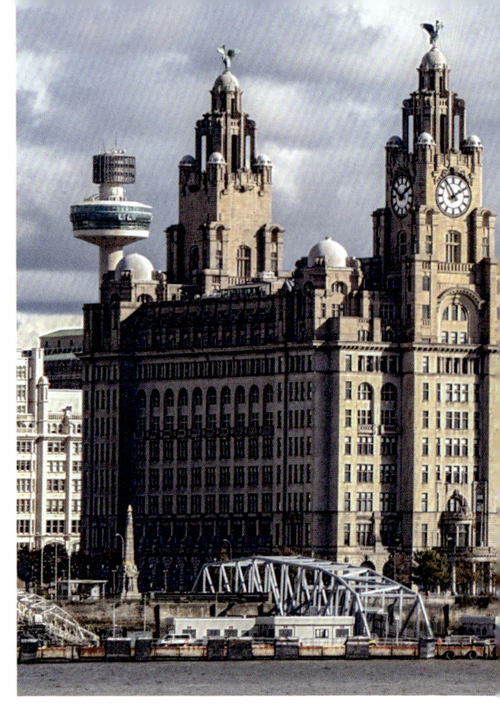

23. 'Pushing the drug dealers back a few streets': the Manchester Climbing Centre at St Benedict's, Ardwick.

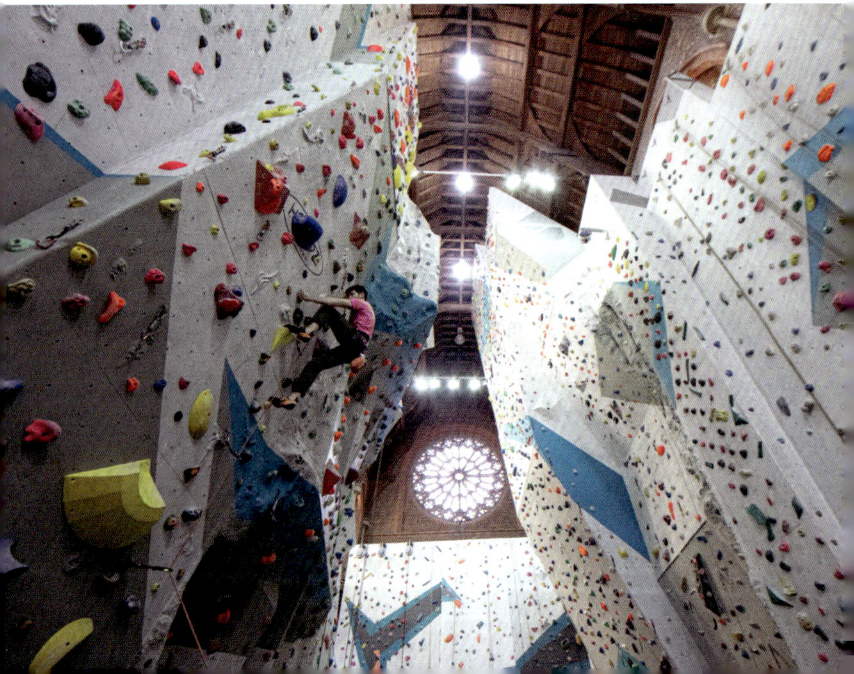

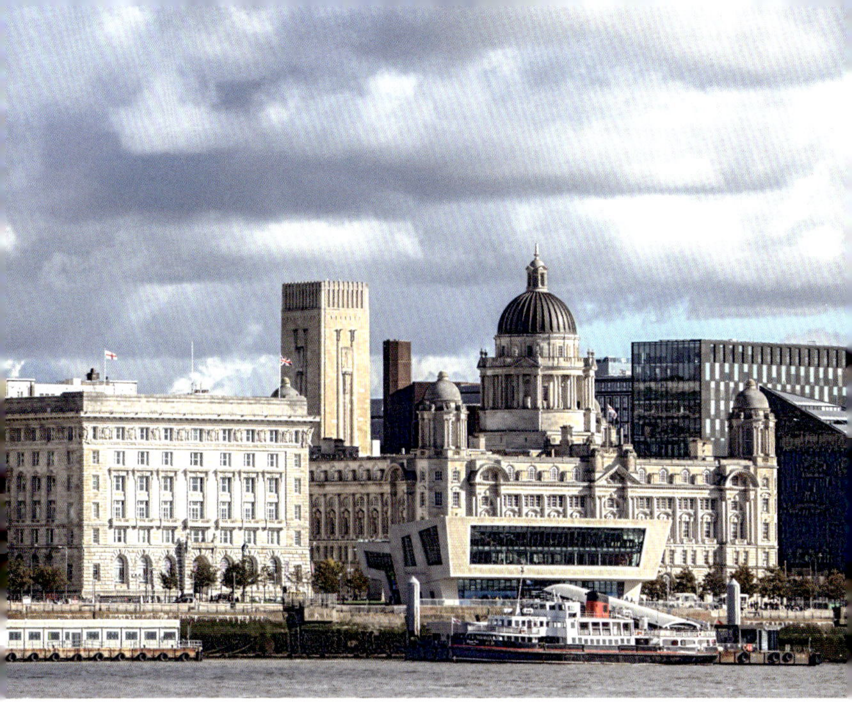

24. Somerset House reclaimed for the public.

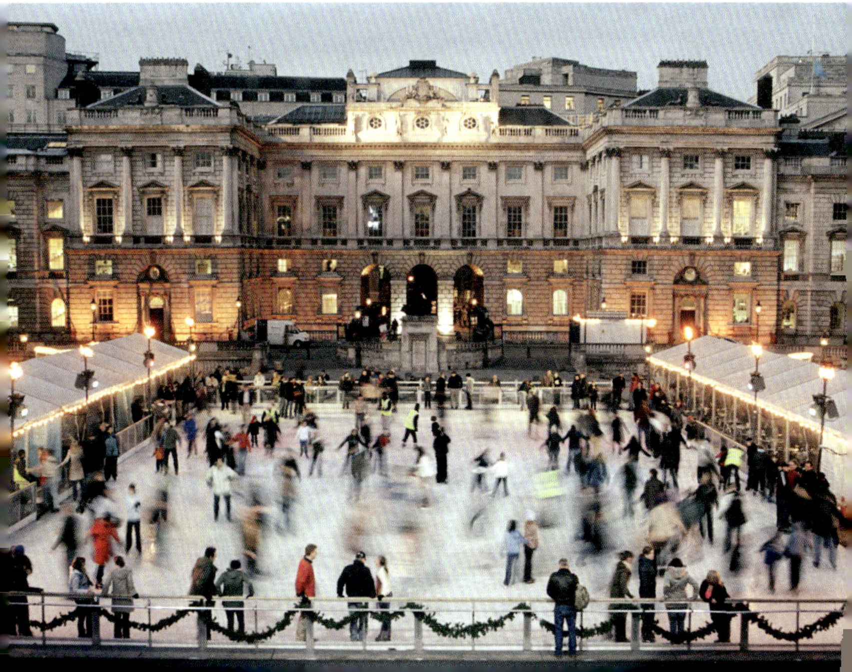

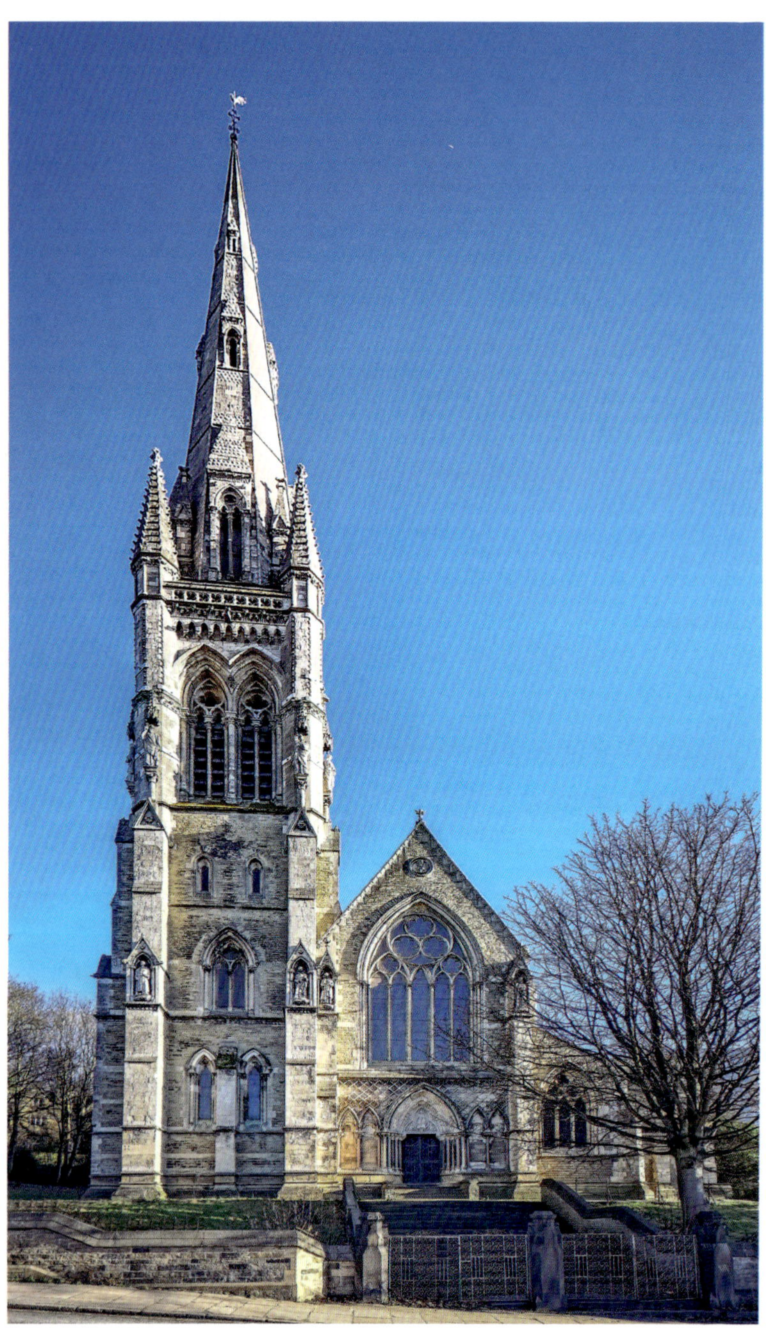

25. All Souls, Haley Hill, Halifax, redundant in 1977.

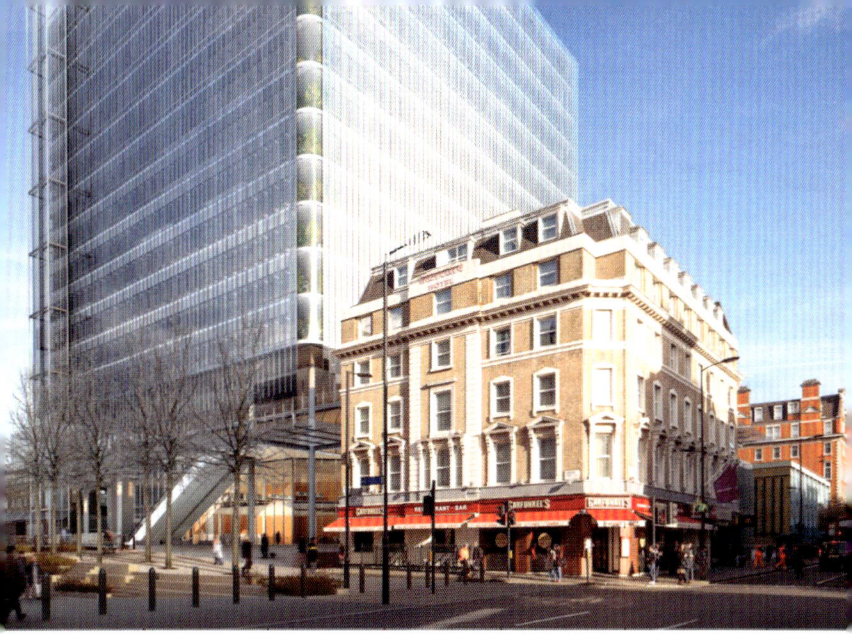

26. Renzo Piano's Paddington Cube.

27. Colston takes the plunge, 2020.

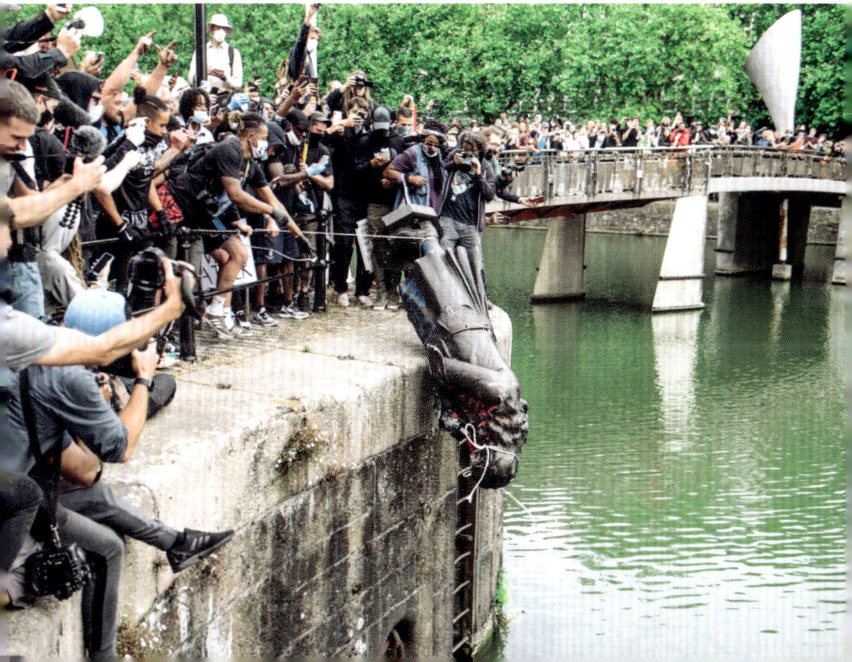

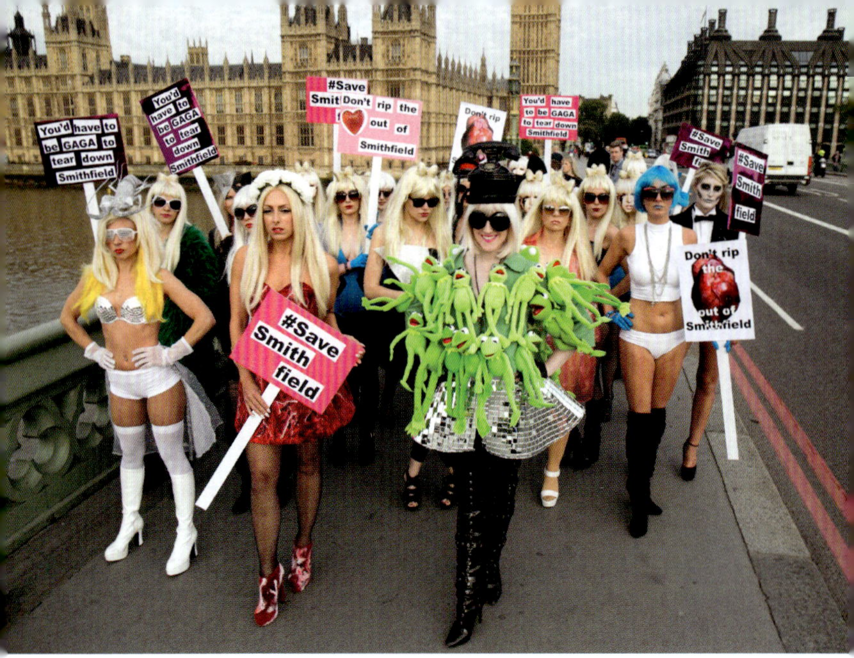

28. Lady Gaga lookalikes saved Smithfield.

29. Climate change: York under water.

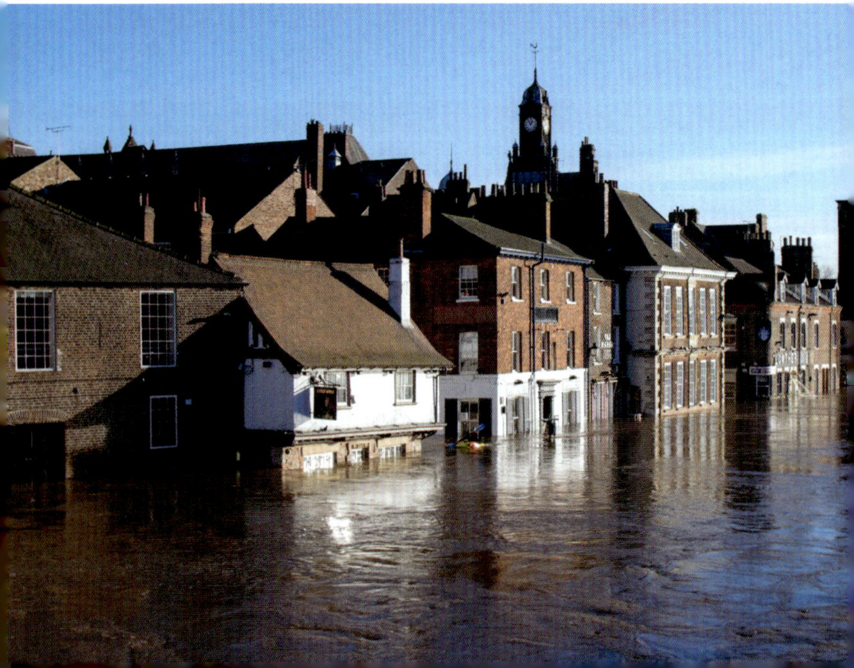

But the rigging had been arranged to prevent enemy boarding, and this meant the crew were unable to escape. Over 400 sailors drowned. This took place before the French fleet, while the king watched from the shore.

In 1836 the wreck was discovered by fishermen who had caught their nets in its timbers. Although divers went down and the wreck was identified, it would take 150 years before the technology existed to bring it safely to the surface. The *Mary Rose* was unusual because so much of the ship had survived, and was visually comprehensible. Moreover, along with the ship, almost half the skeletons, 179, were recovered. A magnificent museum was built in Portsmouth Historic Dockyard (benefitting from the Heritage Lottery Fund) which is a model of its kind, under the tag 'when their world ended our story began'. Public engagement with archaeology reached a new height with the raising of the *Mary Rose*.

The Rose Theatre

It was fortunate that Shakespeare's name was attached to the Rose Theatre in Southwark, an early purpose-built theatre which opened in 1585, but was soon superseded and abandoned early in the reign of James I. It was the proposed redevelopment of a 1950s office building in 1989 that brought the site to light. A two-month excavation had been agreed with the developer and it had been hoped that the remains of the theatre might be discovered. However, when the lost Rose Theatre was indeed identified *The Times* called it 'the most exciting archaeological find since Tutankhamun'. What they found was a fourteen-sided timber structure, coated with lath and plaster, with galleries enclosing an uncovered central yard. One of the unusual aspects of the Rose Theatre story was the ability to cross-reference the results of the excavation with the surviving papers of the theatre's builder, the Elizabethan impresario, Philip Henslowe, stored at Dulwich College.

Since planning permission had been granted – and crucially, without a prior archaeological assessment – under normal circumstances the excavation would have come to a halt after two months, but the theatre world, led by Laurence Olivier, went into action and achieved a reprieve. It was a close-run thing – the lorries were on site to cover the base with gravel, and only prevented by a shield of young people organised by the Danish archaeologist Birthe Kjølbye-Biddle. A galaxy of international acting talent hosted a street party to raise funds. This created a dilemma for the government, which became responsible for compensating the developer. The plans were successfully modified to preserve the theatre under a new stilted design, but the situation had highlighted the problem of getting early access to sites for proper assessment. The recommendations put forward to the minister by English Heritage precipitated a change in the law in 1990 with Planning Policy Guidance 16 (PPG 16). In future it would be the developer who would pay for the excavation, on the 'polluter pays' principle, and not the government. This brought archaeology into the planning process and completely changed the basis of rescue archaeology.

The planning alteration PPG 16 (now superseded) created a new world of competitive archaeological units who would pitch for jobs from developers, usually awarded on the basis of who appeared to be the quickest and the cheapest. Although PPG 16 was probably the right thing to do at the time, it has engendered a degree of cynicism – a section of archaeology has become a commercial entity. Contract or commercial archaeology services have sprung up to meet the needs of developers, and it is estimated that over 5,000 archaeologists (in fifty registered groups) are employed as such. They are sometimes jokingly referred to in the profession as 'Shovelbum'. Today much of archaeology is developer-led, particularly urban archaeology, but there are still shining examples of best practice, notably the work of Oxford Archaeology, which operates across much of England, and the Museum of London Archaeology.

Portmahomack

One of the most romantic of all recent excavations took place on the furthest tip of the Tarbat peninsula on the Moray Firth in north-east Scotland, near the fishing village of Portmahomack. When Martin Carver starting digging there in 1994 it did not seem a particularly promising site – merely a cemetery around a medieval church which served an ancient settlement. But the area exerted a magic allure, for the first millennium carved symbol stones there were long known, and these were associated with the Picts, who have always remained tantalisingly mysterious. Indeed, Carver's findings turned out to be a window into the fascinating world of the Picts – a high-status site that was both monastic and royal, yielding a wealth of material from sculpture to banner scripts. Carver later described Portmahomack as 'a stepping stone in the story of Europe'.[10] Perhaps the biggest surprise was finding evidence from vellum offcuts of a substantial scriptorium.

Aerial photography had first suggested the possibility that an incomplete cropmark beside the old church at Tarbat might actually represent a ditch marking out an enclosure: it was D-shaped in plan, just like a similar arrangement at Iona. Carver had just completed his fieldwork at Sutton Hoo, and Tarbat proved to be the natural successor, casting light not only on the formation of the Pictish kingdom and the role played by Christian conversion and monasticism, but the use of iconography, in the form of the magnificent Pictish sculpture found in abundance in and around the area and across the northern and eastern parts of Scotland. However, success was not a given at the outset, for Tarbat represented a foray into an almost unknown culture which had flourished between the sixth and tenth centuries AD. Over 300 people worked on the excavation, which was a collaborative venture with a host of institutions. Chief among them were the Department of Archaeology at York, Field Archaeology Specialists, the Tarbat Historic Trust, Historic Scotland, and the Heritage Lottery Fund.

The Picts intrigued Carver: 'whatever their inadequacy in

recording their own history or their thoughts, the carved stones, souterrains and hill forts spoke volumes: they were epics, eulogies and threnodies of a people with great heart'.[11] Not only were these people interesting but their period was extraordinary, layered between the Roman Empire and the Christian era. Here was a chance to learn more of their political system. The question that confronted the archaeologist was how to construe the evidence of the material culture.

When Carver started the dig, Duncan Johnson, a retired farmer who had ploughed these fields for over forty years, would enjoy a morning cigarette watching the young people at work. One day Johnson softly asked Carver: 'Now what would you be doing, I wonder?' Carver: 'We are looking for a Pictish settlement.' Johnson: 'What are those devices?' Carver (with added condescension): 'They are electronic devices. We use them to find buried houses.' Johnson: 'Have you found any yet?' Carver (robustly): 'Not yet.' Johnson (after a lengthy pause and a drag on a cigarette): 'Would you like to know where they are?' Carver (on whom reality is slowly dawning): 'Indeed I would!' Johnson (companionably): 'We'll go together then.' The farmer led Carver to where the subsoil turned to pure sand, and his intuition proved correct.[12] The first two evaluation seasons produced promising results but still did not establish the enormity of the project, which traces the rise and fall of a Pictish monastery, along with its workshops and its cemetery.

The sixth- and seventh-century settlements where the story begins were not identifiably Christian. The occupants were farmers of cereals and cattle, and we can gauge their high status by the massive scale of the cyst burials that lie under the tumuli, and by the quality of their jewellery – they may be a people of uncertain religion, but they certainly had links all over Britain. By the eighth century we can be certain that Portmahomack is a monastery from the D-shaped enclosure, from Latin inscription, and from images of apostles carved on stone, and the presence of vellum and sacred vessels. Although we cannot with certainty prove connections to any other monastery, the archaeological work at Tarbat gives us a glimpse of early monasticism, which would have been inspired by Saint Columba's mission to Scotland in the late sixth century AD.

What Carver could see was a settlement in transition: an elite centre, followed by a monastery which brought with it various crafts; the vellum, sculpture and church plate were made here. This period came to a rapid close between *c.*780 and *c.*810 – was it because of a raid? The workshop was burnt down, and when revived was no longer serving a monastic community. But to find a Pictish monastery – wealthy, international, skilful, albeit for a glorious and brief flowering – was extraordinary. As Carver reflected: 'At Portmahomack, the change in emphasis from the leadership of warlords, to faith in the divine, to dependence on commerce, to subservience to centralised governance is particularly vivid...the warrior, the merchant and the monk are not inextricably entangled [...] each has his day in the sun, giving a particular flavour and edge to the political agenda of the time.'[13]

Carver has published extensively on the results of his digs (including the discovery of more of the enigmatic Pictish symbol stones). But his finding evidence for a scriptorium of a scale that could produce something even comparable to the Book of Kells was astonishing. As its new Discovery Centre proves, despite the apparent remoteness of this settlement, during a seafaring era, it served as a major centre of civilisation.

Metal Detectorists

Traditionally many archaeologists had a *de haut en bas* view of metal detectorists and treasure hunters. Their contribution is an intriguing one, potentially both revelatory and destructive, depending on circumstances. Metal detectorists emerged when the mine detector technology of World War II was redeveloped for civilian use, and their growth in popularity during the

1960s held, to archaeologists, all the appearance of a dangerous threat, with various magazines – notably *Treasure Hunting* – encouraging the movement. Holes dug by metal detectorists were of course damaging sites and destroying contextual evidence. Archaeologists believed that fragile sites were only safe in their hands, and with some justification claimed 'ownership' of them. As Charles Thomas pointed out, 'only in Britain is it still possible for unqualified persons to perform a destructive and unrepeatable experiment for fun – an excavation – on part of the common national heritage, with no legal restraint save that of common-law ownership'.[14] Worst of all are the plunderers of existing sites whose 'nighthawking' activities are hated by archaeologists and farmers alike.* Metal detectorists are amateurs with no professional training, but one must also admit that without their dedicated enthusiasm for the past, their determination, and the close cooperation of many of them with archaeologists, important treasures such as the Vale of York Hoard (shown alternately in the Yorkshire Museum and the British Museum) would not have been discovered.

In the 1960s, the reputation of detectorists as being interested chiefly in the cash value of finds and carelessly causing great damage to historical context of vulnerable sites had some truth, but it was not the whole truth. Detectorists were viewed at best as a nuisance and in addition propping up the illegal trade in antiquities. The solution turned out to be not to ban them but to persuade them to report their findings. The passing of the Treasure Act (1996) tightened the law and provides a workable incentive for the treasure hunter to cooperate with landowner, archaeologists and the antiquities market. This successful legislation meant that UK law relating to treasure is the best

---

* A particularly shameful example was the repeated raiding of the Wanborough Roman temple village near Guildford for iron age and Roman coins. See report by Oxford Archaeology and English Heritage 2009: *Nighthawks & Nighthawking: Damage to Archaeological Sites in the UK & Crown Dependencies caused by Illegal Searching & Removal of Antiquities.*

in Europe.* The Portable Antiquities Scheme was founded a year later in 1997 and is administered by the British Museum; it has now catalogued over a million objects. In 2009, a metal detectorist, Terry Herbert, discovered the Anglo-Saxon hoard of gold and silver battle gear and ecclesiastical objects known as the Staffordshire Hoard – a treasure as important as Sutton Hoo. Three years earlier both sides had come together to create a code of practice for England and Wales with the support of both the archaeological and metal detecting organisations. Nobody knows how many metal detectorists there are today, but it is estimated at between 10,000 and 30,000.[†]

The archaeologists have indeed been at the forefront of confronting ethical problems of portable heritage over the last half century. A cynic might point out that they have an extensive history of removing treasures from other countries backed by British economic and political power: the digs of Belzoni, Layard, and Evans, heroic in their time, seem more ambiguous to us today. The overall aim may have moved on from finding treasures to understanding societies, but the legacy remains. The British Museum is on the frontline of this ethical conundrum, but is in a difficult position as far as the return of 'loot' is concerned. Colin Renfrew, a former trustee of the museum, has been particularly vocal in setting out the parameters of acceptability and criminalising the trade in looted treasures. Cleaning up the mainstream art trade had been a success story, but museums are having more difficulty in finding clarity on the moral, legal and cultural questions of what constitutes loot and when it should be returned. Anxieties about provenance have been further fuelled by World War II restitution claims. Overall, it is easier

---

* It should be pointed out that Scottish and Northern Irish law are significantly different and some might argue that they are better.

† Problems were resurfacing in 2020 with illegal excavations at Winchelsea posing as workmen digging up the historic cricket pitch. English Heritage said that year that illegal metal detecting had more than doubled since 2017. Report in *The Times*, 9 July 2020.

to deal with the sins of the present than the past, and the debate continues.

Away from thorny questions of portable heritage, archaeologists are confronted with many other conundrums: when, for instance, to preserve sites from invasive developments (the Rose Theatre was a case in point) and how to treat human remains, for example the recently dug up remains believed to be those of Richard III in Leicester. But most of their problems today mirror those across the heritage sector: archaeology is often managed at a low level by local councils, which no longer have the breadth of personnel let alone enough funding. Local museums, for years the backbone of interpretation and display, now receive less funding.

As we saw in Chapter One, the story of heritage particularly in England as a national asset which the government should intervene to protect and preserve stems from early archaeology, notably the efforts of Lubbock and Pitt Rivers at the end of the nineteenth century. But more than any other branch of the heritage industry, archaeology is a constantly evolving story, as important sites are continuously discovered. For example, some of the most exciting recent finds have not been in towns but prehistoric sites where artefacts have been preserved by proximity to water. In 1999 an archaeologist uncovered a fenland settlement, now known as Must Farm, near Peterborough, which had been built on wooden piles sunk into a river sometime during the Bronze Age, 1000–800 BC. A fire caused the houses to collapse into the waters, which then preserved them, and thus we are presented with a perfect snapshot of the household utensils, domestic metalwork, weaponry and what is regarded as the largest and finest collection of textiles from the British Bronze Age.

Archaeology, like all other branches of heritage, is affected by climate change, but sometimes with rewarding results. An astounding recent archaeological discovery was revealed by coastal erosion at Happisburgh Beach in Norfolk in 2013 – the earliest known hominin footprints outside Africa, which were put down when Britain was still linked to continental Europe.

Archaeologists estimate five adults and juveniles were walking along the mudflats of a large river one day approximately 1 million years ago. With today's tides, weather and sand, the problems of recording these before they vanished were acute, and any attempt at preservation was hopeless, but the moment has been captured. This discovery was the result of coastal change, and we are only at the beginning of this next chapter in the story.

CHAPTER II

Beyond the Town

I thought it would last my time—
The sense that, beyond the town,
There would always be fields and farms,
Where the village louts could climb
Such trees as were not cut down;
I knew there'd be false alarms.

PHILIP LARKIN, 1972

If you had asked anyone in 1945 what they meant by countryside heritage, they would almost certainly have mentioned the Peak District or the Lake District, and they likely would have spoken about the beauty of those landscapes. Many would still agree with that assessment today, but extend the definition to include the way the landscape is managed. A satisfying modern example is the National Trust estate at Fontmell Down, where I met the Trust's ranger, Clive Whitbourn, on a hot July day. This is an idyllic corner of Dorset: Shaftesbury is visible on its hill, and the village of Compton Abbas nestles in the valley. The land was acquired in memory of Thomas Hardy, whose novels are set all about. It is a warm landscape of Bronze Age burial mounds, church towers and with four farms let under agricultural tenancies, mostly dairy and sheep with a little maize. The chalk downlands are said to be the most diverse terrestrial habitat in Britain, with as many as 100 species per square metre of herbs, grasses and other flowering plants, as well as twenty-six types of butterfly on adjoining Hambledon Hill. The 293-hectare estate ticks all the boxes: it's a Site of Special Scientific Interest, and an Area of

Outstanding Natural Beauty.[1] The National Trust stewardship balances a complex matrix of priorities – conservation, access and recreation – while trying to protect and manage these places.

Fontmell Down balances the past, present and future in a happy equilibrium, and that is as much as heritage can ever hope to achieve. With the upsurge in walking and visitors to the countryside it has never been so popular. Today the National Trust thinks a great deal more about people's well-being and sees this as part of its mission. The modern expectation to provide dog facilities, for example, can be challenging, not only in terms of fouling but also in terms of their effect on livestock and wildlife. This is the old balancing act between conservation and access – not quite such a big a problem inland as on the ever-eroding coast. The ranger is unphased by this, commenting that by managing the habitats, everything else falls into place.[*] In this he encapsulates the central tenet of our time, that by saving the habitat we are more likely to save the planet. Few of the chapters in this book are witness to such a dramatic shift in attitude, both locally and globally. The question has moved on from who has access to the land to how we should live on it.

In 1945 the stewardship of the countryside still seemed to be with farmers and landowners, but government wartime intervention did not end with the peace. From now on land became highly politicised and increasingly controversial, whether because of intensive farming, bypasses, housing, or the protection of wildlife. The stereotype of 'country good, city bad' has always run deep in British culture, as in many others. In 1928 the CPRE

---

[*] Today a National Trust ranger needs a broad range of skills: making gates, communicating with the public, conducting biological surveys, writing reports and liaising with the farmers. Clive manages thirty volunteer rangers – see Fontmell Down website. He also manages the forest school sites, which is a Swedish model in which children come for a minimum of six visits over six weeks for day camps and learn respect for each other and nature.

had put out a postcard of St George rescuing the countryside. But who was St George in 1945? The farmers and landowners, or the state? That great nineteenth-century scientist, James Joule, had once proclaimed, 'the grand agents of nature are, by the Creator's fiat, indestructible'. During the period from 1945 to the present day, rightly or wrongly, we have ceased to believe that. Nuclear bombs provided the ultimate destructive weapon, and more insidiously our materialist lifestyle is eroding these elements of nature.

In post-war Britain, the controls of the state came to penetrate every part of life. Land was no exception, as the emergence of 'the 1947 system' demonstrates.[*] Nationalising development rights caused the biggest shift in power between landowning interests and the state in British history, with outcomes that the Historic England website still describes as 'elegant in structure and poetic in outcome'.[2] For planners this was indeed a golden age, producing the first comprehensive framework for land use, and for the creation and protection of national parks. Compared to the present time there was more funding, clearer thinking and a sense of purpose, but seen in retrospect, their aims appear to be at odds with each other: to increase farming production, create nature reserves, and preserve beauty spots for the refreshment of city dwellers. The planners could not foresee the effects of technology – plant breeding, pesticides, intensive farming – let alone take a holistic view of the landscape. The government was riding two horses that were cantering in different directions: increasing food production and upholding spiritual values. The unforeseen erosion of spiritual values in the ordinary countryside by intensive farming contributed to large numbers of visitors

---

* During the war there was a great deal of home-front planning, mostly by the Labour members of Churchill's war cabinet. It was the age of the planning committee and one after another produced their findings: Barlow (1940), Scott (1942), and Uthwatt (1942). They were the stepping stones to what is now referred to as 'the 1947 system'.

increasingly descending on 'honey pot' locations, causing huge damage and traffic problems.*

Nobody could then see that the new powers for the farming industry enshrined in the Agriculture Act (1947), providing state subsidy to increase productivity, were to have such malign environmental side effects. The government wanted to improve the dire balance of payments, decrease food importation and make the country potentially self-sufficient in the event of another war (at the time, a war with the USSR seemed not unlikely). When *The Archers* began broadcasting in 1951, it was a collaborative venture between the Ministry of Agriculture, Fisheries and Food and the BBC, with the aim of informing farmers how to increase productivity during an era of rationing.†

The climate of public and political opinion required a stewardship of the countryside with improved public access. The new Labour government was staffed with ramblers and none more enthusiastic than the chancellor, Hugh Dalton. He established the Land Fund in 1946 to increase the national estate, explaining that although much had been spoiled, he hoped that the 'deep peace of the woodland, the white unconquerable cliffs [...] should surely become the heritage, not of a few private owners, but of all our people'.[3] Announcing the measure in parliament, Dalton recalled the old Liberal song 'The Land', at which point Churchill offered to give the House of Commons a rendition:

The land, the land,
'twas God who gave the land,

---

* This was partly addressed with the creation of country parks nearer towns in the 1968 Countryside Act, to provide that spiritual refreshment closer to home.
† The first broadcast was in 1950.

The land, the land,
The ground on which we stand,
Why should we be beggars
With the ballot in our hand?
God gave the land to the people.

If the 1947 Act had been about exerting control, two years later came the National Parks and Access to the Countryside Act (1949), the object of which was, in the words of Lewis Silkin, the Minister of Town and Country Planning: 'first, to preserve and enhance the beauty of the countryside; and second to enable our people to see it, get to it, and enjoy it.'[4] It has been described as 'the most conscious Act for beauty ever brought about by a British government'.[5] The Act protected those areas with 'conservation' written above the gate, but for the rest of the land, as *Country Life* could look back and lament in 1951, 'the past 20–25 years have witnessed even more widespread destruction of Britain's rural scenery than that which took place when railways and industrialism blighted so much a century ago.'[6] It was a story not dissimilar to our own day; increasing population and housing need, but with the additional requirement of having to build a motorway infrastructure.

Rapid urban development and intensive farming provoked the first stirrings of a movement to protect animals and habitats by the formation of the Nature Conservancy Council (1949) 'for the specific purpose of conserving wildlife on a national basis' on National Nature Reserves, and also Sites of Special Scientific Interest (SSSIs). In future all development (except agricultural) would have to be checked against potential habitat damage. But if one hand lent protection the other was subsidising destruction. An article by Frank Sykes in *Country Life* in 1962 looked at the introduction of chemical agriculture, which was leading to the massacre of birds.[7] Under the banner headline 'Poison in the Air', the *Sunday Post* had already published an article by an Angus gamekeeper which declared that 'a silence is falling over the hills'.[8] In phrases that echo Rachel Carson's great classic that came out the same year, *Silent Spring*, the correspondent wrote: 'many of the songbirds are singing no more'.[9] These bird-deaths could be linked to the new dual-purpose seed dressings to protect crops: dieldrin, aldrin and heptachlor. There was also a mounting concern about the possibility of people being harmed by pesticide residues in their food.

Six years later *Country Life* was emboldened to ask the more fundamental question: 'are farmers and conservationists natural allies, or natural enemies?'[10] The new combine harvesters required large fields to be economic, which in turn led to the removal of hedgerow – approximately 230,000 miles went between 1947 and 1990. *Country Life* maintained that the 'hedgerow is the key to survival of most of the wildlife of Britain, and each hedgerow has its own balance of plants, invertebrate and vertebrate life.'[11] Anybody driving up the A1 motorway through the plains of eastern England could now observe the prairie effect of modern farming: larger fields, the loss of hedgerows, and new factory-like barns.

If the new farming methods endorsed and enabled by government proved a mixed blessing, its upholding of spiritual values became an unambiguous triumph with the creation of national parks. Wordsworth himself had unwittingly set the ball rolling in England when he described the Lake District as 'a sort of national property'; the idea of national parks had been promoted during the 1930s by the CPRE, inspired by the American model of Yellowstone, founded in 1872.[*] The historian G. M. Trevelyan in his booklet *The Case for National Parks* (1938) had proclaimed that it was about more than physical health, but 'a question of spiritual values'.[12] The Attlee government had more ramblers than farmers in its ranks, for whom the glory of the countryside was the scenic brass band of northern England. It all

---

[*] In 1938 the CPRE made a short film, *Rural England: The Case for the Defence*, which was shown in a thousand cinemas (and can still be seen on the internet today) which made the case for national parks by comparing what was done in America and South Africa.

came to fruition in 1949 with the National Parks and Access to the Countryside Act.

The first national parks were the Peak District, followed by the Lake District, Snowdonia, Dartmoor, the Pembrokeshire Coast and the North York Moors, eventually numbering thirteen around Britain. National parks were never as sacrosanct as was supposed, with copper mining in Snowdonia, an oil terminal on the Pembrokeshire coast and an early warning station on the North York Moors. But they were a success from the beginning and form the centrepiece of Britain's countryside heritage. By contrast with America, much of the land within them is privately owned; they are a successful cooperation between farmers, landowners, residents, and the park agencies. The national parks were an acknowledgement that beauty mattered, and as Max Nicholson pointed out 'showed conservation as constructive, rewarding, attractive and even fun'.[13]

If some great inland beauty spots were protected by national parks, it was the National Trust that would be the saviour of the coastline when it launched Enterprise Neptune in 1965 to secure unspoiled stretches. The Trust divided the coastline into three categories: land beyond redemption; land which was managed and in active use but could be restored in future (i.e. Ministry of Defence); and land which was free from development and therefore a target for protection. Of England's 19,491 miles of coastline 900 miles were identified as pristine and these stretches became the Trust's acquisitional target. The hardest area to deal with was the low-lying East Anglian coast, with its caravan parks and holiday villages. The leader of Enterprise Neptune was Commander Conrad Rawnsley (grandson of one the Trust's co-founders) who conceived the appeal as a military operation. Prince Philip was secured as the patron, beacons were lit on St George's Day in 1965, and a great lunch followed in the Mansion House to kick-start the fundraising. Enterprise Neptune was hugely popular with the public; within four years 100 miles of coastline had been added and by 2015, 795 miles.

The largest amount paid by Enterprise Neptune was £500,000

for the acquisition of Orford Ness, which had many attractions. This is an estuary with extraordinary vegetation and birdlife, a Site of Special Scientific Interest, a Special Protection Area, and a Special Area of Conservation. It was also, bizarrely, a Cold War Atomic Weapons Research Establishment and boasted two solid-looking concrete 'pagodas' that seemed as strange and eerie as the Cold War itself. The Trust made the interesting decision that these structures would be allowed to deteriorate without any intervention. But could they adopt the same attitude towards the sea defences? Ownership of the estuary raised questions of responsibility for any potential flooding at the local towns of Orford and Aldeburgh. The Trust would increasingly have to face such dilemmas, particularly how to deal with eroding coastline, notably at Birling Gap on the Sussex coast during the 1980s.* Its policy was to work with nature rather than against it and accept the inevitability of change.

The protection of Britain's coastline has been – with notable exceptions – a success story, especially compared to the continent of Europe. No sooner had the coastline been put on the national agenda, and much of it saved, than the trauma of a coastal catastrophe awoke the British public to its fragility: in March 1967, the oil tanker *Torrey Canyon* sank off the Isles of Scilly, resulting in an oil spillage that devastated miles of Cornish coastline. Thirty thousand tons of oil spilled in the first few hours, and a further 20,000 tons over the first week wreaked environmental havoc. It was an environmental disaster on a scale never previously witnessed in Britain, with an immeasurable loss of marine and bird life. Television news showing pictures of birds paralysed by oil had an enormous impact on the public. The *Torrey Canyon* was 'a symbolic landmark event in the emergence of the

---

* The National Trust had acquired some land with a hotel and some 1840s cottages perched on the edge of a cliff. The intention to demolish the buildings and let nature take its course was opposed by residents who wanted coastal defences. The Trust, however, won the public inquiry on the grounds that whatever the defences, the cottages would eventually fall into the sea.

UK environmental discourse'.[14] People began to wonder whether civilisation was threatened less by nuclear attack and more by man's own impact on nature. Nietzsche was often quoted: 'to sin against God was the greatest sin: but God died and those sinners died with him. To sin against the Earth is now the most dreadful thing'.[15] Environmental radicalism, born in the late 1960s, came of age in the 1970s.[16]

This movement offered an alternative, holistic vision of the world that perceived the preservation of animals, habitats, countryside and environment as global issues. Epitomised by Greenpeace and Friends of the Earth, the movement changed the political landscape and formed the backdrop for the creation of the Department for the Environment in 1970. The oil crisis three years later underlined the reliance on fossil fuels and people questioned the optimism of unbridled wealth creation – confidence in the future was diminishing. With the green movement, landscape became a moral territory in which salvation must arrive through ecological harmony with the environment. A British landmark was Nan Fairbrother's book, *New Lives, New Landscapes* (1970), the biblical text for a generation of landscape architects and environmentalists. Written against a background of affluent consumer demand and rampant change in the urban landscape, the book pointed the finger at new housing estates, shopping centres, motorways, and industrial and business centres.

Fairbrother viewed the countryside as a political issue: 'common ownership was the new revolution, which the former privileged do not like sharing, the former under-privileged do not share responsibly'.[17] But by the 1970s there were those on both sides of the political divide beginning to join hands, epitomised by the Prince of Wales's advocacy of organic farming.* The 'environment' became the new buzzword. Theo Crosby organised an exhibition at the Hayward Gallery in 1973, 'How to

* Prince Charles was later to publish *A Vision of Britain* (1989) which set out his view of urban and rural landscapes, giving emphasis to human scale and aesthetic considerations.

Play the Environment Game', in which he extolled the value of what he called 'the pessimist utopia'. But it was with considerable optimism that Edward Heath created a new Department for the Environment in 1970. It might have been the ultimate Orwellian super-ministry – it was housed in the worst example of 1960s office development – but found unlikely champions. John Betjeman, for instance, declared that in it 'we have a court of appeal against threats to the eyes and noses by builders, engineers and manufacturers'.[18]

A later secretary of state, Michael Heseltine, offered the opinion that the environment ministry was 'perhaps the greatest protector of our heritage and the natural environment in our history'.[19] He succinctly explained this statement to the author: 'It had the power and money to intervene as never before.' Its first secretary of state, Peter Walker, commissioned a study, *How do you want to live?* (1972) intended as a contribution to the UN Conference on Human Environment in Stockholm the following year. Lord Snowdon produced a faintly erotic cover photograph and Philip Larkin wrote the poem printed at the head of this chapter, 'Going, Going'.

The Green Belt

What about the countryside immediately beyond the town where, in Larkin's words, 'there would always be fields and farms'? If you were lucky it might be a green belt. Green belts have often puzzled people. Are they sacrosanct or not? Perhaps the confusion comes because they are government 'policy' and not enshrined in law. This is possibly a distinction that is often overlooked... even by the CPRE. This means they are far easier to build on or nibble away at than national parks.

Unlike national parks, the purpose of green belts was never so crystalline. They were invented not so much to protect attractive countryside as the integrity of the border between the town and the country, a fire-break between the two. Leisure use was never uppermost in the minds of those who promoted them.[*] Their story begins in London, when the City of London purchased Burnham Beeches in 1880.[†] The Green Belt Act of 1938 formally recognised the creation of a ring of land around the capital, designed to limit the spread of its suburbs and to create a buffer between the city and the country. This was extended to most major cities and towns in 1955, when Duncan Sandys brought the Green Belt Act before parliament. Today Britain still has fourteen green belts, which cover over 13 per cent of the country. They are described by the CPRE as 'the countryside next door for more than 30 million people'.

Have they preserved the frontiers of historic towns? Leaving London by train going in any direction except west, one's spirit rises to see green fields and haystacks just ten minutes from King's Cross.[‡] The views of York from Brandsby, of Oxford from Boars Hill, despite Ian Nairn's strictures, and Cambridge from Grantchester have all been protected. Objectors point out that there are often unprotected stretches of scenery more worthy of preservation beyond the green belt, but nonetheless green belts remain as important to the post-war world as ribbon development legislation was to an earlier period. They have protected swathes of countryside and provided lungs for the city. Perhaps the strongest argument for their retention is that once you give permission to build on one, planners will find it harder to refuse the next, more damaging development, and the domino effect comes into play.

A good example is the Oxford Green Belt proposed in 1958 but

---

[*] Green belts have been disappointing as places of pleasure, except in honeyspots like Ashridge or Burnham Beeches where facilities exist.

[†] The concept was advanced by planners such as Ebenezer Howard for Garden Cities to have a *cordon sanitaire*. During the 1930s Raymond Unwin advocated a 'green circle' around London and the LCC purchased land to prevent development.

[‡] As it happened the M25 has swallowed up much of the green belt round London.

not finalised until 1975, sitting across several local authorities.*
There will always be development pressure on successful and
beautiful cities such as Oxford. This might be for housing, new
roads, science parks, superstores, or extending the facilities of the
university and its colleges. The pressure is greatest when farmers
go out of business, notably the dairy farms. The largest single
group of landowners, the Oxford colleges (charitable bodies that
typically must maximise their assets), are especially vociferous
in seeking development. Oxford City Council has occasionally
taken land out of the green belt for development, known as
'safeguarded areas' or 'white land', and this was the catalyst for
the formation of the Oxford Green Belt Network (OGBN),
a protection body which has successfully reversed the trend.[20]
It is the current growth agenda of central government and the
Oxford City Council that are pushing for development, with all
its implications for the scenery.

What are the aims of the OGBN? To protect the historic city
and to encourage the use of brownfield sites within the city itself.
The green belt prevents Oxford City from absorbing nearby
villages, thus protecting their character, and at the same time
it enables the benefits of the city's economic attractions to be
shared more equably with the other Oxfordshire towns. Finally,
by checking the outward sprawl of Oxford's built-up area, the
green belt assists the city council's policy of regenerating its
existing older housing estates. Some claim that land lost to the
inner portion of the green belt can be made up by expanding it

---

* Oxford Green Belt encompasses almost 67,000 hectares and extends
for five miles in all directions. 1,754 hectares are SSSI, and 241 hectares are
open access land. The green belt includes five villages which are subject to
the same planning restraints, except Kidlington by virtue of its greater size.
Seventy-six per cent of the land is in agricultural use and 99 per cent is
maintained 'as landscape character' with 113 hectares of country parks, and
639 hectares registered as (historic) parks and gardens. About 13 per cent is
mixed woodland which is rather higher than the national average of 8 per
cent in green belts. These statistics are taken from the CPRE's 'Green Belts in
England: Key Facts'.

outwards, as has happened at the York Green Belt. But this runs counter to its purpose to keep Oxford in scale with its historic centre. As the OGBN insist, 'the essence of the green belt is its permanence'. Green belts, like Conservation Areas, are today on the frontline of heritage protection.

London's Cublington Airport

The conflicting demands of conservation versus progress would be loudest over new or larger airports and roads, when local and national interests collided. When W. G. Hoskins went to write his classic *The Making of the English landscape* (1955), he chose Steeple Barton in Oxfordshire to find peace and quiet in the seemingly unspoiled landscape but he was surprised and dismayed to be disturbed by the noise from the American air base at Upper Heyford. But the blight caused by airports only gradually became evident, and it was not only sonic. Airports require a huge hinterland for car parks, hotels, terminals, hangars, warehouses, ancillary buildings, and perhaps the most extravagant use of land, a network of new roads and roundabouts to link them to motorways. Local protest movements against the visual and auditory intrusions grew, but governments and the population at large did not offer much sympathy until further runways were required, particularly to cope with London's air transport need. Planning became politically much harder and nothing demonstrated this better than the need for a third airport for London. It represents something of a turning point, for this was the moment when the planners themselves began to put the environment first.

The Roskill Commission of inquiry for the location of London's third airport was set up in 1968 to examine possible sites.[*] A cost/benefit analysis approach suggested a village in the Vale of

---

[*] The inquiry was the most exhaustive to date. It took two and a half years, from May 1968 to December 1970, and cost over £1 million.

Aylesbury, Cublington, as the best site. The village, recorded in the Domesday Book, is typical of most in the area, a fourteenth-century church, some half-timbered seventeenth-century houses and a village pub, the Unicorn. The village sits in one of the last great tracts of empty countryside to the north-west of London. One of the members of the commission, Sir Colin Buchanan, Britain's planner-in-chief, carefully surveyed the area on foot to understand the impact of an airport over an area of 12.5 square miles. He concluded that the social gain was not equal to the environmental and heritage loss, lamenting that 'villages and hamlets, churches and chapels, country houses and cottages, farms, woodland, roads, footpaths and antiquities will all go, as well as the community life gradually developed around these features for over centuries.'[21] He based his new-found conservation values on what he called 'the brotherhood of life, on a compassionate belief that other forms of life have the right to survive too and we should seek to conserve them for their sakes and not, because we find them interesting, for ours [...] I seek to switch the argument for nature conservation from our viewpoint to the viewpoint of the life to be conserved.'[22] This coming from Buchanan sent a very powerful message.

Buchanan gave evidence that 'it would be nothing less than an environmental disaster if the airport were to be built at any of the inland sites, but nowhere more serious than at Cublington where it would lie athwart the critically important belt of open country between London and Birmingham'.[23] His twelve-page note of dissent has been called 'the most powerful case that he or any other planner has made for a comprehensive land use planning system'.[24] It was a plea to protect the environment and to overturn short-term advantages that might have damaging long-term effects. Buchanan expressed grave doubts about the cost/benefit analysis approach, concluding: 'I have no doubt that the things I find of interest in the open background of London are things that will interest many generations to come. I am profoundly certain they are *good* things.'[25] Greenfield sites were too precious – was there a brownfield site? Buchanan favoured Foulness, and his reasoning is an early example of the new impetus that redefined heritage, regeneration. Ultimately all sites proposed in the inquiry were scrapped and Stansted was to become the third London airport some twenty years later.

On the Road

Probably the most destructive form of building in Britain during the 1960s had been the creation of the motorway system, as successive governments put their faith in a car-owning democracy. The first completed stretch was the Preston bypass in Lancashire in 1958 followed by a section of the M1 the next year. By 1964 there were almost 20 million private vehicles on the road. Motorways swallowed up about twice as much land as a railway, consuming about twenty-five acres of land to the mile. Most developments can be shaped according to need, but motorway building is necessarily linear and can only divert at huge expense.

The Ministry of Transport took the self-serving view that roads through beautiful countryside added value by making that beauty more accessible and visible – an argument still brought up by those who do not wish to reroute the A303 from passing so close to Stonehenge. Much of the work of the Royal Fine Art Commission (RFAC) was devoted to the careful routing of motorways and trunk roads through the countryside. The RFAC was a toothless but well-intentioned national committee of taste which, among other interventions, interceded to reduce the damage to the Chilterns by the M40 motorway. The RFAC insisted on a high standard of motorway landscape design which was given direction through the publication of Sylvia Crowe's *The Landscape of Roads* (1960). In one respect British motorways were at the forefront of design – one of the most effective and distinctive contributions is the road signage by Margaret Calvert and Jock Kinneir, whose classic lettering and design remain in place.

The first motorways were not resisted. They were the symbols of the future and widely admired – the new was still in vogue. When the extension of the M3 took traffic away from Winchester, it was a harbinger of the difficult road choices that would, from now on, be vigorously opposed by every side. From the 1970s onwards, roads became a chief battleground for activists. Bypasses were usually more contested than motorways. The bypass was on the face of it the friend of heritage by diverting traffic out of the centre of historic towns, but all too often what saved the town spoiled the countryside. A potentially damaging bypass proposal was that around Petworth in West Sussex in 1973. The town was congested with traffic and for many the obvious solution was to drive a bypass through the Capability Brown park adjoining Petworth House.* The National Trust, the property owner, retained Colin Buchanan to make its case. There were few obvious alternatives except an unspoiled river valley to the east of the town where residents walked their dogs. This was, however, more precious to them than Petworth Park, to which they had only recently been given access. The Trust had to deal with the depressing spectacle of the townspeople supporting the reduction of a Capability Brown park that had been hallowed by Turner.

This case prompted the cultural magus, Kenneth Clark, to write to the minister:

> I can see what a problem this kind of 'democratic' sentiment poses [...] It is certainly an argument against government by referendum. I suppose on the same grounds one could argue in favour of selling the contents of the National Gallery and using the site for a gigantic fun-fair. In these cases, the governments have to understand the word democracy in a philosophical sense rather than a quantitative sense. And on this basis one could

---

* The supposedly inviolate nature of National Trust property came under attack when the six-lane Plympton bypass cut through the park at Saltram in 1970 by obliterating an eighteenth-century carriage drive.

argue that the beauty of Petworth Park will continue to affect men's minds long after the present inhabitants of Petworth have disappeared.[26]

The park scheme was dropped. In future the objectors would no longer be confined to grandees putting pressure on parliamentarians but broader activists, savvy in PR and television, gaining national support.

Never was the debate about conservation versus progress noisier than at the bypass protest which became a green *cause célèbre*, the Third Battle of Newbury in 1996.* The A34 Newbury bypass was planned to cut through countryside described in *Watership Down*, and clip the Capability Brown park at Highclere Castle. In addition the nine-mile route was set to cross over three Sites of Special Scientific Interest, two historical battle sites, and involve the removal of 10,000 trees. Eight thousand protestors took part, many of them green activists involved in a wider 'anti-road' movement to halt road building and thereby protect the environment across Britain. In this they were more extreme than both Nan Fairbrother and Kenneth Clark, two conservationists who believed in the need for well-sited motorways and bypasses.

The figurehead of this protest was a colourful figure, Daniel Marc Cooper, aka Swampy, who felt that direct action was the only way to be heard by the nation and have the desired impact on environmental policy. The Newbury protest brought together many different strata in society. Most striking was the sight of 'well-dressed elderly ladies bringing cake and tea to the crusties and hippies living in "benders" high above the ground'.[27] The involvement of county ladies and business showing solidarity with the green activists sent a message to policymakers that it wasn't just hippies and anarchists that wanted to save the British countryside.

The protests at Newbury generated a series of legal challenges. SAVE mounted a legal case against the Department of Transport's

---

* The first two battles were during the Civil War.

proposal to run the bypass through the park at Highclere, close to the domed Temple of Diana, recently restored with public money. The problem was made more difficult since as a courtier the owner, Lord Carnarvon, felt he could not oppose the road himself. SAVE challenged the minister for refusing to hold a public inquiry.* The judge found in their favour and SAVE got their inquiry – the road was diverted. The Friends of the Earth also went to court to argue the case against the destruction of wildlife habitat, specifically that of Desmoulin's whorl snail. They lost their lawsuit, but thanks to the publicity generated the activists gained a PR victory. It is generally accepted that the protests had a profound effect on transport policy. After Newbury, the Labour government came to power with a manifesto pledge to stop road building and look at the alternatives.

★ ★ ★

At the time of the 2012 London Olympics various polls ranked the countryside on a par with the royal family, the NHS and Shakespeare as what people prized most about England.[28] Today it is the infringement of the built environment on the countryside that is most alarming. To the CPRE, 'Town and Country Planning is now the single most important factor affecting the look of Britain and we meddle with it at our peril!'[29] At present England is losing 27,000 acres annually to urban development, mostly housing. During the second half of the twentieth century the housing stock rose by about 78 per cent, from 13.8 million dwellings in 1951 to 24.6 million in 2000. But it is in the second half of this period, after 1980, that more green fields vanished under development as a percentage of the whole than at any time during the twentieth century. Put another way, in 2010 the extent of Britain's landscape mass that is built up was 7.7 per cent, and by 2020 that figure had increased to 8.3 per cent. As Simon

---

* SAVE put forward an argument that this was a matter of national importance and that the relevant arguments could only properly be examined, considered and challenged in the form of a public inquiry.

Jenkins writes: 'England may have the lowest amount of green space per head of any big country in Europe, but it continues to lavish what is left on the lowest housing densities.'[30]

Anybody seeking to compare the conservation movement in France and Italy since 1945 with Britain would observe that those countries were more successful at preserving their historic towns and cities but have spoiled their countryside, whereas the opposite would be true of Britain. But given the high density of population in Britain,* the preservation of the countryside remains a deep concern, especially with the continuous loss of biodiversity. What is exceptional is the variety of English landscape, so that you can traverse over a saltmarsh into a forest, through meadows and arable land and out onto heaths and downs all within a morning's walk. Jennifer Jenkins, one of the heroines of conservation in the second half of the twentieth century, was right in saying that 'in this small, densely populated island in Britain every landscape matters, the ordinary as much as the beautiful and the historic'.[31] We preserved the great national parks back in the 1960s, and she asked the question: what should we do now? She had no doubt what the objectives should be: 'to improve decent ordinary landscapes; and create good new landscapes where the land has been degraded. The question is how to achieve these objectives?'[32]

---

* Approximately 727 people per square mile lived in Britain in 2020.

CHAPTER 12

The Fall and Rise
of Country Houses

*The end of a thousand years of English history
and culture, as pell-mell the contents are unloaded
into the sale room, the houses handed over to
the government or demolished.*[1]

ROY STRONG, 1974

During the 1970s it sometimes seemed as if heritage was predominantly about country houses. These rural monuments to an earlier age of privilege began to hog the limelight as their owners became the most successful lobbyists in the cultural sector. The period 1945–2000 was the most tumultuous in their long history as they had to adapt to radically altered social and economic conditions. The perils were considerable and many owners simply gave up the struggle in the face of post-war dilapidation, dauntingly high taxation and the loss of staff. Overall, however, the British landowning classes embraced the adaptations required to carry on, and even to flourish. The most pervasive change was the opening of houses to the public on a commercial basis – some aristocrats proved to be natural showmen and palpably relished public attention. In parallel with this was the extraordinary growth of the National Trust, which so often scooped up houses that had simply run out of steam or were financially depleted by death duties. By the 1970s country houses had become something of a cult and the subject of a publicity fest trumpeting their status as a unique British contribution to Western civilisation.

The plight of country houses in the aftermath of World War II was aptly described by a Ministry of Works inspector:

> when the war ended the country was littered with dere-quisitioned houses often in a woeful disrepair. Not only were windows broken, rooms leaking, and gutters blocked but lead had been stolen, ironwork was rusting away and inside, stair balustrades were smashed, treads worn away with hobnail boots and chimney pieces scorched and burned by overheated stoves. There was unpainted woodwork by the yard, and neglect was rampant everywhere: dry rot, wrecked gardens and parks, disbanded staffs, spoiled, moth-eaten, broken or partially burned contents. It is little wonder that no one wanted them.[2]

It was clear that the pre-war country house way of life was at the least seriously compromised and in many cases utterly irrecoverable. Some houses were demolished (10 per cent between 1945 and 1960) while others (as many as 20 per cent) were converted into premises such as schools, nursing homes, hotels or company headquarters.* Nearly all country house studies have concentrated on houses that have retained their contents, but adaptation was necessary, particularly where urban encroachment swallowed country estates, and many mansions became useful as care homes or were successfully divided up to make offices and flats. In Scotland, many fine Victorian baronial houses like Abercairny House were demolished and David Bryce's work at Cortachy Castle truncated.

The incoming Labour government of 1945 petrified the older owners. Lord and Lady Newton of Lyme Park told James Lees-Milne that 'they would never be able to reconcile themselves to the new order after the war. They admitted that their day was done, and life as they had known it was gone forever.'[3] The post-war crisis was in fact anticipated by a far-seeing grandee, Philip Kerr, Lord Lothian, a Liberal peer with an energetic mind

---

* Demolitions reached their peak in 1955 with seventy-six houses lost.

who worked closely with Christopher Hussey of *Country Life*. Together they may be credited with one of the most successful solutions to a heritage problem ever devised, the idea that families could pass their property without tax to the National Trust (necessarily with a hefty endowment) but – crucially – could continue to live in their ancestral home. The Trust was cautious as a result of their chastening experience of taking on two loss-making houses: Barrington Court (its restoration had almost bankrupted them) and Montacute (an empty shell of a house). However, recognising the great and growing threat, the Trust plunged in.

The secretary of the newly formed Country House Committee of the National Trust was the young aesthete James Lees-Milne, whose sympathetic manner and tendency to accept houses on whatever terms he could extract did much to allay the fears of anxious and suspicious owners. Lees-Milne famously expressed his loyalties to the house, the family and the National Trust in that order. From 1940 to 1960 an astonishing seventy properties were accepted, including the Tudor mansions Knole and Hardwick, Jacobean Blickling, two great treasure houses, Petworth and Waddesdon, and the glorious gardens at Stourhead, Hidcote and Bodnant. To give a sense of how effective the National Trust was perceived as a panacea for their problems by apprehensive owners and their trustees, negotiations were opened for several great houses that were to remain in private hands (usually owing to unbreakable entails making the provision of an endowment problematic): Longleat, Harewood, Althorp, Woburn, Holkham and Arundel. The Trust struggled to remain a body of last resort.

Accepting so many great houses and gardens altered the trajectory of the organisation. However, in every generation the National Trust has changed its priorities in line with broader national priorities and threats, and thus it embraced the new and urgent task of saving country houses. This was a relatively short phase in its history which lasted until the 1980s, by which time the Trust was returning to its roots in the landscape. During the early part of their mission to rescue the country house they found themselves both assisted by and in competition with government. The competition came from the Ministry of Works, the nation's curator of monuments. This was brought into focus by the early seventeenth-century prodigy house, Audley End, which was allocated to the ministry. The National Trust felt snubbed and Lees-Milne snootily remarked: 'I am sorry that the NT has not got it because I'm convinced that they will present houses better than the tasteless Ministry of Works.'

The election of the Labour government in 1945 with their nationalising agenda was generally seen to be positive for the National Trust. Hugh Dalton, the chancellor, was not particularly interested in country houses, but he was an enthusiastic rambler and approved of the Trust's mission as an example of practical socialism in action. The Trust would be the major beneficiary of a far-sighted scheme that Dalton set up in 1946, which put aside £50 million from the sale of war surplus equipment as a memorial to those who had died in both world wars, the National Land Fund. If Dalton had landscape and coastline primarily in mind, he had no objection when the scheme was also used to transfer two historic houses, Cotehele in Cornwall and Penrhyn in North Wales, to the National Trust; but where did that leave the contents? The turning point arrived, as usual, with a crisis. Petworth House and its park already belonged to the Trust but *not* the contents, and on the death of Lord Leconfield in 1952, these were threatened with dispersal. The system was amended to allow chattels to be accepted in lieu of death duties while they remained in the house.* The Land Fund enabled such transfers, but it turned out

---

* Since 1910 an Acceptance in Lieu of Tax scheme had operated for land and buildings but had proved unworkable owing to the Inland Revenue's insistence on being paid back for the loss of hard currency. But now Dalton's Land Fund could pay back the Revenue for the loss of tax, which opened up great possibilities.

to be a disappointment in the long run – the Treasury kept hold of the reins, which stifled its full potential.[*]

The number of houses requiring rescue alarmed the government to the extent that Dalton's successor, Stafford Cripps, asked the Ministry of Works for a list of the most important in private ownership which would have to be preserved at all costs – it amounted to fifty-two properties. This was the first occasion that government took a direct interest in the future of the country house. The Ministry of Works sensed an opportunity; it convinced itself that the National Trust did not have the financial muscle to save houses, keep them repaired and provide the necessary expertise. The ministry had the lion's share of visitors: as late as 1962 their sites in England and Wales attracted 5.5 million visitors, compared with 1.2 million for National Trust properties and 4 million for privately owned houses. But many owners, such as Sir Lyonel Tollemache at Ham House, Surrey, would do anything to prevent their homes being taken over by the state, which they felt was over-taxing them and thus the cause of all their misery. Without an endowment, however, Ham House had no choice but to fall under Ministry protection for the time being.[†]

Everybody realised that the National Trust and the Ministry of Works could not accept every great house with or without endowment. Government began to recognise that the solution lay with owners themselves largely thanks to the Gowers Report (1950) commissioned by Cripps: *Houses of Outstanding Historic or Architectural Interest*. This warned of an 'impending catastrophe' as destructive as the dissolution of the monasteries. It strongly supported the view that houses were best preserved

---

[*] Five further properties were accepted by the National Trust through the Land Fund from the Treasury: Beningbrough Hall, Dyrham Park, Hardwick Hall, Saltram House and Sudbury Hall.

[†] Sometimes the ministry acquired a house, such as Cobham Hall, to restore it with a view to finding a new purchaser/tenant – a precedent repeated later at Heveningham, and nearer our own time at Apethorpe.

by the families that occupied and cherished them. The report evidences the special pleading which became the familiar narrative over the next thirty years. The architect Gerry Wellesley (later Duke of Wellington) spoke of 'an association of beauty, of art and of nature [...] seldom, if ever been equalled in the history of civilisation.'[4] The country house is portrayed as a sacred trust to be handed down and the owners as custodians who, in the word of Noel Coward's song, 'scrimp and screw and save'.

The Gowers Report provided a lifeline by recommending that owners of listed properties should be offered grants to embark on a restoration in return for public access. Subsidy rather than nationalisation would be the way forward, and was mockingly referred to as 'doles for dukes'. The Historic Buildings Councils for England, Scotland and Wales were established to administer the cash inducements to restore these or other historic buildings. It stimulated a golden age of houses opening to the public.

The landowners who gave evidence to the Gowers committee favoured tax concessions but played down the possibilities of the tourism that was to rescue so many country houses and by the 1970s to give them such a central position in the heritage story. Most houses had traditionally been open to visitors in return for a tip to the housekeeper, but very rarely commercially. In 1950 only seventy houses were open to the public, but during the 1960s this rose to 350 and has hovered around that number ever since. The ticket money was of course welcome, but during a period of high taxation it was the grants and the ability to set running expenses against tax that proved of most benefit. The first houses to open, in 1946, were Arundel, Burghley and Holkham; in a very dignified manner. The public were often shown round by the butler or a member of the family and it sometimes seemed they were there on sufferance.

Everything changed with the arrival on the scene of the Duke of Bedford and the Marquess of Bath: they invented the modern stately home business at Woburn and Longleat during the 1960s.* These aristocratic showmen took their cue from circus and holiday camp entrepreneurs like Billy Smart and Billy Butlin by opening on their estates hugely successful amusement and safari parks. They worked on the principle of a family day out. It coincided with the rise in domestic tourism encouraged by wider socio-economic factors such as paid holidays, exchange controls limiting the exchange of pounds for foreign currency, and the growing availability of coach tours for day-trippers. The Duke of Bedford's declared aim was to ensure visitors enjoyed themselves and received good service and value for money so they would come back again. This was the language of Butlins. Both peers had a flair for publicity and no fear of commercialism. As the Duke of Bedford, a former *Daily Express* journalist, echoing the breezy Hollywood sex symbol Mae West explained: 'it is better to be looked down upon than be overlooked'.[5]

Lord Montagu of Beaulieu, at the forefront of this new entrepreneurial approach, even wrote a manual for owners: *The Gilt and the Gingerbread: or How to Live in a Stately Home and Make Money.* Country houses began to enjoy a revival after the hopeless 1950s and achieved a certain glamour as the settings for numerous films. There arose a gossip-column fascination in the lives of the owners which chimed with the Swinging Sixties. Even the *Thunderbirds* TV puppet show heroine Lady Penelope was

---

* In 1964, the Marquess of Bath was receiving 135,000 visitors a year at Longleat, well behind the numbers visiting Woburn, Chatsworth, Blenheim and Beaulieu. The circus owner Jimmy Chipperfield promised him 'millions' of people if he opened a safari park. When Lord Bath announced it, all hell broke loose in the press, which conjured up images of lions running wild through Wiltshire, savaging sheep. Joy Adamson objected and *The Times* stated that lions should be confined to heraldry. After the press launch in 1966, the same paper reported – perhaps disappointedly – that 'nobody was eaten here today'. Four years later, the Duke of Bedford followed with Woburn Safari Park, which was a flop until a lioness called Twiggy sank her teeth into a five-year-old girl, Sian Symons Jones. That brought the public in droves.

endowed with her own Palladian stately home and the services of a plucky cockney chauffeur called 'Nosey' Parker. But as always with the 1960s there were several contradictory narratives. If there was an appetite to read about the Duke of Devonshire hosting a ball at Chatsworth, the nearby Duke of Portland had let his pile Welbeck Abbey to serve as an army training college, while the ruined shell of Nuthall Temple, a Palladian Rotunda house, was finally demolished to make way for an extension to the M1 motorway.

The National Trust spent the 1960s digesting the great houses it had swallowed. It adopted a conservationist state of mind and was against enlarging its membership in case the houses were overrun. It nurtured brilliant curators, one of whom, Robin Fedden, jokingly told a colleague: 'you must realise the National Trust has nothing to do with the people'.[6] But awkward questions were being asked about insufficient access to many of their properties. The tectonic plates were shifting, and a fissure developed in 1964 as the Trust began the slow but decisive return to its roots by launching 'Enterprise Neptune' to safeguard Britain's coastline. The rows that erupted – essentially about identity and image – led to the Benson Enquiry (1967) which released the Trust from the control of an oligarchy of amateur aristocratic trustees and adopted a more professional business model. The acquisition of great houses tapered off during the 1970s, but one that got through was Erddig, near Wrexham. The Trust's work there would point the way to the future in the presentation of houses – the discovery of 'downstairs'.

The Yorke family at Erddig had shown their regard for their staff by forming an extraordinary collection of paintings and photographs of workers both inside the house and on the estate. As Merlin Waterson, the Trust curator responsible for its display, explained: 'the house provided an opportunity to re-order the way the National Trust showed its houses. Instead of arriving at the front door, visitors were to make their way through a succession of outbuildings, encountering carpenters working in the joiner's shop, a blacksmith, a baker in the bakehouse, and horses in the stable yard.'* For the first time the staff took centre stage, made possible by the extraordinary surviving archive. In 2007 Erddig was voted the nation's 'favourite historic house'.

The country house narrative was indeed changing. In place of the state rooms with their priceless old master paintings, the treasure houses furnished from the Grand Tour, and the power houses of political fame, we were now offered the story house. Television series such as *Upstairs, Downstairs* (1971–5) had given equal airtime to both sides of the green baize door separating servant and master, and this narrative struck a chord with the public. A 1982 survey revealed that only 9 per cent of visitors gave furniture and paintings as the most important reason to visit, 7 per cent admitted to an interest in architecture, 25 per cent came for 'a day out' or for general interest, while no less than 50 per cent came to find out about 'how people lived in the past'. The new sociological approach was given academic weight by Mark Girouard's *Life in the English Country House* (1978), a transformational study of underlying economic and social structures.

It was just as well that the public interest was more focused on social history, as the art treasures were draining away. There were several causes for this flight to the saleroom: most owners were still farming, an activity that required frequent injections of capital, but overwhelmingly the cause was taxation and, increasingly, divorce. The drain of works of art was alarming, but as Giles Worsley (himself from an art-collecting family) pointed out: 'sales from country houses are always written about as tragedies. In fact, the sale of objects has been a key element in the survival strategy of the country house in the twentieth century'.[7] As far as the mechanisms to save works of art were concerned, the drain was just about manageable – about a half of the important

---

* Waterson p. 196. This approach was pioneered by the brilliant Cornish representative of the National Trust, Michael Trinick, at Lanhydrock in Cornwall in 1969 and later at two Devon properties, Compton Castle and Saltram, where he presented fully furnished kitchens.

works of art were picked up by museums and galleries in Britain, the rest exported – usually to America.[8]

Although the system for saving works of art was noisy and creaking it worked adequately until a new development threatened to overwhelm it. The Labour Party was returned to power in 1974 and published a green paper outlining a proposal for a wealth tax.* This caused panic in the country house world, raising the spectre of an exodus of works of art like that in the 1890s. Owners had for some time realised that they needed more political clout. A few years earlier the British Tourist Authority had formed a committee known as the Historic Houses Committee which warned that taxation was the greatest threat to their survival. Lord Montagu led the formation of the independent Historic Houses Association and became its first president in 1973. It was envisaged as a trade association but immediately became embroiled in a highly political battle to defend its members against the proposed wealth tax. Their most effective propaganda came to them from an unexpected direction the following year, courtesy of the grammar-school educated Roy Strong, director of the V&A, with the seminal exhibition, 'The Destruction of the Country House'.

The exhibition was a dramatic demonstration that country houses were in crisis. The evidence had been accumulating year on year with the startling number of houses demolished since 1945. If there was a flaw in this argument, it was that the evidence presented was actually historic and, despite the threat of a wealth tax, the houses were by this time already more economically resilient and the weakest had already gone to the wall. But in

---

* It would be a mistake to believe that the Labour Party were antipathetic to country houses. As Michael Saunders-Watson, president of the HHA, observed: 'in general I found members of the Labour Party more receptive concerning the heritage [...] the interest in heritage matters shown by the intellectual wing of the Labour Party goes back to the late nineteenth century'. The Tory Party could be surprisingly off-hand about owners, seeing them as a mild embarrassment and assuming their votes were already in hand.

1974 there was a growing sense of gloom, not just among Historic Houses Association (HHA) owners, but across the country at large. Roy Strong himself summed it up: 'the weather has been foul, matching the economic and political situation [...] it's like World War II again [...] everything is in the doldrums'.[9] Britain in 1974 was a country of power cuts, strikes, shortages and political uncertainty. In this miserable social climate, would anyone care about the loss of some country houses?

The response was in fact overwhelmingly of shock and sympathy, except in the Guardian.[10] It was arguably the most memorable and influential exhibition that the V&A has ever mounted. This had much to do with the staging and design: the centrepiece was a 'Hall of Destruction' conceived on the model of the frescoes of falling rocks and pillars crushing giants in the Palazzo del Te at Mantua, in this case representing 319 collapsing country houses. It was pure theatre, with the doom-laden voice of one of the curators, the architectural historian John Harris, reciting a roll call of lost houses. The exact number of houses demolished (or severely truncated) was unknown but the best guesses suggested 250 since 1945 and 1,600 over the previous century. This visual and emotional exhibition coincided with the publication of the more cerebral Cornforth Report, *Country Houses in Britain: Can they Survive?* Written by the respected architectural historian John Cornforth, it offered the most acute analysis of the problem to date and a sober assessment of the challenges ahead.

The impact of the Cornforth Report and the V&A exhibition put country houses right at the top of the heritage agenda. This had some immediate results: capital tax concessions for the transfer of historic houses; and the 1976 Finance Act enabling the creation of maintenance funds; an endowed vehicle in which to place historic houses and their contents – an option embraced by two heavyweights, Arundel Castle and Chatsworth. The spectre of a wealth tax faded away, but this probably had more to do with economic than heritage factors. One important long-term consequence of the exhibition, however, was not fiscal but the formation in 1975 of the influential ginger group, SAVE Britain's

Heritage (SAVE). Its founder, the architectural historian Marcus Binney, was one of the organisers of the V&A exhibition and a former editor of *Country Life*. SAVE proved to be far more than a country house lobby and its most impressive achievements would lie in saving northern mills and other industrial buildings. Its first report focused on the modest terraced house. Perhaps the most consistent theme of SAVE has been to show that any building of whatever type can be adapted, reused and regenerated, given a good architect and the willingness to try.

SAVE and the designer and developer Kit Martin successfully applied this strategy by creating architecturally sensitive, workable domestic divisions at the mansions of Burley-on-the-Hill in Rutland and the Hazels in Bedfordshire. A seemingly hopeless case was the Palladian Barlaston Hall in Staffordshire which was near collapse from a combination of neglect and subsidence caused by coal mining. Its exasperated owners, the Wedgwood pottery company, challenged SAVE to buy the house for £1 if Binney really believed that the house had an economic future. They accepted the challenge, jauntily proffered a 10p deposit and the house was successfully restored. Binney later reflected that its rescue was a collaborative effort of *Country Life* campaigning, the Historic Buildings Council providing grants and SAVE taking the risk. The most intractable of all their country house case histories was the deserted domestic Greek temple, The Grange in Hampshire. Acres of press comment, legal threats to ministers and decades passed before it finally found an unexpected new role as a rural opera house in 1998.[*]

For some historians, the V&A exhibition in 1974 marked the point at which the so-called heritage industry was born. Others point to the establishment the following year of the European Architectural Heritage Year. Either way, heritage was now very much on the public and political radar. In May 1978

---

[*] The longest restoration drama of all is that of Mavisbank near Edinburgh, gutted by fire in 1973 and still waiting in 2020 to be restored for use by the Landmark Trust.

Binney observed that 'never have country houses been more in the limelight than today'. They basked in a new wave of adulation that amounted to a nostalgic cult. Like all cults this required a sacrificial victim, which came in the fattened and spectacular form of an opulent Rothschild mansion owned by the Earls of Rosebery, Mentmore Towers in Buckinghamshire. It was the death of the 6th earl that precipitated a dramatic rescue attempt.

Mentmore was a treasure house *par excellence*, replete with grand French furniture, tapestries, ormolu mounted objects, Marie Antoinette's Sèvres milk pails, etc. – a rich diet for connoisseurs rather than the wider public who cherished Erddig. Henry James was quoted: 'I do not believe that the *Medici* ever were so lodged at the *height* of *their* glory.' The new Lord Rosebery offered the house and its contents to the nation for £2 million, but the frantic efforts to save it proved in vain. The Sotheby's auction went ahead in May 1977, attracting vast international interest. The result was an astonishing £6.25 million for the contents alone. The sacrifice of Mentmore, however, was the turning point that exposed the weakness in the government's heritage policy.

Mentmore was cast as a fiasco and questions were asked in the House of Commons and by the press as to why the nation had proved so incapable of action. Marcus Binney had already identified the root of the problem in an article in *Country Life* before the sale, pointing a finger at the moribund Land Fund, and wondering why it could not be reincarnated to save Mentmore.[11] The lobbying may have been in vain but, as Binney remarked, 'we lost the battle but won the war'.[12] The affair put a spotlight on the Land Fund and its failure to act despite notionally having £18 million of capital. The matter was examined by a Parliamentary Select Committee and a white paper recommended that the Land Fund should be reinvented but distanced from the Treasury and, crucially, with independent trustees.

The result was the formation of the National Heritage Memorial Fund (NHMF) in 1980 with an annual grant that fluctuated between £4 million and £13 million.[*] This new body had the ability to save whatever its trustees thought fit, independent of government (essential when health workers were striking). Perhaps wisely, heritage was never defined – the fund's first chairman Lord Charteris explained that the term would define itself – but in its early years it had a distinctly country house bias. The founding of the NHMF coincided with a generational change that brought several houses to the point of dispersal. This precipitated a last and unexpected round of historic house (and contents) rescues by the National Trust, which were enabled through the fund. The role of the NHMF was usually to provide the endowments which swallowed the lion's share of its grant money during the first decade. Lord Charteris recorded in his 1981/2 report that this 'dominated our thoughts during a period when it looked as though several outstanding large country houses and their contents could need saving simultaneously'.[†]

Charteris was a popular ex-courtier and provost of Eton whose patrician values (and those of his close ally Lord Anglesey) ensured that country houses would receive a sympathetic hearing. In fact, historic properties were enjoying cult status during the 1980s which reached a sentimental apogee with the TV showing of *Brideshead Revisited* (1981), a love letter to Castle Howard, and its international apotheosis with the 'Treasure Houses of Britain' exhibition at the National Gallery in Washington (1985–6). It was the greatest art exhibition ever loaned from Britain and in the words of *The Economist* magazine, 'a shameless sales pitch for

* The NHMF funding is not a clear matter. It started life with a capital base of £10 million to 'look more like the existing capital assets [from the Land Fund] of £17 million by adding a 1980–1 grant of £5.5 million to it'. See Arthur Jones, p. 188. It spent far beyond the income from this capital every year topped up by the minister.

† NHMF Annual Report 1981/2, p. 2. The National Trust was always careful to emphasise that it was not acquisitive of houses for their own sake but only if their survival was at risk, acting in its role as the body of last resort.

the British heritage'. This was truer than the magazine realised, as many of the exhibited works of art would be sold as a result of their international exposure.

The country house *cause célèbre* of the 1980s was Calke Abbey, the counterpoint to Mentmore and expressive of a very different world. The Harpur-Crewe family of Calke were eccentric local squires who pursued their own antiquarian interests. It was their anachronistic character that made the Harpur-Crewes so intriguing. As Patrick Wright wrote: 'the family is distinguished precisely because it lacks any distinction and Calke Abbey is of historical value because it is too sufficiently unremarkable to have survived unnoticed.'[13] Calke represented, in that fashionable phrase, a time warp. Connoisseurs like John Cornforth, who had lobbied to save Mentmore, were lukewarm. The economist Lord Vaizey suggested that the contents were little more than two centuries' worth of junk; all true, but mixed in among it was silver by Paul de Lamerie, an autographed musical score by Haydn, and paintings by Landseer, Lawrence and Ruysdael. Unlike Mentmore, the press clamour over Calke hit a popular note. In his first budget speech as chancellor, Nigel Lawson announced £4 million via the NHMF to save the house for transfer to the National Trust.

During its first decade, as we have seen, the NHMF was to spend the bulk of its money on country houses: Kedleston (£7 million for contents), Weston Park (£6 million endowment to a charitable trust) and Belton (£8 million). Other houses then benefiting from large grants were Canons Ashby, Nostell Priory, Brodsworth, Burton Constable and the gardens of Studley Royal and Stowe. In Scotland Thirlestane Castle was put in a charitable trust and Fyvie Castle presented to the Scottish National Trust, both endowed by the NHMF. Not every application succeeded, and Edward James's surrealist fantasy at Monkton House was turned down. This unexpected NHMF-driven country house rescue phase came to an end with the appearance of the more politically accountable National Lottery. By the time New Labour was swept to power in 1997, the priorities were already changing again towards restoring museums and a contemporary agenda. The following year John Cornforth observed the backlash, and an 'anti-heritage, anti-country house view in the media'. The National Trust firmly announced its policy of acquiring no more country houses and concentrating on land.*

What was happening in the private sector? The Thatcher period brought liquidity to country houses through lower taxation, and notwithstanding the last round of National Trust transfers, in future the private sector would prove to be their rescuer. Houses that had been deserted by the family were reoccupied: Welbeck said goodbye to the army college and became a family home again. Many new owners, both British and foreign, acquired houses without an estate, supported by external financial interests. Existing owners found new income streams, especially corporate entertainment and weddings. Event venues became increasingly popular, and today many houses do little else. Thornton Manor in Cheshire, the former home of Lord Leverhulme, can host three separate weddings in different parts of the house, out of sight and earshot of each other, even providing a separate entrance drive.

At the time of writing there are 1,500 owner members of the Historic Houses Association of which 900 advertise events, weddings, and other commercial activities. In the Edwardian era, houses that existed for house parties and events (usually charity and village occasions) were very much the exception – today this has been reversed. They have created a dual private/public entertainment facility, giving most weekends to commerce and reserving a sufficient number of weekends a year for friends, while the staff and services remain the same. They are effectively hotels. Events have put houses back at the heart of their community, but they have also ripped some of the soul out of them. Perhaps one of the most surprising developments has been the renewal

---

* There would be a dramatic coda to that position when they acquired the great Victorian mansion Tyntesfield in 2002, and Seaton Delaval in 2009.

of country house building, with several architectural practices specialising in this genre.

Taking an overview of the period since 1945, an observer might remark that while privately owned historic houses have been denuded of many of their valuable works of art, their owners have grown immeasurably in confidence, savviness and economic success. More are likely to have had a first career in London. The traditional estate economic model of forestry, agriculture and sporting facilities has been supplemented by new means. A pioneer of commercial adaptation is Roger Tempest, whose family have lived at Broughton Hall near Skipton for thirty-three generations. Tempest changed the way owners used their estates. He was not the first to see that the derelict outbuildings, stables, cow sheds and farmsteads held potential value. Many had converted stables for residential use, but Tempest additionally saw commercial office use opportunities. Technology made working in the country a realistic possibility. Henceforth the economics were about square-footage rather than acreage: 'conservation and development went hand-in-hand', as Tempest has shown. In this he was inspired by the restoration of Salts Mill by Jonathan Silver in West Yorkshire (see Chapter 14).

With the new millennium, the country house story had one more trick to play: bringing economic and social regeneration to a depressed area, an approach pioneered by the Prince of Wales at Dumfries House. This involved granting planning permission to create a community to fund the long-term sustainability of the house remaining open. After negotiations broke down with the National Trust for Scotland, Christie's announced a sale of the contents including the Chippendale furniture made for the house. Prince Charles stepped in to save the estate, house and contents by persuading the Heritage Memorial Fund to contribute £7 million and Historic Scotland £5 million (reversing an earlier decision) towards the full price of £45 million. At the eleventh hour a shortfall of £20 million remained. This sum was loaned by the Prince of Wales's charitable foundation on the understanding that part of the estate would be developed, thus providing regeneration where it was needed. It has had a bumpy ride so far and the economics are far from perfect, but the determination is there.

Today regeneration is the justification for public money provided to Wentworth Woodhouse, the great Whig palace adjacent to depressed Rotherham. This is a partnership tale between SAVE, Rotherham Council, the National Trust, the newly formed Wentworth Woodhouse Trust, and the hereditary landowning family who still own much of the park with its spectacular restored follies and the surrounding estate. Another ambitious stately home project with a wider objective has been initiated by Jonathan Ruffer to restore the former palace of the Bishops of Durham at Bishop Auckland. Although different in character, the project follows a similar ambition, that the house should be the motor of economic regeneration in a depressed locale.

In the Lees-Milne era the National Trust made much of family occupation but by the turn of the millennium this was a polite fiction. The organisation had turned into an educational charity with professional curators, often with a baleful relationship with the donor family (by now doomed to irrelevance in all but a few cases). Although the Trust had come a long way in its presentation of houses, they were still subject to the strict standards of the conservators. Some thought that the houses under its care had a devitalised air. When Simon Jenkins was appointed chairman in 2008, he wanted to loosen things up: throw away the ropes, open the library, play on the billiard table, bash tunes out on the piano and ride the penny farthing. Jenkins wanted visitors to watch conservators at work, children to dress up as workhouse inmates, and to give visitors a feeling of occupation and welcome. The public were invited to a house party. In all this Jenkins was much influenced by the town house of Dennis Severs in Spitalfields – a pioneer of the story home, where the visitor found food on the table and the washing hanging up to dry. Bringing houses back to life has dispelled the old maxim about 'the dead hand of the

National Trust' even if the Trust has occasionally taken matters too far.*

Country houses both private and public appear to be in better condition and more economically sound today than at any time since 1945, but this may be illusory. The traditional preservers of houses and their art collections are far less relevant today. Land ownership has been historically a dependable preserver of the country house and its way of life. Today, because so many are reliant on hedge funds and financial services, they are more vulnerable to economic and fiscal downturns. Those houses not vested in charitable trusts or open to the public are especially exposed to potential wealth taxes. At the time of writing a benign fiscal climate remains, albeit uneasily, and divorce ranks as a higher risk, especially to art collections. Social changes are moving old families closer to a continental model of inheritance with an equal division among siblings and a rejection of the traditional historic preserver of landed estates and art collections, primogeniture, or the first-born takes all.

---

* An example was the swapping of the furniture made for the library at Ickworth with bean bags. One interesting development over the past two decades had been the rise of country house studies as an academic subject, notably at York University (the only new university built around a country house) with the country house partnership, the inspiration of Dr Christopher Ridgway.

CHAPTER 13

The Enthusiasts: Canals and Railways

There is no harm in dreaming dreams and seeing visions. Sometimes dreams come true and visions proved to be prophetic.

THE *EVESHAM JOURNAL* ON THE RESTORATION OF THE LOWER AVON NAVIGATION[1]

In 1945 few would have considered canals and railways as part of the national heritage; but we often fail to recognise heritage until it comes under threat. This was manifestly true in the case of canals and steam railways, two successful heritage movements that arose from popular support, were largely self-financing and almost entirely the work of enthusiasts. No other heritage sectors have been so dependent on volunteer work at all levels. Canals require most labour at the restoration stage, whereas railways represented a challenge hitherto never attempted: a regular supply of skilled volunteer labour available every day of the season – a considerable commitment. However, both movements transformed these picturesque relics of the Industrial Revolution into flourishing leisure industries that greatly add to the pleasure of the countryside and, in the case of canals, also helped to regenerate townscapes. Today there are 562 miles of restored railway, and 3,000 miles of navigable inland waterways in Britain, with canal basins that serve as centres of urban renewal restored and cleaned – some might say too much so, with cappuccino bars and luxury apartments. How did all this come about? Romance and engineering joined forces and found their champion in a man who would, curiously, be present at the birth of both movements, Tom Rolt.

Canals

The canal system is the environmental Cinderella of heritage. They offer a way of life for those who like moving slowly, discovering the country at the pace and height of a horse, and for those who yearn for a refuge and simple life away from the rat race. They are beautiful because they usually follow the natural contours of the land. Canal traffic started to decline in the 1860s when this leisureliness worked against them, and the transportation of goods and people began to be transferred to the speedier, more capacious railway system. Indeed it was the canal's very nemesis, the railway companies, that acquired many of them. Until 1939 England still had a network of working canals, but World War II brought the final blow to the industry: the boatmen left to join the services, the unmaintained waterways became dilapidated, and then after the war most of the remaining haulage business moved to the roads. It is reckoned that in 1941 there were as many as fifty-eight separate canals in Britain,* amounting to 2,500 miles of waterway, much of which had fallen into disuse and disrepair. But what to do with them?

Canals represented a considerable problem – you could legally abandon a canal, but you couldn't physically destroy it without great difficulty; unlike a railway, no one could take it away – and nor would anyone pay to have it taken away. Moreover, a neglected canal was not only an eyesore but a danger to life and health. Part of the problem was one of degree. Railways are either open or closed, but waterways sink gradually into decay and neglect, while still remaining semi-navigable to resolute enthusiasts. It also transpired that attempting to decommission canals created unforeseen problems such as destabilising the

---

* Of which thirty-five were owned by railway companies.

water tables; and they were often still functional for supplying water to factories and farms, as well as for land drainage.

Nonetheless, government policy during the 1950s was that the canals should be abandoned with around half of the navigations threatened with extinction. Local authorities agreed: they saw only the costs and hazards involved in maintaining them. By the 1960s local and central government were in thrall to the mantra: 'close the canal and build a motorway' – which today would probably be reversed. It would take until the 1980s to change official attitudes towards the waterways, establishing them as an important environmental asset, and persuading all parties that restoring them was cheaper than managing the problems that resulted from abandonment. For one thing, it transpired that charitable funds and voluntary labour could be found to help restore them, which would not be the case with abandonment. But the lingering question still remained: what purpose could these restored canals fulfil? Given their forlorn and often dangerous condition, only a determined maverick or visionary could see a future for them. Fortunately, both would appear.

One of the first recorded pleasure trips on a canal was undertaken in 1879 by Peter Willans from the Thames in London to Ripon in Yorkshire. His son Kyrle related the story to a young engineer, Tom Rolt, which inspired Rolt to make a canal trip for himself in the soon-to-become-famous boat that Willans sold him, *Cressy*. As one canal historian has written: 'the impact of this encounter has played a vital role in the revival of the waterways which has developed since 1946'.[2] Rolt's first voyage through the canals of England was during the summer and winter of 1939/40, an inauspicious time to be trying anything new. But he was enthralled by what he found: 'for me they represented the equivalent of some uncharted, Arcadian island inhabited by simple, friendly and unselfconscious natives where I could free myself from all that I found so uncongenial in the modern world'.[3] In 1944 he published his classic book, *Narrow Boat*, at just the point when canals most needed a new sense of purpose, and a champion. The book became something of a cult. Rolt gave up his day job and devoted himself to living on and writing about canals.

Among the many letters that Rolt received following publication of *Narrow Boat* were two from authors who also had an interest in canals: Charles Hadfield (whose *English Rivers and Canals* was published in 1945) and Robert Aickman, the conservationist who was to become the linchpin of the canal movement. On a visit before the war to the theatre at Stratford, Aickman had discovered the old canal basin; his curiosity aroused, he had followed its course, bewitched by this forgotten world. Aickman and Hadfield both suggested to Rolt that they should form some sort of union, suggesting something like the Friends of Canterbury Cathedral.

Accordingly, the three met at Aickman's home in Gower Street, London, where they were joined by others. During that first meeting the doorbell rang, and a stranger enquired: 'is this the meeting of the Inland Waterways Association?' The stranger, whom nobody knew, had just given the new body a name, and was immediately co-opted onto the committee. Aickman provided a room in his house as an office for the new organisation (IWA) and a secretary was hired, none other than the actress and aspiring novelist Elizabeth Jane Howard. The growth and development of the waterway restoration movement was the direct result of the formation of the IWA, which under Aickman's leadership became visionary. For the appeal of the canal movement in its early years owed much to the idea of a lost paradise, a world of overgrown towpaths, viaduct canals and decrepit industrial districts. But it was Robert Aickman who saw beyond this to the future leisure and tourism potential of waterways.

These two charismatic IWA founders, Rolt and Aickman, had very different styles, and were described thus: 'Tom's thin moustache and flattened hair gave an almost military precision to his appearance. In contrast, the pallor of Robert's rather boyish face, and his well-groomed hair, betrayed the life of a city-dweller.'[4] Where Rolt was a superb engineer, Aickman was an intellectual, strategist and publicist. Although both shared a

William Morris-like distaste for industrial progress, Rolt looked backwards to bygone times, where Aickman saw the future. Rolt believed that the IWA should work to revive the traditional commercial traffic of canals and resisted the idea that they should become a precious and 'arty cult'. While both were in search of *la vie de bohème*, for Rolt this meant canalside pubs, old characters and beer, whereas Aickman preferred 'cafés on the continental model'. This clash of styles became evident at meetings, as Tom's practical but impatient temperament came up against Robert's autocratic desire to control every detail.

In its early days the IWA was a far from perfect organisation, riven by petty disputes such as whether, as honorary members, John Betjeman ranked higher on the notepaper than Dame Margot Fonteyn; but its vision for the future of waterways triumphed. It campaigned for a national policy to bring all navigable waterways under one management, and succeeded. An important landmark was the Bowes Report (1958), commissioned by the government and recommending the adoption of many IWA policies, including state support for canals until such time as they could be maintained by private investment. Crucially, the report also recommended that the traditional collection of tolls be replaced by an annual licensing system per boat for each canal to be travelled, an approach strongly advocated by the IWA and still standard today.

The IWA was fortunate to have two founders who were such skilled communicators. Rolt and Aickman knew how to wage campaigns, get letters published, and gather local support – indeed a large part of the success of the movement arrived through their formation of local branches.[*] To their delight they discovered that the press were hungry for canal stories – as early as March 1948, *The Times* ran an article under the headline

---

[*] By 1949 the Inland Waterways Association had over 800 members which doubled in a decade and by 1973 was 11,000. It was incorporated as a company limited by guarantee with neither share capital nor distribution of profits and registered as a charity.

'Holidays Afloat'.[5] The big question was not only whether canals were open, but were truly navigable, with all that that entailed: were there sufficient water levels, working locks, and were they free from impediments? Rolt had already decided to make an exploratory journey to find out.

The Stratford-upon-Avon Canal

Rolt chose the canal that had inspired Aickman; the Stratford-upon-Avon (a spur of the Kennet and Avon), which was owned by the Great Western Railway. Its navigation had been blocked when the raising bridge at Lifford Lane was replaced by a structure that impeded river traffic. Rolt wrote to the Great Western repeatedly for permission to navigate their canal. Then one of the IWA's supporters in the House of Lords, Lord Methuen, extracted an assurance from the Ministry of Transport that with twenty-four hours' notice the bridge could be lifted; an assurance that Rolt decided to test. Such pioneering trips were known as 'canal-busting attempts' and Aickman used them as excellent opportunities to gather publicity. In 1947 Rolt made his way apprehensively along the Stratford Canal. In Aickman's words:

> we rounded a few more corners, and there the crowd was lining both banks several deep; on roof-tops, up trees. A mild sarcastic cheer met our belated advent. The obstruction had been raised by a large gang. *Cressy* passed beneath it, though with a clearance of only an inch or two. The applause became a little warmer. We made statements. We posed for photographs. We accepted cups of tea. We proclaimed a great new future for the canals of Britain.[6]

Despite the cooperation in jacking up the bridge, it was clear to Rolt that the canal was being maintained far below the statutory standard for navigation. It would be a decade before the situation would improve.

The stimulus to restore the Stratford-upon-Avon Canal came in 1958 when Warwickshire Council applied for a warrant of abandonment; their aim was to spare themselves the cost of building a heavy traffic bridge. For the IWA this came at the perfect time, as they were looking for a derelict canal on which to demonstrate that the job could be undertaken by voluntary labour. Aickman, who loved theatre, was full of enthusiasm, believing that if both the river and canal were again fully navigable, Stratford would immediately become the boating centre of the Midlands.* But feeling that they needed some sort of national endorsement, he contacted his friend, John Smith, a brilliant but maverick member of the National Trust board, and suggested that the Trust might get involved. Smith was intrigued, and together they went up to Stratford to meet the person who would become the hero of the story, an architect who had chosen to live on a narrowboat. David Hutchings was a man of unusual determination, and perhaps only somebody as bloody-minded could have achieved the heroic work required.† The IWA appointed him canal manager. But in 1961 nobody knew how to go about restoring a canal: the only precedent was the neighbouring Lower Avon Navigation, which was nearing completion.‡

One important question was whether the IWA should take over ownership of canals, but it was wisely decided that this was too risky; if anybody was to go bankrupt it should be the

---

* It was the southern section of the canal they restored, from Kingswood Junction to Stratford.

† David Hutchings, the central figure in the story of the restoration of the Stratford Canal, was also in the words of the present chairman, Clive Henderson, 'a complete lunatic with almost no awareness of health and safety'.

‡ This restoration which pioneered the use of volunteer labour was the inspiration of Douglas Barwell. In 1950 Barwell joined the IWA and established the Lower Avon Charitable Trust. Aickman described him as 'a really remarkable man – six men in one: charity organizer, council chairman, deep-sea diver, impresario, administrator and leader'.

local associations. Hutchings therefore arranged what he called 'a disturbance', a rally of boats on one of the few sections that held enough water, to proclaim the launch of a new Stratford Canal Trust that would acquire and restore the whole canal. Stratford Town Council were unsupportive, holding negative images of working boats moored near the theatre. They could not imagine the colourful pleasure craft that would enhance the town centre.

The National Trust was cautious – it had been bitten by open-ended projects before. But Smith pointed out that when the Trust was first formed, it had been to preserve landscapes as a recreational resource, and there was no thought of 'owning large numbers of country houses or gardens: but when the need arose we met it: let us now take another step forward, and come to the rescue of a third new sort of property which, like the other two, is at once a source of pleasure and a manifestation of the English genius'.[7] Smith succeeded in brokering a deal whereby the National Trust would take up a lease on the southern section of the canal for five years, with an option to buy the freehold.

Aickman was correct in foreseeing that the Trust's involvement would be important in lending the project credibility – and by extension, the IWA. Over the next three years Hutchings and his team would dredge a quarter of a million cubic metres of accumulated mud, silt and debris. Almost every lock gate had to be replaced, and most onerous of all, many of the brick lock chambers had to be completely rebuilt. Fortunately, the technology was simple; when canals were built in the eighteenth century, they were low-tech and man-sized enterprises, which made restoration using unskilled labour possible.

Making the crucial assumption that the work could be done by volunteers, Hutchins's budget was £42,000. An appeal raised £20,000 and the Ministry of Transport promised the remaining £22,000. The army of volunteers came from many sources: Boy Scouts, Royal Engineers, RAF units and later, a detail of volunteer prisoners from HMP Winson Green.* Work parties also came from other branches of the IWA, including the Waterways Recovery Group, a canal flying squad of available labour. John Smith later said that 'not having taken part in the Stratford project was like not having been at Agincourt'.

By July 1964 the canal was ready for a grand reopening, which was to be done by the Queen Mother from the narrowboat *Linda*. A flotilla of boats headed to Stratford for the opening rally. When the town council prevented them from mooring in the basin or on its own stretch of riverbank, the Stratford Memorial Theatre came to the rescue and offered their riverbank for the expected 200 vessels. John Betjeman wrote a poem to commemorate the day:

Your Majesty, our friend of many years,
Confirms a triumph now the moment nears:
The lock you have reopened will set free
The heart of England to the open sea.

It was exaggeratingly said at the time that the royal reopening probably did more than any other single event to establish the principle of the voluntary restoration of canals.[8] And with the canal so heroically restored, the National Trust decided they would exercise their option to purchase the freehold of a part of the canal, to secure its future.

The Trust did this in the belief that the canal could be managed with two full-time staff, a manager and extra help from volunteers and prisoner work-parties. However, their estimates were woefully inadequate, and they did not reckon on the loss of David Hutchings, who wanted to move on. Throughout

* One replacement bridge made at Wormwood Scrubs from timber and steel was transferred by the Royal Engineers, and installed by the inmates of Winson Green.

the mid-1960s a steady 300 boats a year paid the toll to make the journey to and from Lapworth. The toll was adequate to cover the basic running costs, but not the extraordinary wear and tear, which absorbed vast amounts of money. The Trust also found itself embroiled in the naturally fractious world of inland waterways, where cooperation between such dogged individualists was difficult to muster. Eventually, the Trust threw in the towel and opened negotiations to pass the freehold to the British Waterways Board. In the process they were obliged also to hand over several hundred thousand pounds to cover the maintenance backlog.*

The British Waterways Board had been formed (thanks to the Bowes Report) to serve as the government's regulatory body. Under the 1968 Transport Bill, enthusiastically promoted by Barbara Castle, most of Britain's waterways had been placed within its jurisdiction, with the aim that it should work in partnership with local authorities and voluntary associations to encourage canal restoration. Initially most of this work happened in rural settings, but by the 1980s the regeneration of urban spaces had made canals and their curtilage highly valuable. Waterside apartments and commercial spaces were now highly sought after. One has only to look at hugely successful canalside developments such as Brindleyplace in Birmingham and Salford Basin near Manchester to see the importance of navigable canals in so many regeneration projects over the past twenty years.

What became of Rolt and Aickman? Rolt is best known today for his writings. Aickman has a bronze memorial beside the lock that bears his name on a peaceful reach of the Stratford Canal. Both their wives left them; Rolt's ran off to become an assistant

---

* Today the ownership of the Stratford Canal is vested in the successor body to the British Waterways, the Canal and River Trust (founded 2012), which maintains the infrastructure, with the occasional support of the Heritage Lottery Fund. The canal user's club is Stratford Canal Society, a membership organisation that undertakes the necessary volunteer work. And above these are the IWA, which remains to this day the national lobbyist for canal users.

clown in Billy Smart's circus while Aickman's ended up as a nun in a convent in Hertfordshire. It is a truism that founders are not always the best people to run organisations. Aickman soldiered on at the IWA until 1964, 'running', as he put it, 'this extraordinarily disloyal and ungrateful organization'.[9] However, he looked back with pride on its achievements: 'I'm sure the unique success enjoyed by the Association is derived mainly from the expression that its campaign gives to human needs which are submerged by all the modern agencies of welfare, commerce and din.'[10]

Rolt fell out with his colleagues early in the story: in 1951 he was expelled at a special IWA meeting convened in Birmingham and as a result, he severed all links with canals – he and Aickman did not speak for eighteen years. But his career took an unexpected twist after that fateful Birmingham meeting: 'I left the hall with a decidedly unpleasant taste in my mouth and, by one of those strange coincidences which sometimes occur in life, walked into another and much pleasanter meeting held in a small office in Waterloo Street, Birmingham, a mere 300 yards away. This was one of the first – if not the first – committee meetings of the recently formed Talyllyn Railway Preservation Society.'[11] In short, Rolt was to become the pioneer of the second subject of this chapter, which as he wrote was a 'sequence of events that seems almost miraculously providential'.[12]

The Talyllyn Railway

The origins of the volunteer railway movement could scarcely be dimmer. The Talyllyn Railway was privately owned by a local landowner, Sir Henry Haydn Jones, Liberal MP for Merioneth. Founded in 1864 to provide a rail link between the slate quarry at Bryn Eglwys and the Welsh coast, it was the world's first narrow gauge railway to be constructed specifically for steam traction. With the collapse of the slate company in the 1880s, the railway became a passenger line, adopting its present name. The line was so obscure that it was overlooked when the government rationalised the railways into four companies in 1923 and again when railways were nationalised in 1948. Although loss-making, Sir Haydn vowed to keep the line open during his lifetime.

Rolt first encountered the Talyllyn while holidaying in Wales in 1943. When he attempted to use the line it was out of service, so he walked along the track instead, marvelling that any train could possibly run on such a poorly maintained line. Six years later he read an article about the railway in the *Birmingham Post* which stimulated him to write a letter to the newspaper which in turn generated more correspondence. In July 1950 Sir Haydn died, which brought the future of the railway into urgent focus. Rolt called a meeting at the Imperial Hotel, Birmingham in October of that year which the *Birmingham Post* announced on its front page. As Rolt explained 'the concept of volunteers preserving and running a railway made news because it was then wholly novel. As a result we had a full house.'[13]

With his experience of canals, Rolt knew that he could tap into a great number of enthusiasts. Railway buffs had hitherto been denied any practical creative outlet beyond model making. With the blessing of Sir Haydn's widow, a group led by Rolt took over the Talyllyn. There were no precedents for such a move and these pioneers had to confront the questions that every subsequent volunteer railway faced. What was it exactly they were preserving: the engines, the station or the line? Who were they serving: enthusiasts, tourists or locals? How pure should they be? There were suggestions for instance that Talyllyn should be converted to electricity, which would have made life easier, but that was not the point. It had to be steam or nothing. The railway was in appalling condition and Rolt wondered whether they should change the gauge from 3 feet to a 15-inch gauge tourist line, but his colleagues persuaded him that this would not gain support. The accuracy versus efficiency argument would challenge every future railway preservation society.

It was a considerable achievement to keep the railway running that first season, as Rolt explained: 'against every kind of odds, both human and mechanical, it totally absorbed all my thoughts and energy. That the railway staggered through the season successfully was entirely due to the unfailing support and good advice I received from my predecessor, Edward Thomas, plus the labours of a small and dedicated team of friends and members who stood by me loyally throughout the season.'[14] During the first season Talyllyn carried 15,000 passengers – a record for the line – and this increased to 22,000 the following year.

The main 'human' problem turned out to be the Welsh permanent staff. They had seemed at first pleasant enough and willing, so Rolt was surprised when Edward Thomas warned that they could be difficult. It soon became apparent that they resented the new regime and believed that by undermining Rolt's initiatives they would make the venture's failure certain. He discovered that:

one of them, who lived in a cottage beside the railway, made a jolly practice of pouncing like some old man of the sea, upon new and unsuspecting volunteers who had come down to work on the railway and informing them that I was mad, that my crazy attempt to run a railway which was obviously unsafe was bound to end in disaster, and the sooner they disassociated themselves from the railway and returned whence they had come the better.[15]

Notwithstanding the soothsayers, the pioneering spirit of the line brought out the best in everybody, from the staff to the passengers. The story ignited nationwide interest and inspired two films, *Railway with a Heart of Gold*, and Ealing Studios' popular comedy, *The Titfield Thunderbolt*.

The seed planted at Talyllyn fell on fertile ground and inspired the numerous volunteer railways that sprung up as a result of the Beeching cuts during the 1960s. Talyllyn was effectively taken over as a going concern, and it was a different set of problems that beset the lines closed down by British Railways – they would require new operating organisations.

When BR decided to prune much of the national network, many hoped that the lines and rolling stock could be seamlessly transferred to preservation groups, but that was not the case. Several years usually lapsed between the closure of a line by British Railways and its takeover by preservation groups. In the meantime, locals found new travel arrangements, and so the volunteers were left with a different market, characterised as 'gaily painted locomotives going from nowhere to nowhere'. A more proximate model than Talyllyn for these new railways predated the Beeching cuts: the romantic story of the Lewes to East Grinstead Railway, better known under its affectionate soubriquet, the Bluebell Line.

Bluebell Line

In 1954 British Railways announced the closure of the railway from Lewes to East Grinstead. Despite opposition, it went ahead the following year. Leading the protesters was a local spinster, Madge Bessemer, who took the trouble to study the original 1878 Act of Parliament authorising construction of the line. This revealed a legal obligation to provide a passenger service of four trains a day. Since the Act had not been repealed, the closure was technically illegal without further parliamentary sanction. As a result, the service was resumed in 1956 and Madge Bessemer became a local celebrity, but it was a pyrrhic victory. It became known as 'the sulky service' as it was run in a deliberately inconvenient manner. Two years later British Rail obtained a new Act repealing the clause so that in 1958 the line was closed, seemingly for good.

The next step was remarkable. Four teenage students – Chris Campbell, David Dallimore, Martin Eastland and Alan Sturt – called a public meeting to which 150 people showed up. These young people (the founding generation of preservationists were predominantly young) formed the Lewes and East Grinstead Railway Preservation Society. They persuaded a sympathetic railwayman working at Liverpool Street Station, Bernard Holden, to be their chairman as legally someone over twenty-one was required.* Together they descended on British Railways at Waterloo who had no idea how to deal with such a situation. Nobody had ever asked to acquire a branch railway before, and this did not look like a very promising group. It was obvious the new preservation society would not be able to afford the freehold (offered at £34,000) so it was agreed that they could have a lease for five years at a rent of £2,250 a year with a purchase option available.†

On this basis the railway reopened on 7 August 1960 with just two locomotives and two carriages, cheered on by more than 2,000 people in Victorian dress. The original impetus had been to keep the line open for the locals. Although steam trains were beginning to be replaced by diesel, they were still the norm and it was uncertain that tourists would find them a draw. But as the new railway was only able to open a part of the line, they gave up the original intention of running a daily diesel service and became England's first standard gauge heritage railway instead.‡ They estimated that a daunting 10,000 man-hours a year would be needed to keep the line open. In the first year they carried 15,000 passengers and by 1961 that number had jumped to 91,000. The Bluebell Line caught the public imagination – it was a novelty, chugged through beautiful countryside and bore a memorable name. It is not clear how the railway acquired the Bluebell name. One story has it that during the 'sulky line' period

* Bernard Holden remained the president of the railway until his death aged 104 in 2012.

† The lease came up in 1964 but by now British Railways was asking £65,000 for the freehold. Eventually a purchase price of £43,500 was agreed for the route, including the stations and surrounding land, between Sheffield Park and Horsted Keynes. It would take many more years to run the line to East Grinstead, and Lewes would remain beyond their grasp.

‡ In fact they had been pipped to the post by the Middleton Railway, reopened in June 1960 primarily as a freight line that did not regularly carry passengers for another nine years.

BR ran the line so slowly that you could reach down and pick up the bluebells. A more likely explanation is the proliferation of bluebells in Coneyborough Wood.

Bluebell, as a pioneer in the preservation business, was able to acquire several historic steam locomotives, some straight from service with British Rail. The engines were left in black livery with their new logo while the coaches were painted in the line's own blue livery. It was not until 2007 that the railway admitted diesel locomotives and then made a virtue of it by holding a 'Deltic Gala' in 2015 that was so popular that even *The Railway Magazine* was forced to concede: 'society changes to reflect the tastes of each succeeding generation and I therefore have to admit that the huge crowds boosting the Bluebell coffers when two "Deltics" took over the line in April have made me think again. As long as such events are kept in moderation, they might be a good thing after all'.[16]

How has it all been run? Bluebell reopened as a preservation society. As it grew the railway formed a limited company or plc for administrative purposes but found that it also needed a charitable trust to attract a wider range of funding and collect money in a tax-efficient way. Most of the carriages belong to the plc and half of the locomotives – the other half belonging to several locomotive societies. The societies pool resources to restore engines which they loan to the Bluebell under an operating agreement with a full repairing lease of ten years. This period coincides with the boiler certificate (seven years for a mainline locomotive). The plc is a not-for-profit organisation which nearly breaks even on visitor receipts and the shortfall is made up by subscriptions from the 10,500 members. The railway now attracts some 150,000 visitors a year, of which 85–90 per cent are families on a day out. Bluebell has a turnover of approximately £3 million a year. The charitable trust, which must be heritage-advantageous, can collect up to £1 million in a good year. The railway has sixty full-time paid employees, thirty with part-time contracts and 750 working volunteers (including all drivers and footplate staff). They have three paid young apprentices, who among other things are building a new engine, 'Beachy Head', to keep the skills alive.

One of the most impressive aspects of preservation railways is the scale of the industrial operation that many of them support. Any volunteer railway is – to mix metaphors – both an iceberg and a swan. The surface is a serene operation, often with just one line and one train in sight. Out of view is often a mighty engineering facility. Old steam trains require this resource to repair and rebuild everything from boilers to new carriages, doors, seats and lavatories. Some of Bluebell's colleagues have adopted a specialisation to keep the engineers at work and bring in some extra income. The very successful Severn Valley Railway, which carries 250,000 passengers a year, makes boilers, and such is the scale of their engineering works that they are almost self-sufficient in supplying their rolling-stock needs.

Today the headquarters of Bluebell is Sheffield Park, where among the visitor attractions are a well-stocked museum, a demonstration signal box, and a cafeteria suitably named the Bessemer Arms. It is also home to the railway's locomotive shed, which today can be accessed by the public thanks to a Lottery grant in 2018. Until the Lottery came along there was no government aid for heritage railways. It is easy to understand their support when you take the line, as it chugs through dreamy unspoiled parkland and mature woods with distant views of church spires. Arriving at Kingscote is the closest you will come to experiencing Adlestrop in the modern age.

The Heritage Railway Association is the trade body for heritage railways, which has 280 corporate members in the UK (excluding Scotland) and includes trams and miniature railways. They work with the Heritage Alliance to take up major issues with government. At the time of writing the main topic is coal. For heritage railways the continuing supply of coal under climate change restrictions is a serious problem. It is estimated that heritage bodies burn up to 40,000 tons of coal a year, of which preservation railways use 26,000. Like other heritage sectors VAT on historic building restoration is a sore point. But national and grassroots support for heritage railways remains as strong as ever: 22,000 volunteers (making them after the National Trust the largest employer of volunteer labour in the tourist sector) and 4,000 staff on 130 heritage railways carry 8 million passengers a year, generating an income of £92 million.[17] For most of them the age of steam has never ended. They still adhere to the old railway-man's prayer: 'Good Lord, give us this day thy daily steam and deliver us from all diesels.'

CHAPTER 14

Regeneration: Mills, Housing and Power Stations

Old ideas can sometimes use new buildings.
New ideas must use old buildings.

JANE JACOBS[1]

Up until the 1960s the heritage story had been cathedrals, castles and country houses. For the post-war population, a new political and intellectual agenda identified the heritage of everyman, and in particular of the working man and woman. As Simon Thurley has written: 'the interests of young men and women coming out of the universities, and the more adventurous of their teachers, were now in local history, agrarian history, working-class history, historical geography and economic history.'[2] Henceforth, there would be a new academic interest in industrial and other buildings that reflected working-class history: old warehouses, mills, power stations, dockside quays and factories.[*]

Most of the approaches to conserving heritage were pioneered by the Victorians, but the idea of regeneration is very much of our own time. It has been arguably the most salient aspect of tangible heritage over the last thirty years. Everybody has their own idea of what it means – the definition and the rules change – but

---

[*] Although the pioneer architectural historians writing about industrial buildings often did not fit this description, such as Sir James Richards, and some were in fact off duty from writing about country houses: the *Country Life* journalists John Cornforth and Marcus Binney.

the simplest description is the repurposing of former industrial buildings and their hinterlands, moving from an industrial to a post-industrial world: bringing light to where there was darkness. The success of individual post-industrial conservation projects became recognised as a powerful driver of wider physical and socio-economic regeneration. Heritage-based regeneration begins with the individual reuse of industrial heritage, whether planned or 'organic', and develops into a wider strategic approach as its efficacy is appreciated. This is true of regeneration at its best. But there are other truths too, of regeneration imposing dislocation and managed decline, sometimes becoming a self-serving quangocracy.

Throughout the 1960s the wider public had accepted the belief that contemporary architecture would improve on the past, and architects had felt confident about demolishing otherwise fine and distinguished buildings. But in the 1970s a new notion forcibly took the public, that a building should not be demolished if its replacement were to be inferior. They had observed the poor quality of much of the rebuilding in post-war Britain, half of it driven by ideology and the other half by profit. Architects of many persuasions now began to see a value in old buildings – above all in terms of placemaking. The old and the new must work together. They increasingly realised that improvements to individual houses had only a limited impact, that larger-scale rehabilitation was far more effective, and would encourage the improvement efforts made by individuals, the basis of community repair.

The term 'regeneration' began to creep into government documents in the late 1980s.[3] Officialdom adopted a rather ponderous definition of regeneration: the attempt 'to bring about a lasting improvement in the economic, physical, social and environmental condition of an area that has been subject to change'.[4] Although it is difficult to define, it is obvious to see, and certain pre-conditions work in its favour: fine sturdy buildings, atmosphere, a strong backstory of social history, an engaged local community, a sense that something of value is about to be lost – and that what might replace it would probably be worse. Regeneration embraced many kinds of project: the big mills, the growth of community housing – and the great government-sponsored area reclamations that have transformed cities and are the subject of the next chapter.

The Mills, Warehouses and Former Industrial Buildings

No sight was more poignant in the 1960s and 1970s than the plight of northern textile mills. The mills of West Yorkshire and Lancashire are the most impressive buildings of the Industrial Revolution, which sitting in their gaunt valleys, often near canals, form some the most evocative industrial landscapes in Europe. They exhibit some of the qualities which Edmund Burke identified with the sublime: power, vastness, infinity and uniformity inducing a sense of awe. Painters such Joseph Wright of Derby and Philip de Loutherbourg recognised this character from the beginning, but it took a more homespun modern painter, L. S. Lowry, to view them affectionately within their urban context. For him, the mill chimneys were as important as trees were to John Constable.* And yet in the West Riding of Yorkshire alone, over 300 mills had become redundant in the years 1950–67.[5] Most were demolished.

During the 1960s and 1970s, it was difficult to foresee that mills and warehouses would with time become regenerators of economic activity, and the question was whether to demolish or how to conserve these elephants until they could find a new

---

* Three writers who wrote with appreciation about mill towns in the 1930s were J. B. Priestley, W. H. Auden and John Betjeman. The National Trust was ahead of the curve when they accepted Quarry Bank Mill, Cheshire, as early as 1939 as a working mill from the Greg family who built it as a calico factory in 1784.

economic use.* When Marcus Binney organised the exhibition 'Satanic Mills' in 1979, the problem of their future was very much up in the air. Many were in what planners called twilight uses: small workshops and storage, etc. Their appreciation was in its infancy, both aesthetically and functionally, as highly adaptable spaces. Although they formed much of the character of a town like Oldham, in 1978 its planning officer bluntly stated that 'the retention of mills for other purposes is generally discouraged [...] the clearance of obsolete industrial premises is currently being given a high priority by the authority'.[6] The 1970s witnessed the growth of industrial estates, and every town wanted one. Oldham planned to create 700 acres of brownfield site to attract industry but found that the policy was unsuccessful, and the mills could be more profitably retained. For some of the older local councillors the matter was ideological – they were a relic of a bad past, a reminder of shocking working conditions.

Initially it was small emergent businesses in search of cheap accommodation that began to change this attitude but there were downsides, as often the old mills were in poor condition with less than prestigious entrances and amenities. The ground floor was usually easy to rent, the upper floors less so. Residential use then followed, particularly in Wapping on the River Thames, and as early as 1969 the Landmark Trust converted Edale Mill in Derbyshire into seven flats.† A part of the problem was the reluctance to list industrial buildings until the mid-1980s. The appearance of Conservation Areas could offer some relief and

* Often it was the very vastness of the building and cost of removal that ensured survival. Just dismantling the massive steel frame of the Dunlop Mill near Rochdale took nearly a year. But it was their flexibility that enabled so many to survive. Mill adaptations go all the way back to the 1870s, when a Halifax textile mill was converted to the making of toffee.

† John Smith was something of a visionary when in 1965 he set up the Landmark Trust for historic buildings in good settings which everybody could enjoy as a holiday let. They were usually humble buildings, former railway stations, industrial buildings, as well as apartments in country houses. Smith deserves a separate study.

an early example of the protection of an industrial complex was Saltaire, the Italianate industrial village created by Sir Titus Salt in Bradford during the 1850s.

As late as 1990 Binney could write: 'Enthusiasm for industrial architecture is a new phenomenon. Until recently people have tended to judge industrial buildings by what they represent, rather than what they are.'[7] His organisation, SAVE, had been at the forefront of changing that view. The 'Satanic Mills' exhibition, staged at the RIBA Heinz Gallery, was a major stepping-stone in that appreciation. The photographs by Randolph Langenbach captured the awesome grandeur of former industrial cities like Halifax. The text of the accompanying booklet caught the pathos of the times with the closure and retrenchment of the big West Yorkshire mills. SAVE had concerns that the exhibition would be a reminder of a grim past where people had been exploited. Instead, the exhibition was greeted with enthusiasm, particularly in the north: 'These mills are part of our lives. We don't want them torn down.'[8] English Heritage policy at the time was to schedule only those industrial sites which retained their working machinery, such as Stott Park Bobbin Mill, Cumbria. It viewed them as monuments rather than regeneration sites. The listing of mills was seen politically as one step too far and the change in listing criteria came too late to save many.

Redundant mills, however, offered many advantages and disadvantages: they were highly adaptable and offered enormous square footage cheaply. On the other hand, they required expensive skills, specially made parts and always lurking in every project were the 'unknown unknowns'. The issue was usually the extent of their neglect, their sheer scale, and whether the local economy could sustain the adaptations. One of the seminal restorations was Dean Clough Mills in Halifax, owned by the Crossley family. It had grown with the demand for carpets, and by 1860 the buildings covered no less than eighteen acres. The mill's closure in 1983 presented a massive problem for the town. However, a twenty-year regeneration has created a community which employs 4,000 people and a makeover of the internal spaces which now encompass apartments, a hotel, shopping, art galleries and 150 businesses. Halifax has followed that up with the recent restoration of its great architectural showpiece – one of the wonders of the north – Piece Hall, the only surviving Georgian cloth hall, under the banner of 'trade heritage and culture', with forty-three independent traders (this is close to its original functioning) and an art gallery. Today they talk about the Piece Hall effect.

One of the byproducts of such restorations was the emergence of specialist developers who sought to keep alive the skills and treatments required – none more so than Urban Splash, founded in the 1990s, which has been at the heart of so many regeneration projects in Liverpool and Manchester. They took on the most spectacular of all Yorkshire mills, the Manningham Mills complex in Bradford, with its great campanile-like chimney, restored in 2000. Their philosophy is simple: these mills are priceless, unrepeatable assets that are the pivot around which Urban Splash can build stories for the future. Inspiration came from the great mill towns in New England in the USA, which offered an even greater scale model for Bradford to emulate. Urban Splash acknowledges the importance of the support of Historic England; it may not provide much cash, but its involvement unlocks charitable bodies and other sources of support. There is still much to be done in West Yorkshire and it is reckoned that if all the old disused mills were restored, they would create space for 283,000 jobs.

Scotland offers some appealing and early examples of industrial regeneration. New Lanark is a village south-east of Glasgow that was founded in 1786 by David Dale, who built a village of cotton mills and housing for their workers. Dale worked in a brief partnership with Richard Arkwright and chose the spectacular site for the power provided by waterfalls on the Clyde. The industrial centre worked on 'the belief that if the workers in the cotton mills were provided with good accommodation by the standards of the day, a cooperative shop, a church, an institution for moral improvement and recreational facilities, together with schooling for children, output would rise'.[9] The mills closed in 1968, and after a period of decline, the New Lanark Conservation Trust was founded in 1974 to try to save the village. Today the village is a UNESCO World Heritage Site, Mill No. 1 is a hotel, and the other mills are tourist attractions.

Housing and Community Architecture

Until the 1970s architects and planners had felt confident about demolishing nineteenth-century housing. But architects of all persuasions began to see a value in old buildings, including those that presented anomalous challenges and advantages. They increasingly realised that improvements to small buildings such as individual houses had only a limited impact, that larger-scale rehabilitation was far more effective, and would encourage the improvement efforts of individuals, which is the basis of community repair.

The regeneration of former industrial buildings was now applied to the housing associated with it by the pioneering of community architecture. As Elizabeth Denby wrote with prescience in 1959: 'There is of course no doubt whatever that many very large areas of British industrial development need regenerating, but it is my strong conviction that this must be done sensitively *with* and not *for* or *against* the citizens themselves.'[10]

There is a Victorian forerunner of this movement. Patrick Geddes (1854–1932), a noted Scots biologist and botanist, was ahead of his time in three simple ways: he cultivated waste ground, used volunteer labour, and realised that it was essential to involve communities and volunteers in his projects. The development of the Edinburgh New Town had left much of the Old Town a slum, and during the 1880s Geddes began to buy up the old tenements and lease them as halls of residence to students, helping transform both the environment and the image of the Old Town. The most striking of these was at Ramsay Gardens, at the head of the Royal Mile next to Edinburgh Castle Esplanade.

Scotland remained ahead of the curve, and an early scheme that offered a solution to refurbishment of urban housing was the Scottish Little Houses Improvement Scheme (LHIS), initiated with 'The Little Houses', a 1952 touring exhibition on behalf of the National Trust for Scotland. It took a further eight years for the scheme to be inaugurated in 1960 to 'restore houses of character for re-sale', focusing on the Fife coastal towns. It examined the whole environment of towns and ordinary homes and turned out to be an interesting nexus of conservationist concerns combined with socialist-inspired utopian living. Ian Lindsay addressed the NTS annual general meeting in 1952: 'if you have a picture by Rubens encrusted with dirt and the canvas torn, no sane person throws it on a rubbish dump'.[11] The scheme forged a system (later used at Spitalfields and elsewhere), designed to be self-financing by restoring and selling. Nonetheless, idealists wondered whether social inclusion had been sacrificed to bureaucratic convenience and financial self-sufficiency. Meanwhile, modernist architects were encouraged to design sensitive infill between the regenerated streets, which emphasised an urban ensemble approach uniting old and new in a wider layout. The LHIS began to give interest-free loans to local preservation societies such as that at Crail, and it moved from a partnership model with local authorities to fostering preservation societies, i.e. from statism to volunteerism. The revolving-fund approach got things moving, and saved many houses, even if it didn't always satisfy the rigour of SPAB levels of authenticity.

Community Architecture: England

In England it was a young architect living in Macclesfield, Rod Hackney, who kick-started the community architecture approach during the 1970s. Hackney formed the Black Road Area Residents' Association when their industrial artisan homes were labelled blighted property. Hackney was unusually good at public relations and explained his case to the *Macclesfield Express*.

As an architect he could point out that the properties were not, as the council asserted, in bad condition. Hackney delivered a letter to the council declaring himself a Fellow of the RIBA with a petition with eighty signatures, but the town clerk's department refused to receive or discuss it.

The 1969 Housing Act, passed in the aftermath of the collapse of Ronan Point tower, was the turning point from subsidising high-rise buildings to providing improvement grants for existing housing. The vocabulary changed from 'slum clearance' to 'restoring old artisan dwellings'. This legislation was, as Hackney put it, 'our best friend'. He gained support from his local Conservative MP, Nicholas Winterton, who was one of the few who had read the Act. On examination of the small print Hackney discovered it permitted the preparation of an area report, recommending it for regeneration. The key to saving the houses lay in securing a 'general improvement area' declaration under the terms of the Act. It was clear that Macclesfield Council had not read the legislation. Hackney demonstrated that the cost of improving thirty-three dwellings would be £74,000 but to replace them would cost £207,000. The council refused to respond – everybody was always busy – but when the local papers went into action there was a change of heart and the *Macclesfield Express* declared that 'the Black Road people are to be congratulated on the way they have gone about their "Save Our Homes" campaign'.[12]

The *zeitgeist* was with Hackney – this was the era when people were starting to rethink the way the world's resources were used and E. F. Schumacher's *Small is Beautiful* (1973) would become their text. For Hackney it was not an argument of 'old versus new' but making the best use of the old, a perfect mantra for regeneration. All the political parties saw it as a victory; Labour as a victory for the working man and the Conservatives as a victory for those who help themselves. The council, of course, now wished to take the credit, television crews descended, and the concept of community architecture was established in England. Rod Hackney, however, was summoned by the president of the

RIBA and told that community-led conservation was something that the architectural profession should not concern itself with.[13] But as Hackney realised, 'the role of the architect was changing from that of the authoritarian professional expert to that of interpreter and enabler of residents' wishes'.[14] In 1987–9 Hackney himself became President of the RIBA (having gained, and then lost through loose talk to the press, the approval of the Prince of Wales).

Power Stations

Regeneration of former industrial buildings was not confined to the North. London offers two spectacular cases with landmark buildings on the banks of the Thames: Giles Gilbert Scott's two massive London power stations, one listed and one unlisted. Bankside, the first oil-fired power station in Britain, was decommissioned in 1981. No obvious role could be found for it until it triumphantly became London's largest gallery space, the Tate Modern, in 2000, and the city's most popular new tourist attraction. If everything went right at the unlisted Bankside, Battersea Power Station was a more tortured story. The result is far from perfect, but the best that could be obtained from a set of exceptionally difficult circumstances. But it does underline the persistence of the heritage lobby in the face of what has often been described as the Mount Everest of preservation. When the thirty-two-acre site was sold by the Central Electricity Generating Board in 1984 it offered the greatest challenge to any developer to find a suitable new use. Thus began the long saga finally over in 2022 with many schemes failing along the way, in which, as Rowan Moore put it, 'great visions alternate with bathos'.

'It ranks alongside the Houses of Parliament and Tower of London in the drama of its architecture and riverside setting [...] Eighty years have passed since it was built amid controversy and nearly thirty since it closed and was sold off amid further controversy. Left roofless and rotting for a quarter of a century—longer than it ever worked at full capacity—it remains London's most contentious historic building.'[15] Thus begins Andrew Saint and Colin Thom's entertaining account of Battersea Power Station in the *Survey of London*, published in 2013. Battersea was controversial from its inception. Local residents backed by a *Times* leader mounted objections in 1929 to its erection on grounds of unsuitability in central London and pollution.[*] Although the design is always associated with Giles Gilbert Scott, it was in origin the work of the engineers, Pearce and Halliday, who gave us the four distinctive chimneys.[†] Scott came late in the project, was limited to the exterior, but gave it (chimneys apart – he favoured one central chimney like Bankside) the familiar form that made it as much a part of the image of London as Sherlock Holmes. The quality of his design quelled the critics and it was soon hailed as one of the seven wonders of the modern world.[‡]

Despite its iconic status – many, like Kenneth Clark, regarded it as their favourite modern building in the capital – it was only listed in 1980 in the aftermath of the destruction of the Firestone Factory on the Great West Road. Two years earlier there was an application to demolish Battersea's 1930s Art Deco Turbine Hall, which Marcus Binney described as 'without question the largest hall I had ever entered, 500 feet long, 100 feet wide and 120 feet high'.[16] Binney arrived to see the place being mutilated and the magnificent turbines being carved up for scrap. In 1981 SAVE produced a book entitled *The Colossus of Battersea* suggesting an

---

[*] Even King George V wrote to the prime minister that the whole project was ill-advised.

[†] When his firm addressed the architectural form, they initially called on James Theodore Halliday, not Scott.

[‡] The image of the power station began to take hold in the realm of popular culture. It became a recurrent setting for feature films and music videos, most famously appearing on the cover of Pink Floyd's 1977 album *Animals* with a giant inflatable pig strung between its columns.' Saint and Thoms

alternative use as a sports arena and leisure centre, for which they were given planning consent the following year. A competition for developers was launched to find the best alternative use. Wandsworth Borough Council favoured leisure and recreation over office or retail uses, and thus a theme park scheme devised by the creators of Alton Towers won, with a design that was revised by 'a Texan firm of theme-park specialists that was entirely American in conception, featuring a waterfall, balloon ride, Chinese Emporium, Henry VIII restaurant, a "Ye Olde Souvenir Shoppe", a recreation of a typical Battersea pub, and so on'.[17] The foundation stone of this scheme was laid by Mrs Thatcher in a hard hat in 1988.

As the economic cycles waxed and waned, one scheme followed another, with hotels, housing, shops, cinemas, restaurants and offices being proposed, while consortiums and architects (including Nicholas Grimshaw) came and went, but work ground to a halt.* Rafael Viñoly, architect of one scheme, sighed that Battersea 'was hated to death when it was built; now everyone talks about it as if it was the Taj Mahal'. Saint and Thoms describe the most fanciful scheme:

> a £4 billion scheme included an office development on the former railway land that was to be covered with a plastic 'eco-dome' and crowned by an enormous 1,000ft tall ventilation chimney – apparently the key to the site's carbon-neutral pretensions. Unbelievably, given that a prerequisite of previous applications was that no buildings should exceed the height of the power station, this chimney dwarfed it entirely, and if built it would have been the tallest structure in London.[18]

In 2004 Battersea was placed on the World Monuments Fund's list of 100 Most Endangered Sites of international cultural

---

* In 2005 permission was granted by Wandsworth Council, with English Heritage's support, to demolish and rebuild the four concrete chimneys as 'beyond repair'.

importance. One eccentric but appealing scheme came from Will Self to abandon the power station to a ruin to become an inner city nature reserve. Such was the desperate search for solutions.

The scheme that finally came up with a financially viable proposal and satisfied an almost-despairing English Heritage was led by architect Jim Eyre; an £8 billion project involving 2,000 on-site workers. This has so far been a twelve-year project. Today, the once great brooding giant on the south bank of the Thames has been boxed in and caged by its luxury housing development, leaving only the north and south face visible. This appeared to be the only solution to the problem of raising the funds necessary to save Battersea, and also justifying the astronomically expensive construction of the spur of the Northern Line to overcome the problem of good transport links.[*] For Saint and Thoms, 'perhaps more than any other structure today it represents the impotence of the heritage lobby and planning system when faced with big business at its most rapacious, and also a surprising lack of imagination and drive in what should be a landmark conservation case'.[19] A project on this scale could only really have a satisfactory outcome with government help, and this was made manifest in the great area regenerations further down the Thames and in the north of England.

---

[*] English Heritage came close to accepting an inevitable demolition.

CHAPTER 15

Regeneration: Cities, Docklands and Basins

Cities need old buildings so badly it is probably impossible for vigorous streets and districts to grow without them.

JANE JACOBS[1]

It seemed at points during the twentieth century that former industrial cities were pathologised as sick or failing, notably those with docks: Manchester, Liverpool, Glasgow and Dundee.[2] One symptom of this was depopulation and it took strong planning policies and public subsidy to turn them around. The cultural shift was almost diametric – for seventy years the middle class were leaving by choice or commuting out at night, for example out of Liverpool through the Mersey tunnel to Birkenhead. The working class were relocated to new outlying housing estates, especially in Glasgow. But since the 1990s young people have been returning to cities of their own volition, driven by cultural forces: music, bars, restaurants, cinemas, theatres and clubs. The turnaround of Western cities from places from which to escape to magnetic places where people flock to work, rest, study and play has been an extraordinary shift.[*] What changed? A part of the story is urban

---

[*] This new-found 'cool' in the old urban fabric of cities extended to former slum districts well beyond dockland areas: communities like the Afro-Caribbeans of Notting Hill or Bangladeshis of Brick Lane could become so feted by the fashionable that they were priced out of their own enclaves.

regeneration, and the most successful examples were culture- and heritage-based.

There was a broader historical process at work. The failing industries failed, and new ones took their place: smaller, often creative, requiring well-designed offices and a brand locality, such as the Jewellery Quarter in Birmingham. With the shift from heavy duty 'dirty' industries to clean designer-led businesses came better air quality, cleaner buildings and canal/river water.* A reduction in unemployment, a feeling of security buttressed by a massive injection of government funds, and renewed confidence are all evident in the Liverpool story, told in a separate chapter. But in the way of British narratives, the pendulum swings exaggeratedly from darkness to light – even in Toxteth, things were never as wholly dystopian as the eighties movies or media made out, nor are they always as rosy as today's nostalgic hip implies.

The previous chapter examined the repurposing of mills and other relics of the Industrial Revolution. It was one thing to repurpose a Halifax mill, but what happened when cities faced the collapse of an industrial district, as in the London Docklands, or the collapse of the entire industrial economy at Liverpool, Manchester and Newcastle – moving from the unsustainable in search of a new sustainability? These required a different approach, one in which only central government could break through municipal inertia, override the planning laws, provide infrastructure, and oversee the complex financial structures involved. The approach was pioneered during the early 1980s at London Docklands and Liverpool.

Docklands was at first a faltering story, with multiple demolitions, bankruptcies, community dislocation and clashes with local councils. By contrast Liverpool was the first to demonstrate the importance of cultural and heritage elements in regeneration, which was to be central to the vision at Newcastle's

---

* It is difficult to exaggerate the depressing effect of stinking canals where dead dogs and cats, supermarket trolleys and bicycles were thrown.

Gateshead, Manchester's Ancoats, and Dundee. It is sometimes suggested that the worse things got, the more heritage assets were needed to pull areas out of decline. The formula, however, worked: the preservation of noble old buildings combined with good contemporary architecture and a museum or cultural centre has been successful, and occasionally inspiring.

These and many other regeneration projects share the presence of a waterline: London Docklands, Liverpool Docks, Brindleyplace in Birmingham, Salford and Ancoats in Manchester, Swansea, Cardiff and Hull, not to mention Battersea Power Station and Tate Modern on the Thames. This common thread is not surprising, since historically, industrial enterprise usually required water, whether for power or transport. To the planners of the 1960s, the waterfront was not yet recognised as a desirable element: when the Newcastle Cruddas Park estate was built, the early residents had their gaze turned from the Tyne because its banks were so unkempt. Equally, in Dundee during the 1960s, the River Tay was separated from the city by ring roads and feeders to the new Tay Bridge. Developers were ahead of planners in recognising water's picturesque allure. In many cases it was the sheer filth of the water that was the problem, as Michael Heseltine noted about the Mersey in 1983: 'Today the river is an affront to the standards a civilised society should demand of its environment. Untreated sewage, pollutants, noxious discharges all contribute to water conditions and environmental standards that are perhaps the single most deplorable feature of this critical part of England.'[3] The revival of the urban waterfronts represents a reversal of the exodus to the suburbs, and a return to the wellspring of desirable inner city living. Or it could be more sceptically said that once the factories and workers were shifted out, the middle class felt safe to return.

Often the restructuring of industrial cities during the 1970s – a time of high unemployment – was to be achieved by levelling the ground for new business parks; the perceived conflict between old buildings and jobs was a problem that had yet to be overcome. As late as 1979 it could be said that 'it is still widely believed that conservation and economic growth are incompatible'.[4] However, in America, where legislation passed in 1949 for 'urban renewal' had been through this cycle, it was already known that large-scale demolitions did not always produce the desired benefits. At Lowell in Massachusetts, built in the 1840s as an ideal industrial community, a new approach was pioneered when mills, the locks, canals and machinery were converted during the 1970s to become the poster-boy of such regenerations across the USA. More than anything else what this and the Liverpool chapter demonstrate is that economic growth can be driven by conservation and heritage.

The driver of area regeneration in Britain was to be the creation of Urban Development Corporations (UDCs). As Secretary of State for the Environment, Michael Heseltine announced the first two in 1981: London Docklands and the former docks of Merseyside. These were 'temporary autonomous zones' carved away from local authority control and into the ministry's. They had the potent combination of land freehold, planning powers, money, and Heseltine's political heft.[5] This was certainly not the first attempt to address such area problems, but this time there was more determination.* Both Liverpool Docks and London Docklands exemplify a property-led regeneration which required government intervention on a massive scale, not only to release public money for what Heseltine referred to as 'gearing', but to create the necessary infrastructure to support the incoming workforce and population. Intervention at this national level was also imperative to override local government and existing planning procedures.

This cleansing, or at Canary Wharf, wholesale rebuilding, caused a loss of familiar locale. Some of the romance, the 'decrepit glory' and sense of the patina of old dock quarters, was

---

* A precursor to Urban Development Corporations was the Inner Urban Areas Bill (1978), an inner-city programme that involved twenty-nine local authorities including Liverpool, London Docklands, Manchester and Birmingham. The emphasis was on creating jobs.

lost in the process – gone would be the dark fetid canals and the gaunt and grungy warehouses that appealed to Philip Larkin, who declared that 'deprivation is for me what daffodils were to Wordsworth'. It is difficult today to recall – except through old films and photographs – the black griminess of the industrial landscape, of Ewan MacColl's 'dirty old town'.

London Docklands

Containerisation spelt the slow death for the London docks, which had fallen into decline from the late 1950s. This fate was sealed by the construction of the Thames Barrier, which largely barred very large ships after 1982. Spanning four boroughs, derelict and poverty-ridden, the area was still the responsibility of the Port of London Authority, and the question was long debated as to what should replace them. There was a chronic shortage of cash, with consequent need for developers to fund any scheme – whose interests did not always coincide with either the local residents or the boroughs. The development of a regeneration strategy for docklands was a piecemeal affair dogged by numerous false starts, vested interests, multiple ownerships, and a power struggle between the various boroughs, central government, and the Greater London Council (GLC).

The first move came as early as 1969 with Thomas Telford's St Katharine Docks, next to Tower Bridge, advertised as 'a new Venice'.* The GLC sold the dock to Taylor Woodrow, specifying their requirement for a hotel, offices and apartments overlooking the dock basin. We can only be grateful that they did not fill in the basin, as so often happened in Liverpool. Although St

* The site had a curious history. Queen Matilda had chosen the site to establish her hospital of St Katharine and it remained the personal property of the Queen of England until the Reformation. Sir Patrick Abercrombie had proposed a park on the site to provide a setting for the Tower of London. Williamson, p. 48.

Katharine's functions as a mixed development, it was by later standards poorly done, only retaining a few early nineteenth-century buildings while adding a banal and pseudo-brutalist new hotel and other buildings styled in a warehouse manner – an early example of a developer playing at 'industrial chic' to create a false sense of heritage.

Thereafter Docklands regeneration dwindled during the 1970s, largely because a zoning policy for industrial usage frustrated any development beyond the Thames frontage.[*] The London Docklands Development Corporation (LDDC) changed all that in 1981. It was a tearing up of the rulebook in a breathtaking power seizure of the planning laws by the incoming Thatcher administration, awarding grants directly to developers rather than through local government (who admittedly in most cases were incapable of action). As Michael Heseltine told the author: 'we took their powers away from them because they were making such a mess of it'.[6]

Land was compulsorily purchased, and thus began a period of intense change and development underpinned by infrastructure projects such as the Limehouse Link tunnel, and with the Docklands Light Railway and London City airport both opening in 1987. Although community and a sense of place lie at the heart of most regeneration projects, the LDDC seemed to ignore the community in which it was operating, and local people, especially those on the Isle of Dogs, were not happy.[†] However, the LDDC got things done, and only central government could provide such impetus and infrastructure. There had been American precedents (largely tourism-based), notably the revived waterfront in Boston and the inner harbour of Baltimore, but nothing had been attempted on the scale required at Docklands. LDDC managed 1,756 acres with 417 acres of inlets and dock waters running

---

[*] In 1974 the Docklands Joint Committee was set up to include the GLC and the barriers but little progress was made.

[†] The residents of the Isle of Dogs had a history of plucky independence. In 1970, inspired by the Ealing comedy *Passport to Pimlico*, they declared UDI.

through it, while the stretch of the river amounted to nearer 6,000 acres.[7]

The first indication that Wapping might be more than a bohemian place to live came when Rupert Murdoch bought a thirteen-acre site there in 1978 and was given permission by the outgoing Labour environment minister, Peter Shore, to demolish a group of fine Georgian warehouses for his new print works. Wapping High Street retains some early warehouse conversions to artists' studios and flats, which still look good: in the 1960s, artists – always the pilot fish of taste – had moved in, and gentrification followed during the next decade.

Developments crept eastwards along the Thames, but as it curved south to meet Greenwich, there lay the site of the West India Docks, which offered a chance to do something on a far bolder scale. The LDDC unveiled the first proposals for the new buildings at Canary Wharf in 1985. There could hardly be a greater contrast between the old City of London and Canary Wharf. This site was London's greatest regeneration opportunity since the Great Fire of 1666 and the Blitz. Such projects usually work on an established infrastructure but, apart from the much-altered basins, this was scarcely the case at Canary Wharf. The new project obliterated most of the old site and dwarfed everything. It was a triumph of *laissez-faire* in design terms, breaking all height restrictions and built without reference to anybody. Nobody worried about the effect on views from Greenwich. But if there was little conservation around the central avenues of Canary Wharf, the former Import Dock remodelled with a slightly Vanbrugh-like feel by John Rennie was retained, and successfully holds its own against the giant Gotham City beyond.

If there was not much preservation at Canary Wharf itself, what was happening in the approaches and the hinterland? One of the criticisms about regeneration projects is their 'walled gardens' approach, with some stark contrasts at their boundaries. Compared with the wealth and gigantism of Canary Wharf, the Isle of Dogs gazes from its slightly chaotic low-rise streetscape up to what looks like a city set down by Martians. Its most surprising feature is Mudchute Farm, run as a municipal park on the edge of this Kurt Weill-like Mahagonny. This broad oasis with farmyard animals is as inspired as anything by Octavia Hill – symbolic of the search for Arcadia, and for a better life. With the appearance of Canary Wharf, the residents of 'the Island', as they called it, were divided between the deeply suspicious and those who wanted improved amenities: better shops and public transport. The arrival of the Docklands Light Railway in 1987 was the gamechanger, allowing for easier commuting which altered the nature of the residents, but the fabric of the Isle of Dogs was surprisingly unchanged.

Everything along the river was transformed. Today, Tower Hill to Canary Wharf is one of the most rewarding walks in the capital: flashes of brilliant regeneration, tiny rows of surviving Georgian houses and pubs, intertwined with developer housing (some good, some bad) – a wafer-thin brand of prosperity hugging the river and the old dock basins. The sweep of the river leading to Canary Wharf is majestic, rising Manhattan-like out of the water, somehow inhuman in scale with ant-like figures diving into the over-scaled offices. The energy, wealth and ambition are what strikes the viewer, and the effect ripples upstream. It is a story of putting the river back at the centre of London life, and this was to extend from the Millennium Dome as far down as Waterloo and the London Eye, taking in Tate Modern along the way.

Canary Wharf worked because London's Square Mile is small, and with the 'Big Bang' bringing in foreign banks and transferring trading from floors to screens in 1986, the need for new office space was critical. There is little doubt that the example set, both architecturally and economically, by Canary Wharf meant that the City of London had to up its game and it has spent the years since providing trophy buildings by celebrity architects with huge office spaces at a reasonable rent.[*]

---

[*] Broadgate is usually offered as the most impressive piece of post-war office planning in the City, which arose between 1985 and 1991 with some fine buildings.

Bermondsey, on the south bank, provides a more coherent story of regeneration, as it was completed later, and the quality is generally higher than on the north bank. The walk from St Katharine Docks over Tower Bridge into Bermondsey is now an established trail with an attractive backdrop. It offers an excellent example of the inspiration of an area of characterful warehouse buildings on contemporary architecture, with the two working together to the advantage of both. The centrepiece is Hay's Galleria (1982–6), by Michael Twigg Brown and partners, which roofs over the street of mid-nineteenth-century Hay's Wharf, creating a mall like a Victorian market with iron bracing and pillars. The most admired and reproduced modern housing development is The Circle by CZWG (1987–9), an effective piece of almost Spanish or Italian surrealist architecture in brilliant blue tiles, centering around a de Chirico-like statue of a horse by Shirley Pace. A little further on and Shad Thames becomes one of the most atmospheric streets in London, still criss-crossed by iron bridges and gantries. The old with the new is the main feature of most of the regeneration stories in this chapter.

Gateshead

If London had the most spectacular regeneration project, it was the north that provided the purest examples of heritage-led city regeneration. When J. B. Priestley visited the Newcastle area in 1933, he remarked of Gateshead, 'If anybody ever made money in Gateshead, they must have taken great care not to spend any of it in the town.'[8] Historically, this was a working riverside industrial district. Gateshead used to be described as a narrow lane which led to Newcastle, but today its Baltic Quay is one of the most admired and liveliest arts hubs in the country. Badly hit by industrial decline in the 1980s, the quayside was viewed as an opportunity for ambitious new architecture. Tyne and Wear Development Corporation brought in Terry Farrell, a graduate of Newcastle University, to create a masterplan of mixed development. They also encouraged public art, including Eduardo Paolozzi's *Vulcan*, and most famously Antony Gormley's *Angel* (1994); originally referred to as the Gateshead Angel, but adopted by 'the North', it became a symbol of Tyneside's revival.

At this point Gateshead seems to have got the building bug, and with the Gateshead Millennium Bridge (1995–2001) by Wilkinson Eyre Architects, erected a trophy piece if ever there was one. At the same time the Baltic Centre for Contemporary Art (1998–2002) was converted by Ellis Williams Architects from the shell of a massive former grain silo. This is comparable with Tate Modern as a regeneration project of an old industrial giant into halls for art.* In this Gateshead was following the lead of Bristol, which had already created the Arnolfini gallery from a nineteenth-century former tea warehouse, and Liverpool, where sections of the Albert Dock had been converted into Tate Liverpool. The former Rust Belt had now become a hub for cultural visitors.

One aspect of regeneration pioneered by the Guggenheim at Bilbao is using the assets of the past as a frame for a major piece of contemporary trophy architecture. It is the Sage music centre by Norman Foster that steals the show in Gateshead. Generally admired, the silvery Sage is a superb autonomous building, but opinion is divided as to whether it is too assertive on this prime riverside site. To its critics it screams for attention and upstages its surroundings. Internally, it is like an observatory offering the best views over Newcastle, excepting that of arriving by train over the Tyne bridges. There is no doubting the visitor success of the Gateshead Parnassus, but there are grumblings over the costs to the council.

---

* Baltic has no permanent collection and is therefore an exhibition centre.

Manchester: Salford Quays and Ancoats

In 1979 Ken Powell mused that the prospect of tourists visiting 'Manchester, "City of the Industrial Revolution"' in the same way as they now pour into Florence "City of the Renaissance", seemed fantastic'.[9] The fantastic has come to pass and things have certainly changed, so that one recent observer could write: 'Today, Manchester city centre is a crowded, ebullient labyrinth of glowing Victorian warehouses, long street canyons and redbrick railway viaducts, shaded canals, bohemian narrowboats and lively bars, punctured by lumpen sixties rent slabs and ringed by sci-fi scale construction sites. In places its iron fire-escapes and granite portals evoke mid-town Manhattan, in others the bright yellow trams, tranquil waterways and cobbled squares could be in continental Europe.'[10] If Manchester has few green spaces, it has water. It has based its successful regeneration on adapting the canals and basins (that created its nineteenth-century prosperity).

Salford was the most impressive staging post of the Bridgewater canal, the opening of which precipitated the astonishing growth of the whole Manchester area. However, the regeneration of Salford – a notorious nineteenth-century slum area – has been described as 'more of a commercial than an architectural success'. The new MediaCityUK has been built around the old basins of the Ship Canal – there are very few surviving old buildings, only the watery infrastructure. It boasts, however, two pre-eminent contemporary buildings, the Lowry Centre by Michael Wilford and Daniel Libeskind's Imperial War Museum. The Lowry sits asymmetric, angular and shiny and it is about as far from the Manchester that Lowry painted as can be imagined. The artist would be disorientated by the hyper-modern media city. Salford follows the example of Bilbao and Gateshead in using contemporary trophy architecture to project culture in a historical context.

On the other side of Manchester, Ancoats is a true heritage regeneration. The area, which claims to be the world's first industrial suburb, has two main arteries, the Rochdale and

Ashton canals, lined with the impressive mills and warehouses that left such an impression on the great German architect Karl Friedrich Schinkel on his 1826 visit. As late as the millennium, the old mills were described as 'great cliffs of dereliction' which had been decaying for over seventy years while the wider area had become a byword for crime and contamination, unfairly or not. The area started to be cleaned up for a failed Olympics bid in the 1990s, gathering momentum in the run-up to the 2002 Commonwealth Games with the clearance of the canals and the waterfront made salubrious. Since then the old mills have been adapted to apartments, with new atriums on the inside and restored glazing bars on the outside.

The centrepiece is Cutting Room Square, a good public space, a piazza paved with York stone and the basilica-like Hallé St Peter, a former church, saved and converted for use by the Hallé orchestra, a model of old and new working together. The historic fabric is respected and cleverly leveraged as an asset attracting start-ups, cafés, shops and the symphony orchestra. For the time being Manchester is enjoying prosperity, with sovereign wealth funds falling over themselves to invest money in one of the hottest property booms in Europe.

The outdoor café culture that is such a feature of modern Britain has been a central component of recent regenerations whether at Ancoats, Brindleyplace in Birmingham or at King's Cross in London. The King's Cross regeneration is an imaginative fusion of canals, warehouses and bright new buildings to provide a sense of place. This succeeds thanks to the quality of the public spaces and the way the masterplan connects it all together. It was, however, a slow process and not birthed without pain. The game-changer was the decision to terminate Channel Tunnel high-speed trains at St Pancras. The King's Cross regeneration – involving several adjoining areas – is usually associated with the area around Granary Square, a case of 'industrial luxury', tapping, as the *Guardian* put it, 'into the collective nostalgia for brick sheds and the lure of a bit of bronze trim'.[11] It is inevitably expensive to rent and buy here.

No fewer than thirty-five architects were involved in transforming this post-industrial Elysium of arts organisations, swanky flats, and cafés. Despite the demolition of a working-class housing block, the retention of old structures (particularly eye-catching are the gasometers converted into dwellings) has been essential to its success. Central Saint Martins is in one of them, and its arrival as the first tenant set the creative tone that got the process moving. This area has thrived because it co-locates design, production and consumption in close proximity: the hip café/bar and event space are in tune with the boutique design practice who provide their logo and interior, and the food wholesalers who supply the raw ingredients for their sashimi and accommodate the steady demand from latte-supping flexi workers night and day. Can this dream of an arts-based workplace nirvana work in the low-rent colder climate of Scotland?

North of the border, Dundee, a city that needed some love, has recently embarked on a £1 billion regeneration plan heralded by a spectacular flagship project, the V&A Dundee, which follows the Bilbao model of a trophy art gallery as the locomotive, and Gateshead with its river setting. The River Tay was always the lifeblood of Dundee. As the importance of the port declined in the 1960s the riverfront was effectively separated from the city by a network of roundabouts and feeders for the new Tay Road Bridge.[12] Nobody then could foresee that the riverfront would one day be reclaimed for leisure and culture. In the 1970s the city's factories closed and the oil enterprise went to Aberdeen. Depopulation followed, but Dundee maintained some centres of excellence; the university and Ninewells Hospital, as well as D. C. Thomson & Co Ltd, the creator of *The Beano*. The first stirrings of change came in 1992 with the repatriation of Captain Scott's ship, *Discovery*, from its traditional Thames-side mooring to Dundee, with a museum created alongside. The hope was to lure tourists hurrying between St Andrews and Glamis Castle to stop and spend time in the city. That was not quite enough even with Dundee's other considerable architectural attractions (which it has always underestimated), including a collection of

Victorian churches of national importance, and the first Daniel Libeskind-designed building in Britain.[*]

An outstation of the V&A for Dundee was first mooted by Mark Jones, the London V&A director, with the University of Dundee in 2007. The Scottish government offered support and an international architectural competition was launched, won by the Japanese firm Kengo Kuma and Associates. The building cost £83 million but that does not include the site purchase and raising of the three buildings, a swimming pool, and the compulsory purchase of a casino and the Dundee Hilton. Funding came from many sources: the Scottish government, the Heritage Lottery Fund, Dundee Council, and private sources led by D. C. Thomson & Co Ltd. The museum opened to great acclaim in 2018 and produced a much-needed wave of confidence in Dundee, a sense that 'we can do things'. There is no doubt that the museum, producing an income of £42.8 million, has attracted international visitors who would not otherwise have visited the city. It drew 830,000 visitors within two years of opening.

The first ever dedicated design museum in Scotland, the V&A Dundee acts as an anchor development at the heart of the city's £1 billion proposed waterfront regeneration, which will include residential, office, retail and leisure developments and involves the redevelopment of Dundee railway station and new marina facilities. It is hoped that this activity will produce 7,000 new jobs in the city as well as attracting tourists and further investment – Dundee is now looking at an Eden Project. One prominent Dundonian told the author: 'the V&A Dundee is less a museum than a venue to launch new products and be a lightning conductor for the future'.[13] It remains to be seen whether the money will be forthcoming, but what is certain is that there has not been so much confidence in Dundee since the glory days of 'jute, jam, and journalism'. Has the old Victorian idea that culture follows the money been turned on its head, and does investment now follow heritage? It is certainly true that in the

---

[*] The Maggie's Centre pavilion at Ninewells Hospital.

nineteenth century the great museums and cultural institutions were built when a city had already developed, the philanthropic result of economic success sometimes poured like a sauce over tough meat. Today culture and heritage are harnessed as drivers of economic growth.* Regeneration is where they meet.

As we have seen, there are many kinds of regeneration, each with a different emphasis. At one extreme is Canary Wharf, high-tech office accommodation for international banks where the heritage element is reduced to the old basins, the edges of the wharfs, and a slither of the Old India Dock on its fringes. Similarly, Salford, full of modern offices, sits on the contours of the old basins – they are new cities away from the inner city, 'walled gardens' of prosperity. In addition, MediaCityUK is a cultural hub showcasing heritage in the form of Lowry's paintings, the last great visual poet of the industrial landscape. It highlights the 'Bilbao effect' – the idea that a great museum building can act as a beacon for renaissance and investment. The V&A Dundee is the purest current example of this in Britain, raising the game of the whole city rather in the way that Tate Liverpool achieved at Albert Dock. It is probably too early to fully gauge the success of the arts hubs at Salford MediaCityUK, Gateshead, Dundee, or indeed Margate, but one cannot imagine these places now without them and they have become central to the brand.†

South Bank, Liverpool, Gateshead, Ancoats and Castlefield in Manchester, King's Cross and Dundee all make a case that investment does gravitate towards cleverly curated and repurposed 'heritage'. The change at Ancoats between 2000 and 2020 really

---

* It has become the custom today to locate museums and exhibition centres – some more successfully than others – in poorer or failing cities, encouraged by the government/Millennium Commission/Lottery's social agenda. They have succeeded best when part of a wider urban regeneration project.

† There was even a plan promoted by Mrs Thatcher to place the Thyssen painting collection in a new museum in Docklands, a plan prevented by the desire of Baron Thyssen's wife, who was Spanish, that it should go to Madrid.

is astonishing. And such regeneration brings creative vitality back to the inner city, so that the MTV awards could be hosted on the Mersey docks, and that corporate conferences would move seamlessly from Zurich to Chicago to Liverpool. The sense of inner-city decay was reversed in a remarkably short space of time. Central to this was placemaking, an appreciation of using the historic assets, working to the grain of the existing 'village'. Every Manchester property developer knows that former warehouse apartments sell much quicker than new builds – or as one former planner put it: 'heritage gives a competitive advantage. When used wisely it is a powerful catalyst and accelerant to the making of magical, magnetic places.'[14]

Liverpool Story

*Someday, perhaps, it will be possible to walk through
the streets as among the ruins of another Pompeii [and]
recall the history of a great emporium of the North,
which lived and prospered [...] and then decayed.*

MARIO PRAZ ON LIVERPOOL, 1972[1]

Great ports are romantic, emotional places, and none more so than Liverpool. Few cities have expressed themselves more effectively in poetry and song. Herman Melville called it one of the manmade wonders of the world. But if Liverpool had some grand buildings, it never escaped the endemic squalor of ports, on which Alexis de Tocqueville remarked. No city rose so triumphantly in the nineteenth century or collapsed more dismally during the second half of the twentieth century. Its regeneration from the 1980s onwards is the seminal example of a heritage-led renaissance. Liverpool exemplifies the transition from the collapse of a former docklands industrial base to the rise of a creative base which represents the defining success of Britain over the last half century.

Liverpool had something of the quality of a boom town during the eighteenth and nineteenth centuries. Like all ports it was polyglot and attracted immigrants. At the end of the nineteenth century Liverpool could describe itself as 'the second seaport of the world [...] the principal gateway from the west into Europe'.[2] Its west-facing transatlantic docks and proximity to the industrial cities of the north gave Liverpool an advantage.

The cotton industry was its main wealth, part supported by a slave economy; Liverpool has had to come to terms with having been Britain's leading slave port. Proximity to Ireland and the Irish potato famine of 1846–49 had an enormous impact as refugees poured in, many transiting to North America, while others remained to give the city a unique character, and making it the leading Roman Catholic city in England. For good or ill, Liverpool has always claimed a cultural exceptionalism.

The inner city is studded with superb early twentieth-century commercial architecture by Norman Shaw and his contemporaries. Liverpool's most famous landmarks, the majestic buildings at the Pier Head erected between 1904–17 and dubbed the 'Three Graces', illustrate this scale and ambition. Together, they form an instantly recognisable profile offering a compendium of Liverpool styles. Built in competition with one another, they were designed to catch the attention of passengers on arrival or departure. The tendency towards gigantism of Liverpool architecture attained its zenith not with such commercial architecture, but rather with the designs for its two cathedrals. The Anglican cathedral, the most impressive twentieth-century building in the city, is the work of Sir Giles Gilbert Scott and represents the swansong of the Gothic Revival. It was begun in 1904 and only completed in 1978. How it ever got built and on that scale in a city in decline is something of a mystery, but it equally says something about the loyalty and adherence of the Liverpudlian professional class who largely paid for it.

The seeds of decline were sown when the *Titanic* sailed from Southampton in 1912, spelling the gradual disappearance of the luxury liner traffic. There was still huge ambition in Liverpool between the wars, however, and this is borne out by the construction of the Mersey Tunnels, the airport at Speke, and work on the largest planned cathedrals of the century. The first Mersey road tunnel was said to be a nail in the civic coffin as the middle class deserted the Georgian terraces for life in the Wirral.

The city was exceptionally badly bombed in World War II, with seventy air raids.* Then the post-war decline of local industries, particularly textiles, took its toll on the port. Moreover, whereas Liverpool faced west towards the Irish Sea and the Atlantic, England increasingly turned towards European trade from its easterly ports. Investment melted away from Liverpool, which began to take on the appearance of an imperial mausoleum. Its docks and riverfront were made redundant by the advent of huge container ships which required deep-water terminals, directing commerce elsewhere. The air of idleness and decay pervaded even the city centre.

The streets may have been depressing in appearance, but nonetheless in music and poetry the Merseybeat resounded around the world. Allen Ginsberg could claim that 1960s Liverpool was 'the centre of consciousness of the human universe'. Optimism peaked in 1962, the year the Beatles emerged, and construction began on the new Roman Catholic cathedral (known locally as 'Paddy's Wigwam'). Frederick Gibberd's 'space age' building was of national importance, and has delighted and disappointed people ever since. But in 1963 *The Times* already described the centre of Liverpool as 'like the belly of some mangey stuffed animal with bald patches'.[3] It was Manchester that was to benefit from the office boom of the late sixties.

The planning consultant Graeme Shankland, who was no respecter of Victorian architecture, declared that 'sentimentality is the enemy of understanding: Liverpool's chief inheritance from its nineteenth century is the biggest slum problem in England. Buildings have no merit because they are old or familiar.'[4] The only section of his new road plan that was completed succeeded in separating the city centre from the waterfront. It was variously described as a 'nightmare' and the work of 'Bomber' Harris.[5] However, everyone agreed

---

* Very few buildings were reconstructed, the Blue Coat School, which remains the jewel of eighteenth-century Liverpool architecture, being an exception. It also represents an early example of preservation; Lord Leverhulme bought the building in 1906 to save it from demolition.

that the slums needed to be addressed. The city architect and director of housing, Ronald Bradbury, obliged with more than 110 dismal tower blocks. The creation of three new towns, Kirby, Skelmersdale and Runcorn, also designed to replace the slums, only hastened the decline as the city's population and tax receipts dwindled. Then in 1966 when the housing plan condemned 70 per cent of inner-city dwellings, whole areas of terraced housing, especially in Everton, were simply erased. When in the same year dock strikes finally persuaded Cunard to abandon Liverpool for Southampton, morale sank to new depths. The remaining Georgian terraces of Toxteth, which suffered grievous damage from both bombing and developers, had become a shabby bedsit land. The enforced slum clearances were broadcast to the nation in the television sitcom *The Liver Birds*, with scenes of families fighting off the bulldozers while confronting council officials, and passengers on a passing bus singing 'Land of Hope and Glory'.[6]

The problems multiplied when the Mersey Docks and Harbour Board collapsed into debt in 1971, announcing the city's bankruptcy. Riots broke out the following year, to the belated alarm of Whitehall.[7] The Tory Secretary of State for the Environment, Peter Walker, appointed consultants to study the problem, and was followed by Labour's Peter Shore, who suggested that the city should 'pension off the bulldozers'. Shore, a Liverpudlian himself, found money but never formed a cogent plan. Liverpool was now a problem city, seemingly synonymous with the decline of Britain. As Beryl Bainbridge remarked, 'someone's murdered Liverpool and got away with it'.[8]

Conservation came to Liverpool at the end of the 1960s in the wake of Quentin Hughes's 1964 book *Seaport*, which called out just how much had already been lost. It is a powerful but ambiguous work, written by a senior lecturer at the Liverpool School of Architecture (with a foreword by Shankland – and thus on both sides of the argument). The Merseyside Civic Society, the Royal Fine Art Commission and SAVE all played their part, but it would need more than these worthy organisations to turn such a tide. By the early 1980s Liverpool's core population had fallen below 500,000 and in some districts unemployment rates reached 40 per cent. Clive Aslet described the city centre in 1981 as 'like a morgue full of deserted streets – as if a neutron bomb had been dropped'.[9] During the darkest days of the city's decline the university was a pilot light, continuing to offer a centre of excellence. Moreover, social and spiritual leadership was provided by two great churchmen who worked harmoniously, the Roman Catholic Archbishop Derek Worlock and the Anglican Bishop David Sheppard. They smoothed the cracks between the sectarian and tribal loyalties that were made so evident by the city's other great religion, football.

And then help came. It was from the least expected source: a new Secretary of State for the Environment, Michael Heseltine, a maverick figure in the Thatcher cabinet who had been appointed in 1979. He asked his officials what was the second worst area of urban dereliction after London's East End? Their reply was unequivocal: the banks of the Mersey as it ran through Liverpool. He tells in his memoirs how 'I decided then and there that we should take general powers and designate to specific sites for the first experiment.'[10] His cabinet colleagues favoured a policy of 'managed decline' for Liverpool, but there was a touch of the nineteenth-century activist merchant prince about Heseltine, who would not allow such a policy on his watch. He was to demonstrate what a determined politician can achieve in the face of almost universal scepticism: 'when I first went there I did a lot of listening and I realised there was a problem – everybody knew what was wrong and all had excuses, but there was no leadership'.[11]

Heseltine was like a man possessed who – to the horror of his department – visited Liverpool every week for eighteen months. His strategy was to utilise the city's heritage of historic buildings as a locomotive of regeneration. His hope was that improvement in the built environment would bring back confidence and investment. One of Heseltine's most famous actions was to bring a busload of captains of industry to attract investment by visiting blighted areas of the city: a gambit that was dubbed 'dark tourism'. In an act of architectural homeopathy, he persuaded Wimpey to restore a Georgian street on the edge of Toxteth.

Then he established Merseyside Development Corporation (MDC) in 1981, giving it considerable powers to undertake a programme of regeneration. The Toxteth riots which broke out later the same year – some of the most violent ever seen – gave urgency to these efforts, and gained Heseltine crucial support in cabinet. The first problem to be addressed was the huge expanse of land contaminated by industrial activity. Heseltine backed the idea of an International Garden Festival on a polluted site on the banks of the Mersey. This scheme had the merit that the thirty exhibiting countries would pay for their own national garden and draw visitors. The centrepiece was the Festival Hall by Ove Arup. Out of decay came beauty and morale was lifted – the festival demonstrated that a better world was possible. The people of Toxteth were less impressed, retorting, 'we want jobs not trees'. Visitors to Liverpool in the early 1980s paint an apocalyptic vision of an empty city centre, but that would have been counterbalanced by a visit to the green suburbs where the middle classes continued their comfortable existence. A complicating factor was the arrival in 1983 of Derek Hatton as deputy leader of Liverpool City Council, a member of the Trotskyist Militant group.* Hatton gloried in being philistine, demolishing much of Lancelot Keay's superb pre-war public housing and threatening to sell off the paintings in the Walker Art Gallery. A story has it that officials hid the civic silver collection under St George's Hall to prevent him from selling it.

The crowning achievement of the MDC was the restoration of the long-disused Albert Dock warehouses, which became the emblem of Liverpool's revival. The jewel in this crown was the

---

* In 1983 a 'militant tendency' Labour Party gained control of the council, setting an illegal budget which put them at loggerheads not only with the Tory government but also their own Labour leadership. Today Derek Hatton is a property developer.

establishment of Tate Liverpool, converted by James Stirling. Stirling, himself a Liverpudlian, created a notably restrained and simple plan, perfect for its purpose. Threatened buildings such as the Lyceum and St Francis Xavier's Church were saved from destruction and many in Liverpool began to grasp that its architectural heritage was as important to visitors as its Beatles fame – always the huge tourist draw. Albert Dock precipitated a new wave of waterside development, mostly residential, driven by the dictates of the market. The results, exemplified by Brunswick Dock, were mediocre but at least things were moving. Sadly, despite the superb restoration work, little contemporary architecture of any quality emerged in Liverpool at this time. A group of leading architects, including Richard Rogers and Norman Foster, drew up plans for a 'Fourth Grace' to complement the famous parade of the 'Three Graces'. But the winning design by Will Alsop proved to be too expensive and had no clear purpose. It was cancelled in 2004 and in its place was built the showy new Museum of Liverpool.

The problems of Liverpool's post-war municipal housing schemes led to the rise of housing cooperatives and community architecture. An inspiring example is the Eldonian Housing Cooperative, in which the residents took control of the design. Even the demonised Derek Hatton replaced some of the worst high-rises, and thereby enlarged Everton Park with views over the Mersey. Everton, once a suburb of gentleman's villas, was dotted with twenty-five of Bradbury's towers. Three of them were so unpleasant they became known as 'the Piggeries', where residents went on a rent strike in protest.[12] However, this failure was as much a management issue as a systemic social and architectural shortcoming. Twenty-three of the tower blocks were demolished, and the two survivors were made over to the polytechnic, then inhabited by asylum seekers, and finally sold for a mere £1 to developers. Despite this chequered past, they are today well-maintained and well-regarded private apartments.

The culmination of Liverpool's renaissance came in 2003.

It was Britain's turn to appoint a city as European Capital of Culture; there was strong competition from eleven cities including Manchester, Birmingham and above all Newcastle. The Liverpool bid succeeded with the strapline 'the World in One City'. The announcement was a stimulant to activity: clearing the shops in front of Lime Street station, finishing projects such as the arena and convention centre, and completing road systems, all in preparation for 2008. The year after the announcement UNESCO designated Liverpool a World Heritage Site, calling it 'the supreme example of a commercial port at the time of Britain's greatest global influence'.

The year 2008 was one of celebration, opening with a giant street party hosted by Ringo Starr. Each month offered a different theme, for example, football and tall ships. The number of hotel rooms doubled. This went some way to changing the city's image from one of 'self-pity city' to one of rebirth. One resident sardonically told the author, 'Liverpool is good at bread and circuses even if the rubbish collection doesn't work.' An unexpected legacy is Antony Gormley's haunting figurative sculptures just beyond the city on Crosby Beach, which were sited there for the celebrations but which remained in place, turning a scrappy seafront into a compelling destination.

Among the projects accelerated for 2008 was the massive inner-city shopping development, Liverpool ONE, which the journalist Simon Jenkins described as 'the most sensitive piece of regeneration in England'. It was a Grosvenor Group project stimulated by the local interest of the billionaire Duke of Westminster, whose country estate lay nearby in Cheshire.[13] Liverpool ONE is the most important piece of regeneration since Albert Dock, encompassing forty-two acres and sympathetically incorporating old buildings. Many architectural firms were involved, and the quality of the buildings represented the best in the city at the time. But it is the planning which is most interesting, creating arcades to break the linear shopping streets, opening vistas and making attractive spaces in which to wander.* The cost was £1 billion, and it is perhaps fortunate that Grosvenor was a long-term player, undeterred by the recession which would have caused many developers to scale down their ambitions. Next door is the Rope Walk, an excellent example of the regeneration of old streets – a 1990s masterplan by Building Design Partnership. It is an area of bars and shops that feeds seamlessly into Liverpool ONE. The regeneration company Urban Splash has done excellent work here and elsewhere in the city, notably the stylish conversion of the historic eighteenth-century Roman Catholic chapel of St Peter into the Alma de Cuba nightclub.

But if good things were happening in the city centre, all was not well in neighbouring districts. In the early 2000s post-war-style clearance returned to Liverpool's Granby Street, ground zero of the 1981 Toxteth riots. Under the guise of 'boosting regeneration' a £2.2 billion national scheme known as Pathfinder was promoted by the deputy prime minister John Prescott, who intended it as a housing market renewal programme. The concept was to buy up and demolish terraced properties across the north of England, handing the land to house builders and social landlords for redevelopment. The 'logic' of the Pathfinder scheme was that the houses had only negative value – they would cost more to modernise than they would be worth when the job was completed.† Accordingly, in 2003 Liverpool Council announced its intention to demolish 7,000 terraced houses. They called them zones of opportunity, or 'zoos' for short.

The desire to invest in northern housing was laudable. But as the planning consultant Jonathan Brown observed: 'From the

---

* Not everybody is enamoured with Liverpool ONE. See Minton p. 139, who objects to it 'employing uniformed private guards to police thirty-four private streets'. Others point out the quick turnover of units and the lack of small shops: bakeries, fishmongers, ironmongers etc. in favour of big brands.
† The truth according to Marcus Binney was very different: vested interests. Consultants had already been paid £163 million by 2005. See Binney 2006, p. 32.

start, Pathfinder showed an appetite for destruction. Secretive, top-down and target driven, hundreds of thousands of private homes were condemned in backroom deals between public officials and developer interests, before any proper surveys of their residents or refurbishment potential. The classic English terraced house was demonised as obsolete.'[14] The scheme was exposed in a devastating TV documentary series by Trevor McDonald in 2005 and six years later it was abandoned, but not before many acres of good Victorian housing had been destroyed.[15] The documentary revealed that it cost £60,000 to purchase a house, £17,000 to demolish it and at least £80–100,000 to replace it, but when the programme had the opportunity to repair such a house, this was achieved to a high standard for a mere £24,000 in just four weeks.

In one of the worst affected areas where only four nineteenth-century terraces remained, the residents formed a community land ownership scheme known as the 'Granby Four Streets Community Land Trust' which acquired ten empty houses for renovation as affordable homes. They were close to the so-called Welsh Streets where Ringo Starr had been brought up, and his former house was among those threatened with demolition. Although stopping Pathfinder was a bottom-up movement, it was strongly supported by SAVE and other national bodies.* SAVE won the fight to change policy at a national level, taking several local cases to the High Court. The heritage message was 'let it be'. To everyone's surprise and delight the work at Granby, the work of the architectural collective Assembly commissioned by Xanthe Hamilton, won the 2015 Turner Prize. Visiting the area today is a surreal experience. Ducie Street is still empty by order of the council – trees now grow out of its windows and

* SAVE also fought a valiant battle to save Welsh Streets houses nearby. The houses were earmarked for demolition in 2000. When nearly all the houses were emptied, SAVE was able to buy one to challenge through the courts which led to a public inquiry in 2014 which the inspector recommended against, but he was overruled by Eric Pickles. The terraces from the 1870s and 1880s by Richard Owen still stand.

artists have painted the houses and added decorative accretions. It has become a public work of art.

Liverpool in 2020

How does this leave Liverpool today? It has thirty-six Conservation Areas which cover 9 per cent of the city area, in theory protecting 19,000 properties. The areas within these are better conserved than those without. However, in terms of officer support they are running on empty. Surprisingly few redbrick terraces are covered, despite Liverpool's role in pioneering the by-laws that shaped such late Victorian terraces. Liverpool variously claims to have the highest concentration of Victorian terraces in England as well as the largest number of listed Georgian houses. The 'Georgian listing' trope has become a sort of mantra that allows the city to feel good about itself (albeit a little late in the day, as two-thirds of them have been allowed to perish). But the city does not lavish the same affection on its Victorian terraces, which remain severely at risk. Beyond the centre, listed buildings of great character are being allowed to deteriorate. The shocking state of the block of Arts and Crafts flats in Bevington Street (illustrated by Quentin Hughes in *Seaport*), part of the award-winning Eldonian Village, are a case in point. As the developer has removed its roof, how can they survive? Quirkiest of all is the Arts and Crafts Everton public library, designed in a Jacobean Arts and Crafts style by Thomas Shelmerdine (1896), illustrated in Pevsner – another characterful listed building in decay.

The greatest triumph of Liverpool's regeneration is the Mersey waterfront, now home to museums, exhibitions, and the focus of almost all the city's now-numerous festivals. But even in this protected space a threat is looming. 'Liverpool Waters' is the largest planning application in Britain, a small-scale Canary Wharf, turning derelict docks on both banks of the Mersey into a city of steel and glass. The Peel Group, a property holding company, offer Shanghai as their model, and are seeking Chinese investment. English Heritage and SAVE have objected to the scheme. UNESCO was watching this and other developments in the city carefully, and threatened to withdraw World Heritage Site listing. This happened in July 2020 specifically over the new Everton stadium on the waterfront. It is only the third such deletion in UNESCO's history.* Local opinion is divided over whether this matters. Some on the council dislike the scrutiny, while others recognise that to be the first city in Britain to lose this distinction is a considerable humiliation. As Professor John Belchem put it: 'having led the way in regeneration through conservation, Liverpool has sadly lapsed into polarised and counter-productive opposition between redevelopment and heritage, as if they were mutually exclusive.'[16]

---

* Dresden being the second, with the Waldschlösschen Bridge.

CHAPTER 17

Margate Sands

The sight of abandoned pleasure piers epitomises to us today the plight of seaside towns which have had as precipitous a fall as many former industrial cities.[*] Attempts to revive seaside towns are usually described as regeneration, but are more accurately restoration, rejuvenation and rebranding. There is no better example of this than Margate, with its impressive cultural backstory – here J. M. W. Turner spent his weekends and found that the skies 'are the loveliest in all Europe', Walter Sickert taught at the art school, T. S. Eliot wrote Part III of *The Waste Land* in the shelter on the Promenade, and Tracey Emin has returned to the streets and sands of her childhood. Margate is often cited as the classic example of creativity or arts-led regeneration. In fact the artists and hipsters have reappeared quite recently, and the revival began earlier, with an appreciation of the singular assets of the town. It was eventually crowned with the building of the Turner Contemporary art gallery, which opened in 2011.

During the eighteenth century Margate was transformed from a fishing village at the northern tip of the Isle of Thanet into one of England's earliest seaside resorts. Over the next century it became a popular resort for the East End of London, a poorer version

---

[*] In the nineteenth century there were a hundred seaside piers. Today there are only fifty, of which forty are listed. Many of them are at risk owing to neglect, the increase of storm surges and the effect of climate change.

of Ramsgate. Then it developed a more fashionable new town in the mid-nineteenth century called Cliftonville. The twentieth century saw many fine additions: Margate's own Coney Island, the Dreamland amusement park, with what is now the oldest Scenic Railway rollercoaster in the country (1920), a fine classical railway station by the young Maxwell Fry (1926), and two Art Deco delights, the Thanet School of Art and Crafts (1931) and the Dreamland Cinema (1935). By the 1960s, with the boom in overseas holiday destinations (travel agents promoted 'Malaga not Margate') and the town's consequent decline, Butlin's acquired many of the hotels. During the 1960s, the developer Bernard Sunley built a very tall brutalist tower block on the seafront, Arlington House, which Gavin Stamp described as 'dreadful' before changing his mind and declaring that he saw merit in the building. Still standing in isolation, today it has a totemic quality and is a reminder of a style that is returning to favour.

Several key episodes can be traced back to 1968, when the Margate Civic Society was founded, and the leading Kent conservation architect, Anthony Swaine, was appointed in the first batch of conservation officers after the passing of the Civic Amenities Act the year before. Together they prevented a great deal of demolition, rebutting the usual destructive plan for a gyratory roundabout and fostering an appreciation of the town's remarkable buildings. These include many seaside specials: the underground caves, the Shell Grotto, the fun fair, the Winter Gardens and two theatres. But the major turning point was the arrival of the high-speed trains from St Pancras in 2009, which brought London within eighty minutes, and with it commuters, day trippers, weekenders – and investment. The next three years saw extraordinarily heightened activity, with many projects coming to fruition. The revival of the town was at its most intense between 2009 and 2012.

The Dreamland amusement park was due to be demolished and replaced by a retail park. It was the timely listing of its Scenic Railway that prevented this, and precipitated a complete restoration (£3.8 million came from the DCMS Sea Change programme) and reopening in 2015. Lottery money was used to good effect: the compulsory purchase and restoration of the Art Deco cinema came after it had served its inevitable spell as a bingo hall. Of all restoration projects the most ambitious was Dalby Square, which had been created in the 1860s as part of the move to raise the quality of the town, but by the 1980s found itself in one of the most socially deprived wards in Kent – or even the country – with labels such as 'Sicko Square' and 'Dole on Sea' attached to it. The square was designated a Conservation Area in 2010 and two years later Thanet District Council and the Lottery gave £2.6 million to the 'Dalby Square Project'* for heritage improvements, with fifty-one grants dispersed. In the square itself the central car park was removed and gardens restored, railings were replaced, and building facades renovated. The poster boy of this restoration, 12 Arthur Road, is now available for holiday lets and opened to the public six days a year.

Overshadowing all of these has been the triumphant creation of the Turner Contemporary gallery by David Chipperfield, a water's edge art gallery that John Newman described as 'an architectural image more memorable, perhaps, than any seen in East Kent in all the previous century'.[1] This gallery, which sits at one end of the bay between the town and the sea, has certainly changed the perception of the town and reinforced its artistic status. Margate could now project itself as a creative hub, attracting artists and hipsters. In 2018 the art school, which had been closed since the 1970s, was reinstated, and opened in the former Woolworth's building.† Yet for all this there seems a disconnect between the Turner Contemporary and the work of the local artists.

The restoration of Margate is far from complete and there is still much to be done, notably at the Lido and the Clifton Baths,

---

* The inspiration of Andrew Brown, the south-east regional director at English Heritage.

† In my travels for this book Margate was the only town where I was taken to see the art school.

and the potentially glorious Winter Gardens Theatre. Moreover, the traffic problem, which blights the town's central space, Cecil Square, must be solved. Planning decisions have not been perfect: while the noble classical Sea Bathing Hospital has now been converted into a gated community (groan), its admirable Gothic Revival chapel is being allowed to deteriorate. However, what has been achieved at Margate is impressive and a tribute to the voluntary sector, which keeps the museums and the Theatre Royal going. The Civic Society attempts to keep the council up to the mark, with varying degrees of success. Margate's accent may be on youth, but its backbone, as ever, is age and experience.

The Heritage Industry and the Lottery

*For me the heritage is always about people, which means it's
not always the finest examples of something that need to be saved,
but the ones that have changed – or could change – lives most.
Listing or expert approval is not necessarily a measure
of heritage worth, but of academic preference. Heritage is not
synonymous with excellence.*

PETER LUFF, FORMER CHAIRMAN OF THE
NATIONAL LOTTERY HERITAGE FUND[1]

Sometime during the mid-1970s heritage took off. Some
believe the V&A exhibition 'The Destruction of the
Country House' in 1974 provided the propellant; others
prefer 'European Architectural Heritage Year' the following year,
which gave the concept international recognition. The word
was on everyone's lips, and during the 1980s the Conservative
government rebranded all the main cultural agencies – except
the Arts Council – with a heritage prefix. 'National heritage'
was put at the heart of public arts policy to encourage popular
engagement with historic sites, buildings, monuments and
museums. Formerly elite history was re-examined so that the
excavated wreck of Henry VIII's flagship, the *Mary Rose*, would
relate the tale of ordinary seamen. Everybody now had their
own heritage. Britain's favourite television commercial was
Ridley Scott's 1973 Hovis advertisement, which sought to endow
mass-produced bread with an air of wholesomeness through its

nostalgic evocation of northern working-class life, despite actually being filmed in Shaftesbury in Dorset. In this chapter we will examine the foundation of the three government organisations that constitute the core of the newly coined 'heritage industry'.

The handmaiden of heritage was conservation. The drivers of conservation were no longer exclusively the amenity societies with their influential but limited support. The public became engaged through television and a new educative socio-historical agenda, embodied by the foundation of the Department of National Heritage in 1992 and the Heritage Lottery Fund in 1994. The Lottery established a direct connection between heritage, social values and community benefit. With the arrival of the New Labour administration in 1997, the previous Conservative government's heritage banner was rebranded under the neologism of the 'creative industries'. They could change the name, but not the concept – heritage had seeped deep into public consciousness and was now widely applied by anybody marketing the past.[*]

English Heritage

The visitor success of country houses, whether privately owned or by the National Trust, had not gone unnoticed by the incoming Conservative government in 1979. It wanted to transfer the national collection of buildings and historic sites from the old Ministry of Public Buildings and Works to a shiny brand-new entity that would deliver both the visitor numbers of the National Trust and the commercial success of the private sector. Accordingly, old blueprints were dusted down that would detach both the buildings and many of the regulatory, listing and grant-giving functions from the ministry, which had now been subsumed into the super-ministry, the Department for the Environment. The new secretary of state, Michael Heseltine,

---

[*] The DNH became the Department of Culture, Media and Sport in 1997; it is now the Department of Digital, Culture, Media and Sport.

was unusual for a politician in showing a great interest in conservation, and he sanctioned the creation of a new quasi-independent body. This was formulated in 1982 during a conference at Leeds Castle through the advocacy of Jennifer Jenkins, chair of the Historic Buildings Council. All 880 monuments and sites were duly transferred the following year to the new body under the operating name English Heritage, and similar arrangements were made for Scotland and Wales.

The first chairman was Lord Montagu of Beaulieu – a good choice as he had successfully marketed his own stately home with jazz festivals and a motoring museum. He possessed considerable political and public relations skills. Only the uninhabited royal palaces – the Tower of London, Hampton Court, the Banqueting House and Kensington Palace – were withheld; rumour has it the Queen wished to maintain control owing to concern that Montagu might commercialise them in an undignified manner. They remain part of a separate body, Historic Royal Palaces. Montagu's priority was to improve the presentation of properties – with Stonehenge at the top of the list – and by doing so earn more income at the gate. This was essentially about enhancing the visitor experience by providing popular guidebooks as well as events such as medieval jousts, theatrical performances and similar activities. One of Montagu's many initiatives was to establish a membership body – probably the first in which members of the public could join what remained a government agency. The National Trust were wary of this development, concerned it might dilute their membership and compete with their own commercial activities. English Heritage would never enjoy the membership success of the Trust, but by 2020 it had 2 million members (the National Trust now has 5.6 million).

If the most visible role of English Heritage was its custodianship of the historic buildings and sites now called 'the National Heritage Collection', its principal aim was to protect 'not just a few major monuments but the whole historic environment', as its first annual report ambitiously stated. Much of this essential work is described elsewhere in this book, but it is worth emphasising here the extraordinary progress that has been made in listing and conservation measures. A powerful stimulus to this, one that predated English Heritage, was the storm of protest caused by the demolition of the Art Deco Firestone Factory in Brentford in 1980. Its loss encouraged Heseltine to order that the listing survey be accelerated, particularly with regard to unprotected twentieth-century buildings. The task was estimated to take ten years but Heseltine, perhaps recognising the brevity of political lives, wanted it finished in three. Despite recruiting a team of no fewer than 110 architects and architectural historians at a cost of £45 million it still took seven years to complete. With 500,000 listed buildings, English Heritage was, for the first time, in possession of an inventory of the country's architectural patrimony.

English Heritage was not seeking to increase its estate further, although newly discovered archaeological sites were necessarily taken into care. Apart from improving what it already owned, and listing historic buildings, its most rewarding activity was distributing restoration grants through the Historic Buildings Council. A perusal of their annual reports reveals the range of activities and grants they provided: in the first year a scheme for rundown Victorian terraced housing in Merseyside (the Canning Street Conservation Area). During year two (1985/6) English Heritage spent half of its £52.1 million budget on grants to historic buildings: 2,000 on Conservation Areas and over 400 provided to churches. Over the next few years, English Heritage opened twenty education centres and revised all its guidebooks. By 1992 the incoming chairman, Jocelyn Stevens, acknowledged that the definition of heritage had been widened to encompass industrial monuments. English Heritage had made a promising start with solid achievements, but its destiny was not a happy one. Each successive government, whether Labour or Conservative, wanted either to cut its budget, split it up or sell it off.[*] A happier story unfolded north of the border where the Historic Buildings

---

[*] Between 2010–13 English Heritage saw a reduction in their grant aid of 48 per cent.

Council for Scotland worked harmoniously as an adjunct of the Ministry of Works Ancient Monuments service, until both merged in 1991 to become Historic Scotland.

When New Labour swept to power in the 1997 landslide, many believed that history was consigned to the dustbin. The *Sunday Times* had recently identified a cultural renaissance it dubbed 'Cool Britannia', exemplified by Britpop, the artist Damien Hirst, and the theatre director Nicholas Hytner. This vision of Britain's future was as idealised as heritage had been, but proved seductive to the incoming pop generation prime minister, Tony Blair. New Labour and its spin doctors found the very term 'heritage' Tory-toxic and expunged it from government communications.* The Department of Heritage was accordingly renamed Culture, Media and Sport (DCMS) and the Young British Artists lionised as a potent symbol of cultural virility.

The arts and heritage were repackaged as parts of the 'creative industries': commodities whose subsidy was justified because they were drivers of a much larger process of cultural consumption.[2] New Labour values lay closer to pop music, publishing and broadcasting. There was a tendency to view culture as a business opportunity and place unrealistic expectations on it. The arts and heritage were commandeered to help deliver 'key outcomes of lower long-term unemployment, less crime, better health and better qualifications.'[3] Improvements to investment and the quality of life in Liverpool provided compelling evidence in support of this. The New Labour cultural manifesto was entitled 'Create the Future'. The broadly sympathetic commentator Robert Hewison, author of *The Heritage Industry*, observed: 'The price of the billions that New Labour put towards the cultural sector was a Faustian bargain. In exchange for the money they needed, and which, with some exceptions, they used well, the arts and heritage had to submit to regimes of managerialism, instrumentalism, centralization and oversight that had little

---

* Robert Hewison recalls hearing one official use the word 'heritagenous' as a term of contempt.

to do with their core purpose, and which hampered them in achieving it.'[4]

As far as Simon Thurley, the director of English Heritage, was concerned, New Labour demonstrated unbridled hostility, even if certain individuals, such as the secretary of state Chris Smith, showed some sympathy. English Heritage found itself at the back of the DCMS funding queue and Smith's successor, Tessa Jowell, viewed it as a commercial organisation. She asked Thurley to come up with an idea to prove that heritage was relevant. He and the producer Jana Bennett, the director of BBC Television, conceived the BBC Two series Restoration (2003–4), with a voting system for the public to choose which from a group of building projects should receive English Heritage support. Hosted by the amiable Griff Rhys Jones, the series proved to be popular. The first series voted for the restoration of the Victoria Baths in Manchester. In fact it was the Heritage Lottery Fund that came up with the necessary £3.4 million and, as so often happens in the glare of publicity, the project ran into numerous difficulties.[5] However, the series successfully highlighted the issue of heritage at risk.

Perhaps the greatest problem for English Heritage under New Labour (and David Cameron's coalition government that followed) was maintaining protection of historic buildings and Conservation Areas in a climate that viewed such controls as a blockage in the planning system. Thurley attempted to reform the listing system to place it above criticism. The law was changed so that historic building listing could not be imposed in what some saw as an 'Orwellian' process without an owner first being informed and having a chance to put their case.[*] In fact, the days of English Heritage were almost numbered and the Lottery now had far greater sums to dispose. When David Cameron became prime minister, he asked Thurley: 'could the collection in its care

---

[*] Listing became subject to public consultation after 1992 and the Brunskill Report in an attempt to dispel the mystique that surrounded listing, and the idea that 'the man in Whitehall knows best'.

be given away, sold or dismembered in some way?'[6] That story, however, belongs to another chapter, and we must return to 1980.

The National Heritage Memorial Fund and the Lottery

The creation of English Heritage was one of the few such initiatives not born out of a crisis. If that body streamlined the nation's curatorial and regulatory approach to the built environment, who would deal with the regular crises that occurred when great houses and their contents were sold? Or rescue historic relics such as ships and aircraft, and save historic landscapes that the National Trust could not afford to buy? The system was very hand to mouth. When a crisis arose, the reluctant Treasury had to be prevailed upon and only after considerable political pressure and press clamour might make a special grant. But the problem was of the Treasury's own making, since it had stifled the Land Fund set up in 1946 for this very purpose by the then chancellor, Hugh Dalton.

The matter came to a head over the 1977 sale of the Rothschild treasure house Mentmore Towers, in the Vale of Aylesbury. An alert journalist and art historian, Marcus Binney, called for the Land Fund to be overhauled. This came too late to save Mentmore but the idea prevailed and from the ashes of that crisis arose in 1980 the National Heritage Memorial Fund (NHMF), with an endowment and a fluctuating income that averaged about £8 million a year. The endowment was of enormous importance in its independence from the Treasury under its own trustees, a separation later inherited by the Heritage Lottery Fund.

The new fund was established 'as a memorial to those who have died for the United Kingdom'. It was the veteran MP Tam Dalyell who shrewdly suggested including 'memorial' in the name, partly as a reminder of the Land Fund and because no prime minister could refuse to top up the endowment of a fund in memory of the fallen of two world wars. This proved percipient, and both

Margaret Thatcher and Gordon Brown did exactly that. It was left to the trustees to define what the national heritage might mean beyond a clear link with the United Kingdom. In their first annual report, the chairman, Lord Charteris, confessed: 'we could no more define the national heritage than we could define, say, beauty or art.' Heritage would define itself. As with Kenneth Clark and *Civilisation*, they would recognise it when they saw it. Charteris proved to be an effective chairman by managing to wring more money out of the Treasury than anybody thought possible.

The Trustees interpreted their role as supporting what they perceived to be the most serious threats to the national heritage. They were empowered to give grants to acquire works of art, land, books, manuscripts, and buildings of outstanding scenic, historic, aesthetic, architectural or scientific interest. Crucially, the fund was set up at arm's length from government to spare the political embarrassment of past interventions to save expensive works of art at what always seemed to be financially awkward times or during emotive periods of industrial action. In its early years, the trustees had a patrician hue and its operations were dominated by country house rescues (see Chapter 12). However, to the art world the fund seemed little short of miraculous. The first year's grants set the scene with a wide range of projects: £825,000 for the German Renaissance master Albrecht Altdorfer's *Christ Taking Leave of His Mother* for the National Gallery, £100,000 towards the excavation and recovery of Henry VIII's flagship, *Mary Rose*, and grants to the RSPB, the Suffolk Trust for Nature Conservation, the Blackpool Grand Theatre Trust and the Countess of Huntingdon's Free Church in Worcester.[7]

The second year posed an interesting dilemma when Bernardo Bellotto's *View of Verona from the Ponte Nuova* was offered for sale by the Herbert family, whose home Powis Castle was owned by the National Trust. The National Gallery and the National Museum of Wales both wanted the painting, but preference was given to it remaining at Powis – an early success for the regions over the national collections. By the third year, 1982/3, the annual report noted: 'our role in the more creative, rather than reactive, area of helping with the development of what are, in effect, new "heritage sites". There is a growing realisation in this country of the significance of industrial historical sites', and it accordingly made grants to the Avon Industrial Buildings Trust as well as Ironbridge Gorge Museum.[8] But as the decade unfolded the financial limitations of the fund became more apparent. In 1984 it only managed to save a few of the old master drawings sold from Chatsworth and in 1990 the opulent piece of eighteenth-century Florentine furniture known as the Badminton Cabinet proved beyond its means, as the price tag of £8.7 million would have entirely exhausted its grant that year. With spiralling auction prices, it was becoming obvious that the NHMF could no longer cope with the demands being placed on it. The solution, and the scale of its success, would take everybody by surprise.

The establishment of the National Lottery appeared like manna from heaven. It brought more liquidity into the public cultural sector than at any time since Prince Albert and his post-1851 Great Exhibition bonanza. When John Major announced in the 1992 Conservative manifesto his intention to set up a Department of National Heritage (DNH), one of its main tasks would be to introduce a National Lottery 'to restore the fabric of our nation'.[*] Every major European country already had a lottery and it was pointed out that the Sydney Opera House was financed from lottery revenues.[†] To everyone's surprise Major won the election and the new department of state was carved out of the Office of Arts and Libraries and the Department for the

---

* It was said to be the personal intervention of John Major that ensured that heritage was added alongside the arts and sports list.

† As early as 1978 Victor, Lord Rothschild, in his Royal Commission on Gambling had opined that a lottery would not be socially harmful and suggested that it should raise money for the arts, sport and other deserving causes. The idea, however, grated against Mrs Thatcher's Methodist upbringing.

Environment. To Robert Hewison, the new ministry seemed the ultimate triumph of the heritage industry.[9]

This short-lived ministry had one great achievement, establishing the Heritage Lottery Fund. The new department (DNH) set out two principles for the expenditure of Lottery income: firstly, that it should only be used for capital projects and not revenue. Secondly, it was to provide what was called 'additionality' – something over and above what the taxpayer would normally pay for. The problem, as always, was how to keep Lottery income out of the reach of the Treasury. Who would distribute the money? There were several keen candidates: the Arts Council and the Sports Council were obvious runners, and on the heritage side there was the Museums and Galleries Commission, English Heritage and the National Heritage Memorial Fund (NHMF). The winner was the NHMF, which had experience in all parts of the UK. Moreover, its new chairman, Jacob, Lord Rothschild, was a calmer figure than the volatile Jocelyn Stevens at English Heritage. It was believed Rothschild had the experience and wisdom to steer the transition of an agency of modest size into a behemoth. As Liz Forgan observed, Rothschild 'was brilliant, highly cultured and a centrist'.[10] Rothschild gave the Lottery four touchstones: heritage merit, public benefit, financial viability, and value for money.

The staff of the NHMF/Lottery increased from 7 to 250 to manage their newfound wealth. This transition was well managed and fairly smooth. The increase in grant giving was giddy – during the first year, 1994, it soared from £12 million to £293 million, considerably more than the spend of the NHMF in its entire existence. The two grant-giving panels were kept separate with a different emphasis. They shared the same chair and chief executive with the NHMF having a much narrower focus, less bureaucracy and a very much smaller budget. Much of the bureaucracy that grew at HLF was a consequence of the high level of demand and because of the need to demonstrate fairness and accountability in the disbursal of such large sums.

Like the NHMF, the Lottery was to be at arm's length from

government, but as it soon discovered, it was subject to much closer public scrutiny. Since its money was a percentage of the proceeds from the public (generally the less well-off) there was resistance to it being monopolised by what were perceived as elite pleasures.

The Lottery immediately found itself embroiled in a row over the sale of Winston Churchill's papers, which had been deposited at Churchill College, Cambridge. The crisis arose because his grandson, a Tory MP also called Winston, needed money to fund a divorce. The £13.25 million required to secure the papers created a public relations storm. As well as being seen as 'dosh for toffs', it raised the tricky question of title – didn't state papers belong to the state anyway? It was estimated that about 50 per cent of the Churchill Papers fell into this category, but these were mixed up with personal documents and therefore difficult to retrieve. The newspapers had a field day but the grant was awarded. The Lottery would make mistakes in future, but from now on it would be mindful of the vital importance of appearances.

During its early days, there were numerous arguments about whether the Lottery should take initiatives. A promising example is the Urban Parks Programme. This was set up partly in response to the accusations of elitism prompted by the Churchill Papers and also to counter a perceived bias towards major museum projects. It was believed that 8 million people a day visited public parks, but by the 1990s many were in a poor state. Lord Rothschild remarked: 'this is one area of our popular heritage for which we can really make a difference to people's lives'.[11] For many parks, the programme delivered their first major capital expenditure since Victorian times. The Mughal Garden in Bradford provides an example of a tired municipal park that was brought back to life. In addition to historic importance, the project emphasised amenities such as playgrounds, toilets, cafés and community buildings that enhanced the quality of life. The next problem would be to keep the parks well maintained and the new plants thriving.

There were still critics who thought the developments were

too London-based or did not pay enough attention to small-scale improvements.* Although Lord Rothschild was by instinct a proponent of grand projects, he accepted that 'what people really mean by heritage is the local church, its surroundings, the nearby countryside and farm buildings, the town centre and local green spaces'.[12] This was shown by the responses to numerous consultations. As the Lottery developed, landscape, environment and biodiversity would eventually be treated on a par with historic buildings.

However, the biggest single beneficiary of capital development grants in the first decade were museums and public buildings. These had been starved of investment for decades, to the extent that the infrastructure of some was on the verge of collapse. The 2004 accounts of the Lottery provide a snapshot of expenditure: £9 million to Air Space, Duxford, £13.5 million to Birmingham Town Hall, £9 million to the British Film Institute, £30 million to the Gilbert Collection of *objets d'art* at Somerset House, £9 million to the Football Museum in Preston (later relocated to Manchester), £12.5 million pounds to Kelvingrove Art Gallery in Glasgow, £25 million to the Kennet and Avon Canal, £19.5 million to the Leeds Museum, £17 million to the National Maritime Museum at Falmouth, £32 million to the National Museums Liverpool, £15 million for the Royal Festival Hall, and £25 million for the Mary Rose Museum in Portsmouth. Almost every major museum in Britain received a grant for a new extension or development. The problem for their trustees and directors would now be finding the money to run and maintain their shiny new extensions, but here the Lottery could not help — until its emphasis on capital projects was modified.

The Lottery, like the NHMF, was at arm's length from power but, as Hewison remarked, this distance became a great deal shorter under New Labour. While there is no evidence of direct

---

* To mention a few London projects: the British Museum received £8 million, the British Film Institute £14 million for conservation, the Albert Hall £20 million, the Gilbert Collection £30 million.

political interference, grants became more conditional. Tony Blair's former housemaster, the distinguished educationalist Eric Anderson, recalled that when he was its chairman:

> we were not pushed too hard politically – and never once on a particular project* – but we knew, without as I recall ever saying it at meetings, that keeping reasonably close to the Policy Directions on 'people, activities and access' was likelier to keep our share of the lottery intact. Announcing Urban Parks and Townscape Heritage and the like as special schemes rather than just doing them as part of the overall operation was, I suppose, a way of showing that we were full of ideas for the future.[13]

Even when ministers could be deflected from pushing pet projects, it was more difficult to observe the principle of additionality which became especially blurred when local authorities went bankrupt.

As the Heritage Lottery evolved under DCMS policy direction, it became more socially aware and community driven, with a growing emphasis on education, access and regionalism. When Liz Forgan, previously a journalist and television executive, became the chair in 2001, she recalled a young woman's remark that: 'heritage is your name, where you came from [...] You don't have to earn it. You are born into it.'[14] Forgan mused on 'the sea-change that has come about in people's perceptions of what heritage is and what it means to them'.[15] By providing many smaller Lottery grants to a much wider number of groups, Forgan sought to involve people for whom, in her opinion, 'heritage' might not previously have seemed particularly relevant. The Lottery's annual reports duly recorded fewer works of art and more examples of communities in action.

Since the Lottery shares the same secretariat and cooperates

---

* Colleagues remember this differently and had to steel the naturally collegiate Anderson to have difficult conversations with two secretaries of state about both policy direction and individual recommendations.

closely with the NHMF, many art applications were transferred to the smaller and less socially-driven funding body. In the important case of the Victorian mansion, Tyntesfield, purchased in 2002 by the National Trust, this route was followed partly for reasons of speed but also to show that the financially diminished sister fund remained an active player that could still spend its endowment.[*] As Anthea Case, the HLF chief executive, explained: 'It was an opportunity to demonstrate that the Memorial Fund, which was being slowly starved of funding, had a separate and different role to play from the Lottery.'[16] That traditional high art remained compatible with a more populist approach was shown when the Lottery contributed £8.26 million in 1997 to the purchase of George Stubbs's *Whistlejacket* by the National Gallery and £7.69 million in 1999 towards the acquisition of Botticelli's *Virgin and Child* by the National Gallery of Scotland.

But as one trustee explained: 'grants for works of art were always a bit controversial. Could some of them be said to be *our* heritage? And did the great institutions not have basements stuffed with things no one ever saw? One way to accommodate these objections was by sharing a purchase between a major art gallery and a local museum, as when Gainsborough's *Three Musicians* was acquired jointly by Tate Britain and Gainsborough's House in Sudbury.'[17] Much might depend on the approach of the applicant. An innovative example occurred when the National Portrait Gallery wanted to acquire van Dyck's *Self Portrait* in 2014. The Lottery's Heritage Panel required a detailed proposal that would engage with a wide audience. The gallery encouraged an online audience to paste their own selfies into the elaborate Baroque frame of the van Dyck. Their appeal elicited a record

---

[*] While Tyntesfield was 'saved' by the NHMF, it emptied the coffers and was one of the reasons why the National Gallery applied to HLF for *Madonna of the Pinks*, creating all the attendant public debate about the use of lottery money on this kind of project and requiring the gallery to construct public engagement programmes and a national tour focused on the acquisition.

10,000 individual donors.[18] It may have been inspired by the brilliant refurbishment campaign 'Portrait of a Nation' in which the Scottish National Portrait Gallery showed grids of Scots of many ages and backgrounds with their favourite portrait: a result both inviting and scholarly.

The Lottery fuelled a topsy-turvy museum expansion which brought much-needed reinvigoration to many old regional institutions and created some new ones. In the process there were some failures, mostly of over-ambitious Millennium Commission projects created with the best of intentions to provide opportunities in the depressed North of England. These included the Centre for Popular Music at Sheffield and two projects which received £20 million grants from the Millennium Commission: the environmental visitor attraction Earth Centre in Doncaster and the exhibition centre Urbis, intended to showcase inner-city life in Manchester. In London, while the sequestering of Somerset House for public use proved a brilliant success, the housing in one wing of the Gilbert Collection failed and it was transferred to the Victoria and Albert Museum.

Business plans submitted to the Lottery, often drawn up with the help of advisory organisations that knew little about the day-to-day workings of museums, sometimes proved wildly over-optimistic. Such was the case with the National Heritage Centre for Horseracing and Sporting Art in Newmarket. The Lottery gave considerable support because they saw it as an opportunity to help rejuvenate a rundown market town but little thought was given to the isolation of the venue and the difficulties of getting there. Much the biggest bill the Lottery had to pick up came at the command of government: the cost of the Millennium Dome. This was received via the Millennium Commission, funded out of the Lottery, which did not provide money for any heritage projects in the traditional sense. They favoured community benefit schemes with a slight emphasis towards green initiatives such as the Eden Project, a futuristic botanical garden in Cornwall. For Liz Forgan, 'the Millennium Commission came in like a cuckoo in the nest – first it absorbed all the money, and it had two terrible disadvantages: it was politically motivated and run by politicians, and it had an absolute deadline, so poor decisions were made'.[19]

With the Millennium Dome, New Labour met its cultural Waterloo. This was to be the jewel in the Millennium Commission's crown. There were soaring aspirations when Tony Blair proclaimed in 1998: 'this is Britain's opportunity to greet the world with a celebration that is so bold, so beautiful, so inspiring that it embodies at once the spirit of confidence and adventure in Britain, and the spirit of the future of the world'. The vacuous content of the dome turned out to be a bitter disappointment. Thurley viewed the dome as the nadir in understanding of Britain's heritage, conveniently sidestepping as it did all the awkward baggage of its imperial and colonial history. The Lottery had to provide an eye-watering £628 million, against a budget estimate of £399 million.

Nevertheless, Lottery money was overwhelmingly well spent and it transformed not just the cultural landscape but also what is now referred to as the built environment. Heritage Lottery offices opened in Exeter, Manchester, Birmingham, Nottingham, Leeds, Newcastle and Cambridge in 2002 to better accommodate regional priorities and to deal with smaller grant requests.* Forgan told the author that 'the devolution argument was hotly fought, being expensive, and there was always the possibility of losing control but it was important if people were beginning to see the fund as belonging to them and you got better local projects coming forward'.[20] Advisory committees were established with the devolved governments of Scotland, Wales and Northern Ireland. With growing regionalism, the emphasis shifted from supporting individual buildings and works of art to more ambitious urban regeneration schemes and Conservation Areas, which would formerly have been the purview of English

---

* They were able to dispose up to £2 million grants then; after austerity this was reduced to £1 million.

Heritage. However, by 2004 the gradual squeezing of its funding had put the Lottery in a quasi-leadership role in this sector. An admirable outcome was the restoration of Queen Square in Bristol. However, the largest overall beneficiary was Manchester, which received £520 million in grants from all Lottery sources between 1995 and 2004. Its original grant was increased, after the 1996 IRA bomb, to assist the rebuilding of the city centre, the regeneration of Salford Quays, and the infrastructure for the 2002 Commonwealth Games.

This raises the question of whether such Lottery grants provided 'additionality' or just another way for government to pay for things that should have come out of departmental budgets.* The answer is almost certainly yes; administrations of all stripes steered the Lottery into supporting their social agendas, and by degrees diminished what Liz Forgan calls 'the meat and potatoes' of everyday heritage funding. But examining the success and ambition of Manchester's regeneration, it is hard to imagine this would have happened without the enabling Lottery money. Anthea Case recalls a conference with European colleagues who were amazed that British Lottery funding could be kept separate from the Treasury. It is still too early to assess the cultural impact of the Lottery, but there is no town and city that has not felt its benevolent embrace. If Britons today care more about their surroundings, their museums, their parks, their village halls, and their churches, it is partly because the Lottery has sprinkled its magic dust over them all.

But is heritage holding its own in a changing Lottery climate? There is a cold wind blowing over this sector – an uncertainty where the HLF is heading. The Heritage Fund maintains an allocation of about 20 per cent of all Lottery takings, but its recent name change to the Lottery Heritage Fund sounds ominous. Does this represent a halfway house to it becoming simply the Lottery Fund: one big community fund? The emphasis has shifted from

---

* The regulating ministry, the DCMS, has turned out to be weak and cash-starved. From 2007 to 2020 there was a turnover of twelve secretaries of state.

heritage to community, inclusion and climate change. Nobody could argue against these necessary areas of activity, but one suspects that their growing urgency will leave many built heritage projects far behind.

Churches

John Piper: Why do you suppose that
we all like churches so much?

John Betjeman: Because they're there
whatever happens, aren't they?[1]

Parish share: the annual contribution that funds
priests and the diocese. Benefice: a mutually supporting group of
churches. Quinquennial Inspection Report:
the five-yearly church fabric survey. PCC: Parochial Church
Council that is responsible for the church.

Parish churches are the soul of every village in the land – perhaps the most profound foundation of the nation's historic fabric. Almost half of all Grade I listed buildings in England are places of worship. In most rural settings, the church is the most important local architectural monument. It tells the history of the settlement and offers many pleasures: the ringing of bells, organ music, stained glass, funerary monuments, a habitat for wildlife, a place for prayer and the worship of God. Churches have been called the greatest free museum in the country, an inheritance unrivalled in Europe, and as Pevsner pointed out, England's most characteristic contribution to Gothic art. This chapter is about parish churches, not cathedrals (which are seldom under threat). It looks at examples from the Manchester and Salford dioceses (of several denominations) and Anglican churches in the Norwich diocese, where the demographics are very different, and the emphasis of enquiry differs according to the statistics available.

Although the Church of England is to the public synonymous with its buildings, the organisation has been divided between what a Bishop of Norwich described as 'the complementary viewpoints held both by "church plant rationalisers" and "village church preservationists"'.[2] This binary is often characterised, perhaps unfairly, as 'head office' on the one hand, who want to create a more manageable organisation so as to concentrate on mission (i.e. giving priority to pastoral needs and improving the income of the clergy) and, on the other hand, parishes holding on to uneconomic churches. As one bishop exclaimed: 'I was not ordained to become a museum curator.'[3]

Anglican parishes are, however, self-governing, and only they can decide to close a church unless it has failed to pay the parish share. In that situation a church is put into special measures, and the long redundancy process may be set in motion which involves asking heritage questions. This is not the case with the swifter and more opaque decision-making process in the Roman Catholic Church and Nonconformist churches, for which statistics are not readily available.

Statistics

The Church of England possesses about 16,000 church buildings, of which 12,000 are listed. Of these 9,000 are in rural parishes (8,200 listed). They form one of the largest national networks in the country. To put this in context, in 2020 it was estimated that there were approximately 50,000 pubs in England and Wales, 11,500 post offices in the whole of the UK, 8,500 petrol stations, and 4,900 libraries. Rural pubs and post offices have been closing at a much faster rate than churches.[4]

The average number of Anglican weekly church attendees in 2003 in rural areas was 14 and this rose to 60 on a council estate, 80 in the inner city, 130 in the suburban fringe, and 140 in a small town.[5] Around a quarter of the rural churches now have congregations of fewer than ten and across all of them about

40 per cent of worshippers are over seventy. This is, however, a deceptive statistic, as a village church may have a greater significance to the locality than this suggests. In many villages, after the closure of the pub, the post office and shop, the church and the village hall are what bind the village together, the latter being generally more convenient and easier to heat and use.

Between 1969 and 2002 some 1,630 Anglican churches were made redundant. Approximately 57 per cent of these were adapted to alternative use, 22 per cent were demolished and 21 per cent were preserved in some other form, often by being placed in the care of a preservation body such as the Churches Conservation Trust (CCT).[*] Between 2004 and 2018 there were a further 248 closures, with 300 churches reported as struggling.[6]

Background

Up until 1868 church repairs were paid for under the rates, despite objections from Nonconformists. The system then became voluntary, and there were plenty of pious parishioners and wealthy vicars to support and restore churches; too many, in fact, and the conservation movement was born partly out of a desire to protect churches from over-zealous restorations such as that of Lord Grimthorpe at St Albans Cathedral.[†] William Morris was so alarmed that he founded the SPAB (the Society for the Protection of Ancient Buildings) to curb such enthusiasm and provide sound advice on restoration. Around the same time

* Of the adaptations 14 per cent were to civic cultural or community purposes, 13 per cent residential, 7 per cent for worship by other Christian bodies, and the rest miscellaneous uses: storage, shopping, arts and craft centres, museums, sports shoes, etc. Cooper 2004 p. 64.
† Churches were in fact protected as long ago as 1237 when the pope's legate in England forbade 'rectors of churches to pull down ancient consecrated churches without the consent and licence of the Bishop of the diocese under the pretence of raising a more ample and fair fabric'. Quoted Delafons, p. 120.

the government began to recognise a degree of responsibility for ancient monuments. The Anglican Church fiercely resisted any attempt to include its buildings in any kind of secular legal protection or listing. In 1913 this was formally recognised as the 'ecclesiastical exemption' by excluding church buildings in use from state supervision. Nobody then could conceive a time when the church would not be the best custodian and protector of churches.

Although there were attempts to close churches before World War II – notably in the City of London – the problem became acute after 1945. The situation of churches after the war was less dire than that of country houses, but like their secular counterparts, they had been deprived of any repair work for a decade. Constant appeals to the charitable fund the Pilgrim Trust meant that in 1951 the charity warned that they could not go on paying for what they felt should be the responsibility of the Church of England. By the end of the decade, with the increasing demolition of churches, mostly through inner city area redevelopment and loss of congregations, the Archbishops of Canterbury and York set up a commission in 1958 to advise on redundant churches, chaired by the former Permanent Secretary to the Treasury, Lord Bridges.

The Bridges Report might easily have done for the Church of England what the Beeching Report did to the railways. It accurately predicted that some 790 churches in England would become redundant over the coming fifteen to twenty years and recommended that a new body might take these over if no use could be found for them. Accordingly, the CCT was set up as a statutory body in 1969.[*] Its purpose was, and still is, to care for churches that are too important to be demolished and for which no suitable use could be found – the churches remain consecrated and can be used for occasional services. Its policy has always been to make buildings accessible and explain their

---

[*] Originally called the Redundant Churches Fund.

history.* Nonconformist and Roman Catholic churches can only look to the Historic Chapels Trust, a less powerful body.

The 1970s, 'Change and Decay' and SAVE

During the 1970s, the Church of England wanted the dual advantage of receiving government financial assistance while retaining ecclesiastical exemption. The statistics were alarming – in 1976 the Church Commissioners approved the demolition of one church every nine days, and a crisis was looming. The problem was highlighted in cities like Birmingham, Liverpool, and Manchester, where once a church was closed, it often became a target for vandalism and arson.

A milestone in church conservation was the exhibition at the V&A, 'Change & Decay: The Future of Our Churches', organised by Marcus Binney and Peter Burman in the summer of 1977, which outlined the scale of the threat. This followed the celebrated 'Destruction of the Country House' exhibition, but by now the plight of churches was worse. The publicity generated by 'Change & Decay' was encouraging and the government announced the 'Places of Worship in Use' grant scheme, but with strings attached – threatening to break the tradition of 'no control, no grants'. 'We'll have your blood', said one of the Church of England officials to Marcus Binney at the exhibition preview.[7] But wiser heads saw that independence was no longer possible. Ecclesiastical exemption, although reformed, remains in place to this day.† The price of accepting financial help from the state was that the Anglicans had to accept that once a church building was no longer in ecclesiastical use, it was subject to ordinary listed buildings consent. Binney and his organisation, SAVE, were not only interested in Anglican churches, and its publications

* They receive approximately a quarter of a million visitors per year.
† Ecclesiastical exemption was reformed in 1987 and 1991 under the Skelmersdale Agreement.

included a pioneering appreciation of Nonconformist chapels, *The Fall of Zion; Churches: a Question of Conservation.*[*]

Binney recognised that not every church could be kept in service but wanted to prevent demolitions: 'Experience has taught me', he explained, 'that with effort and persistence, an acceptable solution can be found to the problem of almost all redundant churches.'[8] This view was severely tested at All Souls, Haley Hill, Halifax, one of George Gilbert Scott's finest churches (and his personal favourite), and boasting the second tallest spire of any parish church in England. Declared redundant in 1977, the church faced an enormous repair bill or demolition. Members of the Historic Buildings Council (HBC) inspected it and they deemed that the building did not merit the huge grant required to save it. Was this residual anti-Victorian prejudice? The Church Commissioners' advisory body did not recommend preservation, and demolition seemed the only course of action. The scale of the problem was beyond the resources of the Redundant Churches Fund (who in any case were reluctant to take on an urban church where vandalism was such a problem).[†] The turning point came when Dame Jennifer Jenkins, chair of the HBC, became interested in the fate of the church on account of its townscape value.[‡] They applied to the newly formed National Heritage Memorial Fund, who had a difficult discussion as to whether so large a sum should be spent on a redundant church. The chairman, Lord Charteris, used his casting vote to allocate £250,000 in 1982.[9] Today the church is cared for and opened to the public by the CCT.

---

[*] St Francis Xavier in Liverpool, saved from demolition, even dedicated a stained glass window to SAVE.

[†] The first Victorian urban church the RCF accepted was All Saints', Jesus Lane, Cambridge in 1981.

[‡] All historic building grants were then given by the Department for the Environment on the advice of the HBC, a group of outside experts chaired by Dame Jennifer Jenkins.

English Heritage and the Heritage Lottery Fund

The English Heritage annual report for 1993/4 stated that the two most pressing threats were to Ministry of Defence property and to churches. The next two decades were to be a golden age of state support which would come from several directions: grants from English Heritage and the newly formed Heritage Lottery Fund, and VAT refunds on repairs. The appetite was enormous; the £25 million grant offer launched in 1994 attracted £200 million worth of applications. There was initially a spat between English Heritage (whose power and income were under constant threat from the late 1990s) and the Heritage Lottery Fund over the funding of churches. Since English Heritage funded Grade I and II* listed churches, that left the vastly richer Lottery to fund only Grade II and unlisted churches. However, they sensibly cooperated to set up a joint scheme and in 2003 Anglican churches received £21 million in grants. In 2010 English Heritage, facing a 30 per cent funding cut, withdrew, and the subsequent 'Grants for Places of Worship Fund' was solely funded by the Lottery. Within two years the single largest group of successful applicants to the HLF were churches. This golden age for church grants came to an abrupt end when this ring-fenced fund was abolished after seven years in 2017. When Gordon Brown, a son of the manse, instituted the refund of VAT on church repairs, he presented the argument that churches had a benefit to their wider community and thus were deserving of state help. When this VAT relief comes to an end in March 2022, it will leave places of worship with no public grant funding for the first time in over forty years.

Sales, Conversions and Adaptations

Selling churches is less profitable than one might expect and usually requires significant expenditure on repairs and professional fees. It is certainly easier in most cases to keep a weak congregation going. Churches can be exceptionally difficult to sell – St Peter at Great Birch, a fine 1850 Essex church taken out of worship in 1988, was declared redundant two years later. It was estimated to require £250,000 of repairs at the time, so no buyer could be tempted for fourteen years. At that point residential conversion looked promising with enabling development on adjoining land, but even that has fallen through.[10]

Among the most successful adaptations is perhaps the grandest conversion in England – All Saints, Oxford, now Lincoln College Library, the great baroque church by Henry Aldrich on the High Street. Most churches, as Binney stated, can with imagination be adapted, but in cases such as Booton in Norfolk, where enveloping stained glass makes this near impossible, the Churches Conservation Fund stepped in. Paradoxically, closing churches sometimes means opening them up to a wider public, especially in towns like York and Norwich, which have the highest number of historic churches.

Residential conversion is a more permanent solution than factory or storage and requires more skill. When the interior becomes a set of flats it is harder to articulate the architecture, but there is a good example highlighted below in Hulme. The usual problem with residential conversion is the alteration of the fenestration, of which an egregious example is St Mary, Stamford Brook.

It was often easier to convert Nonconformist chapels with their simple proportions than Anglican Gothic Revival churches. Not all chapel adaptations are domestic: one of the happiest conversions is the Museum of Bath Architecture in the former Countess of Huntingdon's Chapel, in which the building becomes part of the exhibition.

The criterion for most conservationists of a good adaptation is whether the church nave and chancel can still be read as a former church. Sports centres (see St Benedict's below), theatres, dance halls, and night clubs can all work. The oldest Catholic church in Liverpool is now a restaurant and nightclub, Alma de Cuba. Community use is the most fashionable solution, much favoured by the HLF. All Souls, Bolton provides a compelling modern example with a halal café thrown in.

Adapting churches still in devotional use to serve the needs of the parish better has been happening since the beginning of the twentieth century. The seminal example of a crypt conversion was that of St Martin-in-the-Fields by Dick Sheppard, who amid Flanders mud in November 1914 had a vision: 'I stood on the west steps and saw what this church would be [...] I saw it full of [homeless] people, dropping in at all hours of day and night ...and I said to them as they passed: "Where are you going?" and they said only one thing: "This is our home...".'[11] For most churches the most likely adaptation will be the insertion of toilets and a kitchen. Aylsham (a town church) provides a typical example of a pod inserted into a transept to extend the possibilities of the worship and church use. One ingenious installation is to be found at St Peter's, Alstonefield, Derbyshire, where a toilet has been installed in the unused south porch. For this tiny congregation, the toilet was an investment rather than just a cost.[*]

The Church of England has recently accepted the idea of designating some of its church buildings as 'Festival Churches'. There are many variants of the idea, but the core feature of a Festival Church is removal of the requirement for regular services, though the building remains consecrated and available for weddings, baptisms, and funerals.[†] The danger is that no one takes any interest in looking after the building; all this responsibility is delegated to an inadequate group.

---

[*] The whole approval process took two years. The cost was £20,000, of which a quarter was raised locally.

[†] Festival Churches do have to have a minimum of six services a year to be considered 'in use for worship' for grants.

Volunteerism

The secret behind the maintenance and preservation of Britain's rural churches is the army of volunteers – the envy of other European countries. The upkeep of Anglican churches lies in the hands of independent voluntary groups, the PCCs, upon which a diocese is dependent, led by 32,000 churchwardens (giving approximately 1.5 million hours a year). They form the largest voluntary group in the country after the National Trust (at 38,000 volunteers contributing over 2 million hours every year). Churchwardens are the unsung heroes – in many remote places they look after two churches, and often need to be security, cleaner, accountant, fundraiser, secretary, gardener, repairer, flower arranger and much besides. The Diocese of Norwich is a fine example of the power of volunteerism.

It is becoming harder to find people to accept these positions. This shortage makes it difficult to do *new* things – to fundraise for and carry out a large building project or set up new community uses in the church. Support from Friends groups is a recent success story – there are now about 1,000 standalone parish church Friends groups registered with the Charity Commission.* Through activities these groups provide the all-important *pounds, people, and purpose.*

Manchester and Salford Dioceses

The Diocese of Manchester – and its Roman Catholic counterpart, Salford – probably saw more churches built in the nineteenth century than any other, and also more churches closed in the twentieth. It is a relatively small but densely

---

* The income of these groups varies, but half of them raise between £1,800 and £8,000 per year, which is the same order of magnitude as typical annual maintenance and repair bills (as major repairs tend to occur only infrequently).

populated area, mostly covering Greater Manchester.* The most pervasive story is one of population dislocation, changes of context and community, and accordingly, changes of use. The extraordinary growth of the Anglican diocese – formed in 1847 – accommodated the phenomenal industrial development of the city – and also the piety, optimism and sheer vanity of those who built the churches, often on an unrealistic scale, believing in their missionary zeal 'that sooner or later there will be people to bring the building alive'.[12] Today the diocese has 235 listed places of worship, together with 33 for the Roman Catholics and 61 places of worship belonging to other denominations.[13] During the 1950s, both the Church of England and Roman Catholicism continued to flourish, and many new churches were planned which, by the time they were completed, found themselves in a very different social landscape.† Church building was now replaced by church closure, and when so many of the buildings that had served the old working-class fabric of Manchester and Salford were being demolished in the two decades after the war in the name of slum clearance, some sixty Anglican churches went with them. There has been no pattern to these losses. However, following the 2017 Taylor Review, an eighteen-month government pilot scheme was launched across Greater Manchester by Historic England. Several listed Anglican churches have been identified that make good candidates for repair funding to enhance community

---

* Where the population density of the Norwich diocese is about 350 people per square mile, Manchester is about 4,500. There are about 350 churches in the diocese, 90 per cent of which were built after 1820, breaking down as one-third twentieth century and two-thirds nineteenth century.

† It is often forgotten that during the late 1950s and early 1960s more churches were built then than at any time since the 1860s. Harwood 2015, p. 11. As one recent TV programme explained: 'The communities used to gather around the churches, until the estates were pulled down, and the new communities gathered in the pub. Today the young don't want communities, young'uns don't go out with old'uns anymore. All that's gone.' Anne, Thelma and Jackie, older Manchester residents being interviewed in a pub for *Manctopia: Billion Pound Property Boom*, BBC 2, 25 August 2020.

engagement. But since then a diocesan heritage support officer, part-funded by English Heritage, was made redundant, and there is no one to whom a vicar can turn for advice.

★ ★ ★

Most great cities radiate from their cathedral, but by the time the former Cathedral and Collegiate Church of St Mary, St Denys and St George became the Anglican cathedral of Manchester in 1847 the city had already developed southwards to embrace its canals, and the eighteenth-century classical church of St Ann became the city centre church.* There it joined the Cross Street Chapel, first opened in 1694 and though rebuilt four times, still in service today as a Unitarian church. One of the most striking aspects of Manchester was the mutually competitive nature of the religious denominations, with as many as five rival Nonconformist chapels on the same street. The same was true among the Anglicans, and when private patronage became such a feature of church building, this dramatically increased both the quantity and quality.† It was in the industrial suburbs, however, that the great nineteenth-century burst of church building took place, offering, as the Anglican diocesan history states: 'opportunities for service and discipleship very different from such agricultural areas as Hereford [...] which still form the bulk of English church life'.[14]

The foul social conditions of Manchester that made such an impression on Friedrich Engels brought forth a missionary fervour so that a poor suburb like Hulme could boast nine churches in one square mile – typical is St Mary's, whose history reflects the changing pattern of the city. No district has seen more dislocation; the post-war slum clearance was followed by the creation in the 1960s of the famous Hulme Crescents – the Le Corbusian *Unité d'habitation* – which in turn was demolished

---

* Built for Lady Ann Bland, née Mosley, 1707–9, by John Barker in the manner of Wren.

† The Anglican diocese has twelve Grade I churches, forty-one Grade II*.

in the 1990s. As Pevsner put it, St Mary's 'stood through two complete cycles of urban decay, dereliction, destruction and renewal, standing alone amid utter desolation'.[15] It was briefly used by an African Methodist Episcopal congregation before deconsecration. Then the nave was converted into nine flats (sharing the freehold), always a difficult task. St Mary's, however, retains the grandeur of its interior space with the insertion of well-designed wooden pods – one of the better apartment adaptations without compromising the outside fenestration. No one should underestimate the freeholders' responsibility to maintain the enormous tower and spire, the tallest in the city.

One melancholy story of suburban change and decay with an upbeat ending is that of St Benedict's, Ardwick, an Anglo-Catholic church by the local architect, Joseph Crowther, for the Bennett family. Opened in 1878, it was one of eleven Anglican churches in this poor district, designed to bring the faith back into 'the dark places of our awful cities'.[16] During the 1960s the neighbourhood was razed – a 1969 photo shows the church standing alone with its hall (which was about to be destroyed in an arson attack). One by one its neighbouring churches were demolished, all following the same pattern of vandalism and arson. St Benedict's was closed in 2002, at which point a professional climber, John Dunne, saw a sign: 'Redundant: ring this number'. He spent the next three years trying to acquire the church (with all its covenants) and seeking permission to convert it into the Manchester Climbing Centre, accommodating up to 300 climbers at a time. The completed scheme has only nine points where the 'rock face' inserts are bolted to the fabric of the church. At first Dunne wanted to put climbing frames over the rose window and the east end, but soon realised that these are valuable features. In such a deprived area, St Benedict's still performs many of the original social functions of the church – attracting and motivating young people and, as Dunne puts it, 'pushing the drug dealers back a few streets'.[17]

The greatest of Manchester's Victorian Anglican churches is still miraculously in service, in the far-flung suburb of Pendlebury.

St Augustine's is a classic case of a church being built as a monument to family piety in a place where there was insufficient congregation. Grand, noble and sequestered, St Augustine's is like a great stranded whale out of its time and place. Perhaps that was why it appealed to L. S. Lowry, who painted it – a vanity project of the Heywood family – plonked down in a solidly working-class area; hence its moniker 'the miners' cathedral'. The family went to one of the greatest architects of the day, George Frederick Bodley, and their church was built 1871–4 on a vast scale, which in its remoteness almost bestows the feeling of a continental pilgrimage church. Today it has become a district church of St Peter, Swinton, a more advantageously sited church by George Street, which attracts congregations of over 100 – in contrast to St Augustine's maximum of 25. Lack of parking and the impossibility of heating its vastness doesn't help. It survives only because, for now, its two sister churches are happy to support it.* One suspects that if it was not a Grade I listed church by Bodley, it would have closed years ago. One large repair bill will throw its future into doubt – then what will become of it? Grants are not possible with such an uncertain future, and the catch-22 today for so many churches with large repair bills is that small congregations fail the Lottery's standards of public engagement. It is difficult to see what adaptation could work for this nationally important building in such an unpromising position. Until some crisis provokes Historic England, SAVE, and all the various church bodies to work together, it is unlikely that a solution will be found, especially as the Lottery no longer ring-fences money for historic churches.

The Roman Catholics

The Roman Catholics in Manchester had an equally ambitious trajectory, but with less money, they built strictly to need.

---

* All Saints, Wardley, as well as St Peter's, Swinton.

Lancashire had been traditionally a stronghold of Catholic recusancy throughout the penal period and with the coming of emancipation their notables initially provided the financial means to build chapels. They soon proved hopelessly inadequate for the vast influx of migrants (overwhelmingly Irish) that flooded to the city to build the canals and railways, and to escape starvation during the Irish famine. The Salford diocese set up in 1850 was, according to Sheridan Gilley, 'overwhelmingly Irish'.[18]

St Mary's, the so-called 'Hidden Gem', is indeed tucked away in a back street near the town hall. It is the main Roman Catholic church in the city centre, and in origins the oldest surviving – the first church on its site having been built after the first Emancipation Act in 1794, paid for by the de Trafford and Barlow families and middle-class subscribers. This was too small for its swelling congregation, so a rich new church in an eclectic style, part Byzantine and part early-Christian basilica, was built in 1848 by W. G. Weightman and M. E. Hadfield. The surroundings have been rebuilt many times since, and today the church draws its 300–400 Sunday worshippers from across the city. Dry rot forced closure for three months in 1993/4, causing a bill for £750,000.

The same architects – unusually, a Catholic–Protestant partnership – were building the Cathedral of St John the Evangelist (1844–8). Like its Anglican counterpart, it stands at one remove from Manchester's centre, in Salford. This rapidly became the Catholic Church's fastest expanding diocese, but there was always an acute lack of priests, and the diocese relied heavily on Irish imports.[19] The quality of the church building was not as fine as the Anglicans, and it was the Jesuits rather than the diocese who constructed the grandest and architecturally most important church, the Holy Name, opened in 1871.* Designed by the Catholic church architect Joseph A. Hansom & Son (of Hansom cabs fame and Arundel Cathedral), it is almost certainly

---

* The only other Grade I Roman Catholic church in the diocese is E. W. Pugin's All Saints in Barton, built by the Trafford family.

his masterpiece, a church of grand liturgy, continental-inspired devotions and rows of confessionals.

The pace of Roman Catholic church building continued into the twentieth century, and today there are still 118 Catholic churches operating in the diocese which were built in that century (a considerable act of patronage), eleven of them listed. As with the Anglicans, the 1960s were a watershed when the tide turned towards amalgamation, or closure. The most surprising development concerned the future of Hansom's Holy Name. Between the wars its congregation comprised mostly Irish workers, but gradually the university and the hospital took over the area, and in July 1987 the bishop announced the end of the parish and foresaw 'the probability that it will eventually cease to be a building for worship'.[20] Its sale was announced and the only recorded proposal came from Manchester University, which wanted to convert it into squash courts. By March 1989 the matter had become a conservationist cause, with the Victorian Society and SAVE making a plea to save it, citing congregations of 700 on a Sunday.[21] Fr Ray Matus of the Oratory of St Philip Neri stepped in and took a lease on the church and began a programme of much-needed repairs – the Oratorians being one branch of the Roman Catholic Church for whom traditional splendour is still a part of their worship. In 2012, at the request of the bishop, the Jesuits took the church back, and the Oratorians removed to St Chad's, Cheetham Hill, in North Manchester. Holy Name today is the university chaplaincy, run by the Jesuits.

The bravest and boldest adaptation to new use in the Salford diocese is Gorton Monastery – which stands in what used to be the third poorest area in the UK. The Franciscans built the monastery with their own hands to the designs of E. W. Pugin. At that time, the church (begun in 1866) was the largest Roman Catholic parish church in England, with a vast nave worthy of Hogwarts. During the 1960s much of the local nineteenth-century housing was cleared and workplaces went with it, so that in 1989 when the Franciscans withdrew, and the church closed, the building was left isolated and subject to vandalism. The monastery was taken over by a property developer who stripped it of fittings, began a conversion to flats and then went out of business. The building was repeatedly vandalised, and everything of value removed. It seemed a hopeless situation until a former altar boy, Paul Griffiths, obeyed the injunction to St Francis to 'mend my church'. He and his wife Elaine have rescued it. They worked miracles of persuasion, bringing a Preservation Trust into being – a heroic undertaking if ever there was one. In 1999 the monastery was placed on the World Monuments Fund watch list, or as a local newspaper put it: 'Pompeii, Luxor, Istanbul [...] and Gorton'.[22] The restoration has cost £6.5 million and the place is flourishing as an events and leisure venue.

Alas, not all adaptations are as successful as Gorton Monastery. The most important Roman Catholic deconsecration, A. W. Pugin's St Wilfrid's, Hulme, is a travesty. Surrounded by very pleasant modern housing (reminding one visitor of Denmark), the church is a sad sight, both outside and in. This rather low-seated brick building is now an enterprise centre with a set of crudely subdivided rentable offices.

The Roman Catholic diocese has been more managerial in its approach to its church buildings, and congregations are never allowed to fall to the levels of other denominations. When they do so, they are swiftly amalgamated – which reflects above all the scarcity of priests.* Despite further closures, Manchester Catholics remain a healthy community, largely thanks to further arrivals in the city: Nigerians, Brazilians, Poles, Indians, Romanians and Filipinos.

Nonconformity, like Catholicism, had strong roots in the north-west. But their chapels have generally been the Cinderellas of church conservation. Heritage grandee Commander Michael Saunders Watson once turned condescendingly to Marcus Binney, saying, 'when we have saved all the country houses, then we can start on saving some of your Methodist chapels'.[23]

---

* In 2017 the Salford Diocese announced the closure of twenty-two churches, and a hundred parishes were involved in amalgamations.

Nationally, the stock of Methodist buildings in Britain fell from 14,000 in 1930 to under half that number in 1994. Of those that have survived, over half have been adapted for secular use, to which they are usually better suited than Anglican churches.[24] The most romantic survivor is the Fairfield Moravian Settlement in Droylsden, built by the young Benjamin Latrobe, who later found fame in America. The chapel is at the centre of a preserved eighteenth-century village originally designed to be self-sufficient. (The Moravian church claims descent from Jan Hus, a century before Luther.) The stately brick chapel opened in 1785 and still holds services every Sunday.

One Nonconformist church of unusually dramatic proportions soldiers on in the suburb of Ashton-under-Lyne: the Albion Congregational, now a United Reformed Church, dubbed locally as the cathedral of Nonconformity.* Costing £50,000 in 1895 (built by millowners and millworkers), it has suffered the familiar decline in numbers and the difficulty of replenishing congregations, especially since the closure of its church school and its Boys' Brigade. On Sundays it still attracts a congregation of about thirty, and is the responsibility of six elders. Its scale and proximity to so many other large churches in Ashton – a town whose prosperity is fragile – cause anxiety over its future. With a spectacular organ and stained glass windows by Burne-Jones and Morris & Co., it is difficult to see what adaptation would not change its dark and numinous atmosphere beyond recognition. And there is the impressive tower to frighten off potential rescuers. It reminded me of Ian Nairn looking at northern towns: 'I sometimes get the feeling we are just playing out injury time and the final whistle is about to go in about 30 seconds'.[25]

Of the hundreds of Nonconformist closures in Manchester, one stands out – Manchester's Arts and Crafts church, designed by Edgar Wood and built between 1903–7 as the first Church of Christ, Scientist in Britain. Described by Pevsner as 'one of the most original buildings of that time in England, or indeed

* Designed by a Manchester architect, John Brooke.

anywhere', the church closed in 1971 and went through several manifestations until in 1975 it was renamed the Edgar Wood Centre and became an events venue, for which the space is admirably suited. Manchester, having a thriving Jewish population, also built several synagogues, although none can compare with those in Birmingham and Liverpool. The best of them is now the Manchester Jewish Museum, recently restored.

The Twentieth-Century Anglicans

The Manchester diocese has some outstanding twentieth-century churches, especially those by designed by N. F. Cachemaille-Day in the 1930s. Typical is St Michael and All Angels in Wythenshawe, opened in 1937 to serve what was then the largest new council housing estate in Europe. The church is fortunate in its vicar (whose ministry is spread across three churches); she appreciates its architecture and having had a professional career is adept at filling in grant forms – a vital skill these days – but she admits that it is a question of the church living hand to mouth and scrabbling around for money wherever it can be found. With an ageing congregation down to twenty, the future is uncertain. The vast and somewhat featureless suburb of Wythenshawe expanded further post-war with several badly sited new churches. These illustrate the last great era of ecclesiastical building: modernist structures such as Basil Spence's St Francis (1959–61), forced to close and now sadly neglected. The highly original William Temple Memorial Church (1963–5) nearby by G. G. Pace – that so delighted Pevsner – struggles today, too large and un-heatable. Can it survive another decade?*

If many of Manchester's church buildings face a challenging future, some have found excellent solutions. Smirke's classical St Philip's Chapel Street – a Commissioners' church (built after

---

* The sister church of St Michael and All Angels, St Martin, Blackcarr Road (1959–60) has moved the congregation into the parish hall.

Waterloo to combat the growing threat from Nonconformity and 'lest a Godless people might also be a revolutionary one')[26] – was relaunched in 2016 as a resource church supported by the charismatic New Wine Church; it is now popular with all ages and offers the Alpha course.

The big heritage story in Manchester over the last twenty years has been one of regeneration, particularly in the suburb of Ancoats, with the restoration of its famous warehouses and canals. The former Anglican church of St Peter, now Hallé St Peter, today sits on one side of the pedestrianised Cutting Room Square surrounded by cafés, shiny new offices and public space. This Romanesque church of 1859 was deconsecrated during the 1970s and became very dilapidated despite various uses: as a storage facility, a sewing factory, and the Manchester Police even used it to train their dogs. By the 1990s the lead from the roof was gone and the building had become a squat. However these occupants bought it time, preventing demolition until the regeneration of the area provided investment and attracted the famous Hallé Orchestra into the story. After the shell of the church was restored by the Ancoats Building Trust with Heritage Lottery grants, the orchestra took a 999-year lease and moved in in 2013 – adding a good modern extension five years later – to use the building as its practice space as well as running an event business and a café.

The most lauded of all adaptations is that of All Souls, Bolton, at the northern end of the diocese. During the nineteenth century this mill town, known as the Geneva of the north, saw an astonishing burst of building, with no fewer than sixteen Anglican churches, and several times that number of chapels, erected. All Souls, by Paley and Austin, 'the best Gothicists in the north of England', is a wildly unlikely story of resurrection from the dead, and a successful repurposing to meet its community. It is the poster boy of such initiatives with encomiums (and generous grants) from the Lottery and an MBE for the manager. The church was built 1878–81 for the Greenhalgh family, Anglican–Evangelical millowners ('no church attendance no pay'). It is a majestic building in a town where there has always been too much competition for souls.

During the 1960s Bolton's Anglican churches began to close, and the Methodist chapels went even faster. The local population was predominantly Asian, mostly Muslim, by 1986 when the closure of All Souls became inevitable. It was vested in the Redundant Churches Fund (now the CCT) in 1987 but it was invariably kept locked, which did not prevent the lead being stolen from the roof and carted away in wheelie bins.* Its plight, however, moved a local Muslim, Inayat Omarji, who started a campaign to restore it. Several uses were considered, including a doctor's surgery and a public library, but it was as a multiple-use community centre that he won support, with meetings and events spaces, offices and a halal café. It can still hold Church of England services but these are much restricted. It is a hitherto rare case of the CCT passing the management responsibilities of a church to a new trust, the All Souls Community Trust, which has been embraced by local Muslims.

Norfolk Churches

Norfolk is another country – they do things differently there. The long history of radicalism in the city of Norwich stands in counterpoint to the continuity of Norfolk's great country estates. And when radicalism spread beyond the city this spawned religious nonconformity, which became another Norfolk tradition. However, this section is focused on the churches of the

---

* It was vested in the Redundant Churches Fund to save it from the same fate as a neighbouring church, the Saviour, by the same architects: mindless vandalism followed by inevitable demolition. The Saviour story enraged Ian Nairn, whose anger can be seen in *Nairn's Journeys, Football Towns, Preston & Bolton*. He focuses on a smashed memorial tablet – 'This do in remembrance of me' – and shows the various stages of the church's demolition to the sound of the 'Hallelujah Chorus'.

Anglican Diocese of Norwich. It was wealth from the wool and cloth trade in the fifteenth century that was responsible for many of them, built in the Perpendicular style.

The diocese holds an impressive 650 churches – perhaps only in the county of Norfolk can you gaze from one churchyard, St Michael, Booton, across the fields at two outstanding churches, Cawston and Salle. Apart from the sheer number of churches, the most remarkable feature is their resilience. Local congregations are driven by a strong sense of local identity and place. 'No churches been made redundant in Norfolk in the last decade' has been the recent headline story. This contrasts with the period running from the 1960s until the new millennium, during which it seemed that the Bishops of Norwich were at odds with their rural parishioners in wishing to close churches, including many with stable congregations.*

However, some local parishes refused to accept the pattern of closure. They decided to take the initiative back from the clergy and save the churches for themselves. This indomitable spirit was given leadership by one remarkable churchwoman who decided to make a stand over the solitary hilltop church at Corpusty.

Billa Harrod, a human dynamo, was instrumental in the foundation of the Norfolk Churches Trust (NCT) in 1976 and served as its first chair. This was a turning point in the story, and it would be difficult to overstate the importance of its work, indefatigable fundraising, and the support it has provided for so many churches with finance and advice.† Above all it gave other parishioners the confidence to continue the struggle, often against the wishes of the diocese. Today the NCT looks after thirteen redundant churches and chapels in its care (with no ambition to increase this number), and acts as grant-giver, friend and adviser.

As Harrod wrote: 'we suggest holding occasional services in

---

* The problem for the diocese, which remains acute, is the shortage of priests.

† Since it was founded the NCT has awarded grants of approximately £6.5 million towards the repair of churches in the Diocese of Norwich.

remote churches in preference to any alternative use [...] even if there is only a tiny congregation or perhaps no one at all, so that we can have a moment of peace and quiet'.[27] Most recently, Bishop James (1999–2019) made it axiomatic that no churches would fail under his watch, instead placing failing churches into a 'Diocesan Churches Trust', effectively putting them into limbo.* Fifteen churches (which had to be in good condition, diluting the virtue of the scheme) effectively became Festival Churches, with six services a year and given special exemptions. This was one way of avoiding the slow and expensive redundancy process. Opinion is divided on the wisdom of this move – is it merely delaying the inevitable?

On the other hand, one must admit that the occasionally ostrich-like attitude of Norfolk parishes, carrying on regardless, shouldering the burdens of the present while ignoring the perils of the future, has been extraordinarily successful and largely accounts for their resilience. It means accepting discomfort – outside the towns, heating in churches is a rarity. One heritage specialist spoke to the author about working with the building rather than trying to make the building work for us: 'We cannot afford to heat a village church through the winter, and we must cease to think of church as being like our home. We must, like our medieval ancestors, put on more clothes to hear the word of God.'[28]

* The website states: 'Therefore we are launching a Diocesan Church Trust which would enable a limited number of church buildings to be leased to it and which will hold them on behalf of their local community. In practical terms this will mean that the church is still available for occasional services and will continue to have a basic level of insurance and maintenance. This would enable such a church to come back into regular use in a way which would be almost impossible if the building was formally closed and declared redundant.'

St Martin's, Thompson

Like so many Norfolk churches, the first sight of St Martin's, Thompson, is across the fields. The village is set apart, with 350 souls. A numinous fourteenth-century church, Thompson was once highly decorated and colourful, but today is cool and pale, its walls, medieval oak poppyheads and Jacobean stalls bleached by the sun. One of the many surprises about the church is that it has had no resident vicar since 1541, which may partly explain its untouched simplicity.[*] Perhaps its most remarkable feature is the scissor-braced nave roof of forty trusses. Part of a benefice of seven churches, services take place every seventh weekend, attracting an average of thirty to forty worshippers (about ten from the village). In 2000 the quinquennial review revealed that the rain was coming in and much of the timber roof – last restored in 1974 – was rotten. The repairs cost £300,000, paid for with a £250,000 grant from the then ring-fenced Lottery Churches Scheme. The National Churches Trust gave support and £15,000. The parish 'sold' new roof tiles, with the local children paying for one each (thereby earning the right to have their names recorded on one side).

St Mary's, Forncett

Forncett, like a surprising number of Norfolk villages, contains two churches, the picture-postcard pretty St Peter's, a Grade I church (with its distinctive Norfolk round tower), and St Mary's, which once looked as if its days were numbered.[†] Its rescue was essentially thanks to the energy and enterprise of one man, Graham Prior, who understood better than anybody that

---

[*] The Reformation started a period of decline from its rich collegiate church status.

[†] Perhaps its greatest claim to fame was that the Zulu scholar and sometime Bishop of Natal, the Revd John Colenso (1814–83), was the rector.

churches today need activity and partnership if they are to receive support, particularly from the Lottery.

Following redundancy in 1979, the church was put up for sale for £250,000 and many schemes were advanced, including a home conversion and a yoga centre, but there were no takers. Opinion in the village was divided as to whether the village needed a second active church or indeed whether St Mary's was important enough, having a rather mechanical Victorian interior. Undaunted, Graham Prior, a local businessman, kick-started the restoration with a personal loan and set up a Friends group. He secured one of the last HLF grants under their 'Grants for Places of Worship Fund'. Perhaps surprisingly, in 2012 the bishop agreed that St Mary's could become a working church again, one of a benefice of six. Prior understood that to gain national support, 'you have to find a theme',[29] as he put it. He alighted upon partnerships with the Norfolk Wildlife Trust (probably the most actively supported charity in the county after the NCT) and, more unexpectedly, a diocesan Holocaust memorial (with the forming of a Holocaust library in the vestry). A glance at the website indicates an impressive amount of activity in the church.

St Peter and St Paul, Salle

How do you manage a great church when there is virtually no village? Salle is one of the wonders of Norfolk, externally elaborate, and internally light, airy, and perfectly proportioned, with woodwork restored by Ernest Gimson. The cool interior reminds one of nothing so much as a painting by the Dutch seventeenth-century artist Pieter Saenredam. The church survives on its heritage and on music, being an events, concert and recordings destination, and a must-see for tourists. It receives many visitors and is just about coping thanks to three or four classical concerts a year, filling the church with 400 people, and making a profit of £500 on each. It helps that the music enjoys the patronage of the

Prince of Wales. The husband-and-wife vicar team have twelve churches to look after and can manage services twice a month with an average congregation of ten, coming from outside. If the church effectively has no village (sixty inhabitants), it has been fortunate, historically, in having had a safety net with the local landowner, the White family, who financed the exemplary SPAB-inspired restoration of 1910–12.

The church costs £10–12,000 a year to maintain including £7–8,000 parish share to the diocese. It benefits from a dozen small sources of income including weddings and a Friends body. Like so many Norfolk churches, it is dependent on skilled local volunteers who can do the accounts and make the bookings for the events (the organisation for these is undertaken by the lessee). With such a small congregation pool, their biggest looming problem is succession. New facilities, improved lighting, toilets and a kitchen would make events easier and cheaper (without the need for portacabins). But so far Salle PCC has resisted grants because of the interference involved.

St Michael, Aylsham

St Michael, Aylsham fits into the most successful category of Anglican churches, the small-town church around which the local community coalesces. The town has a population of about 8,000, including not only retirees but also the new housing estates which support seven churches of different denominations. On Sundays there are three services at St Michael with 125 worshippers (mixed age thanks to the new residents) and since Covid, an additional 70 via live-streaming. An event such as the annual service for the Royal British Legion attracts a congregation of 600. Aylsham is the mother church of a group of seventeen, served by five active priests and some retired ones. The church costs about £180,000 a year to maintain (including the parish share to the diocese). More startling than the financial cost, to maintain the church with its present arrangements requires approximately

200 hours of volunteer labour every week. Aylsham has accepted HLF grants of £130,000 for the organ (with a scheme for organ scholars). Without a crypt or church hall, a pod inserted into the north transept for meetings and a children's area has transformed the way it functions by providing year-round warm space and allowing for comfortable winter services.

St Mary, North Tuddenham

The Reformation stripped out the colour in most Norfolk churches but at St Mary, North Tuddenham, the Victorians replaced it with stained glass, a stencilled chancel and rich encaustic tiles on the walls of the nave. Surrounded by fields, with only the former rectory nearby, this fourteenth-century Grade I church has no obvious means of support. There was an attempt during the 1970s to close the church which the PCC fought against and won. They were prepared to undertake the thousand hours of volunteer labour required each year.

Today St Mary is in a benefice of six and manages to maintain a service every Sunday attended by twelve regulars (this number has not altered for a generation). It costs £7,000 a year to maintain, of which half goes to the diocese. The weekly plate produces £50 and a fete every second year brings in £2,500. The church has just about managed to stay alive with the addition of concerts and donations. The fabric officer talks about the need for 'events, events and more events'.

The alarm was raised in 2017 when the tower developed cracks on two sides. The NCT gave £15,000 for exploratory work. The parish heroically managed to raise £60,000, of which £40,000 was spent on an investigation which told them they would need to spend a further £350,000 to make the tower safe. Their application to the Heritage Lottery was twice turned down but they were fortunate to receive one of the last substantial church grants that Historic England was able to make, of £280,000. How the last £70,000 will be raised is not clear.

St Lawrence, Hunworth

The economic *coup de grâce* usually comes in the form of fabric wear and tear, but one small rural parish highlighted another problem. With six services a year attracting between ten and fourteen worshippers, this church costs about £4,000 per annum including parish share to maintain, and when they do not break even, the parish share goes down. It is effectively run by a fabric officer husband and churchwarden wife who do all the cleaning, the minor repairs, the gardening and even offer refreshments after the service. Their main anxiety is the lead on the roof.[*] The new insurance premiums are too high without the installation of expensive equipment and surveillance, far beyond the parish's means.

St Agnes, Cawston

St Agnes, Cawston, is a Perpendicular village cathedral, built by an early fifteenth-century de la Pole Earl of Suffolk, one of the great churches of Norfolk with its famous hammerbeam angel roof. The village of Cawston has 1,500 souls with an average Sunday attendance of forty. The annual parish share is £23,000. The church has received £250,000 from the Lottery to redo guttering and rebuild some of the tracery at a cost of £310,000. Among the imaginative fundraising ideas was 'hard hat days', taking visitors up the scaffolding to see the spectacular carved

---

[*] Theft of lead from the roof is the killer for some churches. The insurance and equipment required to qualify for insurance is prohibitive for most small parishes. The repair costs are typically between £35,000 and £50,000 pounds (including replacing the rotten wood underneath) and the thief will probably make £500. In the past English Heritage insisted on replacing the lead but now is beginning to accept terne-coated steel to prevent repeat thefts.

angels closer.* In this case the Lottery accepted that the priority should be the fabric repairs rather than facilities, on the grounds that 'we shouldn't put toilets and kitchens into a building that is leaking'. The church still needs £700,000 spending on fabric repairs. The next phase will be to insert toilets behind an oak screen in the transept which will improve school visits and concerts. The Lottery required an activity plan to increase the number of heritage visitors. It is fortunate that the present vicar comes with professional experience of managing estates and knows how to navigate the grant-giving process, but he admits that the grant-giving landscape is getting much harder.†

St Peter, Corpusty

Corpusty has been described as the grit of the oyster that produced the pearl. At first glance, the church is not an obvious heritage game-changer in the mould of Tattershall Castle or Mentmore. It sits on a lonely eminence, distant from any village, but it is instantly lovable. And one who fell in love with it was Billa Harrod, who ignited a new passion in the county for saving the churches at a time when the diocese was losing interest. She brought her friend John Betjeman to Corpusty, who was moved to write the following lines:

> And should we let the poor old churches die?
> Do the stones speak?
> My word, of course they do.
> Here in the midst of life they cry aloud:
> You have used us to build houses for your prayer
> You have left us here to die beside the road.

* The vicar acknowledges support from the Garfield Weston Foundation who have been especially supportive to churches.
† He is responsible for four churches, including one Festival Church.

The church has a long, chequered history of under-use but in 1900 it was brought back from decay. By the 1950s, the church was being vandalised, but it was the neglect of the Church of England allowing churches to rot that so incensed Billa Harrod. Corpusty appeared to be doomed: the graveyard was overgrown, local people were misbehaving in the graveyard, and most sinister of all, Satanists were gathering there. The screen and altar were ruined. Harrod recognised that only self-help could save the church and she organised working parties, while dragging in such friends as the Prince of Wales and the Duke of Grafton. Corpusty is the perfect demonstration of a great truth, that while it takes many people to close a church, it takes only one determined person to save it.

Corpusty represents a pivot when the locals decided to run things themselves through volunteerism rather than rely on the diocese, but this meant accepting the liabilities. Harrod was fortunate in her connections and brought in her friend, Ivor Bulmer-Thomas, who had recently set up 'the Friends of Friendless Churches', controversial to some (seen as a waste of resources) but a godsend to others. Corpusty was vested in that charity in 1982 before passing to the Norfolk Churches Trust in 2009. The church needed £400,000 to repair the windows and replace broken tracery. Among the excellent ideas for its future is to make it a showcase for contemporary carved inscriptions to raise the quality around the county (mixed at present) and give craftsmen somewhere to show their work. Corpusty is open to the public from Thursday to Sunday and hosts two services a year organised by the NCT.[*]

---

[*] Corpusty received a grant of £112,221 from English Heritage. In 2016 the nave and chancel roofs were repaired with a grant of £98,000 from the DCMS Roof Repair Fund, with the balance of £30,000 provided by the Norfolk Churches Trust. Thanks to two volunteers the church is now open regularly, and the key is also available from the village stores.

St Michael, Booton

An eccentric church by any standards, an astonishing mixture of whimsical amateur oddity and high Victorian excess, St Michael's is in the Victorian collegiate Gothic style and stands somewhere between a folly and a Cambridge college chapel. It was designed by the rector, the Revd Whitwell Elwin, who had the living for fifty years and died in 1900. Today it is vested in the CCT, a national charity which did not accept any Victorian churches until 1981. It would be difficult to pretend that the church is architecturally outstanding, but it *is* a curiosity. Heavily fenestrated with Pre-Raphaelite stained glass, there was little hope of adaptation. How many visitors come in a year, one wonders? But then perhaps civilisation is a state of mind that finds it worth preserving such an idiosyncratic monument. It is one of the twenty-eight Norfolk churches the CCT has in its care.

Norwich Churches

No city outside London built more parish churches within its walls than Norwich, 'the largest collection of urban parish churches north of the Alps' with as many as sixty at the Reformation.[30] Thirty-one Anglican churches survived wartime bombing of which eight, apart from the cathedral, remain in service. Churches have been closing in Norwich since the 1930s slum clearances. In 1973 the Norwich Historic Churches Trust (NHCT) was formed and the diocese transferred a score of churches to the city of Norwich on a ninety-nine-year lease, which in turn passed them to the Trust.* Unlike the CCT it was never the intention of the NHCT to turn the eighteen churches it possesses into museums. Norwich has always seen its role as finding new uses, and as a result they are self-financing.

* The funding was divided between the DoE, the city and fundraising by the Trust and its membership.

At first, the Norwich Historic Churches Trust tried to extract a full commercial rent which did not work until it changed the policy to become more flexible, recognising that the most important point was to keep a building in good order and to have an occupant – the fabric was the priority and the use secondary. St John's Maddermarket, a Grade I church, unsuitable for adaptation, has been left as a church in the care of the CCT, while others such as St Peter Parmentergate contains a stipulation to leave the choir stalls and chancel so that it can still be read as a church. Some adaptations are more successful than others in this respect and a church such as St Gregory's, now a collectables market, has lost its chancel furniture, and its monuments and font are illegible. None have made successful office conversions, except the Trust's own headquarters, St Martin-at-Palace, converted by a previous user. The longest tenant has been at St James Pockthorpe, closed as a church in 1972 and converted six years later for use as a puppet theatre, still operating today.

★ ★ ★

Today churches are in a better condition than they have been at any time since 1914. Until Covid-19 the country has enjoyed a period of exceptional prosperity and sustained attention to conservation. Since 1977 there was a dedicated grant scheme in one form or another for the repair of historic churches. As a result, many churches, particularly in places like Norfolk and Suffolk, are generally in a much better state of repair than before. However, with the closure of the Lottery-funded 'Grants for Places of Worship Fund' scheme dedicated public funding for churches evaporated. The present grant situation is thus very uncertain. The vicar of Cawston echoed the cry of every parish: 'what I find difficult is the ever-shifting grant-giving landscape which makes it so hard to know where to go next'.[31] The survival of nationally important and statutorily protected buildings is left to ever more stretched local priests and PCCs, who may or may not be minded to navigate the ever changing funding and planning criteria with limited central direction or support. The national support systems are increasingly uncertain and diminishing. The loss of funding for Historic England is serious and it reports to the economically weak DCMS.

Ruth Blackman, a Norfolk church conservation architect, commented to the author on the present situation, and I quote her at length:

While there are many smaller grant aiding bodies who generously support minor repairs, the only significant funds available, in recent years, have been from the Heritage Lottery Fund, now the National Lottery Heritage Fund. On occasions, and in absolute desperate circumstances, Historic England will consider offering support. However, since the Lottery Fund became involved in 2013 there has been an additional requirement to 'engage more people' and although this is laudable the demands on parishes are now so high unless they have the skill set to manage such a project, and the majority of PCCs don't. They are appointing professional help at further cost.

In spite of this there is still the requirement for the PCC, as the grant recipient, to demonstrate public involvement, from publishing leaflets, holding events, involving schools, holding skills days, creating walking routes and cycling trails, setting up partnerships with other local voluntary services, putting on exhibitions, to installing new facilities and re-ordering furnishings, etc, all distracting from the main key purpose to simply repair an element of the church. This on top of managing a repair contract, securing Partnership Funding, holding fundraising events and leading their own private lives is taking, and has taken, a toll on the energy, enthusiasm and commitment of many volunteers involved in the church [...] The current situation is that those facing significant repairs to churches, and funding shortfalls, are finding the present requirement challenging to say the least, the public benefit being the greater part of the delivery on the project.[32]

Church closures over the next decade are inevitable, as is highlighted by the foregoing examination of the two dioceses. In Norfolk, sustained by a greater degree of volunteerism, succession is the main problem in the tiny parishes supporting vast medieval churches. In Greater Manchester, St Augustine's, an architectural masterpiece, is left locked six days out of seven, a mile or two from the new £106 million Lowry gallery. It will be a wonder if it survives another decade in its present form.

Everybody agrees that putting churches back into the heart of their community is central to their future, but what if there is no community? Events can go so far, as at Salle, but the real question is less about money and activity – important as these things are – than the continuation of skilled volunteers. Paradoxically, this is easier where the population is smaller, as in Norfolk. Trevor Cooper, chair of the Historic Religious Buildings Alliance, described the present situation to the author in these terms:

> The big shift has been from seeing this merely as a financial problem (pump money into major repairs) to realising we have a major social problem on our hands – who is going to be looking after these buildings, and what is going to be their purpose? The switch in viewpoint has happened over the last fifteen or twenty years and is accelerating. Alongside it there is a rethink of what 'conserving' a church building actually means.[33]

The most recent attempt by government to find solutions was the 2017 Taylor Review, which presented a model of how listed Church of England churches could become more sustainable through regular maintenance, repair and wider community involvement. It endorsed the logic that the more people involved in a project, the more income generated. One of the anomalies of the present position which Taylor recognised is that fabric repairs are not being carried out because 'the repair was not deemed to be sufficiently urgent' when a grant application was initially submitted. Taylor concluded that a maintenance fund for all parish churches is required, and as a result the DCMS set up a pilot scheme to put money into maintenance. This is positive. I finish with the words of Ruth Blackman: 'There is no other collection of buildings more widely available and containing such an extensive and unique collection of artefacts and furnishings and fittings, covering so much of our local and national history, anywhere else in the world that are freely available for anyone to visit at any time without a charge.'[34] They are also, as T. S. Eliot expressed it, temples where prayer has been valid.

Post-Covid

Like all heritage organisations, churches had to find new audiences online during the Covid-19 pandemic and were surprised by how effective this turned out to be. In many cases churches in the benefice now worship together online. In rural North Yorkshire at Ainsty, the Reverend Richard Battersby opined: 'Faith has been made more intense by the pandemic. People on their laptops can actually contribute to the service. Someone from the Congo recently contributed.'[35] The priest spoke about the church being 'shocked into new ways of being' by the pandemic, but he noted that churches that were struggling before have seen an accelerated demise. There are those of course who, using video conferencing over the pandemic, are questioning the need for church buildings, or at least such regular services within them. As the church heritage expert Janet Gough has commented: 'the post-Covid challenge will be encouraging fearful and less confident incumbents and their congregations to reopen their churches for regular services and services for the community – which many believe is the way forward if our church heritage is to be conserved and enjoyed into the future. The recent use of cathedrals as mass vaccination centres during the pandemic has been a marvellous example of church buildings serving the community'.[36] However, based on present estimates more than 350 churches are expected to close over the next five years, a rate eight times faster than before the pandemic.[37]

CHAPTER 20

Museums

*Museums are no longer regarded as schoolrooms
but as laboratories of private and social experience
equipped with all the apparatus of a day trip –
cafes and restaurants and public space, which
simultaneously enhance and diminish the status
of the original collection.*

CHARLES SAUMAREZ SMITH, 2021[1]

A historian of British museums and art galleries examining the period from the arrival of the Lottery in 1994 until the present time is faced with a contradictory landscape, and might wonder what the British really thought about them. More museums were created, restored and revitalised than at any time since the Victorian era – evincing a similar earnest educative mission – and yet it has also been a period of collapsing confidence, soul-searching and funding cuts. Up until the 1970s, museum directors were supremely confident both in their scholarly mission – essentially addressing an educated audience – and in their comfortably secure funding, whether from the state or local government. Paradoxically during the last thirty years, a period when museums have attracted unprecedented numbers of visitors and made impressive strides in finding new audiences and contemporary application, they have been placed at the back of the funding queue and starved of running costs. Any understanding of this history must start with Margaret Thatcher, when she overthrew the post-war consensus that museums had a right to exist in a protected cultural cocoon.

Let us briefly remind ourselves of the pre-1979 world and the new forces shaping museums. 'In the past the museums were great scholarly machines,' Roy Strong, the former director of the V&A, explained to the author, 'a little old-fashioned with displays sometimes but putting on scholarly exhibitions. In this they followed the Arts Council, which pioneered the scholarly exhibition'. Museums in the 1960s were run by distinguished art historians, some of whose careers might start in a provincial gallery before advancing to a national museum.* The furniture expertise in Leeds at Temple Newsam was then on a level with the V&A. Regional museums often showed huge ambition: the brilliant loan exhibitions staged at Norwich Castle Museum on the grand tour, and on Dutch painting, or astonishing to a modern eye, the Greater London Council sponsored series of summer exhibitions on British painting at Kenwood. Their priorities were scholarly and acquisitive – public engagement had barely begun. The post-war generation of museum professionals still took the virtues and values of state cultural provision for granted, and with it an assumption that the state had a duty to provide for the arts.

Margaret Thatcher was the first prime minister with a science degree, and to her the arts like everything else in life had to be measured, costed, and scrutinised for their contribution to the national economy. According to Roy Strong, she saw museums as dead things, piled-up lumber from Britain's past which was now holding the country back.[2] In this she was not so far from some left-wing commentators who saw an obsession with the past and the continuous opening of new museums in the 1970s as a symptom of decline. When Thatcher came to power in 1979 Strong observed that the government's duty to maintain the V&A buildings and refurbish their galleries was taken for granted. Within a decade it had become accepted that up to

---

* Typical was Sir Philip Hendy, who started at Leeds before proceeding to become director of the National Gallery.

50 per cent of running costs had to be raised from the private sector.

The cold wind of accountability led to a more commercial attitude, a need for self-reliance, and the promotion of public–private partnerships. The matter came to a head with the confused fiasco over a new extension planned for the National Gallery, the so-called 'carbuncle affair'. When an adjacent Trafalgar Square site became available for development during the 1980s, the government wanted the wing to be provided by private initiative – in other words the new renaissance art galleries would be sandwiched between shops and offices. The public competition to find an architect was badly mishandled, with echoes of the nineteenth-century 'Battle of the Styles' and the competition to build the Foreign Office. Prince Charles famously intervened, giving his views on the designs and modern architecture in general. Finally, the Sainsbury family stepped in and after a limited competition the postmodern design by Robert Venturi and Denise Scott Brown was selected. The new wing opened in 1991. Such were the problems of creating new museum buildings in the pre-Lottery era. The most debated matter was the imposition of museum charges, seen by nearly all in the museum world as overturning the founding and sacred principle of the right of free entry.[*]

Accountability had taken over, but Strong pointed out that nobody dared to cross government policy: they were still the paymasters. The V&A came under the Department of Education, which Strong found stifling: 'for everything we did – exhibitions, flowers, maintenance – I had to seek permission. It created a dependency culture – the staff saw everything "as of right"'.[3] In transferring the V&A from the Department of Education to a trustee board, Strong would have to raise more money, but at

---

[*] This battle was fought throughout the 1980s and 1990s and finally settled when Chris Smith reinstalled free admission as a civic right and found the cash to support it.

least he thought he would be able to spend it how he wished.[*] He established V&A enterprises and extended the shop. A new language crept in: professionals began to speak about the 'museum experience'. Strong was one museum director already focused on the visitor experience through a pioneering approach to exhibitions (which was still a relatively new idea for the national museums), bringing in designers and thinking of them in terms of performance. 'Cecil Beaton' (1968) during his NPG years and 'The Destruction of the Country House' (1974) at the V&A are still remembered today. Unknown to Strong the idea of museums and exhibitions as theatre would take ever greater hold.

Visitor experience and interpretation were pioneered in a new category of museum that came into existence with the collapse of those industries associated with the Industrial Revolution: open-air and industrial museums. It was the private sector that showed the way with industrial heritage. The Ministry of Works, the precursor to English Heritage, was wary of industrial machinery. By 1974 its inspectors had scheduled 300 industrial sites, but none had been taken into guardianship until the acquisition that year of the Stott Park Bobbin Mill in Cumbria, with displays of the Lancashire weaving and spinning industries. Open-air museums stretch back to nineteenth-century Scandinavia and became popular in England during the 1960s.[†] They were innovative attempts to show audiences what 'their' life might have been like in earlier periods. One particularly influential example was the between-the-wars recreation of Colonial Williamsburg in the USA, presented by guides in period dress.

It was in 1926 that John D. Rockefeller visited Williamsburg and started one of the most remarkable preservation stories that

* The National Heritage Act 1983 established the Victoria and Albert Museum, the Science Museum, the Armouries and the Royal Botanic Gardens, Kew as non-departmental public bodies to be governed by boards of trustees, following the time-honoured arrangements of the British Museum and the National Gallery.
† The first proposal for an open-air museum in England goes back to 1909.

would echo round the world over the next eighty years. Part of the brilliance of this project was to identify the ordinary people who lived in the surviving eighty-eight houses. Williamsburg was to be recreated as a working town at all levels of society with all the concomitant utilities such as a bakery and the saddler. Guides were in costume of the period and cars were forbidden in the historic area. It was not the first museum on these lines; that is generally accorded to be the Norsk Folkemuseum in Oslo, founded in 1894. The full impact of this new approach to presentation of museums and houses would not be felt in Britain until the 1970s, with the new industrial museums, the National Trust's work in creating the backstairs story at Erddig, and Peter Addyman's recreation of the Viking village at York.

The outdoor folk museum and the former industrial works found a successful marriage at Ironbridge Gorge, the crucible of the Industrial Revolution, and almost the definition of a World Heritage Site. When architectural historian Nikolaus Pevsner visited Ironbridge in 1950, he found it 'shockingly sordid'. The artist John Piper described how the 'dead collieries, branch railways, tileworks and iron foundries lie among waste heaps now and then left bare'.[4] However, Ironbridge was not to remain a Piranesian heap of industrial detritus; it was included in the plans for Dawley New Town (conceived in 1963), soon renamed Telford, with a recreational and historic zone incorporating Ironbridge. The museum complex opened in 1967 and spreads over a forty-two-acre site containing thirty-six scheduled listed buildings and monuments with the celebrated 1781 Iron Bridge at its heart. The former industrial buildings were converted into museums, but the most popular attraction, then as now, is the recreated Blists Hill Victorian Town, set in the year 1900. The town (really a village) is run by a mixture of paid workers and volunteers in costume and the shops and cafés reflect the date.

Placing an imaginary recreated village next to important monuments of the Industrial Revolution raised questions. Open air museums may be popular with the public, but they have also attracted academic criticism: they have sometimes lacked historical credibility, appealing to the Hovis mentality and 'fakelore' and begging the question whether heritage has become just another branch of Disney? As one former director of Ironbridge Gorge Museum explained, 'the new wave of industrial museums [...] creates a sort of curious nostalgic, rose-coloured picture of a Pickwickian industrial past which bears no relation to reality but which we like to imagine [...] A lot of what is presented isn't based on scholarship, but upon attitude and emotion.'[5] It was all too easy to forget the 'otherness of the past' and see our forebears as ourselves in different clothing. This played to the new identity heritage.

If 'visitor experience' reflected enjoyment, 'interpretation' became the educative component in museums of all types. This presaged the birth of the 'interpretation centre' and its twin, the 'heritage centre'. The latter came into existence during the 1975 European Architectural Heritage Year when the Civic Trust was invited to curate a series of events in Britain and the first heritage centres were set up in Faversham, York and Chester.[*] Their purpose is to present a theme, rather than display a collection of objects, or in the case of a battlefield, to tell a story. It was this aspect of heritage that persuaded an otherwise sceptical historian, Raphael Samuel, that educationally as well as architecturally, heritage arrived on the scene as a progressive force. However, the perception of heritage as a backward-looking, patrician, 'olden days' concept would not go away. One critical commentator was Robert Hewison whose book, *The Heritage Industry* (1987) questioned the packaging of history reflected at the Jorvik Viking

* Malcolm MacEwen, the press officer to the Royal Institute of British Architects, claims to have invented them: 'As a member of the committee for European architectural heritage year 1975 I persuaded the Arts Council to fund three experimental "architectural interpretation centres", and I was personally involved in the development of the York centre. I still think it was a good idea, although I never liked the name "heritage centre" which was given to it by Lady Dartmouth (later the Countess Spencer and, God help him, the Prince of Wales's step-mother-in-law).' See Samuel, p. 302.

Centre in York and Cadbury World, Bournville. They were, in his view, encouraging a false, repackaged, commodified past that played to a sentimental view of history as a lost golden age. Moreover, Hewison reflected that: 'when museums become one of Britain's new growth industries, they are not signs of vitality, but symbols of national decline.'[6] The contrary view was that countries palpably not in decline like Germany were creating just as many.

In fact, the number of museums in Britain was about to increase further with the arrival of the Heritage Lottery Fund in 1994. Its effect on the museum landscape can hardly be exaggerated. In addition to new museums, almost every significant museum and gallery in Britain expanded with a new wing or extension.[*] There had been nothing like this growth since Victorian times, but the flaw in Lottery largesse was the lack of money to run and maintain these gleaming new buildings. In the short term it provided a massive injection of welcome development cash. Old regional warhorses were given a new lease of life, and a considerable number of new museums were born. Contemporary art museums such as the Lowry at Salford and the Hepworth at Wakefield – serving a new audience hungry for the art of our time – were the most successful. Towering over all of these were two millennium projects: the British Museum Court and the opening in 2000 of Tate Modern to house the nation's holdings of modern and contemporary art.

The conversion of Giles Gilbert Scott's disused Bankside Power Station into Britain's most popular museum of modern art was the great cultural triumph of the era, marking London's recent arrival as a major international destination for contemporary art. The interesting question is how contemporary art swept all before it in London.[†] One day someone will tell us how

---

[*] One aspect of this expansion was filling in courtyards: the British Museum, the Wallace Collection, the Fitzwilliam Museum.

[†] The turnover of contemporary art sales at Sotheby's London amounted to 1 per cent of turnover in 1979 and rose to 30 per cent by the new millennium.

it happened, but till then we can only point to exhibitions at Whitechapel Gallery, Charles Saatchi's interventions, the influx of contemporary minded international collectors, a generational change, the existence of talented native artists, and of course the appearance of Tate Modern itself. All museums had to catch up if they were to bring in younger visitors.[*]

Tate Modern was the brainchild of Nicholas Serota, who came to the Tate after cutting his teeth at the Whitechapel Gallery. Serota (along with Neil MacGregor at the National Gallery and then the British Museum) was the most persuasive cultural operator of the time, adept at keeping governments of all stripe on side. He also succeeded in putting Tate Modern at the heart of the new cosmopolitan society that had settled in London. The opening impressed the world even if it exposed the relative paucity of the Tate's modern art collection when placed beside New York or Paris, something which Serota would work hard to remedy over the next decade. This had much to do with the expectation of visitors to see the work of certain artists leading increasingly to a similar experience in galleries, whether public or private.

The towering success of Tate Modern, however, masked the problems elsewhere in the museum sector. The funding crisis began to bite. Nationals in London, with their vast visitor numbers, access to sponsorship and tourist dollars, were better placed to look after themselves, but for the regions it was, and remains, a massive problem. After 2000, New Labour slightly increased funding for them (particularly for acquisitions through the Acceptance in Lieu scheme), but the Cameron coalition cut funding again during the years of austerity. Commercial activity to compensate for this has greatly increased. Finding sponsorship

---

[*] As one museum director remarked: 'In the United Kingdom you cannot easily obtain a grant for improving the display of Old Masters or ancient art unless you do something to demonstrate its contemporary relevance – which is most easily achieved by ensuring that a living artist add something to the display.'

had already become a large part of a director's job towards the end of the 1990s and has become steadily more important ever since. Sponsors, understandably, require promotion and reliable publicity can be best obtained in a museum by a temporary exhibition or a new building.

All museums today must continuously fundraise, and every director will tell you that finding money is their main problem. The majority of museums belong to one of three categories: national museums supported by central government, regional museums supported by local government, and charitable trusts who in theory live on endowments, admission and retail. Even when a regional museum has the appearance of being independent it is still probably majority funded by the local council.* This fiction enables it to fundraise – some, like the Bowes Museum, for instance, oscillate between council stewardship and independent trust stewardship every decade. Although the Lottery has always encouraged the building of endowments, not least with its occasional matching funding programmes, there is very little tradition in the UK of private giving solely for endowment purposes since the cachet and naming rights that come with capital projects are nearly always more attractive to donors. Here Britain is different from America, where the fiscal incentives are so much greater to support museums and they can rely on regular and successful clarion calls for endowment capital.

Local authority-owned museums are in the most unenviable position, financed by cash-strapped councils struggling to deal with social care while undergoing cuts from central government. Museums are the first services to be reduced and – being municipally owned – find it harder to raise money elsewhere. France spends 4 per cent of local authority spending on culture, compared with the UK's 1 per cent, the lowest in Europe.[7] England alone has 397 local authority museums, most of them

* Exceptions include York Art Gallery, which as a Trust charging an entrance fee has lost most of its local funding. The other funder that should be noted is the Arts Council.

the product of nineteenth-century civic pride. The recent history is telling: according to the Museums Association, sixty-four museums closed in the UK between 2000 and 2016, most of them due to local authority cuts.[8] They are at the mercy of local politicians, who rarely show much interest. Local authority museums, unlike public libraries, are not a statutory service. One former museum curator raised the question: 'if the great local authority museums had remained as great beacons which attracted national and international tourists and were truly a part of the local economy, rather than the demoralised places geared largely to providing community services, would their prospects be better?'[9] Perhaps Bendor Grosvenor is right: 'we, that is, art lovers and museum people, can jump up and down and complain forever that government should spend more on heritage and museums, but they never will, because it's not a priority for the public'. He reaches the harsh conclusion that 'the central reason museums have fewer resources is because they have failed, over decades, to make a strong case to the public, and thus the government, that they deserve their money'.[10]

The reaction by ministers to the museum funding deficit has invariably been the same, the universal panacea of all ministers faced with no money – commission a report. Report has followed report, the means by which an arts minister is seen to be doing something at little cost, in the vain search for remedies. One of the few promising changes came as a result of the Goodison Review (2004): the Cultural Gifts Scheme, introducing *lifetime giving* tax relief for those who offer works of art to public collections, the concept behind the exponential growth of American museums in the twentieth century. Curiously, the funding shortfall has not affected acquisitions. In the past every museum would have had a budget, however small, for new purchases, but as these dwindled the National Heritage Memorial Fund and the Heritage Lottery Fund have made unprecedented sums available. This has created a centralised acquisitions system (more like France) and although it has added a layer of bureaucracy, the outcomes for most museums have been beneficial.

Not all art collections were cash-starved before Covid-19 – one became unexpectedly rich as a result of a tragedy. The Royal Collection, not a museum as such but functioning as one, offers an interesting story. In 1992 there took place one of the greatest devastations to heritage since the war: the Windsor Castle fire. A well-meaning government minister hastily announced that the government would pick up the enormous repair bill. However, the country was in a truculent mood, with royals behaving badly and at the fag-end of a long period of an increasingly dysfunctional Conservative government. The Queen, recognising a PR disaster, stepped in to pay for most of the restoration; her action was to have an unanticipated long-term benefit. The opening of Buckingham Palace to the public was expected to be a temporary measure to raise money for the repairs, but its popularity (and the success of the merchandising that went with it) made it permanent and in the process made the Royal Collection perhaps the best-funded art collection in Britain, as well as the most thoroughly and continuously researched. That was until Covid-19.

The Royal Collection was very badly hit by the pandemic, reliant as it is on foreign visitors. Crucially, it was not able to take advantage of government job retention schemes. At the end of 2020 *The Times* announced that Desmond Shawe-Taylor, Surveyor of the Queen's Pictures (a post created in 1625) was to be made redundant after the annual report recorded a £64 million drop in income.

Funding may be the core problem for most museums, but identity in a multicultural and internet-driven world is another. Museums with ethnography, particularly vulnerable to accusations of looting and restitution claims, have had to re-examine their function and identity – who is addressing whom? Many, following the British Museum example, rebranded themselves as institutions of world art and culture, but this august notion may be past its sell-by date.[11] The British Museum under Neil MacGregor successfully repositioned itself as a museum of societies, a world museum of all people and for all people, the product of the Enlightenment, the visual equivalent of Diderot's *Encyclopedia*. It may or may not have deflected international restitution claims, but certainly provided a moral and intellectual justification for its existence. However, the cover of being 'a world museum' is increasingly under attack and it remains to be seen how long the Benin sculptures remain in Bloomsbury.[12] McGregor reinforced the idea with *A History of the World in 100 Objects*, both on the radio and in book form.

The soul-searching that followed restitution claims and contested heritage caused many questions to be asked about the purpose of museums and their responsibilities to society. This virtuous quest has engendered an idealism about the mission of museums: 'the claim that museums "change lives" represents the enormously positive potential that they have to strengthen communities, make places better, and do things for many kinds of people'.[13] The 2020 Black Lives Matter (BLM) protests brought the question of colonial material into focus, and much besides. One solution is provided by Belgium's African Museum, which has taken steps towards decolonising itself by bringing in contemporary African art and redressing the balance between the colonisers and the colonised. Tristram Hunt at the V&A spoke of 'telling stories that are adequate to multicultural Britain as well as sharing items with their countries of origin'.[14] Museum directors today must acknowledge historical marginalisation and omission. They need to make an honest assessment of their museum's past, its donors, patrons and indeed its purpose. Why are objects on view? So far, the British official response, if there can said to be a national policy, has been to avoid removal of objects but to recontextualise them with new labelling. More sinister to the cultural sector is the propensity of governments to tell museums what they can and cannot do in displaying and interpreting their collections to the public. The age-old principle of 'arm's-length bodies' is at risk, with grants made conditional and trustees politically vetted.

Grants being conditional is not always a bad thing. Lottery grants, requiring museums to achieve a much higher bar of public engagement, have given rise to a more respectful attitude to visitors. Above all the Lottery has required museums to reach new, younger and more diverse audiences. Online audiences have grown accordingly as outreach programmes, especially as a result of Covid, assume greater importance in museum management. Effective examples like that of the Fitzwilliam Museum at Cambridge may focus on a single work of art, such as the Lansdowne relief, exploring context, restoration and provenance. The aim must always be to draw the online visitor into the museum as the power of a work of art must ultimately be felt by standing in front of it. Virtual museum tours can be very enticing in this process, a particularly good example being Portsmouth's Mary Rose Museum. In fact, this might be taken as a model museum of our time with its combination of brilliant architecture, compelling content, rewarding education and sheer visual excitement.

Perhaps the greatest intangible success story of modern museums has been the education programmes, or what one museum director sardonically called 'the cult of infancy'. Art education for children, long pre-dating the Lottery, was pioneered by the Arts Council with the Hayward Gallery schools programme. One former director told the author that it was the arrival of the photocopier that changed everything, aiding interpretation through the ability to provide handouts.[15] There is no doubt that the engagement with young people today is outstanding. The World Museum in Liverpool, as a case in point, shows a film in which a curator engages with young people as to what they would like to see displayed and how. This may be more about appearances than reality but nevertheless shows flair. Museums have consciously or unconsciously become vehicles for the compulsory cultural education for schoolchildren. A significant part of any museum today is made over to educational activities.

And what about presentation? During the 1960s and 1970s museums were decluttered, isolating the object against a white wall. Today we are returning to something closer to the Victorian sense of plenty with the eye unable to rest in comfort for the multiplicity of objects (then) and messages (now) thrown at the visitor. To enter the hall of Kelvingrove Museum in Glasgow is to enter one of the most magisterial entrance halls of any museum. The recent Heritage Lottery-funded restoration is hailed as a great triumph, which it is. It has the stamp of our age in its passion for labelling and explaining, much encouraged by the Lottery. While this is generally a good idea, the nineteenth-century Italian sculptor Antonio Canova observed that the British see art through their ears – they are only interested if a story is attached. Kenneth Clark at the National Gallery was against too much written material on the grounds that visitors preferred reading to looking. Curators today do not always have the confidence to allow art to speak for itself. On the other hand there is now an international school of thought against labelling – taking its cue from Sir John Soane's Museum – that wants to stimulate rather than instruct.* It is moving away from the old encyclopedic model of traversing a museum through the centuries but looking at cross-cultural typologies, or as one director put it, less of a monograph than a short story or poem.[16] There is a suggestion that the main hall of the Fitzwilliam Museum should be hung not with grand portraits of the eighteenth century but objects of world culture. Glasgow and its museums come out top in terms of access with an admirable storage policy – anybody can go and peer at their storeroom racks. How thrilling an ambition that would be at Tate Britain, where 80 per cent of its works of art are in storage.

Tate Britain is a museum looking for love but failing. The problem is identity – rather surprising you might think, as the national collection of British art. If the opening of Tate Modern was a triumph it came at the price of shackling its less glamorous older sibling, Tate Britain, to an uneasy identity that is neither one thing nor another. It became a sad apology for not being Tate Modern with an agenda that has convinced neither those

---

* MONA in Tasmania has no labels and the visitor is handed an 'O' in which you record your thoughts.

interested in contemporary art nor in traditional British art. It has been difficult to draw a large public there in its confused state. What it still needs is an independent trustee body and a director whose heart lies in showing British art in all its richness, and above all allowing the museum to settle comfortably into its own skin. Add to that a willingness to bring works out of storage and circulate the collection with greater regularity.

Exhibitions have been a major part of the museum landscape since the 1960s, but at some point, they became sovereign: as a source of revenue, the means of finding a new public, and attracting publicity. The result is that we have created a world in which we think the public will only react to 'designer label' famous name artists. Hence the obsession with mounting exhibitions devoted to a small number of artists. This has left the permanent collection in some museums looking rather stale and unloved. As one director told the author, 'it is no exaggeration to claim that, if any museum is now thought to be "moribund" or "sleepy" the first remedy (after a Lottery-funded new wing) to be prescribed is to introduce or greatly enlarge a programme of loan exhibitions'.[17] A visitor arriving in London announcing a trip to the National Gallery will elicit the question, 'What's on?' With Covid-19 lending came to a halt and museums were forced to reassess their permanent collections. With the impact of climate change it is likely that CO_2 emissions will be a factor in considering future blockbusters.

At one level exhibitions have succeeded where Margaret Thatcher failed — they have made entrance charges acceptable. By the same token, the old assumptions about visiting a museum and hoping to see a particular masterpiece no longer pertains, as I discovered on a visit to Birmingham. The confusions, dilemmas, strengths and weaknesses at play here are exemplified in two of Birmingham's great museums. Birmingham Museum and Art Gallery is confused. It shows a good collection of old masters (in rather joyless galleries) and a world-class collection of Pre-Raphaelites, of which it is justly proud. On an August visit the Pre-Raphaelites were on exhibition in the USA — not a promising start, no doubt made necessary for making ends meet. That left the old master paintings which the curators awkwardly interspersed with a display: 'Within and Without: Body Images and the Self', a gallery that invites us to consider how public images affect us in our private lives. Charles Saumarez Smith is right: 'museums are no longer places where visitors come to find out, and to be told, about the past: they are no longer treated as public lecture rooms, where works of art are laid out according to strict historical sequence, didactically. Visitors, instead, come to look and to see and discover aspects of the past and the experience of art according to their own independent appetites.'[18] He believes that: 'the priorities of museums are changing towards a much less didactic, instructional approach, away from the past towards the present, away from teaching towards [life] experience'.[19]

Birmingham Museum has a wide range of objects to exhibit – archaeology, local history and fine art – in a building that does not allow much flexibility. The museum's primary attraction, the Saxon treasure known as the Staffordshire Hoard, discovered in 2009, is well done, with story boards, games, models, screens with talking heads and excellent displays. But the museum has no unifying principle. Is this possible to achieve? Historically, great directors at the Fitzwilliam in Cambridge and the V&A were able to bring together equally disparate parts. There is no doubt that the Birmingham Museum is popular with children and locals, but visitors from further afield are more sceptical.

Meanwhile, over at Birmingham University is the Barber Institute, which exemplifies the old-fashioned historical sequence of schools and periods. This is a traditional 'art historian's museum' which like the Ashmolean and the Fitzwilliam thrives best in the groves of academe. The last two university museums maintain high standards of scholarship with excellent presentation. The Ashmolean has succeeded in reinventing itself with a new atrium and wing, vastly increasing exhibition space and now attracting almost a million visitors. If there has been a decline of scholarship generally in regional museums, the inevitable result of managerial policies and the need for fund-raising impresarios, the university museums and nationals keep this flame burning.

Successive governments since the late 1970s have pushed museums to raise more and more of their running costs through private donations. The most successful have been Tate Modern and the National Portrait Gallery, both of which have been raising close to 70 per cent of their funds privately in recent years. This policy is, however, influencing the constituency of the trustee boards of the nationals which are increasingly made up of potential donors in the way American museums always have been. The problem arises, however, when there is an economic downturn and private donations dry up, leaving the 'successful' institutions very exposed – and unlike in the USA the donors will not feel responsible for them.[20] Despite the dwindling percentage of funding coming from government, the political interference is ever greater as museums have become vehicles of social policy.

Perhaps the most inspiring museum story of recent times has been the effect of new museums on depressed and rundown former industrial cities. Britain led the way in this endeavour with the opening in 1988 of Tate Liverpool, beautifully converted from the disused Albert Dock by James Stirling – a museum where you can turn from looking at a Kandinsky to the waters of the River Mersey (see Chapter 16). The opening of the Guggenheim Museum in Bilbao in 1997 endorsed the argument that a cultural institution in striking architecture by a celebrity architect would attract visitors and bring regeneration and economic growth. The most spectacular British example is the recent V&A Dundee, a museum whose contents do not yet match the splendour of its design. The very striking architecture and riverside setting, however, have given Dundee pride and hope.

Better matched with content are two excellent Lottery-funded new museums opened as part of a broader regeneration programme, the previously mentioned Lowry museum in Salford and the Hepworth museum in Wakefield. Turner Contemporary at Margate, an exhibition space rather than a museum, is another example of the talismanic importance of art in the rebranding of old towns. The old Victorian idea that culture follows the money has been turned on its head – now it is investment that follows the heritage. All this speaks of a positive future for museums at the heart of cultural life. But museum professionals are not optimistic, mainly because of ever-dwindling funding. Giles Waterfield, the historian of Britain's regional museums, predicted a bleak future in 2015: 'curatorial expertise dwindles or disappears, opening hours diminish, the fine new buildings and extensions paid for by the Heritage Lottery Fund can be hard-pressed to operate'.[21] People today may wonder whether we have created too many new museums?

CHAPTER 21

Heritage: An Unfinished History

*You can't protect the past if you don't
protect the future.*

EXTINCTION REBELLION POSTER, 2019

This book opens in the second half of the nineteenth century, a time of tumultuous change. Industrialisation, the construction of the nation's railways and the growth of its cities, along with other factors, began forcing people to question the way they were living, and which parts of the nation, and national life, they should protect. At that time there were a few visionaries – prophets such as Octavia Hill, William Morris and John Ruskin – who attempted to provide the answers. Together they set the course of conservation for the next 150 years. Although we think of the conservation movement as mostly concerning buildings and landscapes, it proceeded from addressing broader questions about society – how we should live, and what it is that improves and supports the quality of our lives. Access to nature, greenery and fresh air figured more prominently than old buildings or works of art, but what is striking from today's viewpoint is that the same people were campaigning for all these things together, rather than isolating them into different interest groups.

In the century that followed many more disruptors and threats, mainly deriving from a lack of restraining legislation, have come and gone. We have dealt with them through new laws, ideas, protests and change. In the previous chapters, the boundaries of what can be considered 'heritage' have been widely drawn, in ways that those foundational figures from 150 years ago would have endorsed. As we saw in the first chapter, the conservation group that set off the modern heritage movement was the Commons Preservation Society, formed to prevent landlords removing a shared community amenity. 'Commons' is a word that has recently acquired a new currency at a time when governments are in the grip of commercial interests, especially developers.* Are heritage and commons in fact virtually the same thing, and are the pressures on them fundamentally the same? The concerns of heritage have widened to include town and country, coast and hill, steam ships and railways, high streets and suburbs, in fact anything that we believe contributes to our quality of life and fear may not survive without special help. Thus, while heritage necessarily involves the past, its trajectory is to the future.

Since the 1870s, the heritage story may have seemed like an ascent, climbing one foothill after another, winning height that cannot subsequently be lost. However, this chapter will show that nothing can be taken for granted, and the struggle even to stay in the same place is unending. We are looking at aspects of heritage for which the concept of commons seems especially appropriate, not just covering the paintings in national collections or the properties of the National Trust, but more diverse, everyday things. Commons are not only items that are owned by the state or by great national institutions, but privately owned swathes of land and historic buildings. It is less about ownership than regulation. When ignorance, the profit motive or a loss of amenity affect the common good and regulation is weak, the commons are jeopardised, sometimes forever.

From many perspectives, the heritage sector in Britain today is massively successful. It employs by some accounts 563,000 people and generates £36.6 billion per annum.[1] Tangible heritage

---

* The idea was described by the British economist William Forster Lloyd in 1833, and gained a modern following through the seminal article 'The Tragedy of the Commons' by Garrett Hardin in 1968.

is popular, open to the enjoyment of all parts of a complex society, and adept at mobilising public engagement. Intangible heritage – preserving knowledge and skills that can in turn be passed on – comes with it (the BBC's *Repair Shop* is evidence enough). Yet it faces many threats of a different kind: too much countryside is being consumed by developers, Conservation Areas are being eroded, tall towers built in inappropriate places, high streets are under pressure, while the museums and archaeology, among the principal generators of new ideas and new discoveries, are chronically underfunded. The choices are ultimately political, based on assumptions about priorities. If these are short term or simply hostile to the whole concept, the fragility of the earlier gains is exposed, and political support over the last twenty years has been at best tepid.

The former chairman of English Heritage, Jocelyn Stevens, was right when he mused that 'central government was one of the heritage's deadliest enemies.'[2] No politician today can entirely ignore it, and yet the future looks insecure given the government's continuous undermining of our planning laws, and its acceptance of their ambiguities. During the Covid pandemic of 2020–1, the government can be credited with stepping in and saving many organisations from bankruptcy, but the longer-term trend within all the political parties is not encouraging.

When in 2011 David Cameron's coalition government drew up its National Planning Policy Framework (NPPF) with its presumption in favour of development, it was dubbed the 'developer's charter'.* The idea – coming after a housing slump – was to stimulate the construction industry by simplifying the planning laws – problematic enough in terms of all forms of land use, but more so in relation to anything already deemed to be heritage. Paragraph 134 (updated 195/6) of the NPPF requires 'less than substantial harm to the significance of a designated heritage

---

* Paragraph 173 of NPPF is a get-out clause that allows developers to wriggle out of commitments that won them planning permission if viability is not ensured.

asset' to be weighed against the public benefits of the proposal. This subjective wording leaves much open to interpretation and has opened the door to new building that might in earlier times have been more wisely controlled.

We have a planning system that frustrates local people and entrenches divisive attitudes, leaving all parties dissatisfied. Developers have no more idea than the public whether they will get planning permission because the rules are so ambiguous. Planning officers, slighted by Cameron as 'the enemy of enterprise', have an extraordinarily difficult job interpretating planning law, dealing with an often hostile public, while attempting to serve the needs of their council. These include central government's housing targets, delivered through the arm's-length agency of opportunistic and profit-driven developers whose tail wags the dog of regulation.

According to the CPRE, the deregulation of planning is the gravest threat to the countryside since the 'Wild West' developments of the 1920s and 1930s which brought the organisation into being. Philip Larkin's fears about a degraded landscape save for a few heritage pockets have come back to haunt us, because commons are sacrificed to the legitimate need for housing. The voters in the 2021 Chesham and Amersham by-election sent a welcome message to the government that they don't want to be bullied by house-builders waving their *cartes blanches*. It was widely believed that the Tories lost the election owing to unrestricted development.

It is estimated that, over the last twenty-five years, an area of countryside and green space almost the size of Cornwall has been given to development. Despite holding the lowest density of green space per head of any large country in Europe, England continues to devour 27,000 acres a year. All governments since the 1980s had adopted a policy of brownfield first, that is previously developed recycled land. By 2008, 80 per cent of new homes were being built on brownfield sites until the coalition government of 2010–15 felt that 'brownfield first' was holding back house building and the economy, and scrapped it. As a result, brownfield fell back dramatically just as the rate of house building was increasing, with 700,000 homes earmarked for green belt and open countryside, and brownfield limited to 2,000 homes. New targets for housing on brownfield sites would be a step in the right direction. London has enough derelict sites to accommodate more than 350,000 houses, which is greater than the annual target for the entire country.[3]

If there is a consistent theme running through the heritage story it is the protection of green, open spaces and landscape. Ask anybody in Britain today – whoever they are or wherever they live – what they feel is worth preserving, and it seems like nine times out of ten they will speak of countryside, habitats and scenic landscape, yet curiously this universal priority feels like the least effective, or at least the most confused and threatened area of heritage conservation. Is it because these treasures are so widely spread and the battles to protect them are fought hand-to-hand with inadequate instruments by over-stretched forces?

'The conservation camp falls into two distinct communities,' writes the naturalist Mark Cocker: one lobbying for the preservation of 'landscape beauty', and another which has wild animals and plants as their priority.[4] There are real conflicts at work here, with a growing perception that the familiar and conventionally beautiful upland landscapes, in particular, are preserved to the disadvantage of more varied and robust ecosystems. It is hard to dissent from Cocker's suggestion that forging 'a single blueprint for British nature is an essential prerequisite' of any effort to 'halt and reverse the losses' of British wildlife. These good things must in the end be interdependent and regarded holistically.

In the current hierarchy of safeguarding, it is easier to protect exceptional existing habitats than scenic landscape. At the same time, the relatively new concepts of 're-naturing', or its more radical counterpart, 're-wilding', have captured wide attention, demonstrating the benefits possible by abandoning our received views of landscape beauty, but in this case for beavers rather than house-builders.* Even those scenic landscapes that do have protection are prey to the acceleration of development activity. In 2021 it was reported that there has been a doubling of development in AONBs, particularly in Sussex, Surrey and Kent (with 932 homes approved in the High Weald mostly for large 'executive' properties), in what is described as a 'build and be damned' approach.[5] But as Ruskin put it so eloquently: 'a single villa can mar a landscape and dethrone a dynasty of hills'.[6]

Conservation Areas and Tall Towers

Compared to the powerful mystique of countryside, the arguments for conservation in cities such as Birmingham, Bath and Liverpool have only been slowly and painfully won. There is an adverse turn of the tide here as well, not yet as dramatic as the loss of Georgian terraces, but, like the devouring of green fields, dangerous because gradual. Birmingham Conservation Areas, for example, are subject to attrition through altering of the fenestration, the use of inappropriate rendering, the placing of prominent satellite dishes, or building porches. On an individual basis this has little impact, but in the aggregate, it amounts to a Conservation Area becoming by small degrees a district where it is no longer worth enforcing the rules. Although the 9,300 Conservation Areas administered by local authorities have been one of the outstanding heritage success stories since the 1960s, their foundation in 'the character or appearance of which it is desirable to preserve or enhance' leaves a dangerous degree of wriggle-room. 'Enhance' means different things to different people and, while Historic England guidelines ought to set a standard, subjectivity and political expediency work against them to the extent that applications by local councils are now being lodged to declassify them. It is too much effort to enforce them.

* Many readers will be familiar with Isabella Tree's bible, *Wilding*, stemming from her initiatives at the Knepp Castle Estate.

In 2017 it was estimated that there were 502 Conservation Areas at risk, and many of these have no officer overseeing them.[7] There are no less than 20 per cent fewer planning officers today than in 2008. No single factor will protect a Conservation Area, but a combination of action and public pressure from a local civic society (those watchdogs anticipated in the 1967 legislation) can succeed. The government's proposed expansion of what are called 'permitted development rights' (PDR) gives the matter urgency: this would negate the need for planning permission to be sought, even in Conservation Areas. This expansion is designed to make it easier for shops and restaurants to be converted into flats, and although this has a practical basis, *unchecked* alteration of the historic centres of cities would be a grave mistake. Allowing houseowners to add a storey and change their windows without permission goes against the principle of maintaining such areas under statutory guidance for the greater communal good. Since the 1970s windows have been subject to the depredations of an aggressive replacement industry. They are likely to need more careful negotiation, rather than less, if the subtle beauty that any surviving original glazing patterns bring to an elevation is to be steered through the justifiable needs of thermal upgrading in the face of climate change.

Is the sky a commons? Arguably, tall buildings take it away from people on the street and those viewing for miles around. Somebody is stealing something that belongs to us all. A recent demolition in the Bayswater Conservation Area provides a good case history of how ineffective are the controls that might prevent the theft. Opposite Isambard Kingdom Brunel's noble Paddington railway station, a commercial office development by Renzo Piano known as the Paddington Cube has replaced an Edwardian postal sorting office that in scale and materials had harmonised with its characterful and bustling setting of shops and housing. The tower, reduced from its original proposed height, goes against Westminster Council policy, aside from the sensory domination of such a tall building in a low-rise urban environment. Wind downdrafts and the climatic effects of its glare are further losses of civic amenity. The cash windfalls gained by local councils under Section 106 agreements is a form of covert developer taxation that is the secret driver of many regrettable transgressions.

While tall buildings are spreading in central London, they are more disturbing in a low-rise cathedral city. The recent application to build the Anglia Tower in the Norwich City Centre Conservation Area was supported by the local planning committee, who welcomed the potential investment on an unappealing site. Opposed by Historic England and SAVE Britain's Heritage, the application was called in by the Secretary of State for Housing and Local Government, who, following the procedure open to him, called a public inquiry. SAVE argued: 'this city deserves better. We believe it could be redeveloped in a different way, with low-rise streets and squares that are characteristic of creative quarters that are emerging in cities across the UK.' On the basis of the evidence, which included an alternative low-rise scheme commissioned by Historic England, the planning inspector at the Norwich inquiry recommended the rejection of the application. This view was endorsed by the minister (never a foregone conclusion), and the developer withdrew. However, in November 2021 the developer returned with an amended scheme, still inappropriate, but will it get through?

Tall buildings have their enthusiasts.[8] Public opinion on individual examples is surprisingly consistent – some are liked and others are loathed, for reasons that would be interesting to fathom but seldom seem to inform decision-making. In Manchester, perhaps in continuation of the city's Victorian boosterism, they have become part of the brand, and mayors sometimes regard towers as symbols of civic virility. The buzzword is 'agglomeration', the attraction of high-net-worth earners and the various developments that spring up to attract their investment and service their requirements, such as five-star hotels and international company offices. One tower thus becomes the harbinger and then the nucleus of the next cluster of tall buildings. If the skyline has already been spoiled, as with St George's Tower in Nine Elms, London, a cluster around it, rebranded as the London Plan's Nine Elms Opportunity Area, has spread the effect of damage and even given this formerly nondescript and still unlovable district some *élan*.[*] But given that such towers have tended to provide empty flats for foreign investors, there is the much graver question of their social cost.

In cities such as Tokyo and Paris, tall buildings have been sited with care, confined to business areas. The City of London sold this pass in the 1960s and regretted it later. They imposed height limits until competition with the upstart Canary Wharf triggered a desire to compete in offering modern office space. The construction of Norman Foster's Swiss Re/Gherkin, completed in 2003, was the turning point when earlier ordinances were overruled. Now it is dwarfed by what has followed. Personally, I find the burgeoning collection of skyscrapers exciting and in some ways an improvement on the sometimes dull post-war office buildings that they have replaced, but we have reached the limit of what this fragile area can take. In literal terms, it could be argued that little serious heritage has been harmed. Ancient churches still lie like lapdogs beneath their shadows, but their belittling of St Paul's and the Tower of London remains a serious loss – exactly the sort of thing Paris and many other cities have avoided. Given the narrow medieval street pattern of the City, inserting tall buildings will always be a fraught process, and I doubt whether the area can take more.[†] The inevitable next step has been to cross London Bridge and go south of the Thames, bringing us the Shard by Renzo Piano at London Bridge station.

[*] The fifty-storey Vauxhall Tower, the tallest residential building in Britain at the time, came about because John Prescott overruled the planning inspector who recommended against it.
[†] For Historic England, the 'Tulip Scheme' represented a limit with its proposal to rise 305 metres and harm the setting of the Tower of London. The proposal was rejected by the Mayor of London in 2019 and by the government in 2021, citing 'carbon emissions during construction'.

This in turn has encouraged six more planning applications for tall buildings in Southwark, which will adversely affect and perhaps even wreck the Bermondsey Street and Borough High Street Conservation Areas. Every present mistake licenses the next one.

It used to be said that tower blocks take the pressure off the rest of the built environment, but with a tougher green agenda, they ought to become harder to justify, even if some reputedly green examples exist. It is not just the construction, which is certainly extravagant on CO_2 emissions, but also the maintenance – the higher up a building goes, the more energy is required to service it. It remains to be seen if attempts to curb climate change will succeed in restraining the desire to build upwards.

High Streets

The everyday business of local shopping is valued for good reason. It promotes personal contacts, provides employment, and if businesses are locally owned, it keeps money circulating in the local economy to everyone's benefit. Neglected and allowed to run down while out-of-town stores and online commerce killed them off, high streets are currently receiving welcome attention from heritage and civic organisations because they affect us all. These are among our richest but most vulnerable commons.

Apart from being an obvious indicator of economic and social health, they are the 'front room' of every town or district, contributing to a sense of place. Even before Covid in 2020–1, however, high street stores were closing at a dramatic pace and this seemed like an almost fatal final agony. Apart from high rents that squeeze out the small and quirky, business rates are correctly cited as part of the problem, showing the urgent need to level the playing field with online outlets and ask what gain comes from an empty shop window, although Covid has tended to push rents down, offering younger entrepreneurs a chance. The appearance of an independent bakery often seems to herald a revival – perhaps the history of our times will be written from the standpoint of a loaf of bread. Civic spaces that preserve a strong identity are more likely to prosper, and this is as true for historic towns like Chepstow as it is for Manchester's Chinatown. Outside historic towns, it is character that matters, and this comes with variety. Southall High Street in London with its multifarious Asian shops is a colourful example of vitality without a hint of gentrification. Often it is less obvious places such as Basildon New Town that try hardest in their efforts to remake a successful high street.[9]

To survive, retail may need to cluster defensively, while other shop premises reinvent themselves. The upper floors over shops have often been left empty, and the High Street Heritage Action Zones, of which there are now sixty-nine within existing Conservation Areas, are a timely initiative by Historic England.[*] In Nottingham, the aim is to convert former retail buildings to housing, in the process returning town centres to being the social spaces they once were. Department store closures happened suddenly in large numbers as a result of the pandemic, but these buildings often lend themselves well to domestic conversion.

Official Heritage Bodies

So much for the fragile grass roots, but what is happening higher up the tree? The characterisation of heritage as an industry, suggesting profitability, has increasingly allowed government to slide almost invisibly out of its responsibilities: allowing the Lottery to pay for many of the conservation initiatives of Historic England; making museums dependent on sponsorship; and hiving off the National Heritage Collection to a charity to remove it from government balance sheets. Since the early 1980s, the very

---

[*] This is part of the wider Heritage Action Zones initiative bringing regeneration to towns like Bishop Auckland still wedded to out-of-town shopping.

success of the private heritage sector, whether it be stately homes or volunteer-run steam railways, has made it appear that heritage needs little government support, especially while the former Heritage Lottery Fund bestowed its bounty. But little could be further from the truth.

The Department for Digital, Culture, Media and Sport (DCMS, lately rebranded to include 'levelling up') is the government ministry for heritage matters, a pale shadow of the old Department for the Environment. It is the paymaster of both national museums and Historic England, the latter being their advisor on historic buildings. Until Covid-19 the department had all the appearance of a weak and underfunded ministry with a startling turnover of secretaries of state. It has been the problem rather than the solution, always pressing for cuts. During and after Covid, government support was a lifeline through the Culture Recovery Fund, as previously mentioned, but with the money went a clumsy intervention to ensure a 'positive' angle on interpretation, and the exclusion of more varied narratives that have gained considerable support and might achieve the long-desired widening of the public for heritage.

Britain has a successful record of balancing private and public partnerships because in the past government has always kept its side of the bargain, but the evidence suggests that they no longer want to do so. No prime minister has better expressed such contempt for heritage than David Cameron, when he asked Simon Thurley, then at English Heritage, whether the National Heritage Collection could be given away or sold. The very idea of setting up English Heritage under Margaret Thatcher was to make the running of the nation's historic properties more attractive and therefore economic, and this was achieved to a considerable extent. For Prime Minister Cameron, the logical end of this process was to remove the organisation from the government's balance sheets, so that the management of properties from castles and earthworks to the Art Deco splendours of Eltham Palace went to one branch under the old name, while the regulatory side was rebranded as Historic England.

For the first time since 1913, the government has now shed itself of responsibility for the nation's monuments. The new English Heritage was given what was effectively a severance payment of £85 million to reestablish itself (and pay for its backlog of repairs) – on the condition there would be no further funding after 2023, and always in the expectation that it should wash its face. The result remains to be seen.[*] English Heritage welcomed 6.5 million visitors in 2019 and before Covid was on track to break even by the time funding stopped.[10] Although from its inception it was in competition with the National Trust and the Historic Houses Association, today these organisations see themselves in partnership for a common cause, including campaigning with every heritage and green organisation for the abolition of VAT on building repairs that unfairly favours new construction and often leads to unnecessary demolitions. This has been a long-term, persistent and urgent request from the heritage sector to government, but it has fallen on deaf ears. However well managed the new English Heritage may be, it is unthinkable that governments in France, Germany or Italy would relinquish responsibility for such heritage in this way. The counter-argument – as Roy Strong discovered at the V&A during the 1980s – is that by removing themselves from the annual round of government cuts, English Heritage would be able to plan longer term, avoid government interference, and fundraise more easily. We shall see.

---

[*] Sir Tim Laurence, chairman of English Heritage, comments: 'There are three different interpretations of "washing its face". One category is those which cover the cost of opening to the public and managing them on a daily basis, cutting the grass etc. A second would be to add in the cost of the annual cycle of essential maintenance and conservation. A third would include the major injections of funding which are required from time to time, for instance major roof repairs, a new visitor centre. Remembering that over 300 of our 420 sites are "free to enter", of the rest about 75 break even in the first category, fewer than 20 in the second and only 4 or 5 in category three. Our top four sites in a typical year are: Stonehenge, Osborne, Dover Castle and Tintagel.' Email to author, May 2021.

As the government's adviser on historic buildings, Historic England sends expert recommendations on designation to the secretary of state of the DCMS with advice to accept or reject them, an unpredictable process subject at times to overdependence on media spin or specialists highly paid by developers. It also provides grants for the repair of historic buildings, although since 2010, it has suffered grants cut by 54 per cent in real terms which has left it focusing on how to prioritise its decimated resources. The worst reductions were suffered by the 'Heritage at Risk' grant budget, a fund of last resort reduced over the last decade to £12 million, until it was raised during Covid. Historic England is responsible for determining applications concerning properties designated Grade I or II*. Applications or enforcements for Grade II buildings (the great majority) along with Conservation Areas, are the responsibility of local councils. They are advised by their conservation officers, if they still have any, or otherwise by default the planning committee of elected councillors, often inexpert in such matters and liable to vote against their own advisors. Conservation officer posts have been severely affected by cutbacks over the last five years, with some areas like the East Riding of Yorkshire having lost half of their officers – a situation with all too obvious dangers.

Over the years successive governments have been able to justify reducing the grant-giving capacity of Historic England because the Heritage Lottery Fund has been financing the award of building grants. This is despite the premise of 'additionality' that was so vaunted when the funds first became available. As a result, Historic England has become dependent on the Lottery to fund many excellent initiatives such as the Places of Worship scheme and the High Street initiative. The National Lottery Heritage Fund (as it has been renamed), however, has its own priorities, and they are not the same. When it withdrew from schemes such the 'Grants for Places of Worship Fund', it left churches in a very uncertain position, already subject to declining congregations. There is even scepticism about whether 'church' as an activity needs or wants physical churches.* The vicar of Cawston in Norfolk echoed the cry of every parish: 'what I find difficult is the ever-shifting grant-giving landscape which makes it so hard to know where to go next'.[11]

The threshold of community involvement required by the Lottery is appropriate given the source of the money, but churches cannot satisfy their very different criteria of importance from Historic England. Many significant churches and indeed other buildings fall outside the National Lottery Heritage Fund (NLHF) criteria and are unable to pass its community use threshold. It is a projects-based organisation and cannot take over what are correctly the government's longer-term responsibilities. Fortunately, however, the interests of Historic England and the NLHF intersect at many points and it has proved to be a beneficial partnership.†

That the heritage sector, deprived of footfall and ticket sales, showed such resilience during Covid lockdown must primarily be put down to the government's Cultural Recovery Fund, helped by additional support from the Lottery. In 2020 over £650 million was pumped into 1,500 projects while an alliance between the Arts Council on behalf of the DCMS, Historic England and the NHLF ensured that the distribution was effective. Yet despite this there were 4,000 job losses in the sector and visitor numbers were down by an average of 75 per cent. In the short term the main losers were the big national museums like the V&A that derive so much income from retail and sponsorship. Worst hit was the Royal Collection, entirely dependent on ticket money because it ruled itself out from receiving help through government schemes. Perhaps the biggest gainer in the short

---

* Peter Luff, the former chairman, points out that the National Lottery Heritage Fund ended all its targeted schemes to reduce administration costs in the face of declining lottery income.

† With his background at English Heritage, Simon Thurley's appointment as chair of the NLHF in 2021 is promising, as nobody understands the problems better.

term was Historic England, which saw its grant funding rise in 2021 from £20 to £80 million, although it remains to be seen how this will play out.

Unofficial Heritage Bodies

In the field of the built environment, the amenity societies continue to fulfil their necessary mission of warning and protesting in public and stirring up the media to win attention. There is an ecology in which each organisation has its own niche and *modus operandi*: SAVE marches towards the sound of gunfire, the CPRE attempts to reframe policy for the countryside and planning, while the four main amenity societies – the SPAB, Georgian, Victorian, and Twentieth Century societies – combine small and large casework as needed while educating the public and sustaining a climate of opinion in favour of their particular areas of concern. The world of digital activities during the Covid lockdowns surprisingly brought them new audiences and members. These and hundreds more heritage organisations, with local or specific natural remits that are represented by the Historic Environment Forum and by the Heritage Alliance (founded in 2002). The latter through its seminars and events offers a feeling of solidarity within an otherwise fragmented sector and can campaign for the group as a whole.

As York demonstrates, local civic societies can be effective in holding local councils to account, but there are too few of them and young recruits are hard to find, so that their membership, though dedicated, is elderly. Civic Voice, their membership body, with a total staff of no more than three, is a shadow of the once mighty Civic Trust.[*] If the glory days of the 'heroic period' of

* Civic Voice had 250 civic society members in 2020. They can only realistically operate where there is an existing local body with whom to interact. See their 2018 report, 'What is the Future for our Conservation Areas?'

engagement have passed, we may still find activist bands forming out of local Google and Facebook groups to fight specific issues. Will they stay the course, however, and prove as transformative as the local Civic Trust at Margate? It prevented a great deal of demolition and through fostering an appreciation of the town's remarkable buildings, led the way to regeneration and the creation of a landmark art gallery that added momentum to a vehicle already in motion.

The National Trust

The National Trust must be considered the greatest heritage charity on earth. The organisation has nearly 6 million members, some 10 per cent of the UK's population, attesting to the important role it plays in the life of the nation. Yet that role can be so diverse as to cause confusion and dissent. Simon Jenkins, its former chairman, points out that 'ever since its foundation, the National Trust has argued with itself, and the argument is the same. Is it about gumboots or gutters, rolling acres or gilded cornices, Scafell Pike or Hardwick Hall? At the end of the day, the answer is always the same. Both.'[12] The perception that houses and hills are somehow in opposition and represent different communities of visitors is a false one. Has the Trust too readily swallowed the lazy caricature version of its established supporters? There is no actual contest, only that once houses are perceived as 'an outdated mansion experience', their potential for pleasure and learning is likely to be obstructed rather than opened up.[13]

As so often when there is a lack of clarity about the issues, interpretation comes to the fore. Sometimes the Trust seems to try too hard to solve imaginary problems. There have been tensions for some time between the new 'visitor experience' teams, whose role is to make visits fun and appealing, and the established curators, whose task is to research, understand, interpret and publish the complex histories of properties and collections, yet surely both can co-exist. Initiatives often arise from a virtuous premise, but are carried out in an unthoughtful, and provocative way. Removing the furniture made for the room at Ickworth in order to substitute family-friendly bean bags ignored an important condition for its Acceptance in Lieu of estate duty. This stated that the furniture must be shown to the public or it would be removed from the property – the bean bags quickly departed when this was pointed out. The wider lesson is surely to popularise only with due caution on a temporary and reversible basis.

The Trust has stated its desire to 'dial down' its role as a major national cultural institution. It certainly evinces a reduced enthusiasm for curating its art collections and libraries and even gardens, yet these are no less inalienable under their terms of acceptance as gifts than the hills and streams, and there is no need to neglect them.[14] Putting the growth of the membership (particularly young people and their perceived needs) at the forefront of its mission, along with climate change, well-being and diversity, would certainly have its founders cheering loudly, but it seems a counsel of despair to assume that all ages and conditions might not care equally about all these things and be awake to the Trust's treasures, even if at different points in their supporters' life cycles.

Contested Heritage

That the heritage debate is dynamic is amply demonstrated by the Rhodes Must Fall and Black Lives Matter (BLM) movements, with their rejection of the way British history has been told and a desire to tell the more difficult and polyphonic histories of Britain's imperial past. As the writer Afua Hirsch explains: 'if we were able to see a different version of it [our history] – not a carefully curated, highly selective, politically convenient one, but an honest one, in all its nuances – it might give us all a chance to carve our individual and collective relationship with Britain in a more realistic way'.[15] The Black Lives Matter (BLM) movement gained worldwide momentum following the murder of George Floyd in police custody in Minneapolis in May 2020. In Britain, one of the ramifications of BLM has been to make more prominent those discourses relating to what constitutes truthful history and therefore meaningful heritage. The movement is part of a wider undercurrent of self-questioning, particularly for a younger generation, or what being British means today.[*]

'The summer of 2020 was', as Neil MacGregor observed, 'pretty well everywhere, a tricky time to be a statue.'[16] The desire to topple or deface statues is age old: European history is littered with statues being removed when regimes changed, revolutions took place, or vociferous sections of the public have demanded it, notably during the English Civil War, as well as in Ireland after independence.[†] The present situation, however, goes well beyond that in its global desire to examine historical figures and put history under a moral gaze: was a particular historical figure a hero or a villain?[17] The removal of statues of the previously lauded General Lee in America is a case in point. In fact, the erection of a statue often tells us less about the individual than what virtues were fashionable at the time. British government policy is to retain statues in situ but with an appropriate explanation – 'retain and explain' – and only in extreme cases to remove them to a museum to prevent destruction. At Denbigh in North Wales, there was an attempt to remove the statue of its most famous son, Sir Henry Morton Stanley, for his involvement with King

---

[*] Perhaps not since the Act of Union in 1707 has the question been so potent. The answers then did not dilute local Scots, Welsh or Irish identities and perhaps there is a lesson here. Incorporating different national identities into a common heritage, respectful of all the parts, was achieved but not without pain or a sense of grievance. It was the unifying genius of Walter Scott that papered over the cracks in the Anglo-Scots cultural narrative.

[†] Interestingly, we find an echo in present times of one of the earliest ever pieces of heritage legislation, the Public Statues Act 1854, passed after acts of vandalism to royal statues.

Leopold II's Belgian Congo. A petition to this effect was signed by several distinguished academics, and in 2021 the town council decided to put the matter to a vote. On a low turnout, almost 80 per cent voted to retain the statue.

Present calls for greater diversity and inclusion have strong impetus to a broader approach to history, not dissimilar to the rise of feminist history in the 1970s. It is no longer possible to describe history from a Eurocentric point of view without understanding the collateral effect on the rest of the world. Nobody today will accept the rosy account of history promulgated by the heritage industry during the 1970s – the nostalgic view that so enraged intellectuals like Robert Hewison, who saw it as a sell-out to commercial interests by people who should have known better. Now, country houses, whether privately owned or held in trust for the public good, feel compelled to examine the foundations of their wealth. The family-owned Harewood House in Yorkshire, for example, has gone to some length to tell the story of the sugar plantations on which the family fortune was created. This engagement goes far beyond presentism, and has active programmes with Caribbean stakeholders. The National Trust, having commissioned a report on the same theme for the whole range of its properties, is facing a backlash from conservative interest groups. It met with a similar response when in 2017, with HLF funding, it sought to bring attention to LBGT+ house owners of the past. Insensitive at times to the subtle nuances of the past, at Felbrigg Hall in Norfolk it was a lesson about not jumping to the wrong conclusions.

This wind of contested heritage change has presented the British Museum with a dilemma over its formerly revered founder, Sir Hans Sloane, who for some years worked as a doctor in Jamaica and whose wife's family owned slave plantations. The museum has placed the likeness of Sir Hans Sloane in a secure cabinet alongside artefacts explaining his work in the context of the British empire. This debate will certainly have lasting consequences on how heritage stories are presented and who is writing them. On a positive note, the appearance of 'slavery plaques' has provided a heritage framework for many people who were previously excluded from heritage discussions.* There is no agreed way to write and read history and the challenge is to find the balance between triumphalism, grievance, sentimentality and self-hatred.† It is already clear that most organisations that make up the 'heritage industry' have embraced the need for everyone's voice to be heard.

Social Media Changes the Game

For heritage attractions, social media has come to serve as an effective low-cost marketing tool, and this gear-change was accelerated by Covid. The internet has placed dazzlingly powerful new tools in the hands of the conservation lobby, particularly among them the sharing of information. It is now easier to view planning applications and uncover potentially revealing documents under the Freedom of Information Act. In the past, one of the most effective platforms was the local newspaper, which played a vital role for campaigners, as we saw with Rod Hackney in Macclesfield. Given that 265 newspaper titles have closed in Britain since 2005, the social media alternative has come not a moment too soon. At their best, the digital and print worlds reinforce each other, so that while the platform for local news is now digital and reaches much bigger audiences, the responses are harder to predict.

Petitions are much easier to circulate through social media and help to demonstrate support. When in 2015 King's College London applied to demolish four scruffy-looking nineteenth-century

---

* The National Trust recognised the need to celebrate immigrant community heritage by accepting in 2009 the glorious Wandsworth house of the Kenyan-born poet, artist and writer Khadambi Asalache, decorated by his own hand with the filigree charm of home-made wooden fretwork.

† The Germans coming to terms with their history have been a good example.

buildings on the Strand near Somerset House, to which Historic England had not objected despite their being in a Conservation Area, 10,000 people signed a petition over one weekend. After this was picked up by the BBC, Historic England was compelled to change its position and intervene, so that the buildings were saved. Crowdfunding too has bestowed its blessings: a relatively disadvantaged area like Welsh Streets in Liverpool was able to raise £40,000 in 2014 for its campaign. The role of social media as intermediary and 'matchmaker' is now highly important for heritage organisations, helping to network small and disparate campaign groups, to stiffen morale and multiply their impact.

Celebrities and influencers with large followings, such as the local campaigner 'The Gentle Author', with his 'Spitalfields Life' blog, seed the stories that then run rampant through retweets. This multiplier effect was demonstrated in the campaign to save Smithfield meat market from demolition. At the 2010 MTV Video Music Awards, Lady Gaga had happened to wear a dress made of raw beef, which was referred to by the media as *the meat dress*. Ever resourceful, SAVE had the idea of tweeting her about their campaign to save the meat market, and Lady Gaga's retweet reached 8 million followers. A PR company followed this up by organising a troupe of 100 Lady Gaga lookalikes who crossed Westminster Bridge with the message 'don't rip the heart out of Smithfield', which Lady Gaga retweeted twice in the same day, ultimately reaching 41.6 million people – and copying in the secretary of state. All this was reported on the front page of *The Times*, and in 2014 the market was saved.

Such successes are by their nature unpredictable, but seldom seem to backfire. When Kim Cattrall of *Sex and the City*, an actress who was born in Liverpool, learned of a plan for building houses in Grade I designated Sefton Park, she retweeted this news, expressing her dismay and giving rise to headlines like, 'Hollywood Star Slams Mayor's Plans'. She visited the park and posed with campaign posters.[18] Her actions successfully prevented the development and will make it much harder in future to promote anything similar. The campaign to prevent the erection of the overscaled Anglia Tower in Norwich did not involve celebrities but demonstrated the advantages of a well-designed campaign involving the use of before-and-after visuals. This underlined the importance of an eye-catching image, a compelling headline, the right tone of voice, and smart timing by Historic England and SAVE, once again working with local bodies.

Climate Change – Game Over?

Climate change, where younger people have often taken the lead in sparking grassroots movements (and educating an older generation), looms with urgency above all the other challenges to our countryside and urban landscapes. It is a threat but also an opportunity for heritage because, as one architect commented, 'climate change may supersede heritage as the principal driver of urban conservation'.[19] If in the past the potential destruction of heritage has turned out to be the catalyst for saving it, how might the present worsening emergency reshape the definition of 'saving'?

During the 1870s Octavia Hill recognised that the quality of our lives is predicated on having access to a decent environment and access to green spaces. With climate change we have a reversal of roles. Nature may have been our salvation, but now nature is exacting its revenge. What kind of a world do we want to live in? When William Morris asked himself this question, he drew a picture of a gentle anarchist future without cities in *News from Nowhere.* A political argument as well as one about pre-industrial lifestyles, it has haunted readers for over a hundred years. Can its dream come true in the age of climate emergency? Rob Hopkins's *From What Is to What If* offers a vision of a carbon-free and more democratic, citizen-led future that is both attractive and in the author's view achievable. To demonstrate that his leap of imagination is not merely utopian, Hopkins founded the 'Transition' movement in Totnes, a recipe for local initiatives that has been adopted by groups across the world. They are demonstrating the viability of a shift from high resource use to a community effort to reduce the carbon footprint and ensure resilience in an unknown future, at the same time adding simple pleasures to everyday life. It is a practical enactment of the idea of the commons.

The heritage lobby has embraced the challenges of climate change, with the recognition that 'business as usual' is no longer acceptable, and that there will be grave problems ahead.* When in 2019 the World Monuments Fund co-hosted a conference on climate change and coastal heritage, it reached the sobering conclusion that many things we cherish are going to disappear, literally beneath the waves. But inland water in the form of rivers presents problems of a different order. Mitigation may work up to a point, but there are 240,000 homes in the UK currently in high flood risk areas and their maintenance and repair costs are expected to rise between 20–50 per cent over the decade. The story is just as bad, if not worse, concerning agricultural land at risk of flooding – in England alone, it is estimated to be around 1.3 million hectares, or 12 per cent of the total.[20] Some argue that agriculture itself in its present form is the cause of many of the problems.[21]

Flooding has put heritage on the frontline, with low-lying areas in cities like York under direct threat. Water is not just a problem for vulnerable areas – heavier rainfall is a concern for many old buildings wherever they may be and guttering and run-off cannot cope with the new volumes of rainfall. Climate change also affects heritage in ways that are unexpected: the National Trust suffers a 28 per cent visitor decline in very hot weather, and recently had to close a historic property when it reached 40 degrees centigrade. Ever-cheaper solar energy installations are part of the solution for new buildings, and can be placed in as-yet-untried locations, such as over car parks, or built into

---

* This was certainly the consensus from a conference organised by the Heritage Alliance held in October 2019.

street furniture. Solar farms need not spoil fine landscapes, nor roof panels the visible roof slopes in historic villages – we can be cleverer than this in our survival.

The fundamental question posed by climate change is how we can use the existing environment more intelligently. Buildings produced 34 per cent of all greenhouse gas emissions in 2014, and there is already a focus (regrettably paid only lip service by government) on how to reduce this figure through more efficient insulation, heating and cooling, as well as changing lifestyles. The significance of embodied carbon in existing buildings plays positively in favour of heritage causes. Exchanging new buildings for old ones (with the perverse incentive of VAT exemption for new construction) wastes the material of which the old building was made. Then there is the damaging effect of removing it and finding somewhere to dump it.[22] As the American architect Carl Elefante famously said: 'The greenest building is the one that is already built.'

Retrospect and Prospect

Huge strides have been made over the last 150 years in the protection of heritage. In broad terms, the concept has gained validity. This attests, given the pressure of the last sixty years, to the success of conservationists, especially the buccaneers of the voluntary sector, and the establishment of well-balanced planning laws along with the growth of public awareness that has followed. We are in an immeasurably stronger position today than during the 1960s, when canals needed to be restored from scratch, historic city centres were still being demolished and manic dreams of technological futures induced a crisis of despair. As the architect Serge Chermayeff put it, we needed a space programme for the earth, and we still do. Heritage, even broadly conceived, does not cover all that needs doing, but it has represented an attitude of stubborn resistance, engendering compelling messaging and an ability to get through to government at crucial moments. The enormous acceleration of listing and the creation of Conservation Areas popularised the past and from the 1970s onwards development plans could expect close scrutiny and often vigorous opposition.

But the belief that heritage is sorted is also a part of the problem – a complacent belief that the heritage battle has already been won allows politicians and developers to push the boundaries a little here and then a lot more there, particularly when it comes to the urban landscape. All laws in a democracy must be a balance between the freedom to do something and freedom from harmful action. At present in planning they have been tipped towards the former, but the arguments are not always clear cut – at what point does a high tower interfere with my right to enjoy the sky from my house?

Because Britain has so often operated a crisis system, it works best when the crisis is easily comprehensible and visual: Smithfield Market to be demolished, or a proposed tower block to overshadow a historic cathedral city. The system works less well against the slow erosion of Conservation Areas, the insidious mission creep of developers today, and the loss of greenfield sites on the edge of every town. These rarely impact on public awareness with the same urgency as the sight of the Georgian streets of Bath being felled by the wrecker's ball in the 1970s. Such ad-hoc crisis-driven systems are especially ill-suited to protecting against the rapidly advancing enormity of climate change.

This book has demonstrated the importance, in times of crisis – whether during the Victorian era, the 1960s or the 1980s – of political leadership from any party: a Sir John Lubbock, Richard Crossman, Wayland Kennet, Duncan Sandys or Michael Heseltine. A close study of heritage reveals that it eludes party political identity, although it may at different times have been associated with progressive or conservative forces. In addition to politicians, there were public figures like John Betjeman to corral public support on television and through the press. Without a strong minister prepared to take a stand, conservation values – and by extension towns and countryside – are at risk. No minister since Heseltine has had the strength and vision to go against his cabinet, in his case to push for the regeneration of Liverpool. Today no council is likely to propose the demolition of Albert Dock, but it is the less obvious heritage sites, places where people live, suburban Conservation Areas, and thousands of smaller rural towns that are at risk from the relentless drip, drip of development.

For so many of the heroes of this book, heritage was a passionate cause: for William Morris and Robert Hunter, and nearer our own time, for Ian Nairn, and for the teenagers who saved the Bluebell Line, for Nan Fairbrother and the environment, and for the community protesters who saved Covent Garden, and Marcus Binney at SAVE. How grateful we are to them for ensuring that so much has descended to us. For all of them heritage was about much more than buildings and fine landscapes – they recognised the human values and emotions that such places stir. For Octavia Hill, William Morris and John Ruskin, protection and access to what they would have unashamedly called beauty was a birthright that they wished to bequeath to the future.

Yet we must remain vigilant and hold government to account at both local and national level. Every landscape and townscape is precious. Heritage is a wealth that belongs to us all, 'the commons' that should be shared and enjoyed by everyone, including those who come after us.

Acknowledgements

I would like to thank:

Prof. Sir David Cannadine PBA, Richard Davenport-Hines, Mark Girouard, Stephen Bayley, Francis Russell, Dr Richard Ovenden, David Adshead, Henrietta Billing, Sir Nicholas Penny, Sir Roy Strong CH, Graham Frater who kindly organised a dizzy visit to York where I had the good fortune to speak to Dr June Hargreaves, Sir Ron Cooke, Darrell Buttery, Duncan Marks, Buff Reid and Reyahn King, director of York Museums Trust. Roger Squires (canals), Harry Aubrey-Fletcher, Clive Aslet, John Darlington (World Monument Fund), Ivo Dawney (National Trust), Clive Whitbourn (NT), James Rothwell (NT), Mark Fisher, Merlin Waterson, Adam Nicolson, Lord Heseltine, Sir Laurie Magnus (Historic England), Anastasia Tennant, Gerry McQuillan (former DCMS), Edward Harley (HHA and AIL, Dr Susan Jenkins, Sir Eric Anderson, Prof. Neil Jackson, Dr Norman.W. James, Charles Fitzroy, Charles Sebag-Montefiore, Sir Eric Anderson, Sir Nicholas Goodison, Andy Foster (Birmingham), Tim Bridges (Birmingham), Caroline Kay and Amy Frost (Bath Preservation Trust), Catherine Porteous, Virginia Tandy (NLF), Alan Crookham, the late Peter Ainsworth (Heritage Alliance), Julia Ward (Historic England), Adrian de Ferranti, Sir William Worsley Bt, Ian Scargill (Oxford Green Belt Network), John Harris (Ely), Phil Douce (Worcester Civic Society), Bevis Hillier, Nicholas Coleridge, Richard Ehrman, Dame Liz Forgan, and on Scotland: Sir Brian and Oona Ivory, James Simpson, David Walker, Sir James Dunbar-Nasmith.

Stacey Reed, Anthea Case, and Sir Peter Luff (Lottery), James Hervey-Bathurst and Hugh McQuade (Severn Valley Railway),

Clive Henderson (Stratford Avon Canal), Tony Drake (Bluebell Railway), Dr Martin Postle (Museums), Barbara English (Beverley Civic Society), Dr Janet Barnes, John Pendlebury (Newcastle), the Earl and Countess of Derby, Phil Redmond and David McDonnell (Liverpool), Dr Bendor Grosvenor, Neil MacGregor, Delphine Jasmine-Belisle (Heritage Alliance), Alice Purkiss (Clore Leadership), Sarah James (Civic Voice), Ameer Kotecha, Tom Lloyd, and Dr Ed Weech.

Scilla Latham (Norfolk Churches Trust), Trevor Cooper (Historic Religious Buildings Alliance), Sophie Andreae, Janet Gough, Becky Payne, and for Norfolk churches, Katharine Wolstenholme, Graham Prior, Jolyon Booth, the Revds Helen and Keith Rengert, Revd Andrew Whitehead, Bronwyn Tyler, Peter Shepperd, Keith Brooker, Revd Andrew Whitehead, Ruth Blackman, Charlotte and Henry Crawley, and two experts on Norwich churches, Stephen Heywood and Richard Halsey (for his comments on the churches chapter), Thomas McMahon, former Bishop of Brentwood, Fr Martin Broadley, and Graham Kent. Greater Manchester churches: John Arnold, Bishop of Salford, Revd Canon Nigel Ashworth, Monsignor Canon Anthony Kay, Richard McEwan, Rev Canon Paul Nena, Fr Jeremy Sheehy, Revd Dr Caroline Hewitt, Paul and Elaine Griffiths, Revd Rachel Mann, Bill Wingrove, John Dunne, Fr Brendan Callaghan SJ, Monsignor Canon Anthony Kay, Colin Bell, Richard Miller, Martin Glynn (Hallé), Bill Wingrove and Steven Davies, Gareth Robinson and the team at St Philip's Chapel Street.

Julie Ashdown (Victorian Society), Tom Taylor (Manchester), Margaret Collier (Manchester Victorian Society), David Seker, Dr Simon Thurley, Bruce Anderson, Amanda Satchell, Geoff Orton and Pamela Home, Margate Civic Society, Nick Dermott (Heritage Advisor Thanet District Council). A distinguished group of archaeologists were especially helpful: Professor Martin Biddle, Peter Addyman, Leslie Webster, and Taryn Nixon. On the countryside Sir James Scott, Crispin Truman and Oliver Hilliam (CPRE).

No book is complete without acknowledgement of the London Library and its ever helpful staff, especially Samantha Gibson. I am especially indebted to Dr Brian Allen for stimulating conversations about museums, and the exodus of paintings. The following read all or part of the book and their comments were valuable: Sir Tim Laurence, Dr Mark Evans, Robert Hewison, Sir Simon Jenkins, Dr Peter Mandler, Charles Saumarez Smith, Wesley Kerr, Dr Alan Powers, Dr Christopher Ridgeway, Jonathan Brown, with whom I explored Liverpool and Greater Manchester churches, Dr Martin Royalton-Kisch who vastly improved the manuscript, Professor Peter Davidson and Professor Janey Stevenson who saved me from many pitfalls, and Dr Rory O'Donnell. Having Marcus Binney at the end of an email has been of inestimable value – like checking the gospels with St Peter.

Finally, thanks to my agent, Georgina Capel, publisher, Anthony Cheetham and Richard Milbank, Matilda Singer and Clémence Jacquinet (Head of Zeus). Various researchers dug up treasures for me and I am grateful to Emily Everest-Phillips, Beth Noble, Emma Irving, Lisa Mondiano, Cecilia Riva, Kate Harrison, and Eva James, my assistant, Kate Atkins, and above all to Charity, my first and best reader, who went with me to most of the places described before her tragic death.

Image Credits

1. Hulton Deutsch / Getty Images
2. Jonathan Ryan / Alamy Stock Photo
3. Dave Bagnall Collection / Alamy Stock Photo
4. The Times / News Licensing
5. fotoVoyager / Getty Images
6. Arcaid Images / Alamy Stock Photo
7. Isabella Stewart Gardner Museum / Wikimedia Commons
8. *Traffic in Towns, The specially shortened edition of the Buchanan Report* (Penguin, 1963)
9. Trinity Mirror / Mirrorpix / Alamy Stock Photo
10. Trinity Mirror / Mirrorpix / Alamy Stock Photo
11. Wikimedia Commons
12. LepoRello (Wikipedia) / Wikimedia Commons
13. Evening Standard / Stringer / Getty Images
14. Evening Standard / Stringer / Getty Images
15. © York Archaeological Trust.
16. Mirrorpix / Getty Images
17. Les Zoos dans le Monde
18. Arcaid Images / Alamy Stock Photo
19. Edward Dyer / Alamy Stock Photo
20. steven gillis hd9 imaging / Alamy Stock Photo
21. Iain Masterton / Alamy Stock Photo
22. wellsie82 / Getty Images
23. © Marsha Balaeva
24. Gideon Mendel / Getty Images
25. Alastair Wallace / Shutterstock
26. © Marcus Binney
27. NurPhoto / Getty Images
28. Famous Campaigns
29. Roger Driscoll / Alamy Stock Photo

Endnotes

Preface

1   Fritzsche, p. 207.
2   VW Diary V., p. 346.

Introduction

1   Quoted Tandy, p. 252.
2   Jackson, pp. 101–2.
3   For a full discussion on this topic see
     Astrid Swenson, *The Rise of Heritage:
     Preserving the Past in France, Germany
     and England 1789–1914* (Cambridge,
     2013).
4   Harwood and Powers 2004, p. 9.
5   Merrell Lynd, p. 9.
6   Ibid. pp. 165–7.
7   Standing, p. 90.
8   Miele, p. 2.
9   Ruskin *Modern Painters*, Vol. V 1856.
10   Aslet, p. 50.
11   Waine and Hilliam, p. 7.
12   Ibid, p. 7.
13   Hunter/Stamp, p. 77.
14   Kenneth Clark, *Civilisation* (London,
     1969), p. 320.
15   Nairn, p. 367.
16   Ibid. p. 367.
17   In his preface to the 1973 edition of
     The Sack of Bath.
18   Buchanan, *Mixed Blessings* (1958), p.
     210.
19   Canadine, p. 42.
20   Nicholson, p. 193.
21   Hunter/Stamp, p. 77.
22   Hunter/Stamp, p. 78.
23   Thurley, pp. 251–2.
24   Oliver Wainwright, '"Final Warning":
     Liverpool's Unesco status at risk over
     docks scheme', *Guardian*, 1 July 2017,
     www.theguardian.com/uk-news/2017/
     jul/01/final-warning-liverpools-unesco-
     status-at-risk-over-docks-scheme.
25   Delafons, p. 110.
26   Ibid.
27   Strong, *Scenes and Apparitions*
     (May 1988), p. 8.
28   English Heritage Annual Report
     1998–9, p. 4.
29   Wright, p. x.
30   Quoted in Hugh Clout, 'David
     Lowenthal obituary', *Guardian*, 27
     September 2018, www.theguardian.
     com/culture/2018/sep/27/david-
     lowenthal-obituary.
31   Unpublished coda to *The Heritage
     Industry*, kindly showed to the author
     by Robert Hewison.
32   Peter Luff, email to the author,
     July 2020.
33   Simon Jenkins, *Apollo*, May 2019, p. 23.
34   Ibid.
35   Matthew Parris, 'It's a small point
     but why can I only get medium?',
     The Times, 14 October 2020, www.
     thetimes.co.uk/article/its-a-small-
     point-but-why-can-i-only-get-
     medium-xzh7mw608.
36   Simon Jenkins, *Apollo*, May 2019, p.
     23.
37   Quoted Sandbrook, p. xxv.
38   Jackson, pp. 101–2.
39   Jennifer Jenkins (ed.), p. 28.

Chapter 1: The First Threats

1   John Ruskin, *The Seven Lamps of
     Architecture (849) The Complete Works
     of John Ruskin*, Vol. 8, p. 245.
2   Quoted Bargery p. 106.
3   Swenson p. 273. Swenson points

out that it is a trope of all national heritage accounts that 'regardless of which side they are on in the State-versus-public debate, however, virtually all deplore their own country's delays with regard to other European states'. Swenson, pp. 275–6.

4   Swenson, p. 57.
5   Waterson, pp. 25–6.
6   Gaze, p. 21.
7   *Guide Through the District of the Lakes.*
8   Ruskin Fors Clavigera, Letter 5.
9   *On the Old Road,* vol. II. Ruskin moved to Coniston in 1871. Like Ruskin, Octavia Hill was keen to bring the countryside 'to every landless man, woman and child', but was against the vulgar hordes and what she referred to as 'the London rough'. Swenson, p. 135.
10 Samuel, p. 296.
11 Waine and Hilliam, p. 97.
12 Ibid. p. 39.
13 Ibid. p. 31.
14 Fawcett/Pevsner, pp. 50–1.
15 Fawcett quoted, p. 97.
16 Chamberlin, p. 52.
17 Hunter/Miele, p. 37.
18 Cowell quoted, p. 85.
19 Delafons, p. 25.
20 Thurley, p. 39.
21 Cowell p. 87. To qualify as an ancient monument it had to be uninhabited.
22 Thurley, p. 39.
23 See Swenson, p. 323.
24 Cowell, p. 88.
25 Cowell quoted, p. 89.
26 Thurley, p. 47.
27 Fawcett/Boulting, p. 17.
28 Colin Ward, *Influences: Voices of Creative Dissent* (Hartland, 1991), p. 107.
29 Lucy E. Hewitt, 'Associational Culture and the Shaping of Urban Space: Civic Societies in Britain before 1960', *Urban History,* 39, 4 (2012), p. 596.
30 Andrew Saint, 'How London became a better place', *The Victorian* 68 (November 2021), pp. 4–7.
31 *Punch,* 9 October 1886.
32 Hansard, House of Lords 30 April 1912.

Chapter 2: The Search for Arcadia

1   Priestley pp. 336–8.
2   Thomas Hardy, *Far from the Madding Crowd* (1874) 1919 ed. vol. I, p. 168.
3   Quoted John Pendlebury and Lucy E. Hewitt, 'Place and voluntary activity in Inter-war England: topophilia and professionalization', *Urban History,* 45, 3 (2018) p. 462, first published online 22 August 2017.
4   Strong 1997, p. 30. It began life as *Country Life Illustrated incorporating Racing Illustrated.*
5   This story comes from the memoirs of Thelma Cazalet-Keir, *From the Wings.*
6   Strong 1997, p. 80.
7   Ibid. p. 10.
8   Roy Hattersley, *Guardian,* 24 April 2007.
9   Rowley, p. 35.
10 Kirkham, p. 89.
11 Reynolds, pp. 35–6.
12 Ibid.
13 Strong 1997, p. 117.
14 Ibid., p. 114.
15 Waine and Hilliam, p. 52.
16 Samuel, p. 229.
17 Waine and Hilliam p. 48.
18 Lees-Milne Diaries, 22 May 1945.
19 Cornforth, 1988 p. 35.
20 See Celia Applegate, *A Nation of Provincials: The German Idea of Heimat* (Berkeley, 1990).
21 Rowley, p. 413.
22 Fawcett/Betjeman, p. 58.
23 *See Country Life,* 'Pulling Down London', 16 April 1939.
24 Quoted Bargery, p. 29.
25 Hunter/Stamp, p. 82.

26   Ibid., p.83.

27   Lees-Milne Diaries 11 March 1944.

28   Bargery, p. 7.

29   Youngson, p. 30.

30   Reynolds, p. 76.

31   Waine and Hilliam, p. 104.

Chapter 3: Assembling a National Collection

1   Starkey, p. 230.

2   Richards, p. 94.

3   Heffer, p. 452.

4   Thurley, p. 77.

5   Impey and Parnell, p. 97.

6   Thurley, p. 100.

7   Ibid., p. 135.

8   Ibid., p. 139.

9   Hunter/Champion p. 44.

10   Delafons p. 31.

11   Lees-Milne Diaries 1 June 1945.

12   Address at the 21st Birthday Conference of English Heritage 2005.

Chapter 4: The Exodus of Paintings

1   W. Burger, *Trésors d'Art exposés à Manchester en 1857*, Paris 1857, p. (v).

2   Waterfield, p. 103.

3   Speech to House of Commons, 28 April 1777.

4   Fitzroy, p. 198.

5   Witt, p. 21.

6   Berenson to Mrs Gardner, 10 May 1896.

7   Nicholas Penny to author.

8   Kenneth Clark, lecture, *Art and Democracy*, Tate 8812/2/2/42.

9   Lady Dorothy Nevill, *The Reminiscences of Lady Dorothy Nevill* (London, 1906), p. 105.

10   See NACF's centenary exhibition catalogue *Saved! 100 Years of the National Art Collections Fund* (2003).

11   Witt pp. 18–19.

12   Ibid., p. 31.

13   Conlin, p. 115.

14   Ibid.

15   Saltzman, p. 255.

16   Holmes, p. 333.

17   Ibid., p. 334.

18   For the full story see Penny pp. 229–32.

19   Letter Lord Crawford to Clark, October 1939, Crawford Papers NLS.

20   Letter to James Lees-Milne, 9 June 1977, Yale Beinecke. The owner's names were listed after their pictures, hence the Earl of Raphael for Lord Ellesmere and the Marquess of Reynolds for Lord Lansdowne.

21   'I personally much resent spending huge sums of money on Italian pictures which we do not require and which, if we did not buy them, would not be destroyed but made accessible in some other gallery, when our own great buildings are being pulled down or, in the case of cathedrals, in danger of falling down.' Letter, Clark to Philip Noel Baker, 31 July 1972, Clark archive Tate 8812/1/4/39.

22   Taken from the Cornforth Report, 1974, p. 12.

23   Conlin, p. 195. If one were looking for a foreign precedent for such a popular public fundraising campaign the saving of the Basel Picasso Harlequins would suffice.

24   See Penny, p. 255.

25   Conlin p. 190. In fact, no gallery director since Eastlake and Burton in the nineteenth century had been given the luxury of making foreign collecting their focus – the intervening period was about trying to stem the export drain.

Chapter 5: Brave New World

1   Stamp 2013 p. 28.

2   RIBA, *Rebuilding Britain* (1943), p. 11.

3   Ibid., p. 39.

4   Lees Milne Diaries 5 February 1942.

5   For an interesting discussion on

the rebuilding issues, see Andrew Derrick, 'The Postwar Reconstruction of Wren's City Churches' in *Architectural Association Files* 26 (Autumn 1993) pp. 27–35.

6   Cherry 1981 p. 2.

7   Quoted Cherry 1981, p. 204.

8   Delafons p. 56. Listed building controls as we know them today were only introduced in the 1968 Planning Act.

9   Esher, p. 61.

10   Ibid.

11   Quoted Cherry, p. 108.

12   Transport Report, 1963 letter to Ernest Marples.

13   Transport Report, 1963 letter to Ernest Marples. Further on in the report he was to write: 'it is not a question of retaining a few old buildings, but of conserving, in the face of the onslaught of motor traffic, a major part of the heritage of the English-speaking world' (p. 197).

14   Esher, p. 75.

15   Jenkins, p. 219.

16   Quoted Otto Saumarez Smith, p. 47.

17   Sharp 1968, p. 125.

18   Marriott, p. 32.

19   Ibid., p. 110.

20   Strong, 1997, p. 142.

21   Betjeman letter to Lord Bridges 1958, quoted Bargery, p. 38.

22   Stourton, p. 234.

23   Grindrod, p. 212.

24   Pendlebury, p. 3.

25   Esher, p. 177.

26   Pendlebury quoted, p. 13.

27   See Pendlebury, p. 32.

28   McCombie, p. 79.

29   Quoted by Elain Harwood in *Oxford Dictionary of National Biography*.

30   See Otto Saumarez Smith, p. 1.

31   Kenneth Clark, *Civilisation* (London, 1969), p. 320.

32   Esher, p. 155.

Chapter 6: Birmingham and Anti-Heritage

1   *Nairn's Towns*, p. 9.

2   Price, p. 137.

3   Quoted Stamp, p. 17.

4   Price, p. 187.

5   *Nairn's Towns*, p. 3.

6   Marriott, p. 227.

7   Foster, p. 77.

8   *Guardian*, 1 September 2013.

Chapter 7: The Backlash: The Heroic Period of Conservation

1   Jenkins 1975, p. 268.

2   Hopkins, p. 8.

3   Nairn, 1955, p. 403.

4   Ibid., p. 363.

5   Quoted Harwood and Powers, 2004, Gavin/Stamp,, p. 26.

6   Thurley, p. 234.

7   Crossman Diaries, p. 176.

8   Ibid., p. 311.

9   Pevsner and Bradley p. 452.

10   *The Architects' Journal*, 26 April 1972. In 1974 the GLC adopted a policy of 'least change' for Piccadilly Circus.

11   Hillier vol. 3, p. 28.

12   Fawcett, p. 58.

13   Fawcett/Betjeman, p. 62.

14   Hunter/Stamp, p. 90. These were a pair of *Dancing Girls* by Renoir which were the last special grant given to the National Gallery for works bought from abroad. See Chapter Two.

15   Hillier vol. 3 *Bonus of Laughter*, p. 136.

16   Hunter/Stamp, p. 91.

17   Bradley, p. 159.

18   Ibid., p. 158.

19   Powers 2004, p. 15.

20   Esher p. 144.

21   This followed an influential conference organised by the Scottish Civil Trust in June 1970 – see *The Conservation of Georgian Edinburgh*, Edinburgh 1973 with contributions by John Betjeman, Colin Buchanan and others.

22 Delafons, p. 172.
23 Ibid.
24 Ibid. pp. 172–3.
25 Bevis Hillier, Twentieth Century Society website.
26 Ibid.
27 Powers, p. 133. Sheffield's Park Hill Flats was listed Grade II* in 1998, making it the largest listed building in Europe. An extensive restoration programme overseen by English Heritage with private partnership, especially Urban Splash, is to be completed in 2022.
28 Sherborn, p. 148.
29 Ibid., p. 154.

Chapter 8: Rescuing a City: York
1 Quoted Cooke, p. 14.
2 Pevsner and Neave p. 126.
3 Cooke, p. 20.
4 Civic Trust Report 1958–59.
5 Powers HPC, p. 9.
6 Nuttgens p. 333.
7 Shannon, p. 46.
8 Esher, 1968, p. 8.
9 Esher, p. 205.
10 Nuttgens, p. 333.
11 Park Inn by Radisson on North Street.
12 Esher p. 89.
13 Quoted Cooke, p. 14.
14 York Civic Trust Annual Report and Heritage Review 2018–2019, p. 7.
15 Ibid.

Chapter 9: The Sack of Bath
1 Speech July 1972 Tate 8812/1/4/39. In 1972 Geoffrey Rippon invited Clark to join the council for the Architectural Heritage Year coming up in 1975. He accepted but pointed out that they should not wait until 1975 because so much was being lost every month, particularly in Bath.
2 Peter Smithson, *Bath: Walks within the Walls,* Revised edition (2017).

3 *The Times* Saturday Review, 22 April 1972.
4 Abercrombie, *A Plan for Bath* (1945), p. 64.
5 Fergusson and Mowl p. 68.
6 Ibid., p. 74.
7 Forsyth, p. 232.
8 Fergusson and Mowl p. 16.
9 Ibid., p. 77.
10 Quoted Michael Bloch, *James Lees-Milne* (London, 2009),, p. 287.
11 *A Mingled Measure*, James Lees-Milne Diaries, 12 December 1971.
12 See Adam Fergusson, *The Times* Saturday Review, 22 April 1972.
13 Buchanan 1968, p. 127.
14 *The Times* Saturday Review, 22 April 1972.
15 *The Times*, 26 April 1972.
16 *The Times*, 29 April 1972.
17 Ibid.
18 *The Times*, 3 June 1972.
19 Letter, Clark to Eric James, 3 July 1972, Clark archive Tate 8812/1/4/471.
20 *The Architectural Review*, May 1973, p. 280.
21 See Clark archive Tate 8812/1/4/439B
22 Letter, Clark to Philip Noel Baker, 31 July 1972, Clark archive Tate 8812/1/4/39.
23 Fergusson and Mowl, p. 8.
24 Ibid, p. 78.

Chapter 10: The Archaeologists
1 Biddle, 1973, p. 6.
2 Ibid., p. viii.
3 Ibid.
4 Martin Biddle, 'The Future of the Urban Past' in Ratz pp. 95–6.
5 Much of this account draws from Peter Addyman, 'Creating heritage: Vikings, Jorvik and public interest archaeology', *British Academy Review*, 27 February 2016 pp. 12–16.
6 Interview with author, 2019.

7   Hunter/Stratton, p. 168.

8   Quoted Cooke, p. 11.

9   Richard Griffith quoted in Alan Bennett's diary, 29 March 2013, *Keeping On Keeping On* (London, 2016), p. 304.

10   Carver, p. 1.

11   Ibid., p. 18.

12   Ibid., p. 31.

13   Ibid., p. 221.

14   Charles Thomas, 'Archaeology in Britain 1973' in Ratz p. 8.

Chapter 11: Beyond the Town

1   For a fuller description see 'Reserve Focus: Fontmell and Melbury Downs, Dorset' in *British Wildlife*, December 2015, pp. 104–9.

2   Hugh Ellis, 'The Rise and Fall of the 1947 Planning System', Historic England website.

3   Waine and Hilliam, p. 105.

4   Reynolds, p. 30.

5   Ibid.

6   Strong, 1997, p. 164.

7   Frank Sykes, *Country Life*, November 1962.

8   *The Sunday Post*, 9 April 1962.

9   Sheail, p. 114.

10   John L. Jones, *Country Life*, December 1968. See Strong, p. 183.

11   *Country Life* 19 December 1968.

12   Reynolds, p. 76.

13   Nicholson, p. 37.

14   John Sheail, 'Torrey Canyon: The Political Dimension', *Journal of Contemporary History* 42, 3 (July 2007), p. 485.

15   Friedrich Nietzsche, *Thus Spake Zarathustra* (1883).

16   Sir Frank Fraser Darling gave the 1969 Reith Lectures, 'Ecology and the Crisis of Population Growth and Pollution', and two years later the Friends of the Earth produced *The Environmental Handbook, Action Guide for the UK*.

17   Powers HPC/Wartnaby p. 70.

18   Aldous, p. 7.

19   Heseltine, p. 232.

20   See website: Oxford Green Belt Network.

21   Esher, p. 152.

22   Buchanan, 1972, p. 71.

23   Buchanan's Note of Dissent to Roskill Commission.

24   Cherry, 1981, p. 212.

25   Buchanan's Note of Dissent to Roskill Commission.

26   Letter to Rt. Hon. John Peyton, 21 September 1973, Tate 8812/1/4/335.

27   Ed Douglas, *Statement: The Ben Moon Story* (2015).

28   Jenkins, 2013, p. 337.

29   Waine and Hilliam p. 80.

30   Simon Jenkins in Jennifer Jenkins (ed.) pp. 106–7.

31   Jennifer Jenkins (ed.), p. 260.

32   Ibid.

Chapter 12: The Fall and Rise of Country Houses

1   See article by Ruth Adams: https://journals.le.ac.uk/ojs1/index.php/mas/article/view/219

2   Sherborn, p. 131.

3   Lees-Milne Diaries, 23 December 1943.

4   Quoted Cowell, p. 115.

5   *New York Times* obituary, 29 October 2002.

6   Gaze, p. 242.

7   Giles Worsley, 'Beyond the Powerhouse: Understanding the Country House in the Twenty-first Century', *Historical Research* 78, 201 (August 2005), p. 425.

8   See Cornforth Report, 1974, pp. 12–13.

9   Strong Diaries, 1967–87, p. 142.

10 See Caroline Tisdall, 'Englishmen's Castles', 9 October 1974.
11 *Country Life* 10 March 1977, p. 575.
12 Binney to author.
13 Wright, 2009, p. 35.

Chapter 13: The Enthusiasts: Canals and Railways

1 Bolton, p. 77.
2 Squires, p. 20.
3 Rolt Part II, p. 80.
4 Bolton, p. 4.
5 *The Times*, 4 March 1948.
6 Quoted Squires, p. 27.
7 Gaze, p. 199.
8 Ransom, p. 50.
9 Bolton, p. 94.
10 Ibid., p. 228.
11 Rolt Part II, p. 176.
12 Rolt Part III, p. 17.
13 Ibid., p. 13.
14 Ibid., p. 18.
15 Ibid., p. 19.
16 Quoted Long, p. 105.
17 Brown, p. 12.

Chapter 14: Regeneration: Mills, Housing and Power Stations

1 Jane Jacobs, *Death and Life of Great American Cities* quoted by Randolph Langenbach in *Satanic Mills*, p. 21.
2 Thurley, p. 217.
3 See *State of the Arts or the Art of the State: Strategies for the Cultural Industries* (Greater London Council, 1985); *An Arts and Cultural Industries Strategy for Liverpool: A Framework* (Liverpool City Council, 1987).
4 Peter Roberts and Hugh Sykes (eds), *Urban Regeneration: A Handbook* (London, 2000), p. 17. This is a useful book for anyone interested in the nuts and bolts of regeneration.
5 Binney, 1990, p. 19.
6 Binney, 1979, p. 31.

7 Binney, 1990, p. 9.
8 Binney, 2006, p. 18.
9 Maurice Lindsay, *Thank You For Having Me* (London, 1983), p. 196.
10 Letter, Elizabeth Denby to Lionel Brett, 8 June 1959, quoted Otto Saumarez Smith, p. 135.
11 Harwood and Powers, 2004, Diane Watters, p. 116.
12 Hackney, p. 67.
13 Waterson, 2019 p. IV.
14 Ibid.
15 Draft essay online, Andrew Saint and Colin Thom, *Survey of London Battersea: Public, Commercial and Cultural*, vol. 49, 2012.
16 Binney 1984, p. 234.
17 Ibid.
18 Saint and Thom.
19 Ibid.

Chapter 15: Regeneration: Cities, Docklands and Basins

1 Jane Jacobs, *Death and Life of Great American Cities* quoted by Randolph Langenbach in *Satanic Mills*, p. 20.
2 I owe much of this chapter to discussions and travels with the former Liverpool planner, Jonathan Brown.
3 www.merseybasin.org.uk/
4 Binney, 1979, p. 42.
5 See Brown: www.architectsjournal.co.uk/news/opinion/michael-heseltine-was-there-in-liverpools-hour-of-need
6 Lord Heseltine to author.
7 Williamson, p. 52.
8 Priestley, p. 263.
9 Ken Powell in Binney, 1979, p. 43.
10 Jonathan Brown *Mancunian Odyssey*, an unpublished account of a trip made with Marcus Binney in June 2019 around Greater Manchester.

11   Oliver Wainwright, *Guardian*, 9 February 2006.

12   A good account of attempts in the 1980s to rectify the road planning separating the city from the river is given in A. J. Youngson's *Urban Development and the Royal Fine Art Commissions* (Edinburgh, 1990) pp. 157–62.

13   Christopher Thomson to author.

14   Jonathan Brown to author.

Chapter 16: Liverpool Story

1   Mario Praz, *On Neoclassicism*, a book of reprinted essays mostly from the 1930s, English edition, 1972, p. 118.

2   Quoted Stamp, p. 107.

3   *The Times*, 6 April 1963.

4   Foreword to *Seaport*. Raphael Samuel described Shankland as 'The butcher of Liverpool'.

5   By Gavin Stamp and Simon Jenkins respectively.

6   Some residents in Eldon and Granby resisted redevelopment and preferred to stay in the historic neighbourhood, and thus began the move towards housing associations and cooperatives which have been successful. Also see *Who Cares*, a documentary examining the problems of slum demolition and removal of people to new housing blocks, allowing the inhabitants speak for themselves: www.screenonline.org. uk/film/id/820087/index.html

7   See Jonathan Dimbleby, documentary for Thames Television, 1972, at https://player.bfi.org.uk/free/ film/watch-liverpool-8-1972-online

8   Quoted Sharples p. 37.

9   In conversation with the author.

10   Heseltine, p. 212.

11   For a good account see Jonathan Brown, 'Michael Heseltine was there in Liverpool's hour of need', *The Architects' Journal*, 21 March 2017.

12   See Lord Denning's description in Liverpool City Council v Irwin, available on the internet.

13   The Duke of Westminster personally underwrote the project. A good description of the project is David Taylor's *Liverpool: regeneration of a city* (undated).

14   See www.savebritainsheritage.org/ news/item/191/Housing-Scandal-Pathfinder-A-Post-Mortem

15   For the first of three programmes see: https://vimeo.com/25137004

16   Prof. John Belchem quoted by Oliver Wainwright, *Guardian* 1 July 2017.

Chapter 17: Margate Sands

1   John Newman, *Kent: North-East and East* (Yale, 2013), p. 96.

Chapter 18: The Heritage Industry and the Lottery

1   Peter Luff, email to the author, July 2020.

2   Hewison, 2014, p. 28.

3   Ibid., p. 29.

4   Ibid., p. 7.

5   A glance at the Wikipedia entry for the Victoria Baths will provide an outline of the problems.

6   Thurley, p. 4.

7   NHMF Accounts 1980/81.

8   NHMF Annual Report 1982/83, p. 3.

9   In a coda to *The Heritage Industry*.

10   Interview by the author, 2020.

11   Tandy, p. 221.

12   Annual Report HLF and NHMF 1996/97, p. 8.

13   Email to author, 26 April 2019.

14   Annual Report HLF and NHMF 2000/2001, p. 2.

15   Ibid.

16   Interview with author, 7 May

2020.
17 Interview with Catherine Porteous.
18 Tandy, p. 197.
19 Interview with author, 7 May 2020.
20 Interview with author, 2020. Today approximately 70–80 per cent of the LHF money is in the gift of the regional committees.

Chapter 19: Churches
1   Quoted Cooper, 2004, p. 1.
2   Harrod, p. 5.
3   Binney, p. 159.
4   Cooper, 2004, p. 20.
5   Cooper, 2004, p. 18.
6   Guy Braithwaite, *Struggling, Closed and Closing Churches* Research Report, commissioned by the Church Buildings Council (2020).
7   Binney 1984, p. 155.
8   Ibid., p. 156.
9   Ibid., pp. 165–72.
10 Cooper, 2004, p. 17.
11 Sermon, Archbishop Rowan Williams, 28 April 2008, at St Martin-in-the-Fields.
12 Dobbs, p. 181.
13 Taylor Review, p. 34.
14 Dobbs, p. 1.
15 Pevsner, *Lancashire: Manchester and the South-East* (2010), p. 451.
16 Quoted McEwan, p. 64.
17 Conversation with author, 2020.
18 Sheridan Gilley, 'The Years of Equipoise 1892–1943' in V. Alan McClelland and Michael Hodgetts (eds), *From Without the Flaminian Gate: 150 years of Roman Catholicism in England and Wales* (London, 1999) pp. 21–61.
19 Ibid.
20 *Manchester Evening News*, 24 July 1987.
21 *Manchester Evening News*, 31 March 1989.
22 *Manchester Evening News*, 25 July 1999.
23 Marcus Binney to author. It should be noted that Methodists call their places of worship churches, and do not consider themselves as Nonconformists.
24 Saunders TAMS, p. 107.
25 See *Nairn's Journeys*; *Football Towns, Preston & Bolton*.
26 Dobbs, p. 138.
27 Harrod, p. 39.
28 Conversation with author, 2020.
29 Graham Prior to author, 2019.
30 Groves pp. 9–11. There were over 500 pubs.
31 Talking to the author in October 2020.
32 Ruth Blackman email to author, 16 October 2020.
33 Trevor Cooper email to author, 28 October 2020.
34 Ruth Blackman email to author, 16 October 2020.
35 The *Telegraph Magazine*, 9 January 2021, p. 13.
36 I am grateful to Janet Gough for sharing her views with me on this subject, 2020.
37 Report in *The Times* 13 October 2021.

Chapter 20: Museums
1   Charles Saumarez Smith, p. 231.
2   Roy Strong, *Diaries*, 1967–1987, p. 231. Mrs Thatcher's biographer, Charles Moore, disputes this view and believes that she was very proud of the nation's museums and galleries.
3   Interview with author, 2019.
4   John Piper and John Betjeman, *Shropshire: A Shell Guide* (1951), p. 26.
5   Quoted Hewison p. 138.
6   Hewison p. 84.
7   See Alistair Brown, 'Civic Values', *Apollo*, June 2019, p. 47.
8   Ibid.
9   Former museum curator to author.

10 Email to author.

11 See Nicholas Thomas, 'What are Museums For?' *Apollo*, October 2019 pp. 47–8 and *The Art Newspaper*, June 2021, p. 5.

12 See Dan Hicks, *The Brutish Museum* (London, 2020). An alternative view is set out in a book review by Gilead Cooper QC in *Trust and Trustees*, 2021 pp. 1–13.

13 Nicholas Thomas, 'What are Museums For?', *Apollo* October 2019, p. 48.

14 Radio 4 *Today Programme*, 16 June 2020.

15 Janet Barnes to author.

16 Charles Saumarez Smith, 2021, p. 224.

17 Nicholas Penny to author.

18 Charles Saumarez Smith, 2021, p. 231.

19 Quoted in *The Art Newspaper*, April 2021, p. 22.

20 Brian Allen, conversation with author.

21 Waterfield, p. 322.

Chapter 21: Heritage: An Unfinished History

1 See Historic England 'Heritage Counts' on behalf of the Historic Environment Forum.

2 English Heritage Annual Report 1998–99, p. 4.

3 See The State of Brownfield CPRE 2021.

4 CPRE Big Read, Spring 2019.

5 *The Times*, 22 April 2021, p. 4.

6 Quoted in Geoffrey Madan's *Notebooks*.

7 Information from Civic Voice.

8 See Skyscraper City website.

9 See Basildon Council Regeneration Strategy.

10 This is according to their chairman, Sir Tim Laurence.

11 Talking to the author in October 2020.

12 Simon Jenkins, *Country Life*, 7 October 2020, p. 75.

13 Leaked internal NT document, 2020.

14 See Stephen Anderton on the National Trust and gardens in *The Times*, 27 October 2021, p. 28.

15 Hirsch, p. 86.

16 *The Art Newspaper*, September 2021 p. 5.

17 See Alex von Tunzelmann for full debate on this subject, London 2021.

18 Sex and the City star Kim Cattrall in row with mayor of Liverpool over green space in the city', Telegraph, 24 November 2014, www.telegraph.co.uk/news/celebritynews/11249718/Sex-and-the-City-star-Kim-Cattrall-in-row-with-mayor-of-Liverpool.html

19 James Simpson, *The Times*, 7 February 2020, p. 30.

20 Information from the Environment Agency, 2018.

21 George Monbiot, 'Micro-Consumerist Bollocks', *Guardian*, 30 October 2021 www.theguardian.com/environment/2021/oct/30/capitalism-is-killing-the-planet-its-time-to-stop-buying-into-our-own-destruction

22 'There's No Place Like Old Homes: Re-use and Recycle to Reduce Carbon', Historic England, February 2020, https://historicengland.org.uk/content/heritage-counts/pub/2019/hc2019-re-use-recycle-to-reduce-carbon/

Select Bibliography

www.open.edu/openlearn/history-the-arts/history/heritage/what-heritage/content-section-3.3

Abercrombie, Patrick, *The Preservation of Rural England* (Liverpool, 1926).

Abercrombie, Patrick, *Unpublished Memoir* (Liverpool University Library).

Adams, Ruth, 'The V&A, The Destruction of the Country House and the Creation of "English Heritage"', *Museum and Society* 11, 1 (2013) pp. 1–18.

Aldous, Tony, *Goodbye Britain?* (London, 1975).

Amery, Colin and Cruickshank, Dan, *The Rape of Britain* (London, 1975).

Applegate, Celia, *A Nation of Provincials: The German Idea of Heimat* (Berkeley, 1990).

Aslet, Clive, *The Real Crown Jewels of England* (London, 2020).

Bargery, Robert, *Design Champion: The Twentieth Century Royal Fine Art Commission 1924–1999* (London, 2019).

Biddle, Martin, *The Future of London's Past: A Survey of the Archaeological Implications of Planning and Development in the Nation's Capital* (Worcester, 1973).

Biddle, Martin, 'The Rose reviewed: a comedy (?) of errors', *Antiquity* 63 (1989), pp. 753–60.

Biddle, Martin, *The Search for Winchester's Anglo-Saxon Minsters* (Oxford, 2018).

Billingham, Nick, *Stratford Canal* (Stroud, 2002).

Binney, Marcus and Burman, Peter, *Change and Decay: The Future of Our Churches* (London, 1977).

Binney, Marcus, Ken Powell and others, *Satanic Mills*, (London, 1979).

Binney, Marcus, *Our Vanishing Heritage* (London, 1984).

Binney, Marcus, Machin, Francis and Powell, Ken, *Bright Future: The Re-use of Industrial Buildings* (London, 1990).

Binney, Marcus, *SAVE Britain's Heritage 1975–2005: Thirty Years of Campaigning* (London, 2005).

Binney, Marcus, *Big Saves: Heroic Transformations of Great Landmarks* (London, 2016).

Bolton, David, *Race Against Time* (London, 1991).

Bloch, Michael, *James Lees-Milne* (London, 2009).

Borley, Lester, *Dear Maurice: Culture and Identity in late 20th Century Scotland. A Tribute to Maurice Lindsay on his 80th Birthday* (East Lothian, 1998).

Boughton, John, *Municipal Dreams: The Rise and Fall of Council Housing* (London, 2018).

Bradley, Simon, *St Pancras Station* (London, 2007).

Bragg, Melvyn, 'Heritage', *In Our Time*, Radio 4 (18 July 2002) (www.bbc.co.uk/programmes/p00548j4).

Breeze, David (ed.), *Studies in Scottish*

Antiquity Presented to Stewart Cruden (Edinburgh, 1984).

Bridgen, Tom, *Value in the View: Conserving Historic Urban Views* (London, 2018).

Brown, Jonathan, *The Railway Preservation Revolution: A History of Britain's Heritage Railways* (Barnsley, 2017).

Buchanan, Colin, *Traffic in Towns: The specially shortened edition of the Buchanan Report* (Harmondsworth, 1964).

Buchanan, Colin, *Bath: A Study in Conservation* (London, 1968).

Buchanan, Colin, *The State of Britain* (London, 1972).

Cannadine, David, *In Churchill's Shadow: Confronting the Past in Modern Britain* (London, 2002).

Cannadine, David, *Making History Now and Then: Discoveries, Controversies and Explorations* (London, 2008).

Cannadine, David, *Victorious Century: The United Kingdom 1800–1906* (London, 2017).

Carman, John, *Archaeology and Heritage: An Introduction* (London, 2002).

Carrington, Noel, *Industrial Design in Britain* (London, 1976).

Carver, Martin, *Portmahomack: Monastery of the Picts* (Edinburgh, 2016).

Chamberlin, E. R., *Preserving the Past* (London, 1979).

Chapman, David and others (ed.), *Region and Renaissance: Reflections on planning and development in the West Midlands* (Redditch, 2000).

Charlton, Susannah and others (ed.), *100 Churches 100 Years* (London, 2019).

Cherry, Bridget and Robey, Anna (eds), *Rediscovered Utopias: Saving London's Suburbs* (London, 2010).

Cherry, Gordon E., *Pioneers in British Planning* (London, 1981).

Cherry, Gordon E., *Birmingham: A Study in Geography, History, and Planning* (Chichester, 1994).

Childe, V. Gordon and Clarke, D. V., *Skarra Brae* (Edinburgh, 1988).

Conlin, John, *The Nation's Mantlepiece: A History of the National Gallery* (London, 2006).

Cooper, Trevor, *How Do We keep Our Parish Churches?* (London, 2004).

Cooper, Trevor (ed.), 'For Public Benefit: Churches Cared for by Trusts', *Ecclesiology Today* Issues 49 & 50 (2014).

Cormack, Patrick, *Heritage in Danger* (London, 1976).

Cornforth, John, *Country Houses in Britain: Can They Survive? An Independent Report* (London, 1974).

Cornforth, John, *The Search for a Style: Country Life and Architecture 1897–1935* (London, 1988).

Cossons, Neil, 'English Heritage: The First 21 Years', *Conservation Bulletin* 49 (Summer 2005).

Cowell, Ben, *The Heritage Obsession: The Battle for England's Past* (Stroud, 2008).

Crawford, James, *An Inventory for the Nation* (Edinburgh, 2015).

Crossman, Richard, *The Diaries of a Cabinet Minister*, vol. 1 1964–66 (London, 1975).

Crowther, Sir Geoffrey and others, *Traffic in Towns: a study of the long-term problems of traffic in urban areas: Reports of the Steering Group and Working Group appointed by the Minister of Transport* (London, 1963).

Daniel, Glyn, *A Short History of Archaeology* (London, 1981).

Delafons, John, *Politics and Preservation: A Policy History of the Built Heritage 1882–1966* (London, 1997).

Dobb, The Rev'd Arthur J., *Like a Mighty Tortoise: A History of the Manchester Diocese* (Manchester, 1978).

Dodd, Phillip, *The Battle Over Britain* (London, 1995).

Esher, Lionel, *A Broken Wave: The Rebuilding of Britain 1940–1980* (London, 1981).

Esher, Lionel, *York: A Study in Conservation* (London, 1968).

Evans, Graeme and Shaw, Phyllida, *The Contribution of Culture to Regeneration in the UK: A Review of Evidence* (London: DCMS, 2004).

Fawcett, Jane (ed.), *The Future of the Past* (London, 1976).

Fawcett, Richard and Oram, Richard, *Melrose Abbey* (Stroud, 2004).

Fergusson, Adam and Mowl, Tim, *The Sack of Bath – And After: a record and an indictment* (Bath, 1989).

Fitzroy, Charles, *The Rape of Europa: The Intriguing History of Titian's Masterpiece* (London, 2015).

Forshaw, Alec, *1970s London: Discovering the Capital* (Stroud, 2011).

Forsyth, Michael, *Bath* (Pevsner Architectural Guide) (New Haven, 2007).

Foster, Andy, *Birmingham* (Pevsner Architectural Guide) (New Haven, 2016).

Fritzsche, Peter, *Sranded in the Present: Modern Time and the Melancholy of History* (Harvard, 2004).

Gaze, John, *Figures in a Landscape: A History of the National Trust* (London, 1988).

Girouard, Mark, *The English Town* (New Haven, 1990).

Goodison, Nicholas, *The Goodison Review: Securing the best for our Museums: Private Giving and Government Support* (Richmond, 2004).

Grindrod, John, *Concretopia: A Journey Around the Rebuilding of Postwar Britain* (London, 2013).

Groves, Nicholas, *The Medieval Churches of the City of Norwich* (Norwich, 2010).

Hackney, Rod, *The Good, the bad and the Ugly: Cities in Crisis* (Oxford, 1990).

Hall, Peter, *Cities of Tomorrow: An Intellectual History of Urban Planning and Design in the Twentieth Century* (Oxford, 2002).

Harrod, Wilhelmine, *Norfolk Country Churches and the Future* (Norwich, 1972).

Harwood, Elain and Davies, James O., *England's Post-War Listed Buildings* (London, 2015).

Harwood, Elain and Powers, Alan, *The Heroic Period of Conservation* (London, 2004).

Harwood, Elain and Powers, Alan, *Buildings for Business* (London, 2020).

Haskell, Francis, *History and its Images: Art and the Interpretation of the Past* (New Haven, 1993).

Haskell, Francis, *The Ephemeral Museum: Old Master Paintings and the Rise of the Art Exhibition* (New Haven, 2000).

Heffer, Simon, *The Age of Decadence, Britain 1880 to 1914* (London, 2017).

Heseltine, Michael, *Life in the Jungle: My Autobiography* (London, 2000).

Hewison, Robert, *The Heritage Industry: Britain in a Climate of Decline* (London, 1987).

Hewison, Robert, *Cultural Capital: the Rise and Fall of Creative Britain* (London, 2014).

Hillier, Bevis, *John Betjeman*, vols 2&3 (London, 2002 and 2004).

Hirsch, Afua, *British: On Race, Identity and Belonging* (London, 2018).

Holmes, C. J., *Self & Partners (Mostly Self): Being the Reminiscences of C. J. Holmes* (London, 1936).

Hopkins, Owen, *Lost Futures: The Disappearing Architecture of Post-War Britain* (London, 2017).

Hopkins, Rob, *From What Is to What If: unleashing the power of imagination to create the future we want* (London, 2019).

Hughes, Quentin, *Seaport, Architecture & Townscape in Liverpool* (London, 1964).

Hunter, Michael (ed.), *Preserving the Past: The Rise of Heritage in Modern Britain* (London, 1996).

Impey, Edward and Parnell, Geoffrey, *The Tower of London: The Official Illustrated History* (London, 2000).

Inglis, Angela and Buckner, Nigel, *King's Cross: A Sense of Place* (London, 2012).

Jackson, J. D., *The Necessity For Ruins* (Amherst, 1980).

Jameson, Conor Mark, *Silent Spring Revisited* (London, 2012).

Jenkins, Jennifer (ed.), *Remaking the Landscape* (London, 2002).

Jenkins, Simon, *Landlords to London: The Story of a Capital and its Growth* (London, 1975).

Jenkins, Simon, *England's Thousand Best Churches* (London, 1999).

Jenkins, Simon, *A Short History of London: The Creation of a World Capital* (London, 2019).

Jones, Arthur, *Britain's Heritage: The Creation of the National Heritage Memorial Fund* (London, 1985).

Kadish, Sharman, *Jewish Heritage in Britain and Ireland* (Swindon, 2015).

Kennett, Wayland, *Preservation* (London, 1972).

Kirkham, Pat, *Harry Peach* (Leicester, 1986).

Kitchen, Paddy, *A Most Unsettling Person: An Introduction to the Ideas and Life of Patrick Geddes* (London, 1975).

Klemek, Christopher, *The Transatlantic Collapse of Urban Renewal: Postwar Urbanism fromNew York to Berlin* (Chicago, 2010).

Knox, James, *Robert Byron* (London, 2003).

Lees-Milne, James, *The National Trust: A Record of Fifty Years' Achievement* (London, 1945).

Lees-Milne, James, *Ancestral Voices* (London, 1975).

Lees-Milne, James, *Prophesying Peace* (London, 1977).

Lees-Milne, James, *The Enigmatic Edwardian: The Life of Reginald 2nd Viscount Esher* (London, 1986).

Long, Richard C., *Lewes & East Grinstead Railway: The Bluebell Line* (Surrey, 2016).

Lowenthal, David, *The Heritage Crusade* (Cambridge, 1968).

Lowenthal, David, *The Past is a Foreign Country – Revisited* (Cambridge, 1985).

MacCarthy, Fiona, *William Morris: A Life for Our Time* (London, 1994).

Malone, Caroline, *English Heritage Book of Avebury* (London, 1989).

Mandler, Peter, *The Fall and Rise of the Stately Home* (New Haven, 1999).

Marriott, Oliver, *The Property Boom* (London, 1967).

McEwan, Richard I., *None Will Remain:*

Five Lost Churches of Manchester (The Anglo-Catholic History Society, 2014).

McCombie, Grace, *Newcastle and Gateshead* (Pevsner Architectural Guide) (New Haven, 2009).

Merrell Lynd, Helen, *England in the Eighteen Eighties: Towards a social basis for Freedom* (London, 1968).

Miele, Chris (ed.), *From William Morris: Building Conservation and the Arts and Crafts Cult of Authenticity 1877–1939* (New Haven, 2005).

Miller, Mervyn, *English Garden Cities* (Swindon, 2010).

Minton, Anna, *Ground Control: Fear and Happiness in the Twenty-First Century City* (London, 2012).

Moffat, Alistair and Rosie, George, *Tyneside: A History of Newcastle and Gateshead from Earliest Times* (Edinburgh, 2006).

Moir, Esther, *The Discovery of Britain: The English Tourists* (London, 1964).

Mount, Ferdinand, *English Voices: Lives, Landscapes, Laments 1985–2015* (London, 2016).

Nabarro, Sir Gerald, *Steam Nostalgia* (London, 1972).

Nairn, Ian, *Outrage* (London, 1955).

Nairn, Ian, *Nairn's Towns* (first edition 1967) edited, updated and introduced by Owen Hatherley (London, 2013).

Nicholson, Max, *The New Environmental Age* (Cambridge, 1989).

Nicolson, Adam, *Regeneration: The Story of the Dome* (London, 1999).

Nuttgens, Patrick (ed.), *The History of York: From Earliest Times to the Year 2000*, (Pickering, 2007).

Pendlebury, John, 'Alas Smith and Burns? Conservation in Newcastle upon

Tyne City Centre 1959–1968', *Planning Perspectives*, 16, 2 (2001), pp. 115–141.

Penny, Nicholas, *National Gallery Catalogues: The Sixteenth Century Italian Paintings Vol II Venice 1540–1600* (London, 2008).

Pevsner, Nikolaus and Bradley, Simon, *Buildings of England: London 6: Westminster* (New Haven, 2003).

Pevsner, Nikolaus and Neave, David, *Buildings of England: Yorkshire: York and the East Riding* (New Haven, 2005).

Pevsner, Nikolaus and Richmond, Ian, *Northumberland* (New Haven, 2002).

Powell, Ken and de la Hey, Celia, *Churches: A Question of Conversion* (London, 1987).

Powell, Kenneth, *Powell and Moya: Twentieth Century Architects* (London, 2009).

Powers, Alan, *Britain: Modern Architecture in History* (London, 2017).

Price, Frank, *Being There* (Leicestershire, 2002).

Priestley, J. B., *English Journey* (London, 2018, 1st edition 1934).

Ransom, P. J. G., *Waterways Restored* (London, 1974).

Ratz, Philip (ed.), *Rescue Archaeology* (London, 1974).

Rawnsley H. D., *A Nation's Heritage* (London, 1920).

Reynolds, Fiona, *The Fight for Beauty: Our Path to a Better Future* (London, 2016).

RIBA, *Rebuilding Britain* (London, 1943).

Richards, Julian, *Stonehenge: The Story So Far* (Historic England, 2017).

Rolt, L. T. C., *The Landscape Trilogy: The Autobiography of L. T. C. Rolt* (London, 2005).

Rowley, Trevor, *The English Landscape in the Twentieth Century* (London, 2006).

Rule, Margaret, *The Mary Rose: The Excavation and Raising of Henry VIII's Flagship* (London, 1982).

Saltzman, Cynthia, *Old Master, New World: America's Raid on Europe's Great Pictures* (London, 2008).

Samuel, Raphael, *Theatres of Memory: Past and Present in Contemporary Culture* (New York and London, 2012).

Roberts, Charles (ed.), *Treasure for the Future: The Norfolk Churches Trust 1976–2001* (Norwich, 2001).

Saumarez Smith, Charles, *The National Gallery: A Short History* (London, 2009).

Saumarez Smith, Charles, *East London* (London, 2017).

Saumarez-Smith, Charles, *The Art Museum in Modern Times* (London, 2021).

Saumarez Smith, Otto, *Boom Cities: Architect-Planners and the Politics of Radical Urban Renewal in 1960s Britain* (Oxford, 2019).

Saunders, Matthew, 'How certain is the victory of conservation? Indeed, have we won?', Lecture to the Historic Religious Buildings Alliance (London, 2019).

Saunders, Matthew, 'Nonconformist Chapels; a Conservation Overview', *The Transactions of the Ancient Monument Society* 63 (2019).

Saunders Watson, Michael, *I am Given a Castle: The Memoirs of Michael Saunders Watson* (Norfolk, 2008).

Shannon, John, *York Civic Trust: The First Fifty Years* (York, 1996).

Sharp, Thomas, *Town Planning* (Harmondsworth, 1940).

Sharp, Thomas, *Town and Townscape* (London, 1968).

Sharples, Joseph, *Liverpool* (Pevsner Architectural Guide) (New Haven, 2004).

Sheail, John, *Nature Conservation in Britain: The Formative Years* (London, 1998).

Sherborn, Derek, *An Inspector Recalls: Saving our Heritage* (Sussex, 2003).

Skene, Prue, *Capital Gains: How the National Lottery Transformed England's Arts* (London, 2017).

Smith, Brian and others, *Inherit: Investing in Heritage – A guide to Successful Urban Regeneration* (Norwich, 2007).

Smith, Chris, *Creative Britain* (London, 1998).

Spiers, Shaun, *How to Build Houses AND Save the Countryside* (Bristol, 2018).

Squires, Roger, *Canals Revived: The Story of the Waterway Restoration Movement* (Wiltshire, 1979).

Stamp, Gavin, *Britain's Lost Cities* (London, 2007).

Stamp, Gavin, *Anti-Ugly: Excursions in English Architecture and Design* (London, 2013).

Standing, Guy, *Plunders of the Commons: A Manifesto for Sharing Public Wealth* (London, 2019).

Starkey, David and others, *Making History: Antiquaries in Britain 1707–2007* (London, 2007).

Stourton, James, *Kenneth Clark: Life, Art and Civilisation* (London, 2016).

Strong, Roy, *Strong Points* (London, 1985).

Strong, Roy, *Country Life, 1897–1997: The English Arcadia* (London, 1997).

Strong, Roy, *Garden Party: Collected Writings 1979–1999* (London, 2000).

Strong, Roy, *Passions Past and Present* (London, 2005).

Strong, Roy, *Scenes and Apparitions: Diaries 1988–2003* (London, 2016).

Sweet, Rosemary, *Antiquaries: The Discovery of the Past in Eighteenth-Century Britain* (London, 2004).

Swenson, Astrid, *The Rise of Heritage* (Cambridge, 2013).

Sykes, Olivier and others, 'Liverpool City Profile', *Cities* 35 (2013).

Tallon, Andrew, *Urban Regeneration in the UK* (London, 2010).

Taylor, Nicholas, *The Village in the City* (London, 1973).

Thomas, Suzy and Stone, Peter G. (eds), *Metal Detecting and Archaeology* (Woodbridge, 2009).

Thurley, Simon, *Men From the Ministry: How Britain Saved its Heritage* (New Haven, 2013).

Tinniswood, Adrian, *Noble Ambitions: The Fall and Rise of the Post-War Country House* (London, 2021).

Tunzelmann, Alex von, *Fallon Idols: Twelve Statues That Made History* (London, 2021).

Waine, Peter and Hilliam, Oliver, *22 Ideas that Saved the English Countryside: The Campaign to Protect Rural England* (London, 2016).

Waterfield, Giles, *The People's Galleries: Art Museums and Exhibitions in Britain 1800–1914* (New Haven, 2015).

Waterson, Merlin, *A Noble Thing: The National Trust and Its Benefactors* (London, 2011).

Waterson, Merlin, *Rescue & Reuse: Communities, Heritage and Architecture* (London, 2019).

Watkin, David, *The Rise of Architectural History* (London, 1980).

Williams, Stephanie, *Docklands* (London, 1993).

Williams-Ellis, Clough, *England and the Octopus* (London, 1928).

Williamson, Elizabeth and Pevsner, Nikolaus, *London Docklands: An Architectural Guide,* (Pevsner Architectural Guides) (London, 1999).

Wilson, David, *The British Museum: A History* (London, 2002).

Witt, Robert, *The Nation and its Art Treasures* (London, 1911).

Wright, Patrick, *On Living in an Old Country: The National Past in Contemporary Britain* (Oxford, 2009).

Yougson, A. J., *Urban Development and the Royal Fine Art Commissions* (Edinburgh, 1990).

Index